Where Sin Abounds

Where Sin Abounds

The Spread of Sin and the Curse in the Book of Genesis with Special Focus on the Patriarchal Narratives

Robert R. Gonzales Jr.

WIPF & STOCK · Eugene, Oregon

WHERE SIN ABOUNDS
The Spread of Sin and the Curse in the Book of Genesis with Special Focus on the Patriarchal Narratives

Wipf & Stock
An imprint of Wipf and Stock Publishers
199 W. 8th Ave., Suite 3
Eugene, OR 97401

www. wipfandstock.com

ISBN 13: 978-1-60608-747-3

Manufactured in the U.S.A.

לְיֵשׁוּעַ הַמָּשִׁיחַ
אֲשֶׁר חַסְדּוֹ גָּדוֹל מִכָּל־חַטָּאתִי

To Jesus Christ,
whose grace is greater than all my sin!

Contents

Tables

Acknowledgements

SELF-CONGRATULATION AND PRIDE AT the completion of a project like this might indirectly support the thesis of this study (i.e., sin abounds since Adam's fall), but such attitudes would not reflect reality or serve the aim of this project, which is to give glory and praise to God. Ultimately, therefore, the triune God deserves the credit for any wisdom reflected in these pages. Paul's rhetorical question "What do you have that you didn't receive?" (1 Cor 4:7) reminds us that we are stewards of divine truth, not fountains.

I must thank my fellow pastor, Jeffery Smith, and the members of Covenant Reformed Baptist Church for twelve months of partial sabbatical, without which I am not sure how I could have completed this project. I'm also grateful for the valuable suggestions from Drs. Robert Bell, Kenneth Casillas, Randy Jaeggli, and Samuel Saldivar, as well as my editor, Mr. Dennis Cone. Of course, I take credit for any deficiencies in the final product. Finally, I'd like to thank God for a wonderful and supportive family. My wife, Becky, has proven herself a God-ordained "helper" in countless ways, and my five wonderful children never gave up praying for daddy's book.

Abbreviations

AASOR	*Annual of the American Schools of Oriental Research*
AB	*The Anchor Bible*
ABD	*The Anchor Bible Dictionary*
ACCS	Ancient Christian Commentary on Scripture. Edited by Thomas C. Oden. *Genesis 1–11 (vol. 1).* Edited by Andrew Louth. *Genesis 12–50 (vol. 2).* Edited by Mark Sheridan. Downers Grove: Inter-Varsity Press, 2001–2002.
ANEP	*The Ancient Near East in Pictures.* Edited by James B. Pritchard. Princeton: Princeton University Press, 1969.
ANET	*Ancient Near Eastern Texts.* 3rd ed. Edited by James B. Pritchard. Princeton: Princeton University Press, 1969.
ANF	*The Ante-Nicene Fathers.* Edited by Alexander Roberts and James Donaldson. 10 vols. Grand Rapids: Wm. B. Eerdmans Publishing Co., 1956.
AOTC	*Apollos Old Testament Commentary*
ASV	American Standard Version
BA	*Biblical Archaeologist*
BabTalmud	*The Babylonian Talmud.* Edited by Isidore Epstein. 6 parts with index. 35 vols. London: Soncino Press, 1935–48.
BCBC	*Believer's Church Bible Commentary*
BDB	The Brown-Driver-Briggs Hebrew and English Lexicon
BDCE	*Baker's Dictionary of Christian Ethics.* Edited by Carl F. H. Henry. Grand Rapids: Baker Book House, 1973.
BN	*Biblische Notizen*
BibSac	*Bibliotheca Sacra*
BSC	*Bible Student's Commentary*

BST	*Bible Speaks Today*
CANE	*Civilizations of the Ancient Near East*. Edited by Jack M. Sasson. 2 vols. 1995. Reprint, Peabody, MA: Hendrickson Publishers, 2006.
CBQ	*Catholic Biblical Quarterly*
CSB	Christian Standard Bible
CTJ	*Calvin Theological Journal*
DRA	Douay-Rheims Bible
DSBS	*The Daily Study Bible Series*
EBC	*The Expositor's Bible Commentary*
EBCE	*Encyclopedia of Biblical and Christian Ethics*. Edited by R. K. Harrison. Nashville: Thomas Nelson Publishers, 1987.
EBS	*The Encountering Biblical Studies*. Edited by Walter A. Elwell.
Enoch	*The Book of Enoch*. Translated by Robert H. Charles. Oxford: Clarendon Press, 1912.
EQ	*The Evangelical Quarterly*
ESV	English Standard Version
GBH	Paul Joüon. *A Grammar of Biblical Hebrew*. Translated and revised by T. Muraoka. Rome: Editrice Pontificio Istituto Biblico, 1992.
GKC	*Gesenius' Hebrew Grammar*. Edited by E. Kautzsch. Translated by A. E. Crowley. 2nd ed. Oxford: Clarendon Press, 1910.
GR	*Genesis Rabbah: The Judaic Commentary to the Book of Genesis*. Translated and edited by Jacob Neusner. 3 vols. Atlanta: Scholars Press, 1985.
GTJ	*Grace Theological Journal*
HALOT	L. Koehler and W. Baumgartner. *The Hebrew and Aramaic Lexicon of the Old Testament*. 2 vols. Translated and edited under the supervision of M. E. J. Richardson. Study edition.
Herodotus	*Herodotus*. Translated A. D. Godley. Cambridge: Harvard University Press, 1961–1964.

HOTC	*Holman Old Testament Commentary*
HS	Ronald J. Williams, *Hebrew Syntax: An Outline.* 2nd edition. Toronto: University of Toronto Press, 1976.
IBHS	B. K. Waltke and M. O'Connor. *An Introduction to Biblical Hebrew Syntax.* Winona Lake, IN: Eisenbrauns, 1990.
ICC	*The International Critical Commentary*
Illiad	*Homer's The Iliad.* Translated Robert Fitzgerald. Garden City, NY: International Collectors Library, 1974.
Int	*Interpretation*
ITC	*International Theological Commentary*
ISBE	*The International Standard Bible Encyclopedia.* 2nd ed. Edited by Geoffrey W. Bromiley. 4 vols. Grand Rapids: Wm. B. Eerdmans Publishing Co. Publishing Co., 1979–88.
JAAR	*Journal of the American Academy of Religion*
JAOS	*Journal of the American Oriental Society*
JBL	*Journal of Biblical Literature*
JETS	*Journal of the Evangelical Theological Society*
JNES	*Journal of Near Eastern Studies*
Josephus	*Antiquities of the Jews.* In *The Complete Works of Josephus.* Translated by William Whiston. Grand Rapids: Kregel Publications, 1981.
JRT	*Journal of Religious Theought*
JSNT	*Journal for the Study of the New Testament*
JSOT	*Journal for the Study of the Old Testament*
JSOTSup	*Journal for the Study of the Old Testament Supplement Series.* Sheffield: Sheffield Academic Press, 1997.
JSS	*Journal of Semitic Studies*
JTS	*Journal of Theological Studies*
Jubilees	*The Book of Jubilees.* Translated by Robert H. Charles. London: Adam and Charles Black, 1902.
Judith	*The Book of Judith.* Translated by Morton S. Enslin. Leiden: E. J. Brill, 1972.
KJV	King James Version

LCBI	Literary Currents in Biblical Interpretation.
LSGEL	*A Greek-English Lexicon*. Edited by Henry George Liddell and Robert Scott. Oxford: Claredon Press, 1968.
LW	*Luther's Works.* Edited by Jaroslav Pelikan. 56 vols. St. Louis: Concordia Publishing House, 1958–1966.
LXX	Septuagint
MT	Masoretic Text
NAB	New American Bible
NAC	*The New American Commentary*
NAU	New American Standard Bible (1995)
Neofiti	*Targum Neofiti 1: Genesis*. Translated by Martin McNamara. Vol. 1A of *The Aramaic Bible*. Edited by Kevin Cathcart, Michael Maher, and Martin McNamara. Collegeville, MN: The Liturgical Press, 1992.
NET	New English Translation
NJB	New Jerusalem Bible
NIB	*The New Interpreter's Bible*
NIBC	*New International Biblical Commentary*
NICNT	The New International Commentary on the New Testament
NICOT	The New International Commentary on the Old Testament
NIDOTTE	*The New International Dictionary of Old Testament Theology and Exegesis*
NIGNTC	*New International Greek New Testament Commentary*
NIV	New International Version
NKJ	New King James Version
NLT	New Living Translation
NPNF	*The Nicene and Post Nicene Fathers of the Christian Church*. Edited by Philip Schaff. 38 vols. Grand Rapids: Wm. B. Eerdmans Publishing Co., 1956.
NRSV	New Revised Standard Version
NSBT	*New Studies in Biblical Theology*
NT	New Testament

OBT	*Overtures to Biblical Theology*. Edited by Walter Brueggeman and John R. Donahue.
Onkelos	*Targum Onkelos to Genesis*. Translated by Moses Aberbach and Bernard Grossfeld. Denver: Ktav Publishing House, 1982.
OT	Old Testament
OTS	*Oudtestamentische Studiën*
Philo	*Philo*. Translated by F. H. Colson. 10 vols. Cambridge: Harvard University Press, 1966.
PNTC	*Pillar New Testament Commentary*
P-Jonathan	*Targum Pseudo-Jonathan: Genesis*. Translated by Michael Maher. Vol. 1B of *The Aramaic Bible*. Edited by Kevin Cathcart, Michael Maher, and Martin McNamara. Collegeville, MN: The Liturgical Press, 1992.
RBTR	*Reformed Baptist Theological Review*
TB	*Tyndale Bulletin*
THOTC	*The Two Horizons Old Testament Commentary*
TLOT	*Theological Lexicon of the Old Testament*
TNK	Tanakh
TNTC	*Tyndale New Testament Commentaries*
TOTC	*Tyndale Old Testament Commentaries*
TWOT	*Theological Wordbook of the Old Testament*
VT	*Vetus Testamentum*
VUL	Vulgate
WBC	*Word Biblical Commentary*
WTJ	*Westminster Theological Journal*
ZAW	*Zeitschrift für die alttestamentliche Wissenschaft*
ZPEB	*The Zondervan Pictorial Encyclopedia of the Bible*. Edited by Merrill C. Tenney. 5 vols. Grand Rapids: Zondervan Publishing House, 1975–1976.

Introduction

A PRIMARY FUNCTION OF Scripture is to impart a proper understanding of sin. The apostle Paul underscored this function when he noted in Romans 3:20 that "through the law comes knowledge of sin." The context (3:9–19, 21) suggests that Paul is referring not to the Decalogue or five Books of Moses in particular but to the OT Scriptures as a whole as they function to reveal God's moral demands for humanity.[1] However, later in the epistle the apostle narrows his focus to the first book of the Hebrew canon, namely, Genesis. In Romans 5:12–14, Paul uses the redemptive-historical narrative recorded in Genesis, which he describes with the phrase "from Adam to Moses," to expound sin's primeval origin, universal scope, and ultimate consequence (Rom 5:12–21).[2] Following

1. As Murray remarks, "It is not Pauline . . . to regard the law that is epitomized in the ten commandments as a law that can be segregated; the OT in its entirety is permeated with the requirements and judgments which are summed up in the ten commandments." *Epistle to the Romans*, 105–6. See also Cranfield, *Romans 1–8*, 195; Hendricksen, *Exposition of Paul's Epistle to the Romans*, 124–25; Hodge, *Epistle to the Romans*, 80–86; Moo, *Epistle to the Romans*, 204–10; Leon Morris, *Epistle to the Romans*, 169–72; Schreiner, *Romans*, 168.

2. Some commentators note Paul's dependence on the Genesis 3 account of man's "fall." See, for example, Bruce, *Epistle of Paul to the Romans*, 129; Cranfield, *Romans 1–8*, 114; Godet, *Commentary on St. Paul's Epistle to the Romans*, 205; Murray, *Epistle to the Romans*, 181. Hendricksen suggests that Paul "may have been thinking, among other things, about the deluge, which destroyed almost the entire population of the world." *Exposition of Paul's Epistle to the Romans*, 179. It is probable, however, that Paul's reference to "death reign[ing] from Adam to Moses, even over those whose sinning was not like the transgression of Adam" is an allusion to the entire primeval and patriarchal epochs as they are recorded in Genesis. This is noted, but not developed, by Lenski, who observes in commenting on 5:14, "Abel was killed by his own brother. The history of every one of those ancients ends with *wayyamoth*, 'and he died.' . . . These are the facts that stand out in the story of Genesis 'from Adam to Moses.'" *Interpretation of St. Paul's Epistle to the Romans*, 363. Kline is certain Paul has the Genesis narrative in view. He writes, "These bounds ['from Adam to Moses'] are not simply temporal, as if Paul said 'until the days of the Hittite empire' or 'from the paleolithic to the late bronze age.' But the *terminus ad quem*, 'to Moses,' and the *terminus a quo*, 'from Adam,' are epochal turning points in the history of divine-human relationships, or, in more Biblical terms,

Paul's reasoning, one would expect the motif of sin to play a major role throughout *the entire narrative* of Genesis.

WHAT EVER BECAME OF SIN (IN THE PATRIARCHAL NARRATIVE)?

Nearly all scholars divide Genesis into primeval and patriarchal history, though they debate the precise point of division.[3] Interpreters offer various reasons to justify the division. First, the primeval narrative focuses on human history in general, whereas the patriarchal narrative focuses on Jewish history in particular.[4] Second, the primeval narrative follows a fast pace and spans long periods of time, whereas the patriarchal narrative slows the tempo and spans only four generations.[5] Third, many scholars see a shift in thematic emphases.

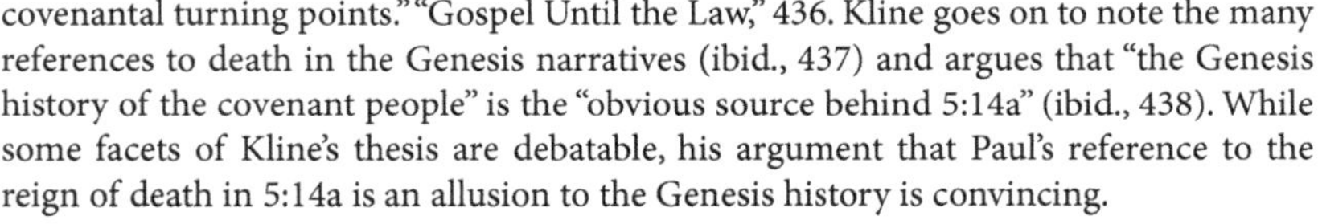

covenantal turning points." "Gospel Until the Law," 436. Kline goes on to note the many references to death in the Genesis narratives (ibid., 437) and argues that "the Genesis history of the covenant people" is the "obvious source behind 5:14a" (ibid., 438). While some facets of Kline's thesis are debatable, his argument that Paul's reference to the reign of death in 5:14a is an allusion to the Genesis history is convincing.

3. A number of biblical scholars and commentators conveniently locate the dividing point between Genesis 11 and 12. More commonly, however, interpreters mark the division between 11:26 and 11:27. A few make the division as early as 11:9. Von Rad carries primeval history through 12:9 and begins patriarchal history at 12:10. *Genesis*, 5–7.

4. Westermann argues that Genesis serves as an introduction to the Pentateuch and may be viewed as two concentric circles around Israel's birth as a nation at the exodus event: "While the stories of the patriarchs, Gen 12–50, present the history of Israel before it became a people, the story of the primeval events has a far wider horizon. It gives the events which take place in the middle of the Pentateuch a far wider horizon, extending them to world events in the broadest sense of the word." *Genesis 1–11*, 2. See also Gowan, *From Eden to Babel*, 3–6; Mathews, *Genesis 1—11:26*, 43–44; Sarna, *Genesis*, xii–xiii.

5. According to the ages given in the genealogies of Genesis 5 and 11, primeval history (Gen 1–11) spans no less than two thousand years and probably somewhere between twenty-five hundred and three thousand years. For a detailed discussion of the significance of these genealogies for chronology, see Benjamin Shaw, "Genealogies of Genesis 5 and 11 and Their Significance for Chronology." On the other hand, the events recorded within the patriarchal history (Gen 12–50) occur within a three-hundred-year period. The following interpreters note the slowed pace: Dever, *Message of the OT: Promises Made*, 66–67; Hamilton, *Genesis 1–17*, 10–11; Speiser, *Genesis*, lxx; Thomas, *Genesis*, 113.

The Sin Versus Grace Dichotomy

In primeval history, the narrator focuses on the origin and spread of sin, as well as God's consequent curse and judgment on humanity. Although God's blessing begins the narrative (1–2) and his grace surfaces from time to time after the fall, the main emphasis of primeval history is on sin and the curse. In patriarchal history, however, the spread of sin theme falls off the radar of most scholars. Here, it is generally argued, the narrator shifts the emphasis to God's promise of blessing in the lives of his chosen people, the family of Abraham. A few interpreters argue that this shift occurs immediately after the Flood.[6] Most scholars locate the shift of emphasis sometime after the Tower of Babel story (11:1–9) with the introduction of patriarchal history. Gerhard von Rad, for example, contrasts "the Jahwist's great hamartiology in Gen. III-XI" where "sin broke in and spread like an avalanche" with patriarchal or "sacred" history where "the promise of the possession of the land of Canaan, and the promise of an innumerable posterity" become the central motifs.[7] Following von Rad, John Gibson sees the "main thrust of the [first] eleven chapters" as "negative" because "they have portrayed sin spreading like a virus and infecting mortally not only humanity but the very physical creation." With the commencement of patriarchal history, however, "the call to Abraham which will set the Gospel story in motion is about to be issued."[8] According to Gordon Wenham, chapters 1–11 reveal "the hopeless plight of mankind without the gracious intervention of God." "But the promises first made to Abraham in 12:1–3," argues Wenham, "begin to repair that hopeless situation."[9] Victor Hamilton also views the patriarchal history (12–50) as the solution to the sin problem as outlined in the primeval history (1–11) and thus traces the progression of the

6. Keil and Delitzsch, *Pentateuch*, 1:34; Rendtorff, "Genesis 821 und die Urgeschichte des Jahwisten," 69–78; Clark, "Flood and the Structure of the Pre-patriarchal History," 184–211; Fretheim, *Creation, Fall, and Flood*, 112–13.

7. Von Rad, *OT Theology*, 152–54.

8. Gibson sees God's activity in the first eleven chapters as "a rearguard action as desperately [God] defends his Kingdom against [sinful man's] usurping hands." But beginning in chapter 12, "God Launches His Counter-Offensive," *Genesis*, 1:212–13.

9. Wenham goes on to expand this contrast: "Sin had apparently frustrated God's purposes for mankind [chs. 1–11]: the promises give hope that they may indeed by realized [chs. 12–50]. The primeval history thus explains the significance of the patriarchal story: though apparently of little consequence in the world of their day, the patriarchs are in fact men through whom the world will be redeemed." *Genesis 1–15*, li.

narrative "from generation (chs. 1–2), to degeneration (chs. 3–11), to regeneration (chs. 12–50)."[10] More recently, Allen Ross has concluded that the curse predominates in the primeval history while the blessing holds preeminence in the patriarchal narrative.[11] As a result of this tendency to contrast the primary theme(s) of primeval narrative with patriarchal narrative, the spread of sin motif fails to receive adequate treatment in Genesis 12–50.[12]

The Plaster-Saint Syndrome

Another factor that sometimes blinds scholars to the spread of sin theme in the patriarchal narrative is an inordinate emphasis on or exaggeration of the piety of the patriarchs. Of course, the patriarchal narratives as well as the rest of Scripture bear witness to the exemplary faith and obedience of these saints.[13] Yet Jewish and Christian exegetes have sometimes

10. Stating it from a different angle, Hamilton avers, "After the series of sorry examples presented in chs. 1–11, we are meant to read chs. 12ff. (patriarchal history) as the solution to this problem," *Genesis 1–17*, 11.

11. In Ross's words, "In Genesis the curse is prominent in the first eleven chapters, for that part of the book traces the spread of sin once humans came to know 'good and evil.' The emphasis on the curse is replaced in the patriarchal narratives by the prominence of the blessing, except for the warning of a curse for those who oppose God's program and God's people (Gen 12:1–3)," *Creation & Blessing*, 67.

12. Noting the use of narrative typology in the Pentateuch in which the narrator highlights how earlier redemptive events anticipate later ones, Sailhamer compares the "Spread of Sin" motif of Genesis with the theme of the "Defilement of the Camp" in Lev 11–16. But in Sailhamer's analysis, the "spread of sin" theme is limited to the first eleven chapters of Genesis. *Pentateuch as Narrative*, 39–41. Genesis 1–11 depicts "an endless cycle of chaos, evil, and destruction," according to Arnold. "But a significant turn occurs with the call of Abraham in chapter 12. The problem of human sin finds partial resolution through covenant relationship with God," *Encountering the Book of Genesis*, 200. T. D. Alexander remarks, "While the early chapters of Genesis concentrate mainly on the terrible consequences of these initial developments [i.e., human disobedience, alienation from God, and divine punishment], the rest of Genesis, from chapter 12 onwards, moves forward with the hope that humanity may yet be reconciled to God." *From Paradise to the Promised Land*, 98. See also Driver, *Book of Genesis*, lxx–lxxi; Roop, *Genesis*, 88, 93–94; Stigers, *Commentary on Genesis*, 34–35; Westermann, *Genesis 1–11*, 66–68, 604–5.

13. In the patriarchal narrative, Abraham is commended for his faith (15:6), pious fear (22:12), and obedience (22:16; 26:5). Not surprisingly, later Scripture writers refer to him as God's "servant" (Ps 105) and "friend" (2 Chr 21:7; Isa 4 1:8; Jas 2:23), and he is held up as a paradigm of piety for NT believers (John 8:39–40, 56; Rom 4:18–24; Gal 3:7, 9; Heb 11:8–17; Jas 2:21–24). The Scriptures also refer to Isaac and Jacob as God's "servants" (Exod 32:13; Deut 9:27) and attribute the same quality of faith to them

stressed patriarchal piety to the point of minimizing or excusing the patriarchs' faults. For example, the Book of Jubilees, a second-century BC Jewish work, alludes to the manifold trials and temptations Abraham faced in the Genesis narrative and asserts that "in everything wherein [God] had tried him, he was found faithful."[14] Another Hellenistic apocryphal work reads, "Therefore you, O Lord, God of the righteous, have not appointed repentance for the righteous, for Abraham and Isaac and Jacob, who did not sin against you, but you have appointed repentance for me, who am a sinner" (Odes 12:8, NRSV).[15] The Genesis Rabbah, a fourth-century AD conflation of the Genesis stories, portrays Abraham's personal merit as the ground of God's blessing on him and his descendants.[16] The Babylonian Talmud stresses the merit of the patriarchs and

(Heb 11:19–20) as well as to Joseph (Heb 11:21), whose moral integrity is especially highlighted in the patriarchal narrative (39:8–9).

14. The larger context reads: "And the Lord knew that Abraham was faithful in all his afflictions, for he had tried him through his country and with famine, and had tried him with the wealth of kings, and had tried him again through his wife, when she was torn (from him), and with circumcision; and had tried him through Ishmael and Hagar, his maid-servant, when he sent them away. And in everything wherein He had tried him, he was found faithful, and his soul was not impatient, and he was not slow to act; for he was faithful and a lover of the Lord" (17:17–18). Later the author describes the patriarch as "perfect in all his deeds with the Lord and well-pleasing in righteousness all of the days of his life" (23:10a). *Jubilees*, 121–22, 145.

15. This is the twelfth of fourteen Odes that are appended to the Psalms in the Greek manuscript codex Alexandrinus (fifth century AD) and bears the title, "The Prayer of Manasseh." Although its earliest known appearance is found in a third century AD writing known as the *Didascalia*, most scholars date the original work in the first or second century BC. See Metzger, *Introduction to the Apocrypha*, 123–28.

16. In Parashah 44:5 (commenting on Gen 15:1–21), Abraham reasons with God: "Lord of the ages, you made a covenant with Noah that you would not wipe out his children. I went and acquired treasure of religious deeds and good deeds greater than his, so the covenant made with me has set aside the covenant made with him." Then God is portrayed as answering the patriarch: "Out of Noah I did not raise up shields for the righteous, but from you I shall raise up shields for the righteous. And not only so, but when your children will fall into sin and evil deeds, I shall see a single righteous man among them who can say to the attribute of justice, 'Enough.' Him I shall take and make into the atonement for them all." Jacob Neusner, the translator and editor, interprets this to mean that the "merit of Abraham will protect Israel in time to come, and, in future ages, there will be someone in the model of Abraham, who will serve as atonement for Israel." According to Parashah 48:8, the patriarch possesses sufficient merit to deliver any Israelite from the fires of Gehenna: "In the age to come Abraham will sit at the gate of Gehenna, and he will not permit a circumcised Israelite to go down there. Then what will he do for those who sinned too much? He will remove the foreskin from infants who died before they were circumcised and will place it over [Israelite sinners] and then lower them into Gehenna [protected by the skin]." *GR*, 128–29, 182.

their invulnerability to the power of sin.[17] Perhaps to a lesser degree, some of the early church fathers so emphasized the godliness of the patriarchs that they found it necessary either to allegorize or to provide a positive interpretation of passages that appear to depict the patriarchs as engaging in sinful behavior.[18] Even the Reformers tended to overemphasize the patriarchs' piety and minimize their faults.[19] Štefan Porúbčan's thorough study of sin in the OT provides a more recent example of this tendency.[20] The author includes a summary of the historical development of sin in each major redemptive epoch. After treating man's fall into sin (404–32) and the subsequent spread of sin through antediluvian society (432–38), Porúbčan turns his attention to the patriarchal history

17. For example, *Berakoth* of *Seder Zera'im* attributes the efficacy of Daniel's prayer (Dan 9:17) to the merits of Abraham (7b). *Baba Bathra* represents the rabbis as teaching that "evil inclination had no dominion [over] Abraham, Isaac, and Jacob" (17a). *BabTalmud*, 35. See also Edersheim's survey of the Talmudic literature in *The Life and Times of Jesus the Messiah*, 1:271–72.

18. When explaining Abraham's descent into Egypt and wife-sister ruse, Didymus the Blind (circa 313–398) can write, "On the literal level Abraham made an intelligent compromise with the lustfulness of the Egyptians." But "as for the spiritual meaning, those who pass from virtue to vice are said to descend to Egypt. . . . It does not say 'he descended' but 'he entered.' His descent is an entrance, because every zealous man condescends to those who fall without falling with them . . . to deliver them from their fall. Just as one becomes Jewish for the sake of the Jews without being a Jew, and ungodly for the sake of the ungodly without being ungodly, so one comes into Egypt without living as an Egyptian." *ACCS*, 2:7. Chrysostom portrays Rebekah's deceptive scheme to secure the blessing for Jacob as "a mother's affection" and equates it with "God's designs." According to Chrysostom, it was God "who prompted her to make plans and also made sure all turned out well." *ACCS*, 2:169. When Isaac assesses Jacob's act as deceptive (Gen 27:35), Augustine assures the reader that Isaac is only using the term in "a figurative sense" since in reality "a guileful, deceitful man . . . would deserve a curse." *ACCS*, 2:179.

19. Martin Luther begins his exposition of the patriarchal narratives well by noting Abraham's deliverance from idolatry and interpreting it "as proof for the doctrine of grace over against the worth of merits and works." *Lectures on Genesis*, 2:246. Yet throughout his lectures, Luther is quick to commend Abraham and his descendants for their piety, while at the same time excusing or minimizing their sins. John Calvin also commences his treatment of the patriarchal narratives by underlining "the gratuitous mercy of God" in Abram's call. *Genesis*, 1:343. But he, like Luther, feels compelled to emphasize the godliness of the patriarchs and to downplay their faults. The present study will highlight instances of this tendency in Luther and Calvin when relevant passages in the patriarchal narratives are analyzed.

20. Štefan Porúbčan, *Sin in the Old Testament: A Soteriological Study*. At the time of its publication, Porúbčan claimed, "So far there is no thorough and comprehensive study of sin in the OT" (xiii).

(438–44). He begins this section with a statement that conditions his entire perspective on the patriarchal narrative: "Here *we are not dealing with a sinner*, but with a particularly righteous man, a friend of God [emphasis added]." In the paragraphs that follow, he fails to mention a single patriarchal sin (!) and concludes by according Abraham's personal merit equal weight with divine grace as a ground or basis for God's covenant promise.[21] Victor Hamilton also overplays Abraham's piety when he writes, "Will there be more Adams and more tower builders? Or is there a way out of this dilemma [i.e., human sin in primeval history]? The obedient model of Abraham contrasts to all the sorry models who have gone before him."[22] As these examples demonstrate, an overemphasis on the virtues of the patriarchs has sometimes kept interpreters from seriously considering their vices.

Removing the Rose-Colored Glasses

However, there are at least four good reasons why the interpreter of Genesis should see the "spread of sin" as a major theme not only of primeval history but also of patriarchal history. First, the distinction between primeval and patriarchal history is not as sharp as sometimes alleged. Recent studies have demonstrated the integrity of the book as a whole and suggest that the central themes of chapters 12–50 actually are grounded in chapters 1–11.[23] The unity of Genesis would seem to suggest

21. Comparing Abraham with Noah, Porúbčan notes that "the covenant is built upon God's favour and mercy, and at the same time upon the acknowledged righteousness and unshaken faith and faithfulness of the man Abraham. We can note the enormous influence of a righteous man with God." *Sin in the Old Testament*, 440. While Porúbčan's assessment of the patriarchal history and of Abraham's piety is not devoid of truth, his failure to mention any patriarchal sin in a section purporting to be a history of sin is an obvious deficiency of his work. The author's desire to emphasize Abraham's merit (an emphasis consistent with his Roman Catholic theology) has to some degree blinded his eyes to the real and frequent portrayals of patriarchal sin in this period of redemptive history.

22. *Genesis 1–17*, 11. Hamilton references Coats who makes the same superficial contrast: "Genesis 1–11 seems uniform in presenting man as a creature who seeks divine power but whose search comes to ruin in confrontation with God. . . . One might well ask, on the basis of the disobedient model, what an obedient model would look like. The primeval history leads naturally to the history of God's relationship to Abraham." "The God of Death: Power and Obedience in the Primeval History," 234.

23. Clines appropriately notes, "In the final form of Genesis, therefore, there is at no point a break between primaeval and patriarchal history. What follows immediately upon the Babel story (11:1–9) is the genealogical table leading from Shem to Terah

that important themes developed in primeval history (e.g., spread of sin) will receive further treatment in patriarchal history. Second, as noted in the introductory remarks, the NT assigns a sin-revealing function to the entirety of the OT (Rom 3:10–20), especially the Torah, which includes the book of Genesis (Rom 5:12–21).[24] Third, the NT writers portray the patriarchs not only as saints but also as sinners saved by grace. In particular, Paul describes Abraham as an "ungodly" (ἀσεβῆ) man whom God justified. Since this description carries negative moral overtones[25] and cannot be limited to Abraham's pre-conversion state,[26] it is likely

(11:10–26). But who Shem is can be learned only from the Table of Nations, where his family is detailed . . . (10:21–31), or from the Noah story . . . (9:26). So the Shem genealogy is firmly linked into the primaeval history. On the other hand, it is plain that the goal of the genealogy is Abram (11:26–30). Its function is equally to trace the ancestry of Abram—so it is attached to what follows—and to follow the line of descent from Shem—so it is attached to what precedes." *The Theme of the Pentateuch*, 84–85. Based on the *toledot* structural device, Mathews argues, "The composition forms an Adam-Noah-Abraham continuum that loops the patriarchal promises with the God of cosmos and all human history." *Genesis 1–11:26*, 41. See also Childs, *Introduction to the OT as Scripture*, 136–60; Mann, "All the Families of the Earth," 341–53.

24. Scholars often overlook the fact that the book of Genesis functions both as a witness to pre-Torah revelation and also as a part of Torah revelation. Hence, the events recorded in Genesis occurred *before the law* (Rom 5:13–14; Gal 4:17–18), yet they also constitute the revelation *of the law*, which has as one of its functions the revelation of human sin (Rom 5:12–21; see also Rom 4:15; 7:7–9; Gal 3:19, 22).

25. Some, such as Dunn, attempt to tie the term in this context to Abraham's covenantal standing (i.e., he was justified while *outside the covenant*) and disconnect it from any negative moral connotations. *Romans 1–8*, 204–5. The basic meaning of the word ἀσεβῆ, however, demands a negative moral description of the person in view (see also Gen 18:23, 25; Exod 23:7; Deut 25:1; Ps 1:1, 4–6; 9:23; 11:5; 17:9; 26:9; Prov 1:10; 2:22; 10:20; Isa 5:23; 13:11; 55:7; Ezek 20:38; 33:8, 9, 11, 12, 14; Rom 5:6–8; 1 Tim 1:9; 2 Pet 2:5–6). This is further confirmed by the inclusion of David's words (4:7–8) from Psalm 32:1–2, which bear biographical witnesses to the kind of "ungodly" person God justifies (i.e., in David's case, an adulterer and murderer). The point of Paul's argument is not merely that God declares people righteous who are outside the covenant (i.e., Gentiles) but that God declares people righteous who do not merit that accreditation.

26. Note that Paul bases his portrayal of Abraham as an ungodly man justified in Genesis 15:6, a text characterizing the patriarch some time after his initial conversion (compare Gen 12:1–6 with Acts 7:2–4; Heb 11:8). Although Abraham was justified once-for-all years prior to his act of faith described in Genesis 15:6, that simple faith remained paradigmatic of the patriarch's first act of saving faith. Moreover, the blessing attributed to Abraham in 15:6, namely, being credited as righteous, continues to contemplate his state as "ungodly," that is, as a sinner in need of saving grace. Similarly, Paul's citation of David's words in Psalm 32 certainly applies to David's post-conversion experience (Ps 32:1–2; Rom 4:7–8).

Paul saw the patriarch's vices as well as virtues when he read the Genesis text.[27] Finally, and most importantly, a careful exegetical and theological analysis reveals an equal if not greater emphasis on the pervasiveness of human sin in the patriarchal narrative than that found in the primeval narrative.

FALLING SHORT: LITERATURE REVIEW

A review of relevant biblical studies reveals that a detailed and comprehensive exegetical and theological analysis that focuses particularly on the theme of sin in the patriarchal narrative does not exist.

Commentaries

As noted above, nearly all commentators fail to perceive a major role for the sin motif in the patriarchal history. The majority of these commentators do not ignore the sins of the patriarchs. Hamilton, for instance, notes the numerous sins and shortcomings of the patriarchs in his exposition of chapters 12–50. But he argues that the narrator's (and God's) silence concerning their sins implies a shift of emphasis from human sin to God's faithfulness and electing grace.[28] To Allen Ross's credit, he does not ignore the theme of sin and evil in the patriarchal narratives and assures the reader that "in [his] exposition of Genesis . . . the motifs of blessing and cursing and good and evil appear repeatedly, tracing the theological message of the book." Nevertheless, his general summary of thematic emphasis cited above (n. 11) betrays a common tendency to downplay the spread of sin theme in the patriarchal narratives.[29] Kenneth Mathews provides a "theology of Genesis," highlighting the themes of the promised blessing, seed, and land. Though he devotes only one paragraph to the theme of "sin" in his theology of Genesis,[30]

27. In other words, Paul's characterization of Abraham as "ungodly" is based not merely on the patriarch's pre-Canaan life (Josh 24:2; Neh 9:7) but embraces the totality of the patriarch's life as depicted in the patriarchal narrative. With respect to Abraham's legal status and moral condition before God, he is always viewed, to use Martin Luther's coined expression, *simul iustus et peccator*. See *Lectures on Romans: Glosses and Scholia*, 63; *Lectures on Galatians 1545: 1–4*, 232.

28. *Genesis 1–17*, 38–50.

29. *Creation & Blessing*, 69. Even the title of his commentary directs the reader's focus away from sin and the curse.

30. *Genesis 1—11:26*, 54–63.

Mathews's second volume, which covers patriarchal history, gives a slightly greater emphasis to the topic of sin, devoting almost six pages to the motifs of sibling rivalry, deception, and alienation. Yet he makes it clear that these sin motifs are subordinate to the overarching theme of God's promissory blessings.[31] Bruce Waltke comes closer to providing a unified reading of the entire Genesis narrative that incorporates the sin motif. But Waltke, like the commentators above, places the accent on redemption rather than on sin.[32] While a reading of Genesis that sees divine grace overruling human sin is generally sound (Gen 50:20), it can hinder the reader from fully exploring and appreciating the pervasiveness of sin that permeates the patriarchal narrative.

Articles, Essays, and Monographs

Numerous journal articles and essays explore the theme of sin in Genesis. Those focusing on narrative sections within the larger patriarchal narrative are limited in scope.[33] Monographs that explore the theme of sin include various literary analyses of stories[34] or themes within the larger

31. *Genesis 11:27—50:26*, 72–80. See also Mathews's theology of Genesis in the *New Dictionary of Biblical Theology*, 140–46. Mathews does list "crime and curse" as one of the major themes in the book, but he confines his discussion under this heading to passages in the primeval narrative.

32. Says Waltke, "God's promise to establish his kingdom through his grace that overcomes human sin is the governing theme of Genesis." *Genesis*, 50.

33. The literature here is too vast to cite exhaustively, but a few examples include Berg, "Der Sündenfall Abrahams und Saras nach Gen 16:1–6," 7–14; idem, "Nochmals: ein Sündenfall Abrahams—der erste—in Gen 12:10–20," 7–15; Doyle, "The Sin of Sodom: yāḏaᶜ, yāḏaᶜ, yāḏaᶜ?" 84–100; Kirsh, "What Did Sarah See?" 107–10; Daube and Yaron, "Jacob's Reception by Laban," 60–62; Tucker, "Jacob's Terrible Burden: In the Shadow of the Text," 145–58; Friedman, "Deception for Deception" 131–44; Caspi, "The Story of the Rape of Dinah," 25–45; Kessler, "Genesis 34—An Interpretation," 3–8; Bechtel, "What If Dinah Is Not Raped? (Genesis 34)," 19–36; Shapira, "Be Silent: An Immoral Behavior?" 232–44; Fewell and Gunn, "Tipping the Balance," 193–211; Nichol, "Genesis xxix.32 and xxxv.22a: Reuben's Reversal," 536–39; Schimmel, "Joseph and His Brothers," 60–65; White, "Reuben and Judah," 73–97; Ackerman, "Joseph, Judah, and Jacob," 2:85–113; Mathewson, "An Exegetical Study of Genesis 38," 373–92; Wildasvsky, "Survival Must Not Be Gained Through Sin," 37–48; Hilgert, "The Dual Image of Joseph in Hebrew and Early Jewish Literature," 5–21.

34. Alter provides a brief analysis of the Judah-Tamar story in *Art of Biblical Narrative*, 3–12. Gunn and Fewell provide a more detailed investigation of this story as well as the stories of Abraham and Sarah in *Narrative in the Hebrew Bible*, 34–45, 90–100. Fokkelman explores the Jacob cycle in *Narrative Art in Genesis*, 46–81, as does Fishbane in *Text and Texture*, 40–62. Sternberg provides an extended analysis of the

patriarchal narrative. Devora Steinmetz provides a literary analysis of the phenomenon of ethical conflicts between fathers and sons in the patriarchal narratives as the promise and blessing is passed on from one generation to the next.[35] David and Diana Garland focus on the moral abuses suffered by some of the matriarchs in the patriarchal narrative.[36] Burton Visotsky, a Jewish rabbi, provides a more comprehensive analysis of sin committed within the patriarchal family extending from the story of Abraham to Dinah's rape in Shechem.[37] There are also character studies that comment on the sins of the patriarchs.[38] Iain Duguid has written two books that highlight both the failures and the triumphs within the families of Abraham, Isaac, and Jacob. He stops at Genesis 35, however, and his work is written on a semi-popular rather than scholarly level.[39] Similarly, Ian Toppin's study of family dysfunctions within the patriar-

---

story of Dinah's rape in Genesis 34. *Poetics of Biblical Narrative*, 445–75. Ryken examines the stories of Abraham, Jacob, and Joseph in *Words of Delight*, 62–71, 71–81, 100–05.

35. *From Father to Son*. Although Steinmetz's analysis is primarily literary in character, it operates under the normative assumption of modern psychoanalytical and anthropological theories, which she discusses in her introduction. Ibid., 11–34.

36. In particular, they explore the theme of sin as it affects the lives of Sarah, Hagar, Leah, Dinah, and Tamar in *Flawed Families of the Bible*, 19–124.

37. *Genesis of Ethics*. However, Visotsky's analysis is flawed since it rejects the Scriptures as the normative basis for ethics. According to Visotsky, "Even God's law must stand the scrutiny of human ethics." Ibid., 208. Not surprisingly, he views the stories simply as a helpful means to elicit discussion concerning moral dilemmas, which in turn promotes moral development. In his own words, "It is not the narrative of Genesis that makes the work sacred. Rather it is in the process of *studying* Genesis that the transformation takes place." Ibid., 11 (emphasis his). Visotsky follows a reader-centered hermeneutic, at times offering several interpretations for the same passage and considering them valid ways to view the text. Some of his readings will be noted in this present study.

38. Such would include Getz, *Abraham*; idem, *Jacob*; idem, *Joseph*; Jordan, *Primeval Saints*, 61–149; LaSor, *Great Personalities*, 13–49; Whyte, *Bible Characters*, 65–123. In some cases, important characters are not discussed. For example, neither Getz nor LaSor includes a treatment of Isaac, Esau, or any of the matriarchs. Whyte's study excludes Judah. Moreover, some of these studies tend to be written on a more popular level and often lack sufficient exegetical discussion. Jordan's treatment, while reflecting a degree of scholarly reflection, is marred by an overly positive view of the patriarchs reflected in his attempts to justify many of their sins. The study below will interact with some of Jordan's attempts to exonerate the patriarchs and matriarchs of certain wrongdoings.

39. *Living in the Gap Between Promise and Reality*; idem, *Living in the Grip of Relentless Grace*.

chal community, though spanning from Adam through Jacob's sons, suffers from brevity and a lack of exegetical and theological depth.[40]

Dissertations

A few doctoral dissertations examine the theme of sin in Genesis, but most of these limit their analysis of sin to the primeval narrative.[41] Those that do extend beyond the primeval narrative limit their focus to a particular dimension of sin within the Genesis corpus. John Ronning sees the Cain-Abel narrative as the first fulfillment of the divinely-imposed enmity between these "seeds," and he traces successive fulfillments of Genesis 3:15 throughout the narrative, noting several striking parallels between, for example, Ishmael and Isaac, Esau and Jacob, and the ten brothers (especially Judah) and Joseph.[42] Michael Williams identifies and analyzes those narratives in Genesis involving deception, with the aim of determining whether evaluative patterns in the text itself indicate the rightness or wrongness of the deceptive act.[43] While these studies

40. *Biblical Patriarchs and Their Legacy of Family Dysfunctions*. The book includes 116 pages of exposition. Toppin provides little exegetical analysis of the Hebrew text and no interaction with secondary literature.

41. Bratcher builds on the earlier studies of von Rad, Westermann, and Clines. She notes a formal pattern of episodes of sin, discovery of sin by Yahweh, judgment speech, mitigation of the judgment, and execution of the judgment in Genesis 1–11. She concludes that the narratives focus on the human violation of God's will and God's response to expose sin and correct it with judgment and grace. "The Pattern of Sin and Judgment in Genesis 1–11." Lim's *Grace in the Midst of Judgment* is a slight revision of the author's doctoral dissertation that was published in 2001. Lim employs a "theological hermeneutic" and analyzes the narratives of Genesis 1–11, concluding that "grace in the midst of judgment" not only characterizes the theme of these chapters but continues throughout the OT canonical literature. Shank studies the theme of sin in Genesis 1–11 in light of the Cain and Abel narrative. He concludes that the central theme of primeval history is not the spread of sin and grace [contra von Rad, Westermann, Clines] but rather the "self-limitation of God." Applied to the Cain and Abel account, "God permits sin to exist as an independent entity with a desire for Cain which he can master. Furthermore, within the context of the God-Cain relationship, sin emerges as a human responsibility" (iii). "The Sin Theology of the Cain and Abel Story."

42. "The Curse on the Serpent (Genesis 3:15) in Biblical Theology and Hermeneutics," 143–78, 184–211. Although Ronning's dissertation is actually concerned with the curse on the Serpent and its intertextual connections throughout the entire Bible, he does provide helpful analysis of the themes of hatred, strife, and violence throughout Genesis.

43. *Deception in Genesis*. In this edited and republished version of his PhD dissertation. Williams notes that while the narrative evaluates most deceptive events negatively, it assesses deception positively "when the perpetrator deceives one who has previously

make significant contributions to a theology of sin in the patriarchal narrative, none of them provides a comprehensive picture.

THE BOOK OF GENESIS: WHERE SIN ABOUNDS

The objective of the present study is to meet the need for a comprehensive and detailed exegetical and theological analysis of the spread of human sin in the patriarchal narrative of Genesis. More particularly, the study will examine both the varied expressions of human sin (i.e., sin proper) as well as the effects of human sin (i.e., the divinely imposed consequences for sin). The study will be "comprehensive" in that the patriarchal narrative as a whole will be analyzed.[44] The study will also deal with grammatical particulars and theological nuances within the text and thus be "detailed." Moreover, the study will engage in theological exegesis, which accepts the text's own self-attestation as divine revelation and which attempts to formulate from that revelation doctrine normative for human faith and life.

MARKING THE BOUNDARIES

The nature of this study requires certain delimitations. First of all, questions of authorship, intended audience, and historical setting are important components for interpreting any piece of ancient literature. To achieve the objective of this study, however, it will not be possible to engage the source-critical debate regarding the pre-textual history,

---

wronged him in order to restore his own condition to what it would have been had it not been disrupted, while, at the same time, not harming the victim." That is, "deception is justified when it is used by one previously wronged against the one who has done the wrong in order to restore *shalom*" (56). After analyzing the material in Genesis, Williams examines deception in other key OT passages. Then he looks at evaluations of deception in later Jewish tradition, Ancient Near East literature, and parallels in folklore. He concludes that "deception in Genesis is a phenomenon with significant differences from its occurrences in the rest of the Bible and in other cultures ancient and modern" (223). Williams goes on to suggest as an "avenue of inquiry deserving further study and reflection . . . the question of the purpose for the preservation of so many deception accounts in Genesis" (224).

44. An attempt is made to analyze all the major passages in which human sin or the divine curse is present. The study, however, is not exhaustive in the sense of including detailed discussion on every explicit or implicit mention of sin or the curse in the Genesis narrative. Space did not permit such an exhaustive coverage. However, the appendix includes a table featuring all the noted instances of sin or the curse in the entire Genesis corpus.

authorship, date, and integrity of the book of Genesis. Such a pursuit is beyond the scope of this study, and there are already useful works that critique the philosophy and many of the conclusions of modern source criticism.[45] The writer proceeds from the conviction that the entire book of Genesis is a unified literary work authored by Moses[46] written to the newly formed nation of Israel sometime between the exodus from Egypt and conquest of Canaan. Second, sensitivity to the literary art and structure of a text is also helpful in establishing the meaning of a text.[47] But again, the objective of this study will not permit an extended analysis of the literary devices or the overall structure of the patriarchal narrative, though the writer will seek to incorporate insights gleaned from the available literary and structural analyses.[48] Third, many questions regarding the historicity of the patriarchal and especially the primeval narratives have arisen in modern times. These questions cannot be ignored since denial or affirmation of the historical accuracy of the Genesis narra-

45. For critiques of the documentary hypothesis and source criticism, see Allis's classic *Five Books of Moses.* For more recent critiques, see T. D. Alexander, *From Paradise to Promised Land*, 3–94; Garrett, *Rethinking Genesis.*

46. For a defense of essential Mosaic authorship, see Archer, *Survey of OT Introduction*, 99–147, 173–89; Dillard and Longman, *Introduction to the OT*, 38–48; Garrett, 47–83; Harrison, *Introduction to the OT*, 495–541; Young, *Introduction to the OT*, 42–46; Youngblood, *Book of Genesis*, 9–15. As these works demonstrate, a traditional defense of Mosaic authorship does not preclude the possibility that Moses may have utilized some earlier sources or that there may be some "post-Mosaica" glosses in Genesis. The current tendency among evangelicals, though, as Dillard and Longman note (47–48), has been to speculate more about possible pre-Mosaic sources underlying the Genesis text or to concede too much post-Mosaic redaction.

47. On the value of literary analysis for biblical studies, see Alter, *Art of Biblical Narrative*; idem, *Art of Biblical Poetry*; Sternberg, *Poetics of Biblical Narrative*; Gunn and Fewell, *Narrative in the Hebrew Bible*; Ryken, *Words of Delight*; Ryken and Longman, *Complete Literary Guide to the Bible.*

48. Some more recent commentaries provide helpful examples of literary and structural analyses of Genesis. For example, a number of commentators see the repeated use of the formulaic phrase אֵלֶּה תּוֹלְדוֹת/ʾēlleh tôlēdôt (2:4; 6:9; 10:1; 11:10; 11:27; 25:12; 25:19; 36:1; 36:9; 37:2), or its variant, זֶה סֵפֶר תּוֹלְדֹת/zeh sēper tôlēdôt (5:1), as a major structuring device. See Ross, 69–88; Waltke, 18–21; McKeown, *Genesis*, 2–3. For a structural analysis of the entire book of Genesis and its relationship to the larger Hebrew canon, see Dorsey, *Literary Structure of the OT.* For examples of literary analysis of individual sections within the larger Genesis narrative, see Gunn and Fewell, *Narrative in the Hebrew Bible*, 34–45, 90–100, 194–205; Fishbane, *Biblical Text and Texture*, 40–62; Fokkelman, *Narrative Art in Genesis*, 11–241; Ryken, *Words of Delight*, 62–105; Sailhamer, "Genesis," in *Complete Literary Guide to the Bible*, 108–20; Sternberg, *Poetics of Biblical Language,* 131–85, 285–308, 349–54, 394–400, 445–75.

tives profoundly influences one's exegetical and theological conclusions. Nevertheless, space will permit neither a careful analysis of the objections raised to the historicity of the primeval and patriarchal narratives nor a comprehensive defense of their historical reliability. Many sound defenses having been set forth,[49] the present study will proceed on the assumption that the Genesis narratives convey historical information that is both real and also reliable.

THE MODUS OPERANDI

The Genesis narratives address such topics as the origin, nature, spread, and divine restraint of human sin, but space does not permit a comprehensive and detailed exploration of these. Instead, this study will focus primarily on *the spread of human sin*. Of course, it will be necessary to address briefly the origin and nature of sin, especially as revealed in the Fall narrative in order to provide the historical backdrop and theological framework for understanding sin's spread. Furthermore, the divine curse on sin will be briefly examined in the Fall narrative, and its outworking will be explored in the subsequent narratives inasmuch as it contributes to the overall theme of sin's spread. God's restraint of human sin takes one into the realm of common grace and special grace. Though these are important counterbalancing themes to the spread of human sin, they will not be the focus of this study. Moreover, though this study will explore sin's beginnings in the Fall narrative and its subsequent spread through the primeval narrative, its primary focal point will be the patriarchal narratives.

Part one, a chapter that investigates the Fall narrative, first situates mankind's fall into sin in its creational and covenantal context. An analysis of the serpent's temptation and the human fall into sin then follows. The chapter also addresses the essential nature of this first human transgression, concluding with an examination of God's inquest, curse, and banishment of the human couple from the Garden of Eden.

Part two is a chapter exploring the spread of sin and the curse themes in the primeval narratives in order to uncover certain patterns

49. Kitchen, *On the Reliability of the OT*, 1–5, 313–72; 421–500; Garrett, 47–83; Hamilton, *Book of Genesis: Chapters 1–17*, 56–67; Mathews, *Genesis 1–11:26*, 109–11; idem, *Genesis 11:27–50:26*, 22–55; Ross, *Creation & Blessing*, 50–64. For a discussion of the larger question of historicity and the OT, see Long, "Historiography of the OT," 145–75; idem, *Art of Biblical History*, 281–429.

and motifs that will serve as narrative types to evaluate the patriarchal narratives. In this way, the second chapter prepares the reader for a deeper exploration of these themes in the patriarchal narratives.

Part three consists of six chapters. Chapter three examines the spread of sin in pagan society as revealed in the patriarchal narrative. Chapters four through seven provide a detailed analysis of the spread of sin in the patriarchal community, moving from the first to the fourth generation of the patriarchal family. Finally, chapter eight investigates the spread of the divine curse in the patriarchal narrative, which complements the theme of the spread of sin.

The study concludes with a summary and synthesis of the findings. In addition, the conclusion highlights important contributions to one's view of the overall thematic structure of Genesis, as well as to one's understanding of the doctrines of sin, grace, justification, and sanctification.

PART ONE

Sin and the Curse in the Fall Narrative

1

The Beginnings of Sin and the Curse in the Fall Narrative

In the beginning, the God of gods (אֱלֹהִים),[1] creates "all things of nothing, by the word of his power, in the space of six days, and all very good" (Gen 1:1–31).[2] But this "beginning" is only *the beginning* of King Elohim's empire-building program because into the midst of his pristine creation, the heavenly Suzerain, also known as Yahweh (יהוה), places his image (צֶלֶם), that is, his visible resemblance and representative. As Yahweh-Elohim's image, man (אָדָם) stands in covenant relationship to his Sovereign and is commissioned to subdue the earth as a loyal vassal and vice-regent to his Creator (Gen 1:26–28; 2:15–17). That is, from the *terminus a quo* of Eden's Holy Mountain garden sanctuary (2:8–15), humanity's task is to advance God's kingdom centrifugally over the entire earth, following his Creator's work-rest cycle (2:1–3), until the whole earth is filled with Yahweh-Elohim's glory (Isa 43:7; Rom 11:36; 1 Cor 15:24–28; Rev 4:11). Had mankind fulfilled his imperial commission in a way that accurately reflected his holy Suzerain's character and that visibly manifested absolute submission to and dependence on the divine will (2:15–17), he would have inherited fullness of life as a royal grant

1. This is the plural form of אֱלוֹהַּ, which grammarians appropriately designate as the plural of majesty (GKC § 224c) or the honorific plural (*IBHS* § 7.4.3). Waltke and O'Connor explain, "In this usage (sometimes called the *pluralis majestatis*) the referent is a singular individual, which is, however, so thoroughly characterized by the qualities of the noun that a plural is used" (*IBHS* § 7.4.3). Thus, in the case of God the idea expressed is something like "the very essence or epitome of Deity." See also this plural used of God when he is referred to as "the Holy One" (Prov 9:10) or as "the Lord" (Exod 15:17; Deut 10:17; Ps 8:2. Cf. *GBH*, § 136d–e).

2. The words within quotation marks, which concisely summarize the content of Genesis 1:1–31, are taken from the Westminster Shorter Catechism's answer to the question, "What is the work of creation?" Schaff, *Creeds of Christendom*, 677.

and joined his Creator-King in an eternal Sabbath-rest (Heb 4:1–11).[3] What should have been, however, was disrupted when human sin and the divine curse entered the world. This chapter will focus on the beginnings of sin and the curse depicted in the Fall narrative of Genesis 3.[4]

3. For a fuller development of the covenantal and eschatological themes reflected in this paragraph, see the author's "The Covenantal Context of the Fall," 5–32. The following works also provide helpful analyses of the covenantal and/or eschatological themes and ramifications of the creation narratives: Beale, *Temple and the Church's Mission*, 81–87; Dempster, *Dominion and Dynasty*, 55–77; Dumbrell, *Covenant and Creation*, 11–46; Griffith, "Eschatology Begins with Creation," 387–96; Kline, *Kingdom Prologue*, 8–117; Merrill, *Everlasting Dominion*, 277–97; Vos, *Biblical Theology*, 27–40; idem, *Eschatology of the OT*, 73–76; Ward, *God & Adam*, 17–29; Wisdom, *Royal Destiny*, 5–44.

4. Traditionally, both Jewish and Christian interpreters have read Genesis 3 as the tragic account of Adam and Eve's "fall into sin." For example, the apocryphal work Wisdom of Ben Sira (Sirach) alludes to Eve's transgression and declares, "Sin began with a woman, and thanks to her we must all die" (25:24, NJB). Another apocryphal work, Wisdom of Solomon, shifts the blame one step further and asserts, "Death came into the world only through the Devil's envy" (2:24, NJB). The apostle Paul also alludes to the Serpent's seduction of Eve (2 Cor 11:3; 1 Tim 2:14) but brings Adam into the picture when he writes, "Therefore, just as sin came into the world through one man, and death through sin, and so death spread to all men because all sinned" (Rom 5:12; cf. 12–21; 1 Cor 15:21–22, 45–49). Modern scholarship, however, has tended to question or deny that this narrative is about a primeval "fall into sin." In many cases, the idea of a primeval fall-event is rejected on the basis of a rejection of the historicity of the early chapters of Genesis. At best, these early chapters portray existential, not historical realities. See Ricoeur, *Symbolism of Evil*, 233; Hanson, *The Serpent Was* Wiser, 41; Westermann, *Genesis 1–11*, 275–78. This study proceeds on the scripturally self-attested assumption that the events portrayed in the primeval narrative reliably reflect actual historical events. Especially relevant are the genealogies of the chronicler (1 Chronicles 1–9) and Luke, who both treat Adam as the historical progenitor of the promised "seed," whom Luke identifies as Christ (Luke 3:23–38). If one yanks the thread of primeval narrative from the cloth of history, he runs the risk of unraveling the entire garment of redemptive history and undermining the gospel. The testimony of Psalm 136 is also important as the psalmist extols God's mighty deeds in the historical context of the Exodus (136:10–15), the wilderness (136:16), the conquest of Canaan (136:17–22), and his own day (136:23–25), and he links them with God's mighty acts in Creation (136:5–9), drawing from the very language and sequence of the Genesis creation account. Finally, according to the NT writers, both Jesus and his apostles interpreted the early chapters of Genesis as real history. In Matthew 19:4–6, Christ bases the theological warrant for marriage on the historical origin of marriage as recorded in the primeval history (Gen 2:22–24). He also alludes to the historicity of the original temptation in John 8:44. In several places, the apostle Paul clearly treats Adam as a historical individual (Rom 5:12–14; 1 Cor 15:21, 22, 44–49; 2 Cor 11:3; 2 Tim 2:13–14). Of special interest is Paul's use of the Genesis account of Adam and Eve's creation to support male headship: "For it was Adam who was *first* (πρῶτος) created, and *then* (εἶτα) Eve" (1 Tim 2:13, emphasis added). Paul bases his theology of male-female roles on the as-

THE TEMPTER AND THE TEMPTATION

Genesis 3:1 introduces a new character into the Eden narrative and signals a shift in the plot.[5] He is introduced as "the serpent." Initially, the reader may picture nothing more than a legless reptile (suborder: *serpentes*).[6] But additional information in the account suggests that this entity is more than a mere snake. This creature talks with the humans and entices them to sin (3:1–5). As a result, he and his "offspring" are cursed by God (3:14–15). The mixture of animal and supra-animal characteristics raises the question of the real identity of this "tempter," the answer to which is vital for a proper interpretation of the text.

The Identity of the Serpent

Some modern scholars suggest that the narrator's portrayal of a talking animal classifies the text as ancient folklore and myth, and it serves both an etiological as well as a moralistic function.[7] Others compare the narrative with ancient Near Eastern serpent mythology and argue that the serpent is a symbol of immortality, wisdom, or chaos.[8] Still other

---

sumption that the Genesis creation account presents real historical sequence. These and other examples (1 Cor 11:7–9; Heb 11:3–7; 2 Pet 3:3–6; 1 John 3:8; Jude 14) demonstrate that Christ and the apostles treated the early chapters of Genesis as real history. A few modern scholars, however, have attempted to reject Genesis 3 as a "Fall narrative" on the basis of exegetical and literary analysis. See, for example, Barr, *Garden of Eden and the Hope of Immortality*, 1–20. For a rebuttal of Barr's arguments, see Fretheim, "Is Genesis 3 a Fall Story?" 144–53.

5. Note the disjunctive *waw* at the beginning of 3:1, which serves to mark a new stage in the story (see *IBHS* § 39.2.3).

6. The Hebrew term נָחָשׁ is generally used to refer to a type of a reptile, usually a legless reptile such as a snake (Num 21:6; Deut 8:15; Ps 58:4; Prov 23:32; Isa 65:25; Jer 8:17; Amos 5:19; Mic 7:17).

7. Herman Gunkel opines, "The myth belongs to the category of myths and fairy tales very common in antiquity and among primitive peoples which tell how certain animals came by their unusual characteristics, 'why the flounder has its oblique mouth, the donkey its long ears, and the bear its stumpy tail.'" *Genesis*, 21. See also Skinner, *Genesis*, xi; von Rad, *Genesis*, 92; Westermann, *Genesis 1–11*, 259.

8. See Joines, *Serpent Symbolism in the OT*, 16–31. While acknowledging parallels between the serpent in Genesis 3 and ANE mythology, others understand the portrayal of the serpent in Genesis 3 as a kind of demythologizing polemic against such mythological stories. Sarna, for example, notes that the serpent here is described as merely a creature, as mortal, and as too insignificant to speak in God's presence (24). Wenham believes that there may be an allusion to the ANE myths with a polemical aim to correct the falsehood of those myths and to present the truth. *Genesis 1–15*, 72–73. Wenham

modern commentators propose that the serpent be seen as a symbol for the evil impulse that resides within human beings[9] or a metaphor for whatever in God's good creation serves to facilitate options for human decisions for or against God.[10] There are, however, significant problems with these modern views. The historical character and non-symbolic nature of the other Edenic referents (i.e., the trees, rivers, animals, humans, etc.) render the interpretation of the serpent as a mythical symbol[11] or as the personification of evil impulse untenable. The fact that Moses attributes personal qualities (i.e., speech, intelligence, ethical capacity) to the serpent (3:1–5) and portrays him as an entity liable to divine judgment (3:14–15) precludes treating the serpent as a mere metaphor. Such an interpretation is incompatible with the textual data.

The Serpent as an Instrument of Satan

Traditionally, Bible scholars have taken the serpent as a real snake that becomes the instrument or organ through which Satan entices man to sin.[12] The fact that the serpent is compared to "the beasts of the field"

---

interprets the serpent as an "anti-God symbol" that "symbolizes sin, death, and the power of evil." Ibid., 80. He acknowledges that later biblical writers identify the serpent with the person of Satan, but he does not believe the Genesis narrator possessed this understanding. Instead, the narrator intended simply "the powers of evil," and later revelation, by virtue of *sensus plenior*, expanded the referent to Satan. Ibid., 81.

9. Driver interprets the snake as "representative of evil thoughts and suggestions." *Book of Genesis*, 47. Similarly, Cassuto sees "the serpent" as a kind of latent crafty impulse in man himself. Accordingly, "The duologue between the serpent and the woman is actually, in a manner of speaking, a duologue that took place in the woman's mind, between her wiliness and her innocence, clothed in the garb of a parable. . . . By interpreting the text in this way, we can understand why the serpent is said to think and speak; in reality it is not he that thinks and speaks but the woman does so in her heart." *From Adam to Noah*, 142–43.

10. Fretheim, "Is Genesis 3 a Fall Story?" 149; idem., "Genesis," 365–66; Gowan, *From Eden to Babel*, 51–52.

11. The reality and prevalence of serpent mythology in the ANE is undeniable. But some features of ANE myth may be better understood as legend, that is, as containing an admixture of fact and fiction. Arguably, the ANE myths about serpent-like superhuman beings or gods, associated with immortality, wisdom, and evil, reflect the faint yet corrupted memory of a primeval tradition passed down from antiquity. If that is the case, then Genesis 3 may be viewed, at least partly, as a polemic against pagan mythology and a true representation of the origin of evil in the world.

12. A sampling of commentators and theologians includes Luther, *Lectures on Genesis*, 1:151; Keil and Delitzsch, *Pentateuch*, 91–92; Berkhof, *Systematic Theology*, 224; Vos, *Biblical Theology*, 44; Henry Morris, *Genesis Record*, 106–09; Reymond, *New Systematic Theology of the Christian Faith*, 441–42.

(3:1, 14)[13] seems to suggest an ordinary snake. That the serpent is styled as "crafty" does not necessarily disqualify the entity from membership in the animal kingdom since the Bible elsewhere attributes sapient qualities to mere creatures (Prov 30:24–28), including the snake (Matt 10:16). The data also suggest, however, that there is an intelligent and malicious personality at work behind this creature (3:1, 4–5; 14–15).[14] Therefore, the majority of commentators identify the evil persona behind the serpent as none other than Satan,[15] also called the devil,[16] the dragon,[17] and significantly "the ancient Serpent" (Rev 12:9; 20:2).[18] According to Scripture, Satan can enter, possess, and influence both animals and humans (Matt 8:28, 31–33; Mark 5:12–16; Luke 8:32–36).[19] God's curse in 3:14–15 may be viewed as addressing the real culprit (i.e., Satan) through

13. There is some debate about whether this comparison implies that the serpent was an animal with more wisdom than the animals he is compared to (*positive comparison*, or *superlative comparison*, *IBHS* § 14.4d, 14.5d) or whether the serpent is in a class by itself, possessing a kind of shrewdness the other animals did not possess, i.e., "the serpent was shrewd as none other of the beasts," (*comparison of exclusion. IBHS* § 14.4e; GKC § 119w). In any case, it is argued that the syntax represents the serpent as belonging to the same class as the "beasts of the field."

14. Accordingly, Collins avers, "A competent reader from the original audience would have been able to infer that the serpent is the mouthpiece of a Dark Power." *Genesis 1–4*, 172.

15. The Hebrew שָׂטָן may refer simply to mere human adversaries (1 Sam 19:22 [Heb 23]; 29:4; 1 Kgs 5:4; 11:14, 23, 25; Ps 109:6) or to the Angel of Yahweh who opposes a false prophet (Num 22:22, 32). Both the Old and New Testament canons, however, employ the term for the Adversary par excellence, the infamous antagonist of God and His people (Job 1:6–9, 12; 2:1–4, 6–7; 1 Chr 21:1; Zech 3:1–2; Matt 4:10; 12:26; 16:23; Mark 1:13; 3:23, 26; 4:15; 8:33; Luke 10:18; 11:18; 13:16; 22:3, 31; John 13:27; Acts 5:3; 26:18; Rom 16:20; 1 Cor 5:5; 7:5; 2 Cor 2:11; 11:14; 12:7; 1 Thess 2:18; 2 Thess 2:9; 1 Tim 1:20; 5:15; Rev 2:9, 13, 24; 3:9; 12:9; 20:2, 7).

16. Matt 4:1–11; Luke 4:1–13; John 8:44; 1 John 3:8, 10; Rev 12:9, 12; 20:2, 10.

17. Isa 2 7:1; 51:9; Rev 12:3, 4, 7, 9, 13, 16, 17; 13:2, 4; 16:13; 20:2.

18. Both texts in Revelation use the phrase ὁ ὄφις ὁ ἀρχαῖος, which has been variously interpreted as the "ancient serpent" (NIV, ESV, NET, CSB), the "old serpent " (KJV, DRA, ASV, NAU), or "that primeval serpent" (NJB). The fact that these texts juxtapose this phrase with the titles "dragon," "devil," and "Satan" clearly indicates that the author of Revelation saw more than a mere snake in Genesis 3.

19. The example of Balaam's talking ass is sometimes adduced as analogous to the talking serpent (Num 22:28, 30), though in the case of the donkey, it was not Satan but God who opened its mouth.

the instrument (i.e., the serpent), comparable to Jesus's rebuke of Peter, "Get behind me, Satan" (Matt 16:23).[20]

The Serpent as a Title for Satan

There is, however, another way of viewing the serpent of Genesis 3. When NT writers associate the serpent with Satan or the devil, they do not explicitly represent that association as a semi-divine "dark power" manipulating an animal as a mere organ of temptation. Instead, "the serpent" seems to function as a descriptive title, at the same level as "the dragon," "the devil," or "Satan" (2 Cor 11:2, 14; Rev 12:9, 14, 15; 20:2).[21] Since later revelation identifies Satan as a fallen angelic creature (Job 1:6–9, 12; 2:1–4, 6–7; 1 Chr 21:1; Zech 3:1–2; Matt 4:1–11; Luke 4:1–13; 10:18; 2 Cor 11:14; Eph 2:2, 6:11, 12; Rev 12:9), then perhaps what Adam and Eve saw and heard in the Garden was no mere snake but a serpent-like creature belonging to a higher order than the ordinary "beasts of the field." Several considerations lend support to this view.

First of all, the serpent obviously bears qualities that are superior to the animal life, namely, intellectual, communicative, and moral capacities. The use of the *min* comparative to describe the serpent as wiser than the ordinary animals (מִכֹּל חַיַּת הַשָּׂדֶה) indicates a *contrast* and need not imply that the serpent *in fact* belonged to the same class of beings with which he was being compared.[22] Hence, the narrator's syntax seems to place the serpent into a class of his own.[23] Moreover, one may read what some commentators interpret as an etiological allusion to the ordinary

20. Some scholars who adopt this reading doubt the original audience would have been able to discern this meaning but think it became an appropriate inference from later revelation. See Eichrodt, *Theology of the OT*, 2:405; Payne, *Theology of the Older Testament*, 216, 291–95; Shuster, *Fall and Sin*, 22; Walton, *Genesis*, 210.

21. Similarly, Buswell suggests, "The words 'the Serpent' . . . should be read as a proper name, or as a title functioning as a proper name. The Genesis account has nothing to say about a biological reptile." *Systematic Theology of the Christian Religion*, 1:264.

22. When Solomon pledges to build Yahweh a great temple, "for our God is greater than all gods [מִכָּל־הָאֱלֹהִים]" (2 Chr 2:5), he does not intend to place God in the same class as the false deities of the pagan nations. When the Psalmist declares, "I have more understanding than all my teachers [מִכָּל־מְלַמְּדַי]," he views himself as a pupil, not as a teacher (119:99). Similarly, "the serpent" of Genesis 3:1 may *appear* to belong to the class of animals with which he is compared but *in fact* does not.

23. Ward agrees that "the words may be read as placing the serpent outside the category of 'the wild creature of the field,' in which case another cunning creature, but not an ordinary snake, is meant. The creature is Satan himself, a fallen angel." *Foundations in Genesis*, 100. See also Stigers, *Commentary on Genesis*, 73–74.

snake's legless locomotion (Gen 3:14) as a metaphorical description of disgrace and defeat (Lev 11:43; Ps 72:9; Mic 7:17).[24]

Second, the superiority of the serpent over the humans also suggests an angelic creature. In Genesis 2, Adam is portrayed as wiser than the animals in that he is appointed to rule over them (1:26, 28) and has the capacity to name them (2:19–20). Indeed, among all the livestock, birds, and beasts, there was found no equal to Adam (2:20).[25] But in chapter 3, "the serpent" assumes the role of humankind's teacher and superior. As many commentators point out, the description of the serpent as "crafty" (עָרוּם) (3:1) is probably a word-play on the previous description of Adam and Eve as "naked" (עֲרוּמִּים) (2:25). Although Adam and Eve are portrayed as wiser than the animals, they are also depicted as lacking a higher kind of wisdom, symbolized by the Tree of Knowledge (2:9, 16–17; 3:5–6).[26] Accordingly, the reader should interpret their עֲרוּמִּים as a reference to ethical innocency and immaturity.[27] They do not yet possess that Elohim-like quality and prerogative that characterizes angelic beings (2 Sam 14:17) and later earthly monarchs who function

24. The etiological interpretation of this passage seems quite trivial and out-of-step with the serious theological intentions of the inspired author. For one thing, snakes, as the Israelite reader well knew, did not really "eat dust." And is it not better to view the snake's legless movement as a wonder of God's creative activity—a part of the original "very good" (1:31)? Moreover, human-reptile antipathy is by no means universal; some people are very fond of snakes, and there are other animals (like certain insects) that produce a far greater aversion in humans than do snakes. Consequently, it seems more natural to interpret God's curse on the serpent as addressing an intelligent, supernatural being who would "father" a race of spiritual rebels that would oppose the race of the godly, physically born of Eve but spiritually born of God (see Gen 4:2–8; John 8:44; 1 John 3:8–12; Jude 1:11). See Hamilton, *Book of Genesis: Chapters 1–17*, 196–97.

25. "But for Adam there was not found a helper fit for him." The Hebrew term translated "fit" [כְּנֶגְדּוֹ] refers to that which corresponds in stature or capacity. The point is not merely that Adam needed a suitable biological partner with which to procreate but that the animals lacked the intellectual, spiritual, and moral qualities necessary to serve alongside Adam as vice-regents to fulfill God's creation-mandate.

26. For the interpretation that sees "the knowledge of good and evil" as a kind of ethical maturity (i.e., "wisdom") that pertains primarily to those in kingly authority who have the right to exercise judgment, see Clark, "A Legal Background to the Yahwist's Use of 'Good and Evil' in Genesis 2–3," 266–78.

27. Ethical immaturity need not connote a flaw in Adam's human nature or the presence of sin. The NT implies that Jesus Christ progressed from a lower state of ethical maturity to a higher state of ethical maturity (Luke 2:40; Heb 5:8–9) without the slightest taint of ethical flaw or sin (2 Cor 5:21; Heb 4:15; 7:26; 1 Pet 2:22).

as judges (2 Sam 14:17; 1 Kgs 3:9).[28] The serpent, however, does possess that quality. Although the Hebrew עָרוּם may sometimes convey negative connotations (Job 5:12; 15:5), it predominantly denotes one who possesses wisdom (Prov 14:8) and is contrasted with ethical folly (Prov 12:6, 23; 13:16; 14:18) and naïveté (Prov 14:15; 22:3; 27:12).[29] So the narrator portrays the serpent as wiser than the humans.[30]

Third, the use of the definite article with the noun "serpent" (הַנָּחָשׁ) suggests an entity already well-known to the original Israelite audience.[31] Of course, this may imply nothing more than that the Israelites already knew the Genesis 3 story about a talking serpent that tempted the first humans. On the other hand, biblical evidence indicates that Moses's original audience may have been aware of a class of angelic creatures called "seraphim" (שְׂרָפִים) to which the serpent of Genesis 3:1 may have belonged. Though the term is sometimes applied to ordinary snakes,[32] it

28. As additional support for the proposal that human judges exercise a God-like prerogative and function when they render judicial decisions, one should note that Scripture sometimes refers to mere human judges as ʾelōhîm, even when their judgments fail to represent accurately divine justice and equity (Ps 82:1–7).

29. Likewise the cognate verb (ערם) may connote the negative idea of devious scheming (Job 5:13; Ps 83:3) or the positive idea of wisdom (Prov 15:5; 19:25).

30. Interpreters and theologians debate at what point the serpent's עָרוּם became corrupted into anti-God or "worldly" wisdom. Most locate Satan's fall sometime prior to the Genesis 3 narrative so that his cunning in verse 1 is interpreted negatively. See Chafer, *Satan*, 3; Unger, *Biblical Demonology*, 15, 18, 20, 42, 184–217; Waltke, *Genesis*, 90. Others argue that Satan's fall occurred in connection or close proximity with man's fall. See Payne, *Theology of the Older Testament*, 294; Jordan, "Merit Verses Maturity," 200, n. 38. Arguments in favor of Satan's "fall" occurring about the time of man's fall include (1) the fact that at the end of the sixth day God assessed the creation as "very good" (Gen 1:31), which would seem to preclude the presence of evil in the universe at that point, and (2) the fact that God pronounces a penal curse on Satan *at the same time* that he pronounces a curse on fallen humanity (Gen 3:14–19).

31. The usage is not anaphoric since there is no previous mention of the serpent in the context; nor is the usage generic since it is not a class or species of animals in view but a single entity. Instead, according to Waltke and O'Connor, the articular noun designates "*a well-known thing or person*; the combination is close to constituting a name (cf. 13.6)" *IBHS* § 13.5.1.c (emphasis theirs).

32. Aside from Isaiah's vision, wherever the noun שָׂרָף appears in the OT, it seems to refer to a venomous snake (Num 21:6, 8; Deut 8:15; Isa 1 4:29; 30:16). The noun derives from the Hebrew verb "to burn" (שָׂרַף) and may denote the burning sensation from their venomous bite (cf. LXX, δάκνων), but more likely it refers to their shiny or luminous appearance. Even the term נָחָשׁ which appears to be related to the word for "bronze" (נְחֹשֶׁת) may "suggest a shiny and luminous appearance, which would arrest Eve's attention." Hamilton, *Book of Genesis: Chapters 1–17,* 187. The two other Isaiah references (14:29;

is also used in Isaiah's vision for the dragon-like angelic beings with wings and limbs that flanked Yahweh's throne (Isa 6:2, 6). Such semi-divine creatures find counterparts in the legends and mythology of the ancient Near East. In her study of serpent symbolism in the OT and its relation to ancient Near Eastern serpent symbolism, Karen Joines notes the striking resemblance of form and function between the seraphim of Isaiah 6 and the winged serpents that stand erect, wear crowns, and flank the throne of the fourteenth-century BC Egyptian Pharaoh Tutankhamen. She also refers to the many Egyptian scarabs that feature winged serpents, most of which date to the eighth and ninth centuries BC.[33] While the Israelite reader would have rejected the mythological distortions of his pagan neighbors, he would have no serious obstacle in viewing the serpent of Genesis 3 as a supernatural being of angelic status that had rebelled against Yahweh and had become the supreme Antagonist to the divine will. The fact that the angelic guardian-creatures called "cherubim" (כְּרוּבִים) were also present in the Garden of Eden (Gen 3:24; Ezek 28:12–15)[34] lends further support to the view that the "primeval serpent"

30:16) describe the שָׂרָף as מְעוֹפֵף., which some versions translate as "flying" (KJV, NAU, ESV, CSB) and others as "darting" (NIV, NET). Interestingly, the fifth-century BC Roman historian Herodotus wrote of "the winged serpents [that] are nowhere seen except in Arabia, where they are all congregated together." Book III, Chapter 109 of *Histories*, cited in Joines, *Serpent Symbolism*, 8. Some modern evangelicals have conjectured that these texts may be referring to the now extinct pterosaur, a "prehistoric" flying reptile. See Goertzen, "Bible and Pterosaurs: Archaeological and Linguistic Studies of Jurassic Animals that Lived Recently"; Ham, *Great Dinosaur Mystery Explained!*, 45.

33. *Serpent Symbolism*, 49–51. Moreover, she discusses recent archaeological evidence of divine or semi-divine serpent creatures in ancient Near Eastern mythology and legend dating in some cases to the third-millennium BC (17–31, 62–73, 109–21). These mythical concepts of semi-divine dragon-like creatures may reflect the nations' faint memory of that primeval serpent creature in Eden. In light of this abundant archaeological evidence, Ronning remarks, "It is ironic to note that the key argument used by rationalists to turn the tide towards a naturalistic interpretation could not be made today. That is the argument that Israelites could not have known of a Satanic being such as the dragon of Revelation equated with the Genesis 3 serpent until the exile. For some strange reason, the discovery of the ancient Near East evil anti-God dragon figure, predating Moses by almost 1,000 years (or more), has not caused a reevaluation by scholars of the identity of the Genesis 3 serpent, even though we have seen strenuous efforts to interpret Leviathan as a supernatural dragon even where he is clearly portrayed as a created animal. In this respect (as in all others touching on the interpretation of Genesis 3:15), we see the New Testament well ahead of modern scholarship." "The Curse on the Serpent (Genesis 3:15) in Biblical Theology and Hermeneutics," 380–81.

34. The pseudepigraphal First Book of Enoch also associates the seraphim and the cherubim in paradise and as guardians of the throne of God (1 Enoch 20:7; 71:7; 61:10).

(Rev 20:2, NJB) was not an ordinary snake but an angelic being who was about to lead the vice-regents of Yahweh-Elohim into cosmic mutiny.[35]

The Nature of the Temptation

After entering the stage of the narrative, the Serpent proceeds to raise a question about God's prohibition (3:1b). Following Eve's initial response (3:2–3), he boldly asserts that God will not carry out his threat of punishment for disobedience (3:4) and insinuates that God is unfairly withholding from the humans something that is rightfully theirs (3:4–5). Traditionally, the Serpent's actions have been understood as a "temptation," that is, a solicitation to evil. Recently, some interpreters have attempted to construe the Serpent's actions in a positive light. Richard Hanson, for example, proposes that the Serpent actually may have been acting on God's behalf and daring the human to "become what [he was] destined to be: a creature who bears God's image."[36] This study, however, will demonstrate that the narrator portrays the action of Adam and Eve in an entirely negative light. Therefore, the traditional understanding of the Serpent's role as "tempter" is correct (Matt 4:1, 3; Mark 1:13; Luke 4:2; 2 Cor 11:3; 1 Thess 3:5; 1 Tim 2:14; Rev 20:10). Nevertheless, recalling Scripture's affirmation of God's sovereignty[37] should lead the reader to interpret this event also as a divinely directed "test"[38] intended to prove

35. One might object to viewing the serpent as an angelic being rather than a snake on the basis of Genesis 3:15, which seems to portray a human stepping on the head of a snake. Scripture, however, elsewhere speaks of the placing of one's foot over one's enemy as a symbol of victory (Josh 10:24–25; 2 Sam 22:29; 1 Kgs 5:3; Ps 18:38 [Heb 39]; 47:3 [Heb 4]; 110:1; Mal 4:3; Matt 22:44; Mark 12:36; Rom 16:20; 1 Cor 15:25, 27; Heb 2:8). The reference, therefore, need only imply a victory for the woman's seed at the cost of a serious wound from a vanquished enemy.

36. Hanson, 43–49. This reading shares affinities with some modern feminist readings of the Genesis 2–3 narrative, as well as ancient Gnostic interpretations. For further examples, see Jones, *Spirit Wars*, 126–30.

37. Yahweh's absolute control over all events, including the good and evil actions of humans, is affirmed throughout the Hebrew canonical literature (Gen 45:5, 7; 50:20; Ps 103:19–22; Prov 16:33; Isa 4 5:1–8; 46:9–11; Amos 3:4–6; Dan 2:21; 4:24–25, 34–35).

38. For the theological distinction between a "temptation" and a "test" as it relates to the Fall narrative, see Shuster, *Fall and Sin*, 21; Youngblood, *Book of Genesis*, 52–53. For a discussion of the theological difficulties that relate to divine sovereignty and goodness, human responsibility, and the so-called "problem of evil," see Carson, *How Long, O Lord?*, 15–36, 39–49, 117–73, 177–203; Frame, *Apologetics to the Glory of God*, 149–90; Murray, "Fall of Man," 2:72–76.

whether Yahweh's image would remain loyal to his Suzerain and receive the royal grant of full sonship and immortality.

The Serpent's "Question"

Satan begins his attack by posing what most translations take as a question: "Has God indeed said, 'You shall not eat of every tree of the garden'?" The exact construction אַף כִּי is not found elsewhere in the OT rendered as a question. Genesis 18:13 employs הַאַף in a question—"shall I *truly* bear a child?"—but, unlike Genesis 3:1, it contains the *he* interrogative. Cassuto believes the כִּי itself carries the interrogative element and the אַף is shifted forward for emphasis.[39] Keil calls it an "interrogative of surprise."[40] Speiser suggests that Satan is not really asking a question but making an incomplete statement that provokes the woman's rejoinder: "Even though God told you not to eat of any tree in the garden . . ."[41] Hamilton takes it as an expression of surprise, "Indeed! To think that God said you are not to eat of any tree of the garden!"[42]

However one understands the syntax, most agree that the Serpent is attempting to induce the woman (and the man) to reflect on the divine prohibition (2:17). The negative particle לֹא with the Hebrew מִכֹּל can mean "not every" (KJV, DRA, NKJ) or "not any" (ASV, NAU, NIV, NET, NLT, ESV, CSB). The latter idea is more restrictive and is analogous to Abraham's oath to the king of Sodom, "I will not take a thread or a sandal thong or anything [מִכֹּל] that is yours" (Gen 14:23, NAU). If this is the idea intended by the Serpent, then he blatantly misrepresents God's prohibition.[43] His words imply an unreasonable restrictiveness, which in fact is contrary to the exegetical emphasis on divine generosity (Gen 1:29; 2:9, 16). If, however, the Serpent intended the first idea, then the form of his question contains no misrepresentation of God's prohibition per se. A similar though not exact parallel would be the text where God commands Moses, "Tell your brother Aaron not to come whenever

39. *From Adam to Noah*, 144; see also Stigers, *A Commentary on Genesis*, 74.

40. He lists 1 Samuel 23:3 and 2 Samuel 4:11 as examples, though the syntax is not identical. *Pentateuch*, 94.

41. Speiser, *Genesis*, 21, 23.

42. Hamilton, *Genesis 1–17*, 186. For other suggestions on the precise meaning of the construction, see Skinner, *Genesis*, 73; von Rad, *Genesis*, 86; Kidner, *Genesis*, 67; Mathews, *Genesis 1—11:26*, 235 n. 179.

43. Gesenius lists Genesis 3:1 under this meaning (GKC § 152b).

[בְּכָל־עֵת] he chooses into the Most Holy Place" (Lev 16:2, NIV). Obviously, God is not saying the High Priest can *never* enter the Most Holy Place. Rather, he is limiting permission to the time God himself designates. Paul Joüon thinks the Serpent's question should be interpreted in this sense, in which case his attack would be subtler.[44] The primary element of misrepresentation would be contained in the Serpent's expressed "surprise" at the prohibition, conveyed by the Hebrew אַף ("indeed"). This more stealthy beginning seems a preferable reading, given the Serpent's characteristic subtlety.[45]

Eve's Initial Response

Eve responds to the Serpent's query (or accusation) in two parts. First, she assures him, "We may eat of the fruit of the trees in the garden" (3:2). Her words are almost identical to God's statement to Adam in 2:16, except she leaves out the infinite absolute (אָכֹל) which serves to underscore God's generosity: "you may *freely* eat." This may indicate a subtle shift in Eve's mind away from God's generosity and towards the prohibition, which she addresses in the next verse. "But God said," Eve adds, "'You shall not eat of the fruit of the tree that is in the midst of the garden, neither shall you touch it, lest you die'" (3:3). Once again, her representation of God's original statement is close but not exact. She fails to include another infinitive absolute that stresses the certainty of God's threatened penalty: "for in the day that you eat of it you shall *surely* [מוֹת] die" (2:17). Perhaps Eve is already questioning the seriousness of God's warning or his ability to carry it out. Some have argued that Eve's use of the negative particle פֶּן also betrays a degree of uncertainty in Eve's mind: "lest we *might* die."[46] She also adds an extra clause: "neither shall you touch it [וְלֹא תִגְּעוּ בּוֹ] which nearly all commentators interpret as an exaggeration of the prohibition and therefore an indication that Eve was construing the prohibition in an entirely negative way.[47]

44. *GBH* § 160k.

45. Leupold is probably correct when he says of the first, more restrictive idea, "The exaggeration would be too gross and crude. The devil would have completely overshot his mark and roused a feeling of resentment at the coarse insinuation." *Exposition of Genesis*, 144.

46. So Currid, *Study Commentary on Genesis*, 1:118; Ross, *Creation & Blessing*, 135.

47. "All in all," says Currid, "the woman distorts and mistreats the Word of God" (1:118); see also Aalders, *Genesis*, 1:100; Calvin, *Genesis*, 1:149; Hartley, *Genesis*, 65; Leupold, *Exposition of Genesis*, 148; Mathews, *Genesis 1—11:26*, 235–36; von Rad,

It is equally possible, however, to read Eve's initial response in a more positive light. Her omissions may simply be examples of abridging a previous statement. Moreover, the element of contingency expressed by the particle פֶּן is related to the condition of their eating the fruit, not to any perceived uncertainty of God's threat.[48] Furthermore, Eve's "addition" was probably a *correct inference* from the divine prohibition against eating since God's prohibitions sometimes include the injunction, "Do not touch" (Exod 19:12; Num 16:26; Deut 14:8; see also 2 Sam 6:1–8; Exod 29:37; 30:39).[49] When Christ responds to the devil by quoting Scripture, he does not cite the passage verbatim in every case, but sometimes modifies, adds, or drops a word.[50] Hence, faithfulness to God's Word does not demand *ipsissima verba* but *ipsissima vox*.[51] Satan's quick rejoinder to Eve in 3:4, "You will not surely die," seems to indicate that he interpreted Eve's first response as in *basic agreement* with God's original warning.[52] Finally, since Eve does not experience shame and guilt until *after* eating the fruit (3:7), it is premature to assign the beginnings of human sin to this point of the narrative. As a result of these considerations, Eve's initial

---

Genesis, 88; Ross, *Creation & Blessing*, 131, 134–35; Waltke, *Genesis*, 91; Wenham, *Genesis 1–15*, 73; Westermann, *Genesis 1–11*, 239–40.

48. Edom's warning to Israel, "You shall not pass through, lest [פֶּן,] I come out with the sword against you" (Num 20:18) was certainly not intended to be read, "I *might perhaps* come out," but as an unyielding threat.

49. Cassuto notes that the Hebrew verb "to touch" often "has a graver connotation than mere touching" (e.g., Gen 20:6; 26:11) and argues that "the clause *neither shall you touch it* is simply synonymous with the preceding clause *you shall not eat thereof*." *From Adam to Noah*, 145.

50. In Matt 4:10 and Luke 4:8, Christ cites Deut 6:13, changing the verb "fear" (φοβηθήσῃ, LXX) to "worship" (προσκυνήσεις), adding the word "alone" (μόνῳ) and excluding the clause, "and swear by his name (καὶ τῷ ὀνόματι αὐτοῦ ὀμῇ, LXX)."

51. Ross acknowledges, "The changes that were made between this verse and the giving of the commandment are within the legitimate range of interpretation." *Creation & Blessing*, 135. Yet Ross still insists on viewing her "imprecise" quotation in a negative light!

52. Walton begins by appropriately noting, "The narrative does nothing with [Eve's] miscue." But Walton then argues that by dropping the infinitive absolute from God's warning, Eve "has blurred an important nuance," a fact which the Serpent notices and on which he "capitalizes" by "negating Eve's version rather than God's." *Genesis*, 204. The only similarity between Eve's assertion and the Serpent's claim, however, is the plural form of the verb. Furthermore, the devil actually uses the infinite absolute, which resembles God's original wording more than Eve's representation. Therefore, it seems more likely that the Serpent is directly contradicting both the divine warning as well as Eve's representation of that warning.

response to Satan's attack appears to be an appropriate response (cf. Eph 6:17).

The Serpent's Attack on God's Integrity and Goodness

In the Serpent's second communication with the woman, he advances an attack against the veracity of God's word and the goodness of God's character. His rejoinder begins with a *waw* adversative and, as noted above, assumes that her response was a basically accurate portrayal of God's original prohibition (at least of the threat): "But the Serpent said to the woman, 'You will not surely die [לֹא־מוֹת תְּמֻתוּן]'" (3:4).[53] At first glance, Satan's attack seems too bold and confrontational to win Eve's sympathy. He immediately follows his direct attack against the veracity of God's word, however, by suggesting the rationale behind the prohibition, which sows seeds of suspicion in Eve's mind regarding God's benevolent intentions. According to the Serpent, two results will ensue from their eating the fruit: their eyes will be opened, and they shall become like God(s), knowing good and evil (3:5).[54] The reader should note that both of these predicted results are confirmed by the subsequent context. Adam and Eve's eyes are "opened" upon eating the fruit (3:7), and they do become like ʾelōhîm, knowing good and evil (3:22). Moreover, Adam and Eve do not appear to die "in the day" they eat from the tree. The Serpent's claims, therefore, have a prima facie semblance of truth.[55]

53. Normally, the negative particle occurs between the infinite absolute and finite verb. In this case, however, the negative precedes both the infinitive absolute and the finite verb. Gesenius describes such a construction as "exceptional" and lists Psalm 49:8 and Amos 9:8 as the only other two examples (GKC § 113v). Ross argues that the shifting of the Hebrew negative לֹא forward is done for emphasis: "Not—you shall surely die" *Creation & Blessing*, 135. See also Leupold, *Exposition of Genesis*, 149.

54. It is unclear whether the second use of Elohim (כֵּאלֹהִים) should be interpreted as a singular, i.e., "as God," or as a countable plural, i.e., "as gods" (cf. LXX, ὡς θεοὶ). The latter seems plausible in light of the fact that the participle translated "knowing" (יֹדְעֵי) is plural. But the plural may also hark back to Adam and Eve. As Mathews suggests, "Ambiguity here may be purposeful since the whole tenor of the Serpent's speech is marked with clever devices" (236 n. 183). See also Hamilton, *Genesis 1–17*, 189.

55. Shuster captures the deceptive cunning of the Serpent's temptation when she notes, "It is, first of all, artful and designing; it raises doubts and questions about what God said, putting a fatal gap between hearing God's command and obeying it, a gap in which one's own reasonings reign supreme. . . . More particularly, it involves distortion of the truth . . . [and] it has the appearance of good. A lie would not work unless it contained a great deal of truth. Traditional rat poison seduced its prey by being 96 percent good corn meal and only about 4 percent arsenic." *Fall and Sin*, 22–23. Cornelius

Nonetheless, it is equally clear that the Serpent distorts the truth. Yahweh-Elohim desired his vassal-son to obtain the wisdom that the tree of knowledge symbolized. But the vassal-son must acquire this wisdom "in the fear of the Lord" (Prov 1:7; 9:10) and in obedience to God's commands (Deut 4:6; 11:26–27; 30:19–20).[56] It is not, therefore, as the Serpent insinuates, that Yahweh selfishly wants to keep man from experiencing what is good and desirable.[57] And as Adam and his descendants learn, God's death-threat (2:17) was not empty.[58] In summary, the reader should interpret the Serpent's claim as deceitful and not offered in man's best interests. He is proposing nothing less than that Adam and Eve should pursue the way of counterfeit wisdom (1 Cor 1:20, 21; 3:19; Jas 3:15), which is based on creaturely autonomy—man acting as his own god.[59]

Plantinga also highlights the tempter's subtle trickery when he remarks, "To prevail, evil must leech not only power and intelligence from goodness but also its credibility. From counterfeit money to phony airliner parts to the trustworthy look on the face of a con artist, evil appears in disguise. Hence its treacherousness." *Not the Way It's Supposed to Be*, 98.

56. As Fretheim notes, "The command seems to forbid an immediate acquisition of knowledge, though without suggesting that humans should not have wisdom. The issue involves the way in which wisdom is gained. The fear of the Lord is the beginning of wisdom (see Rom 1:20–21). By using their freedom to acquire wisdom in this way, they have determined that the creational command no longer applies to them." "Genesis," 361.

57. Writes Kline, "Satan's claim was that God, because of a jealous reluctance to share his honor with others, had lied about the probation tree to prevent man from becoming like him in respect to the knowledge of good and evil (Gen 3:5). With subtle artistry the devil painted a complete falsehood, a total distortion of reality, portraying God in his own devil-likeness and representing himself in the guise of divine virtue and prerogative." *Kingdom Prologue*, 124.

58. Chapters 2 and 8 will highlight he fulfillment of Yahweh's death-threat curse.

59. Kidner aptly remarks, "The climax is a lie big enough to reinterpret life (this breadth is the power of a false system) and dynamic enough to redirect the flow of affection and ambition. To be *as God*, and to achieve it by outwitting Him, is an intoxicating programme." *Genesis*, 68. Hamilton, *Genesis 1–17*, is also on target when he writes, "Whenever one makes his own will crucial and God's revealed will irrelevant, whenever autonomy displaces submission and obedience in a person, that finite individual attempts to rise above the limitations imposed on him by his creator" (190).

THE FIRST HUMAN SIN

In response to the Serpent's slanderous insinuation of God's malevolent intentions toward the humans and his deceitful claim about the benefits of disobedience, Eve now focuses her attention on the tree.

An Autonomous Assessment

The woman begins to assess the forbidden fruit independently.[60] Eve observes three distinct aspects of the fruit. But the syntactical structure of the sentence explaining her assessment distinguishes the third description,[61] making the motivation for her taking the fruit actually two-fold. First, the woman evaluates the fruit as physically appealing, "good for food" in terms of flavor and nourishment. The phrase "good (טוֹב) for food" echoes both God's appraisal of creation as good (1:4, 10, 12, 18, 21, 25, 31) and his provision of vegetable produce for humankind as part of his "blessing" (1:29–30; 2:9, 16). She also saw the visually appealing quality of the fruit. The Hebrew word תַּאֲוָה ("pleasant") is used elsewhere to describe someone's "favorite dish" (Job 33:20). In one sense, Eve's assessment of the fruit is accurate. God did create the fruit "pleasant to the sight [נֶחְמָד לְמַרְאֶה]" (2:9). Her assessment, however, now assumes an autonomous posture. She wrests Yahweh's own appraisal of the tree out of context and misapplies it to her situation.[62]

Second, the woman assessed the fruit of the tree as psychologically appealing: "The tree was to be desired to make one wise."[63] Eve now views the tree as an instrument for obtaining wisdom, and in a sense she is correct. "The knowledge of good and evil" does refer to ethical maturation

60. As Brueggemann notes, "The rhetoric of fidelity has given way to analysis and calculation. The givenness of God's rule is no longer the boundary of a safe place. God is now a barrier to be circumvented," *Genesis*, 48.

61. Genesis 3:6a reads, וַתֵּרֶא הָאִשָּׁה כִּי טוֹב הָעֵץ לְמַאֲכָל וְכִי תַאֲוָה־הוּא לָעֵינַיִם וְנֶחְמָד הָעֵץ לְהַשְׂכִּיל. Note that first two clauses begin with כִּי and are coordinate, while the last clause appears without the כִּי and stands off as the ultimate motivation.

62. As Waltke notes, "In light of chapter 1, [Eve's assessment of the Tree] is surely ironic. Good is no longer rooted in what God says enhances life but in what people think is desirable to elevate life." *Genesis*, 92. See also Sarna, *Genesis*, 25.

63. The Hebrew word translated "to make wise" (לְהַשְׂכִּיל) is the Hiphil of שׂכל, a word related to wisdom and success (Ps 32:8; Prov 16:23; 21:11; Dan 9:22; Neh 9:20). Most translators and commentators take the Hiphil as causative (i.e., to impart wisdom), but some, such as Speiser, *Genesis*, 23–24, argue for an intransitive meaning (i.e., to become wise).

and is to some degree synonymous with wisdom. This quality may be virtuous or evil. It all depends on the way one obtains it. When obtained in dependence on and in consistency with God's revealed word, "the knowledge of good and evil" is a virtue that God ultimately intends for mankind. When obtained independent of and in contradiction to God's revealed word, this knowledge becomes a vice and something God never intended for mankind (cf. 1 Cor 1:26ff.). Now comes the fatal moment of choice, which stands at the very heart of the narrative.[64]

A Proud Partaking

The second half of 3:6 reveals the first human sin in a concise, matter-of-fact fashion: "She took of its fruit and ate, and she also gave some to her husband who was with her, and he ate." The prepositional phrase describing Adam as "with her" (עִמָּהּ) often connotes mutual participation (Gen 30:16; 39:10; Exod 22:15; Deut 22:23, 25, 28, 29; 2 Sam 11:4; 12:24) and sometimes implies physical proximity (Judg 13:9; 1 Kgs 17:20; Esth 2:13).[65] Clearly the narrator wishes to implicate Adam in the crime. Moreover, the Serpent's repeated use of the second person plural (3:1, 4–5) may also be an indication that Adam was at Eve's side throughout the entire temptation.[66] Certainly, God's initial interrogation of Adam

64. Walsh has analyzed the Eden narrative (2:4b—3:24) as consisting of seven scenes arranged concentrically, the fourth of which is Adam and Eve's partaking of the fruit (3:6), marking the structural center of the narrative (169–71). Thus concludes Walsh, "The central word of the entire narrative is at once the man's sin and his acquiescence in and affirmation of the perverted chain of influence it achieves." "Genesis 2:4b—3:24: A Synchronic Approach," 176–77.

65. Joüon interprets the preposition *her* as a nominal attribute, which implies that Adam is viewed as the one present with Eve during the temptation (*GBH* § 132a).

66. So argue Keil, *Pentatuech*, 95; Cassuto, *From Adam to Noah*, 148; Sarna, *Genesis*, 25; and Walton, *Genesis*, 206. Aalders seems to think that 1 Timothy 2:14 ("the man was not deceived") requires that Adam was not physically present. *Genesis*, 1:102. Leupold also believes that the placement of the phrase "with her" in the sentence suggests that Adam was not with Eve at the outset of the temptation but only joined her at this point. *Exposition of Genesis*, 152–53. But Walton argues that the placement of the prepositional phrase actually proves Adam was with her since otherwise it would have been connected with the verb "eat" rather than "gave." *Genesis*, 206. Of course, one might argue that the narrator could have been clearer and said something like, "so she took some of its fruit and gave to her husband, and they ate it." This would remove the ambiguity but might sacrifice the author's emphasis on the personal responsibility of each.

(3:9, 11) and the rest of Scripture lay the blame equally if not more so on Adam (cf. Rom 5:12ff.; 1 Tim 2:14).[67]

As to the nature of this first human sin, a number of modern writers seem intent on defending or minimizing the human action. Gunkel describes the action as "harmless and childish desire."[68] Susan Niditch argues for a feminist reading of the narrative: "Together with the snake, [Eve] is a bringer of culture."[69] Francis Watson encourages the reader to view "the Serpent as the liberator, Eve as heroine in her courageous quest for wisdom, and the Lord God as a jealous tyrant concerned only with the preservation of his own prerogatives."[70] Other, less radical, proposals suggest "mistrust,"[71] "folly,"[72] or "disobedience"[73] as opposed to the stronger idea of "rebellion." While these descriptions of the primordial sin are true enough, they fail to identify the root cause behind man's sin as well as to highlight its aggravated nature.

At the root of humankind's first sin is hubris or pride. The Serpent suggested to the humans that they, not God, controlled their destiny (3:4), and therefore, that they were free to determine independently

67. Higgins goes too far in attempting to exonerate Eve from blame, even arguing that God only addressed Adam in the prohibition (2:17) and that God's final words to the woman (3:16) may be read as a prophecy rather than a judgment. "The Myth of Eve: The Temptress," 645. On the other hand, she does offer several plausible reasons for viewing Adam as present during the Serpent's temptation (645–47).

68. *Genesis*, 17. See also Barr, *Garden of Eden and the Hope of Immortality*, 11–12.

69. "Genesis," 14.

70. "Strategies of Recovery and Resistance," 103.

71. According to Fretheim, "The primal sin may be best defined as mistrust of God and the word of God." "Genesis," 366. Fretheim is correct to note that Adam and Eve failed to trust God and His Word. But *mistrust*, in itself, is a somewhat neutral word. For it to be sinful, there must be some evil disposition that dissuades the individual from trusting one who is trustworthy.

72. Sailhamer argues that their sin should not be viewed as rebellion but as folly: "There are several features of this story that suggest the author wanted to draw a relationship between the Fall and man's quest for wisdom. Man's disobedience is not so much depicted as an act of great wickedness or a great transgression as much as it is an act of great folly." He concludes, "Thus, the temptation is not presented as a general rebellion from God's authority. It is rather portrayed as a quest for wisdom and "the good" apart from God's provision." "Genesis" 50–51. But Sailhamer's assessment misses the point. To pursue wisdom apart from and in disobedience to the expressed will of God *is* rebellion!

73. Roop, *Genesis*, 43. But this too is open to the objection that in the context of a Suzerain-vassal relationship, disobedience to the Suzerain's command is viewed as rebellion.

what was right or wrong, beneficial or harmful (3:5). By heeding Satan's words, Adam and Eve chose to disregard God's word because they were motivated by an aspiration to God-like prerogatives that were inappropriate for them to possess as mere creatures.[74]

This interpretation of pride as the motivating factor behind the first human sin finds intertextual support from three other passages of Scripture. First, Ezekiel's oracle against the king of Tyre not only accuses the monarch of hubris and of assuming the prerogatives of deity (Ezek 28:2–10) but also likens him to primeval man in Eden, whose heart "was proud" and who "corrupted [his] wisdom" (Ezek 28:12).[75] Second, the apostle Paul's acclamation of Christ, the Second Adam, "who, though he was in the form of God, did not count equality with God a thing to be grasped" (Phil 2:6)[76] provides the polar opposite portrait of the First Adam's action in Eden. It was Yahweh-Elohim's intention to exalt his human vassal-son and to give him a name above every name in keeping with his ultimate design for humanity (Gen 1:26–28).[77] But Adam "grasped" at kingship prematurely and disobediently.[78] Because of this pride, Adam disqualified himself and his seed from the eschatological

74. As Dumbrell rightly observes, "By eating of the fruit man was intruding into an area reserved for God alone, and the violation of the command is tantamount to an assertion of equality, a snatching at deity." *Covenant and Creation*, 38.

75. Some interpret the proud entity of Eden as a possible allusion to Satan. For example, see Feinberg, *Prophecy of Ezekiel*, 160–64; Unger, *Biblical Demonology*, 15. Even if Satan is in view, however, one may still infer that Adam and Eve were drawn away from God by the same kind of hubris since Satan tends to beget children in his own likeness (John 8:44; 1 John 3:8, 10, 12). Even so, a number of scholars have advanced good reasons for viewing the Edenic entity to whom Ezekiel compares the king of Tyre as Adam, who falls into sin because of pride. See Leslie Allen, *Ezekiel 20–48*, 89–96; Blenkinsopp, *Ezekiel*, 123–25; Duguid, *Ezekiel*, 344–47; Gowan, *When Man Becomes God*, 69–92; Keil, *Ezekiel*, 410; Taylor, *Ezekiel*, 195–97; Zimmerli, *Commentary on the Book of the Prophet Ezekiel*, 90–95. Though most of these authors are quick to find many elements from the Genesis 2–3 account in Ezekiel's description, a number of them stumble over Ezekiel's reference to "the Holy Mountain of God" (Ezek 28:14, 16), alleging the concept to be alien to Genesis 2–3. Such a conclusion completely misses the topographical implications of Genesis 2:10–14.

76. The Greek word translated "a thing to be grasped" [ἁρπαγμὸν] refers to what is taken by force or snatched away (see Matt 13:19; John 6:15; 10:12; 2 Cor 12:2).

77. This ultimate design is further elaborated in texts such as Ps 8:3–9; Matt 19:28; Luke 22:30; 1 Cor 6:3; Col 2:10; 2 Tim 2:12; Rev 4:4; 5:10; 11:16; 20:4, 6; 22:5.

78. Contrast Christ's refusal to accept Satan's offer to grant him "the kingdoms of this world" (Matt 4:8; Luke 4:5), which were rightfully his inheritance (Ps 2:8) but which had to be obtained according to the will and timing of his Father.

reward (2:9; 3:22).[79] Third, the apostle John appears to have Genesis 3:6 in view when he characterizes the "love of the world" (another way to describe "sin") as "the lust of the flesh and the lust of the eyes and the boastful pride of life [ἡ ἀλαζονεία τοῦ βίου]" (1 John 2:16, NAU).[80] If John is alluding to the Fall as a paradigm for human sin, then he interprets Adam and Eve's quest for autonomous wisdom (3:6) as ultimately springing from hubris.[81] In conclusion, pride is the root that motivates human sin.[82] This pride, in turn, prompts unbelief in the veracity of the divine word,[83] the violation of which constitutes rebellion or a breach of covenant.[84]

79. Thankfully, the Second Adam has opened the way back to Eden and the tree of life (John 3:16; 11:25–26; Rev 2:7; 22:2, 14, 19).

80. The Greek word ἀλαζονεία refers to "arrogance" (Jas 4:16) and its connection with "life" [βίος] suggests not mere materialism but a cocky presumption of being the existential center of the universe and the controller of one's destiny (see Jas 4:13–17).

81. As noted above, the syntactical structure of Eve's three-fold assessment of the tree actually emphasizes the third feature of appeal, namely, "that the tree was to be desired to make one wise" (3:6).

82. Merrill agrees with this analysis of the first human sin: "This episode describing the first attempt to undermine the sovereignty of God sets the tone for all subsequent human history, for history, in the final analysis, is reducible to a record of human hubris and sin, a condition redeemable only by God's own gracious interposition." *Everlasting Dominion*, 41. See also Augustine, *City of God*, 460–62; Hoekema, *Created in God's Image*, 173–74; Shuster, *Fall and Sin*, 52–55.

83. Some writers insist that unbelief gives rise to ambition and pride. Spurgeon calls it "the monarch sin . . . the egg of all crime, the seed of every offense." and argues that "everything that is evil and vile lies couched in that one word—unbelief." "The Sin of Unbelief." According to Calvin, "unbelief has opened the door to ambition," and "ambition has proved the parent of rebellion." *Institutes of the Christian Religion*, 1:153, 1:245. Keil seems to agree with this sequence when he writes, "Doubt, unbelief, and pride were the roots of the sin of our first parents, as they have been of all the sins of their posterity." *Pentateuch*, 96. But it seems more likely that *ambition and pride* are what give rise to unbelief.

84. Two eighth-century BC prophets allude to a primeval covenant and define human sin in terms of covenant breaking. Hosea brings his fellow Israelites before the bar of God because "like Adam [כְּאָדָם] they transgressed the covenant [בְּרִית]" (Hos 6:7). Some translations render the Hebrew "like men" (LXX, GNV, KJV, NKJ) and others translate the text "at Adam" (NET, NJB, NRS), a town in northern Israel (Josh 3:16). But, as Reymond notes, the former rendering introduces "an inanity into the text, for how else could Hosea's contemporaries transgress than 'like men'?" *New Systematic Theology of the Christian Faith*, 460. The latter requires an emendation to the text, changing the prefixed preposition from a כְּ to a בְּ. The word שָׁם, which begins the second half of the verse, usually means "there" and might seem to lend credibility to a locative interpretation. But in some places, it may have the force of an interjection, "Look there!"

A Guilty Conscience

Prior to Adam and Eve's sin, their nakedness was unaccompanied by shame (2:25). Following their sin, however, their nakedness is now associated with "opened eyes" (וַתִּפָּקַחְנָה עֵינֵי שְׁנֵיהֶם), a metaphor for acquired knowledge, and with a newfound impulse to cover their nakedness (3:7). Interpreters offer various explanations for the newly acquired knowledge and urge for clothing.[85] The most contextually responsible interpretation is to view the knowledge acquired as a form of ethical maturity but in a negative form. They now know good and evil but *in disloyalty to the divine will*, and the resulting knowledge (i.e., bad conscience) has produced the unpleasant feeling of shame (3:7b)[86] and fear (3:8–9), the opposite of their experience prior to the Fall (2:24–25).

(Pss 36:13; 48:7; Ps 132:17; Zeph 1:14), which would make perfect sense here (see NET). Consequently, there appears to be no substantial reason for an emendation of the text, and the translation "as Adam" (VUL, DRA, NIV, NAU, NLT, ESV, CSB) is preferred. For a helpful discussion of this text, see Curtis, "Hosea 6:7 and Covenant Breaking like/at Adam," 170-209; McComiskey, *Hosea*, 95; Warfield, "Hosea vi.7: Adam or Man?" 116-29. The prophet Isaiah universalizes Hosea's verdict, applying it to all the nations: "The earth is polluted because of its inhabitants, who have transgressed laws, violated statutes, broken the ancient covenant [בְּרִית עוֹלָם]" (Isa 24:5, NAB). The fact that Isaiah's indictment is directed to "all the nations" preludes a reference to any of the Jewish covenants. Some scholars opt for the Noachic covenant. But John Oswalt is correct when he notes that "while the *eternal covenant* may have specific reference to the Noahic covenant in Gen 9:1–17 with its prohibition of bloodshed, its broader reference is to the implicit covenant between Creator and creature, in which the Creator promises life in return for the creature's living according to the norms laid down at Creation." *Isaiah 1–39*, 446. See also Young, *Book of Isaiah*, 2:156–58.

85. Gunkel sees a transition from ignorance to enlightenment: "One may say that the narrator already has a very vague notion, although he does not attain clarity regarding it in his presentation, namely that enlightenment, maturity can only be achieved through sin" (18). Similarly, Driver argues that the knowledge gained was the transitional experience of moving "from the innocence of childhood in to the knowledge which . . . belongs to adult age." *Book of Genesis*, 46. Building on these ideas, Bonhoeffer has suggested that the knowledge refers to a "sexual awareness" that the couple did not possess before eating from the tree. *Creation and Fall*, 78–81. But as Henri Blocher appropriately notes, "Genesis 2 simply does not depict the man and the woman as two children before the age of puberty, and casts no shadow across the marriage union; on the contrary, the text provides the charter of this gift from the Creator." *In the Beginning*, 129. This is not to deny the element of sexual shame that their attempt at covering their nakedness reveals. But such sexual shame is only the tip of the iceberg, perhaps a synecdoche. See Stigers, *Commentary on Genesis*, 75–77.

86. Since the urge to cover their nakedness indicates a reversal of the condition described in 2:25, then one should infer that the humans now experience "shame" (בּוֹשׁ), which in the OT can refer to a disappointment felt because of unrealized expectations

INQUEST, JUDGMENT, AND BANISHMENT

After the first human sin there is a juridical inquest (3:8–13), a pronouncement of the curse-sanction (3:14–19) that is followed by an act of faith (3:20) and a response of forgiveness (3:21). Finally, there is a formal expulsion from the Garden of Eden (3:22–24).

The Juridical Inquest

When Yahweh-Elohim begins his inquest in 3:8, the humans respond immediately with fear and attempt to hide among the trees of the Garden. The divine inquest is clearly theophanic, though recent interpreters question the traditional rendering of the text that portrays Yahweh on a peaceful routine stroll through the Garden "in the cool of the day"[87] and suggest instead something like a terrifying storm-theophany comparable to Yahweh's manifestation at Sinai.[88] Yahweh formally summons

(Job 6:20; Isa 4 2:17; Jer 14:3; 22:22; Hos 10:6), to a disgrace felt because of defeat at the hand of one's enemies (Ezra 9:6; Isa 1:29; 30:5; Jer 2:36; Dan 9:7; Mic 1:11) or because of immoral or imprudent actions of a relative (Prov 10:5; 12:4; 14:35), or to feelings of guilt for sin committed (Job 19:3; Jer 2:26; 6:15; 8:12). Note also this last meaning in the apocryphal Sirach 41:17. Since this "shame" has come as a result of disobedience, it is most natural to interpret it in the last sense, as feelings of guilt.

87. Traditionally, the phrase לְרוּחַ הַיּוֹם has given translators and interpreters some difficulty. Most translators have understood this as a time reference. The phrase, as it stands, would seem to suggest, in the context and climate of the Middle East, some time in the early morning or late afternoon/early evening. Some suggest, the "wind of the day" refers to sometime in the late afternoon when the breeze blows. The LXX seems to interpret the phrase this way by using the Greek word for "afternoon" (τὸ δειλινόν). Cassuto suggests that the noun רוּחַ be understood as a verb related to Arabic and Ugaritic cognate verbs signifying "to be in the period after midday." In this case, the added הַיּוֹם would hark back to God's warning in 2:17. Thus, the point of 3:8 would be to underscore the fact that God did not let the day of Adam's transgression pass before carrying out His judgment. *From Adam to Noah*, 153–54.

88. Jeffrey Niehaus argues on the basis of comparative philology that Hebrew יוֹם corresponds to the Akkadian ūmu, which means "storm." In this case, the phrase would be translated "in the wind of the storm" and would suggest theophanic judgment. *God At Sinai*, 155–59. Yahweh's קוֹל is often associated with "thunder" in poetic texts (Pss 18:14 [13]; 46:7 [6]; 77:17) and with God's theophanic manifestation at Sinai (Exod 20:18; Deut 5:25). Note also the combined use of קוֹל and רוּחַ in Jeremiah to refer to Yahweh speaking (metaphorically) in a thunderstorm (10:13; 51:16). Nevertheless, interpreters have been reluctant to adopt Niehaus' rendering because of the lack of lexical support for יוֹם as "storm" (though *HALOT* does list Song 2:17; 4:6 and Zeph 2:2 as possible instances). See Grundtke, "A Tempest in a Teapot? Genesis iii 8 Again," 548–51. Kline offers another interpretation, first asserting that רוּחַ in 3:8 should be understood in light of Genesis 1:2, which he interprets as a reference to the "Spirit of God," that is, a theo-

the man to a judicial hearing,[89] where Adam correctly interprets God's query "Where are you?" (3:9) as carrying the sense of "What has happened to you? Give an explanation."[90] Adam admits that the sense of Yahweh's special presence and his newfound discomfort with nakedness have caused him to hide (3:10). Yahweh then replies with two more questions (3:11) designed not to solicit information otherwise unknown to God but (1) to link Adam's perceived nakedness to the act of eating from the tree of knowledge, and (2) to elicit from his prodigal son a penitent confession of wrongdoing. Hence, Yahweh's inquiry carries both a juridical and redemptive design. In the same fashion and to the same end, he interrogates the woman (3:13a).[91] Eve's response to their holy Suzerain is virtually identical in form to Adam's (3:12, 13b). Both consist of two parts: an explanation of the circumstantial factors that gave rise to the crime and a confession of wrongdoing. Most scholars interpret the explanation as a form of blameshifting and therefore discount the

---

phany, not merely a primordial wind. Kline then suggests that the *lamed* preposition indicates "in the capacity of" and cites several passages that appear to use the preposition in this way (Num 22:22, 32; 2 Chr 18:21; Isa 4:6; 11:10). Thus, argues Kline, one should read the first part of the verse as, "They heard the sound of Yahweh God traversing the garden as the Spirit of the Day." *Images of the Spirit*, 106. Kline then connects "Spirit" and "day" with God's special creative activity in Genesis 1:2 and God's eschatological judgment activity, which is developed later in the Old and New Testaments as "the day of the Lord" (106–31). See also Kline, *Kingdom Prologue*, 128–31.

89. The verb "to call" (קרא) when used with the preposition "unto" (אל,) often bears the sense of "summons" (Gen 28:1; Exod 10:24; 24:16; 34:31; etc.; cf. קרא + ל. in Gen 12:18; 20:9; Deut 25:8). The meaning would place God's inquiry in the category of lawsuit. It is also significant that Yahweh addresses the man rather than the woman. Cassuto argues that the "man was the first to be tried, because the primary responsibility rested upon him, and he was the first to receive the Divine command." *From Adam to Noah*, 155. Indeed, the earlier context suggests that God addresses Adam first because God had originally addressed the prohibition to him and not Eve (2:16). This fact would seem to highlight Adam's representative role as covenant head. God first addresses the man because he holds a special and representative role in fulfilling the covenant stipulations. Eve's failure is ultimately his failure. And Adam's failure will have implications for his descendants to follow, as the subsequent context of Genesis will make clear. Collins highlights several other ways in which the narrator underscores the man's covenant headship. *Genesis 1–4*, 173–74.

90. Likewise, God's question to Cain, "Where is Abel your brother?" (4:9) actually means something like, "What have you done to your brother Abel? Explain to me."

91. "What is this that you have done?" (3:13) does not function primarily as a quest for information. The phraseology is used elsewhere in Genesis and carries the sense of a formal accusation of wrongdoing (Gen 4:10; 12:18; 20:9; 26:10; 29:25; 31:26; 44:15).

confession.[92] The reader must concede that the charge of blameshifting is grammatically and syntactically justifiable.[93] Nevertheless, he should also note that Adam's and Eve's respective explanations are factual: the events are retold as they actually transpired.[94] Moreover, they each admit guilt in violating the prohibition. Elements in the ensuing narrative seem to indicate that Yahweh, at least in part, accepted their confession of guilt.[95]

92. Concerning Adam's explanation, Hamilton remarks, "He points the finger of blame both at his spouse—she . . . gave me—and at God—the woman whom you placed by me. Through rationalization the criminal becomes the victim, and it is God and the woman who emerge as the real instigators in this scenario. Adam plays up their contribution in his demise and downplays his own part. By postponing his own involvement until the last word in this verse, Adam attempts to minimize his part in this sin." With respect to the woman's testimony, he writes, "The woman's answer to God's question is similar to the man's. She too must exculpate herself. Neither of them exhibits any sign of contrition." *Genesis 1–17,* 194. For similar assessments, see Aalders, *Genesis,* 1:104; Calvin, *Genesis,* 1:164–65; Cassuto, *From Adam to Noah*, 157–58; Currid, *A Study Commentary on Genesis*, 1:125–26; Hartley, *Genesis*, 68; Keil and Delitzsch, *The Pentateuch*, 1:98; Kidner, *Genesis*, 70; Luther, *Lectures on Genesis*, 1:177ff.; Mathews, *Genesis 1—11:26,* 241–42; von Rad, *Genesis,* 91; Sailhamer, "Genesis," 54; Sarna, *Genesis,* 26; Waltke, *Genesis*, 93; Wenham, *Genesis 1–15,* 77–78. Westermann concedes that the man and woman are attempting to defend themselves, but he justifies their responses as "legitimate freedom to defend themselves." *Genesis 1–11,* 255.

93. Adam's testimony begins with a nominative absolute or *casus pendens* ("the woman whom you placed by me"; הָאָדָם הָאִשָּׁה אֲשֶׁר נָתַתָּה עִמָּדִי), which serves to highlight an element in the main clause (GKC § 135c; *GBH* § 156e; *IBHS* § 4.7; 8.3a; see also Gen 15:4; 24:7), and he adds the resumptive pronoun ("*she* gave to me"; הִוא נָתְנָה־לִּי). Hence, Adam's points to Yahweh's gift of the woman who herself had offered him the fruit as the catalyst for his crime. Similarly, Eve's testimony places "the serpent" first in the clause (הַנָּחָשׁ הִשִּׁיאַנִי), which is often done for emphasis (*HS* § 573). Like Adam, she seems to shift the emphasis to another party as the catalyst for her crime.

94. Adam explains, "The woman whom you gave to be with me, she gave me fruit of the tree" (3:12a); Eve tells Yahweh, "The serpent deceived me" (3:13b). The reader should not miss the fact that Yahweh accepts these explanations as true and responds accordingly. He queries the woman in response to Adam's testimony. He curses the Serpent in response to Eve's testimony. Therefore, Yahweh accepts their testimony as formally true even though the couple may have framed their testimonies in such a way so as to partially mitigate the degree of their guilt. Also noteworthy is the fact that the apostle Paul treats Eve's explanation as factual (1 Tim 2:14).

95. Ross notes, "Eventually, they did confess, and it was sufficient." *Creation & Blessing*, 144.

Yahweh's Penal/Remedial Curse

Now begins God's judicial sentence pronounced on the three culpable parties. The order of the sentencing actually follows the historical order of sinful action: the Serpent, the woman, and then the man (3:14–19).[96] That God first addresses and condemns the Serpent seems to indicate that the humans' shift of the blame ultimately to the Serpent was formally correct.[97] Thus, Yahweh-Elohim's "curse" (אָרוּר אַתָּה) on the Serpent exceeds in severity the general curse on humans and beasts[98] and functions as a doom-oracle (3:14).[99] Of special interest is the timing and manner of the Serpent's ultimate demise. Genesis 3:15 portends a divinely imposed hostility between the Serpent's "offspring" and the woman's "offspring" that will issue in mortal combat, resulting in the Serpent's ultimate defeat.[100] That the man and woman are yet to multiply, fill, and subdue the

96. One may also note the chiastic structure of the narrative. In the inquest, Yahweh begins with the man and ends with the Serpent (3:8–13). In the sentencing, Yahweh begins with the Serpent and ends with the man (3:14–19).

97. This does not imply that Yahweh relieves them of personal responsibility for their role in the crime, as the subsequent narrative demonstrates. At the same time, Yahweh does not identify Adam and Eve's "blameshifting" as a crime in addition to their eating of the fruit.

98. Yahweh does not curse either Eve or Adam directly, but only indirectly. Some interpret the מִן preposition in the clause מִכָּל־הַבְּהֵמָה וּמִכֹּל חַיַּת הַשָּׂדֶה as an ablative, "designating movement *away from* a specified beginning point" (*IBHS* § 11.2.11b). Thus, God is *banishing* the Serpent from the other animals. See Brichto, *Problem of "Curse" in the Hebrew Bible*, 82–85; Speiser, *Genesis*, 22, 24. This assumes, however, that the Serpent is merely a species of the animal kingdom and is destined to live a solitary life. But the exegesis presented above has already demonstrated that "the tempter" is more than a mere beast. On the other hand, one may interpret the מִן preposition in Genesis 3:14 as a comparative marker (*IBHS* § 11.211e), denoting a *comparison of degree*, i.e., "cursed are you more than" (*IBHS* § 14.4d) or a *comparison of exclusion*, i.e., "cursed are you rather than" (*IBHS* § 14.4e). In this case, Yahweh curses the Serpent *instead of* the animals or *more than* the animals. The latter option makes better sense here since the animal kingdom (and all creation) suffer the effects of the Fall (3:17–18; 6:7, 13, 17; 7:21–23; Rom 8:20–22). Hence, God's curse on the Serpent is *graver* than his judgment on the humans and the rest of creation.

99. The substance of the curse, "on your belly you shall go, and you shall eat dust all the days of your life," should not be interpreted in a literal sense—as if the verse provides a prescientific explanation for why snakes have no legs or why snakes "eat dust" (which even the ancients would not have taken literally!). The words should be understood, as elsewhere in Scripture, as a metaphorical description of disgrace and defeat (Lev 11:43; Ps 72:9; Mic 7:17). Thus, Yahweh's statement here puts beyond a shadow of a doubt the outcome of the struggle depicted in 3:15. It is, consequently, a doom-oracle.

100. Some scholars read 3:15 as nothing more than a perpetual struggle between the respective offspring with no clear victor indicated. Gerhard von Rad offers a pessimistic

earth (3:16–19) suggests that the battle will be protracted. The Serpent's eventual defeat will come through the agency of woman's offspring. This vital detail implies (1) a divinely effected realignment of the allegiance of at least a portion of humanity away from the Serpent and towards Yahweh[101] and (2) a reversal of the Serpent's plan to thwart Yahweh's creation intentions for humankind. So a redemptive blessing arises from the midst of a penal curse![102] And with justification, the reader may interpret the curse upon the Serpent as the proto-evangel.[103]

God next renders a judicial sentence on the woman (3:16). On the one hand, her punishment may be viewed as punitive in nature.[104]

---

reading, "The terrible point of this curse is the hopelessness of this struggle in which both will ruin each other." *Genesis*, 93. Walton's interpretation is not much brighter, "The verse is depicting a continual, unresolved conflict between humans and representatives of evil" *Genesis*, 226. These readings ignore the already portended defeat of the Serpent in 3:14 (i.e., laying on one's belly and licking the dust) and discount the significance of the Serpent's "underfoot" position, which elsewhere signals defeat (Josh 10:24–25; 2 Sam 22:29; 1 Kgs 5:3; Pss 18:38; 47:3; 110:1; Mal 4:3; Matt 22:44; Mark 12:36; Rom 16:20; 1 Cor 15:25, 27; Heb 2:8).

101. Here, then, is the first reference to a monergistic work of regeneration. Divine imposed enmity (וְאֵיבָה אָשִׁית) towards Satan is the flipside of divinely restored love and loyalty towards man's heavenly Suzerain (see Deut 30:6; Jer 31:33; 32:40; Ezek 36:26; John 1:13; 3:3, 5–7; Eph 2:1–10; 1 Pet 1:3, 23).

102. Indeed, as subsequent revelation demonstrates, redemptive blessing (i.e., saving grace) *must* come through the divine curse (i.e., the satisfaction of divine justice and pacification of divine wrath). For this reason, Christ's propitiatory death becomes a consequent necessity in order that God might be just and the justifier of the one who believes in Jesus (Rom 3:23–26; Gal 3:13; Heb 2:9–10, 17).

103. Gage neatly summarizes the gospel message implied in the curse: "It was by the death of the last Adam that the Serpent of old encountered death and the first Adam found life. The nails that pierced the feet of Christ would bruise the heel, but they would crush the head of the Serpent (1 Cor 2:8). The last Adam wore the thorns of the first Adam, but by these wounds he was healing his people (Isa 53:5). Christ knew the nakedness of Adam, but by this shame he was clothing his people in righteousness (Gal 3:27). For the first Adam the tree of knowledge brought death. But the last Adam knew death upon the tree bringing life (1 Pet 2:24). Adam had made a grave of a garden, but Christ would make a garden of a grave (Luke 24:5)." *Gospel of Genesis*, 46–47.

104. Some commentators try to play down the punitive nature of God's sentence on the woman and the man. Cassuto, for example, sees God's pronouncements here as in effect taking up where the account of man's creation in Genesis 1:26–27 left off. In other words, the choice between taking of the tree of life vs. the tree of the knowledge of good and evil was a choice between simple immortal existence vs. responsible freedom and morality. The human couple chose the latter against Yahweh's counsel, yet Yahweh remedies the situation by giving the woman and man power to procreate and survive as a species in the hostile environment outside of Eden. *From Adam to Noah*, 161–64.

She will suffer pain[105] in connection with motherhood. The first clause literally reads, "I will surely increase your pain and your conception" (author's translation). The infinitive absolute (הַרְבָּה) preceding the finite verb (אַרְבֶּה) may serve either *to affirm the certainty* of an action or outcome (*IBHS* § 35.3.1f) or *to intensify* the idea expressed (*IBHS* § 35.3.1i). The former may be rendered, "I will surely multiply" (ESV), and the latter, "I will greatly increase" (NIV). The prepositive position of the infinitive absolute favors the former sense, namely, God affirms the certainty of the punishment. On the surface, it would appear that an increase in pain *and an increase in pregnancy* are the result of God's curse. However, it does not seem appropriate to view increased "fruitfulness" as a facet of the divine curse since the narrative has already identified it as a result of God's blessing (1:28). David Tsumura has argued that וְהֵרֹנֵךְ derives not from הֵרוֹן, the noun for "conception," but from the root הרר, meaning "trembling."[106] But the synonymous parallelism favors the traditional reading of "conception." The reader should interpret the two nouns as a hendiadys and translate them, "your painful conception" or "your pain in conception." The fact that the event of conception does not involve physical pain need not preclude this interpretation since both conception and giving birth function here as a synecdoche for the woman's entire role as mother.[107] Furthermore, the woman will also suffer

---

This interpretation, however, mingles the blessing of Genesis 1 with the curse of Genesis 3 in a way that erases any real distinction. It is true that Yahweh's curse on the Serpent is direct, whereas his curse on the man and woman is indirect. God does not curse Adam and Eve per se, but he curses their vocations, relations, and environment. But the "indirectness" of the curse on humanity does not preclude a punitive element. The curses God threatened on Israel for disobedience and covenant infidelity were also indirect (Lev 26; Deut 28), yet they were clearly to be viewed as acts of divine retribution and punitive in nature.

105. The first expression for "pain" (עִצָּבוֹן) may refer to physical (Gen 3:16; 5:29) and psychological pain (Pss 13:3; 146:3; Prov 15:13) and can lead one to despair of life itself (Job 7:15). The second word (עֶצֶב) usually refers to psychological pain (see especially 6:6; 34:7; 45:5; 1 Sam 20:3, 24; 2 Sam 19:3 [Heb 3]; 1 Kgs 1:6; Neh 8:10, 11; Pss 78:40; 127:2; Prov 10:22; Isa 54:6). It can also refer to the pain God feels in response to human sin (Gen 6:6; Pss 78:40; 139:24; Isa 63:10). It is significant that God does not merely describe what will happen but pledges to take an active part: "I will surely multiply [הַרְבָּה אַרְבֶּה] your pain." Hence, human pain must not be interpreted as merely natural phenomenon but as the consequence of God's penal activity.

106. "A Note on הרון (Gen 3, 16)," 398–400.

107. Moreover, the nouns and along with the cognate verb may denote emotional pain (Gen 3:17; 5:29; 6:6; 34:7; 45:5; 1 Sam 20:3, 34; 2 Sam 19:3; Neh 8:10; Prov 10:22; Isa

disharmony in connection with her relationship to the man. The noun describing the woman's "desire" (תְּשׁוּקָה) for her husband is only found in two other contexts. In the Song of Solomon, it describes the *sexual craving* of a man for a woman (7:11). Accordingly, some interpret this statement as an affirmation of Eve's ongoing sexual desires for her husband despite the pain that will result from the childbearing.[108] But the other place where תְּשׁוּקָה is used (4:7) precludes the sense of *sexual* desire. Moreover, neither Scripture nor common human experience suggests that a woman's libido is stronger than a man's. If anything, the opposite is true (Matt 5:27–30). Others suggest that the woman's desire is simply a reference to her innate longing for appropriate intimacy. Therefore, the curse resides not in the woman's orientation towards her husband but in his orientation toward her: "but he shall rule over you," that is, the man will abusively oppress the woman.[109] More recently Susan T. Foh has compared the vocabulary and syntax of 3:16b with 4:7. In Genesis 4:7, God warns Cain, "[Sin's] desire is for you, but you must rule over it" (וְאֵלֶיךָ תְּשׁוּקָתוֹ וְאַתָּה תִּמְשָׁל־בּוֹ). In this case, sin desires to have its way with Cain. Similarly, argues Foh, the woman will desire to dominate her husband.[110] That leaves the question of how to interpret the husband's response: וְהוּא יִמְשָׁל־בָּךְ. Looking again at 4:7b, וְאַתָּה clearly appears to be adversative ("but you"), and the imperfect verb with its object—תִּמְשָׁל־בּוֹ—may have an *obligatory* force ("you must master it," *IBHS* § 31.4g) or a *potential* force ("you are able to master it," *IBHS* § 31.4c). The latter rendering would introduce an inanity into 3:16b (i.e., of course the man can dominate the woman!). The former makes sense: the woman will desire to have her way with the husband, but the man must retain his

---

54:6; 63:10) as well as physical pain. Hence, the woman's punishment will entail a broad spectrum of suffering and misery in connection with her role as mother.

108. See Driver, *Book of Genesis*, 49; Gunkel, *Genesis*, 21; Skinner, *Genesis*, 82–83.

109. See von Rad, *Genesis*, 93; Westermann, *Genesis 1–11*, 262. Some who adopt this reading, identify male headship as a facet of the curse. Phyllis Trible, for example, writes, "[The husband's] supremacy is neither a divine right nor a male prerogative. Her subordination is neither a divine decree nor the female destiny. Both their positions result from shared disobedience. God describes this consequence but does not prescribe it as punishment." *God and the Rhetoric of Sexuality*, 128. See also Sarna, *Genesis*, 28; Walton, *Genesis*, 228–29. The Vulgate apparently has a similar idea in view and renders 3:16b: *et sub viri potestate eris et ipse dominabitur tui*. The LXX does not help matters when it apparently reads תְּשׁוּקָה as תְּשׁוּבָה and translates with the noun ἀποστροφή ("returning"?).

110. "What Is the Woman's Desire," 376–83.

God-given headship over her.[111] On the other hand, the imperfect verb with its object in 3:16b (יִמְשָׁל־בָּךְ) may, in contrast with 4:7b, have a *future* or *predictive* force ("but he will master you," *IBHS* § 31.6.2). In this case, God may be predicting the potential abuse of male authority without necessarily denying its proper place. The verb משל ("rule") can denote a lordship that is either *benevolent* (Gen 45:8, 26; Ps 22:28; Prov 17:2) or *oppressive* (Judg 14:4; Prov 22:7: Isa 1 9:4). Context must decide.[112] This interpretation preserves most of the symmetry between 3:16b and 4:7b while also recognizing that part of the woman's curse will include not merely a difficulty on her part to submit to her God-ordained head (see Isa3:12) but also, at times, an oppressive retaliatory response on the part of her husband. The apostle Paul alludes to this dual aspect of the curse when he exhorts the Christian wife to submit to her husband and the Christian husband to love his wife (Eph 5:22–29; see also 1 Pet 3:1–7).

On the other hand, a remedial or redemptive element appears in Eve's punishment. Yahweh has not completely withdrawn the creation blessing of fruitfulness. She will bear children. Moreover, she will mother an offspring who will realign himself with the interests of Yahweh's kingdom and eventually overcome the works of the Serpent. It is likely that Adam discerned these redemptive implications in Yahweh's punishment of the woman and responded by assigning her a new name (3:20). Adam "called his wife's name Eve." The Hebrew name Eve (חַוָּה) occurs only here and in 4:1. The LXX translates the name here as "Life" (Ζωή), but in 4:1 transliterates it (Ευαν), which the apostle Paul follows (2 Cor 11:3; 1 Tim 2:13). In light of the reason given for Adam's assigning her this name and in light of the apparently etymological relationship to חיה, it seems likely that the name derives from the Hebrew noun for "life." The fact that the Hebrew חַוּה has a median *waw* rather than a median *yod* may suggest that it derives from a more primitive form of the word. In support of this possibility, it may be noted that the Ugaritic verb "to live" contains the medial consonant *yod* in the Qal form but the medial

111. See Foh, Ibid., 383; Collins, *Genesis 1-4*, 159–60; Culver, "Traditional View," 40–41; Mathews, *Genesis 1—11:26*, 250–52; Ortlund, "Male-Female Equality and Male Headship," 108–9.

112. Scripture and history bear witness to both good and bad examples of male leadership and female submission.

consonant *waw* in the Piel. This fact suggests a *factitive* meaning for Eve, such as "giver of life," or the *intensive* idea of "propagator of life."[113]

Yahweh concludes his judicial sentencing with Adam (3:17–19). God's curse on the man, as the woman, is indirect. He does not pronounce the man אָרוּר, as he did the Serpent. Instead, he curses the ground (אֲרוּרָה הָאֲדָמָה). Collins argues, "Nowhere does [the curse] imply that somehow human sin has distorted the workings of the natural elements; rather, agriculture is the arena in which God brings his chastisement upon human beings."[114] But just as "childbearing" is a synecdoche for the woman's larger role of mother and wife, so "the soil" does not limit God's curse merely to the sphere of agriculture. On the contrary, the curse here pertains to the entirety of man's task "under the sun." Thus, the reader should interpret the punishments on the woman and man together: God is withdrawing his unqualified blessing and imposing a curse upon *the filling* and *the subduing* of the earth, that is, humankind's creational mandate (1:26, 28). Collins' concern to limit the curse to Adam's agricultural task is probably motivated by scientific objections to the idea of God interjecting new elements into nature that did not previously exist (e.g., "thorns and thistles"). It is difficult, however, to evade Paul's all-inclusive assessment of the scope of the curse: "For the creation [ἡ κτίσις] was subjected to futility" and is in "bondage to decay." Moreover, "the whole creation [πᾶσα ἡ κτίσις]," analogous to the woman, "has been groaning together in the pains of childbirth until now" (Rom 8:20–22). Hence, Paul, following the teaching of Genesis and the rest of the OT, believed human sin had ecological ramifications.[115] Thus, God touches Adam at

113. Hamilton argues for the factitive, *Genesis 1–17*, 205–6, and Sarna for the intensive, *Genesis*, 29.

114. Collins, *Genesis 1–4*, 164.

115. For a further development of the ecological ramifications of human sin in the OT, see Dyrness, "Stewardship of the Earth in the OT," 50–65. Bible interpreters debate the precise manner in which human sin brought about changes in man's environment. Creationary scientist Henry Morris suggests that God, by removing his blessing, allowed mutations that would give rise to changes in physical structures, resulting in phenomena such as thorny plants, carnivorous teeth, or deadly viruses. *Genesis Record*, 125–26. Taking a different approach, Kline agrees that the curse involved the entire creation but argues, "Man's state of blessedness is thus seen to be primarily a matter of God's providential authority over creation, controlling and directing every circumstance so that everything works together for man's good and nothing transpires for his hurt or the frustration of his efforts. God gives his angels charge over the one who stands in his favor lest he should dash his foot against a stone (Ps 91:12). Blessing consists not in

that point in his life related to the primary focus in his role of fulfilling the creation mandate.[116] Man was to rule over the ground joyfully and successfully. Now the ground will rule over him. He will enjoy the fruit of his labor only through painful toil (בְּעִצָּבוֹן).[117] And this painful toil will haunt man's steps all the days of his earthly existence (כֹּל יְמֵי חַיֶּיךָ) until it reaches its inevitable end in human death (3:19). The phraseology "until you return to the ground" obviously alludes to human death and the dissolution of the body. Many modern commentators understand human death to be a natural phenomenon and part of God's original intent for man. Therefore, these words are merely descriptive, indicating that mankind will find no reprieve from the curse the entire duration of his earthly life.[118] Some conservative commentators believe mortality was man's original created lot and that immortality or freedom from death was only possible by means of immediate access or future access to the tree of life.[119] However, both Old and New Testament writers link

---

the absence of the potentially harmful stone, but in the presence of God's providential care over the foot. Adam's world before the Fall was not a world without stones, thorns, dark watery depths, or death. But it was a world where the angels of God were given a charge over man to protect his every step and to prosper all the labor of his hand." *Kingdom Prologue,* 56–57; see also Walton, *Genesis,* 236–38. Perhaps the moral state of pre-fallen Adam may serve as an analogy of the natural state of creation prior to the fall. Adam was created without moral defect (innocent) with the ability to refrain from sin (*posse non peccare*) but also with *the potential* for moral defect (sinfulness) and sinning (*posse peccare*). Similarly, it is possible that the genetic elements that would give rise to aberrant and harmful facets of nature were already *potentially* present in the original creation but held in bay by God's beneficent providence.

116. Hamilton observes, "Both divine messages are directed to a point of highest fulfillment in the life of the female and the male. For the female that is, among other areas, her capacity of mother and wife. For the male that is, among other areas, his capacity of breadwinner and family provider" *Genesis 1–17,* 203.

117. As with the woman's pain in childbearing, the pain here envisioned is both physical (Gen 3:16; 5:29) and psychological (Pss 13:3; 146:3; Prov 15:13) and can lead a man to despair of life itself (Job 7:15). Thus, man's quest for eschatological fullness (i.e., ultimate meaning, fulfillment, and purpose of life) will now meet with frustration. The canonical book of Ecclesiastes explores this theme of human frustration in a curse-world more fully. See W. Anderson, "Curse of Work in Qoheleth," 99–113; David M. Clemens, "Law of Sin and Death," 5–8; Starikov, "Mercy of Vanity," 124–30.

118. See Fretheim "Genesis," 364; Skinner, *Genesis*, 84; Vawter, *On Genesis*, 85; von Rad, *Genesis,* 95; Westermann, *Genesis 1–11,* 266.

119. See Munday, "Creature Mortality: From Creation or Fall?", 51–68; Collins, *Genesis 1–4,* 160–62; Kline, *Kingdom Prologue,* 56–57; Hamilton, *Genesis 1–17,* 203–4; Walton, *Genesis,* 183–85.

human death with God's wrath and curse and identify it as a consequence of human sin (Ps 90:3–12; Ezek 18:4; Rom 5:12ff.; 6:23; 8:6; 1 Cor 15:21–22; 56a; Heb 9:27; Jas 1:15). Nor is it possible to limit Yahweh's death-sentence sanction to "spiritual death,"[120] since 3:19 clearly includes physiological death as part of Yahweh's *punitive sentence* on humanity. Hence, Yahweh's words should be read as *prescribing* man's punishment not merely *describing* the outcome of man's disobedience.[121] Moreover, the very language employed of being taken from the dust (creation) and returning to the dust (uncreation) is suggestive of judgment (see Gen 6–8).[122]

But just as a remedial or redemptive design resided within Eve's punishment, so too with Adam's. The fact that Yahweh does not terminate Adam's commission to subdue the earth suggests that the Creator has not abandoned his original intentions for humanity and the rest of creation. Moreover, one may infer that just as Yahweh would raise up a deliverer-offspring to defeat the Serpent's kingdom of darkness *through the woman's painful childbearing* (compare 3:15 with 3:16), so too God's chosen deliverer would attain that victory, ironically, *through man's (i.e.,*

120. Contra Collins, *Genesis 1–4*, 175.

121. Contra Walton, *Genesis*, 236–38.

122. With respect to the question of whether man's original constitution prior to the fall was mortal or immortal, one may again use the analogy of Adam's original moral condition. In his original state, Adam was neither sinful nor indefectibly holy. Similarly, Adam was neither mortal nor immortal. The "seeds of mortality" were not *naturally active* at the point of Adam's creation, only held in bay by access or potential access to the tree of life. *Mortality*, like human sin, only existed as *a potentiality*. Likewise, *immortality* only existed as *an eschatological potentiality*, a royal grant to be conferred for fealty rendered in man's accomplishment of his covenantal obligations specified in Genesis 1:26–28 and 2:15–17. This explanation is at least as old as Theophilus of Antioch, who lived in the last half of the second-century AD. Theophilus writes, "But some one will say to us, 'Was man made by nature mortal?' Certainly not. 'Was he then immortal?' Neither do we affirm this. But one will say, 'Was he then nothing?' Not even this hits the mark. He was by nature neither mortal nor immortal. For if He had made him immortal from the beginning, He would have made him God[-like]. Again, if He had made him mortal, God would seem to be the cause of his death. Neither, then, mortal or immortal did He make him, but, as we have said above, capable of both; so that if he should incline to the things of immortality, he should receive as reward from Him immortality, and should become God[-like]; but if, on the other hand, he should turn to the things of death, disobeying God, he should himself be the cause of death to himself." *ANF*, 2:105. For an extended treatment of the subject of human mortality before the Fall, see Terreros, "Death Before the Sin of Adam."

the deliverer-offspring's own) painful death[123] resulting in the reversal of Yahweh's curse, the restoration of blessing, and the fulfillment of God's original intentions for humanity and the world. That Adam evidenced hope in a redemptive reversal that would emerge from Yahweh's curse is suggested in his naming of Eve, which Moses positions immediately following the curse-sanction (3:20).[124] That Adam's response is an act of saving faith is intimated by Yahweh's reciprocal action of clothing the human couple to hide their nakedness, which signifies that Adam and Eve's "fig-leaf" coverings (3:7) were inadequate to cover their nakedness. Human nakedness, which in this context includes guilt and shame, can only be remedied by a covering that God himself provides (cf. Exod 28:42), which covering signals the expiation of guilt (3:21).[125]

123. Yahweh's oracle that the woman's offspring would crush the Serpent's head signals the Serpent's ultimate demise. Nevertheless, the fact that the Serpent would strike back and bruise the offspring's heel suggests the possibility of a mortal wound. The immediate and typical fulfillment of this prophecy, as seen in the Cain and Abel story, demonstrates that the Serpent (through his offspring, i.e., Cain) may mortally wound the woman's offspring (i.e., Abel). Therefore, though Adam and Eve may not have initially read "and you shall bruise his heel" as a reference to death, they later would have both the grammatical and also the historical warrant for such an interpretation. Eve's celebration of Seth's birth as "the offspring" to replace Abel (4:25) suggests that she may have drawn that hermeneutical conclusion.

124. That Eve would become the mother of all the living [human beings] is an obvious biological fact arising from God's creative design for the man and the woman. Thus, her name signals the perpetuation of God's original creation blessing despite the curse. See Hamilton, *Genesis 1–17,* 206–7. There is, however, reason to believe that Adam intended more in his name conferral. It seems more likely that Moses would have placed Adam's giving the woman a new name in the context of chapter 2 or 4 if the name merely served to highlight her biological function. If someone objects and argues that Moses placed it after the curse simply because he wanted to reflect historical sequence, one may counter that argument by noting that (1) Moses is highly selective in his narrative of the creation and Fall, usually only including what serves a theological aim, and (2) Moses elsewhere inserts statements dischronologically for thematic purposes (e.g., 2:19). If Moses wanted to highlight the woman's biological function as *Urmutter*, he probably would have placed Adam's statement in chapter 2 or 4. But since Moses places Adam's giving of his wife the new name *immediately after the curse*, he seems to want his audience to read the seeds of hope in Adam's expression (i.e., through the woman "Life" would be restored). See Kline, *Kingdom Prologue*, 150; Waltke, *Genesis*, 95; Reymond, "An Investigation of the Covenants of the OT and their Significance in the Theocratic Program of God," 149.

125. As Brueggemann remarks, "With the sentence given, God does (3:21) for the couple what they cannot do for themselves (3:7). They cannot deal with their shame. But God can, will, and does," *Genesis,* 50. Moreover, since Yahweh's covering of the couple's nakedness counters the exposure of their nakedness (3:7), it would seem quite natural

Banishment from the Garden

Verses 22–24 bring closure to the Fall narrative and are key for understanding man's sin and its consequences. The text contains three thematic elements: divine assessment of the fallen human condition, divine alarm at the fallen human condition, and divine action towards the fallen human condition.

Divine Assessment

What the Serpent claimed would happen Yahweh confirms has happened. Man has become *like God* (3:22a)! Some demur and interpret this statement as divine sarcasm.[126] There is irony here, but not the kind of irony some commentators suppose. Yahweh's words are depicting reality. Man assumed the divine prerogative to decide *autonomously* what was good and what was bad for him and his destiny.[127] According to Scripture, God does confer the privilege and ability of knowing good and evil on certain individuals, particularly kings (2 Sam 14:17; 1 Kgs 3). But God reserves the right to delegate this prerogative; it must not be usurped. Moreover, man must exercise this prerogative in the fear of Yahweh and in conformity with the divine word. Hence, man's experience of becoming "like God" was not what he expected. In this irony lies the distinction between Satan's prediction and God's assessment.[128]

---

to interpret Yahweh's action redemptively. God's act of clothing the man and woman signifies or symbolizes a divinely instituted remedy for guilt and shame, and it portends God's redemptive intentions for the fallen human race. See Hamilton, *Genesis 1–17*, 207. Some commentators believe that the implied death of animals in order to acquire the skin-coverings would have suggested the institution of animal sacrifice to the original Israelite reader. See Kline, *Kingdom Prologue*, 152; Mathews, *Genesis 1–11:26*, 255; Ross, *Creation & Blessing*, 140; Schaeffer, "Genesis in Time and Space," 75.

126. Calvin, *Genesis*, 1:182–83; Vos, *Biblical Theology*, 33.

127. As von Rad notes, "The guiding principle of his life is no longer obedience but his autonomous knowing and willing, and thus he has really ceased to understand himself as creature" *Genesis*, 97.

128. Hamilton captures the irony: "Man has become like God. But one suspects that these words in the serpent's mouth convey one thing and the same words in God's mouth say another. The serpent held out to the couple the prospect that being like God would bring with it unlimited privileges, unheard-of acquisitions and gifts. . . . Alas, rather than experiencing bliss, they encounter misery. Rather than sitting on a throne, they are expelled from the garden. Rather than new prerogatives, they experience only a reversal. The couple not only fail to gain something they do not presently have; the irony is that they lose what they currently possess: unsullied fellowship with God. They found nothing and lost everything." *Genesis 1–17*, 208. Blocher's comments are also worth

Divine Alarm

The last half of 3:22 has occasioned much discussion among interpreters. The expression is incomplete, and most interpreters treat it as elliptical. The elliptical form has the effect of stressing alarm and urgency.[129] Some modern commentators see an allusion here to the jealousy of the gods as represented in pagan mythology. In other words, they see this verse as confirming the Serpent's suggestion that Elohim's prohibition betrayed a selfish desire to retain immortality for himself and to keep it from humanity. A better interpretation of Yahweh's alarm and prompt action to prevent mankind from partaking of the tree is to view it as redemptive in motive and purpose. Partaking of a divine sacrament appointed for blessing in an unworthy manner results in judgment rather than blessing (1 Cor 11:27–29). Similarly, for Adam and Eve to partake of the tree of life apart from the outworking and accomplishment of Yahweh's redemptive design might have resulted in an eternal existence but certainly not life as God intended. As taking from the tree of knowledge resulted in a counterfeit wisdom, so taking from the tree of life apart from the permission of God would result in a counterfeit life, which would be no life at all since man would remain alienated from his Maker. To borrow from NT theology, Yahweh would not allow Adam and Eve to sidestep the cross any more than Jesus would allow Satan to persuade him to do so (Matt 4:1–11; 16:22–23; Luke 4:1–13). Once man fell into sin, God determined a new pattern—blessing through curse. By expelling Adam and Eve from the Garden, God acts in mercy on them

interesting

---

noting: "The verse expresses the paradox of life under sin; it is a kind of autonomy by which mankind apes the independence of God, though this autonomy is illusory and is actually alienation" *In the Beginning,* 131.

129. The ESV renders the ellipsis as follows: "Now, lest he reach out his hand and take also of the tree of life and eat, and live forever—." Gerhard von Rad classifies it as an anacoluthon (97), that is, an abrupt change in the middle of a sentence used for rhetorical affect. Wenham offers a better suggestion. The elliptical expression is an aposiopesis (*Genesis 1–15,* 85), that is, "a sudden breaking off of a thought in the middle of a sentence, as though the speaker were unwilling or unable to continue." *American Heritage Dictionary of the English*, 4th ed. (Boston: Houghton Mifflin, 2006), s.v. Hence, the narrator is not simply employing a rhetorical device to underscore the speed of God's action, but he has also tried to portray something of the emotional upheaval within the divine heart. It is as if Yahweh becomes choked up when assessing man's action and contemplating his danger while remaining within reach of the second sacramental tree. Moved with strong emotions, he quickly carries out the solution (3:23–24) rather than stating it.

and their offspring, and he insures that his redemptive pattern remains intact.[130]

Divine Action

Yahweh sends האדם[131] into exile. The verb "sent away" (וַיְשַׁלְּחֵהוּ) in verse 23 may connote the idea of breaking off a (legal) relationship, as in the case of divorce (Deut 21:14; 22:19, 29; 24:1, 3; Jer 3:8; Isa 50:1; Mal 2:16) or banishment (Gen 12:20; 21:14; 25:6; Isa 27:10; Oba 1:7). The parallel verb "drove out" (וַיְגָרֶשׁ) in the next verse is also used with reference to divorce (Lev 21:7, 14; 22:13) and more commonly forced exile (Gen 4:14; 21:10; Exod 6:1; 10:11; 11:1; 12:39; 23:28–31; 33:2; 34:11; Num 22:6, 11; Deut 33:27; Josh 24:12, 18; Judg 2:3; 6:9; 0:41; 11:2, 7; 1 Sam 26:19; 1 Kgs 2:27; 1 Chr 17:21; Job 30:5; Ps 78:55; Jonah 2:4; Mic 2:9; Zeph 2:4). Both ideas of divorce and exile assume the breach of a covenant[132] and serve to mark the formal enactment of Yahweh-Elohim's juridical penalty. Hence, the epoch of primordial paradise has ended, and sacred or redemptive history has officially commenced. Though man must now reside east of the Garden, his future destiny lies in the west (12:1–3).

130. Bramer writes, "If man were to decide that the good thing to do would be to eat from the tree of life, he would forever experience a living death. Man's knowledge was not accurate or sufficient, but he might think it was. God, in grace, would not allow fallen man to make a temporal decision that would prevent him from accepting God's provision for his predicament. In the future, when man's sin would be dealt with through redemption, the tree of life would be placed in the new earth for man to eat (Rev 22:2)." *Genesis*, 47. See also Dumbrell, *Covenant and Creation*, 37; Ross, *Creation & Blessing*, 149; Ward, *Foundations in Genesis*, 115.

131. The narrator's use of the singular masculine pronoun in 3:23 as the object of "sent" and his use of אֶת־הָאָדָם in 3:24 as the object of "drove out" serves to underscore Adam's representative role and covenantal headship. God's banishment of Adam from the Garden means banishment for his wife as well as his offspring. See Collins, *Genesis 1–4*, 173–74; Mathews, *Genesis 1–11:26*, 256; Ward, *Foundations in Genesis: Genesis 1–11 Today*, 114–15.

132. The parallel between Adam's and Israel's exile provides another argument for viewing Adam's sin as a breach of covenant since his punishment mirrors Israel's.

PART TWO

Sin and the Curse in the Primeval Narratives

2

The Spread of Sin and the Curse in the Primeval Narratives

MANKIND WAS EXPELLED FROM Eden's Garden as a result of his sin (3:22–24). Yet he was not immediately banished from the land of Eden itself, nor was he completely barred from access to God's presence and favor. Just as Yahweh-Elohim's covenantal threat-sanction of death (2:17) included an implied promise-grant of eschatological life (2:9, 22), so Yahweh's judicial curse-penalty (3:14–19) contained an implied reinstatement of the original promise-grant of life by which the Serpent-initiated rebellion would be reversed and the original prospects of eschatological fullness would be restored (3:15). However, as the curse-promise portended and as the events subsequent to mankind's tragic fall revealed, God chose not to reestablish his original kingdom objectives instantaneously. Instead, the Creator-now-turned-Redeemer opted, according to his wisdom, to display the riches of his grace against the backdrop of the fullness of human sin. Accordingly, postlapsarian history unfolds a story of the spread of human sin. As surely as mankind multiplies and fills the earth, so human sin advances in stride.[1] This sad story of human depravity in turn provides the foil against which divine justice and mercy are gloriously displayed.[2]

1. In the words of Blocher, "Sin proliferates along with mankind. It takes on new aspects as human life develops in new directions." *In the Beginning*, 197.

2. The drama of redemptive history always assumes human sin as its backdrop. Consequently, a proper analysis of both primeval and patriarchal history as revealed in the Genesis narrative must include a focus on the spread of sin motif in order to fully appreciate God's grace.

BROTHER KILLS BROTHER

The record of life outside the Garden begins with a birth-notice of Adam and Eve's firstborn son, Cain, and Eve's maternal response (4:1). The birth of a second son, Abel, is also recorded but without any accompanying maternal response (4:2a). The asymmetry may suggest that the firstborn child occupied Eve's special attention.[3] More likely, though, it is the narrator who is especially interested in Cain, evidenced by the fact that he refers to Abel not as Eve's "son" but as Cain's "brother." The following verses confirm that Cain is the main actor in the plot. From the brothers' births, Moses quickly moves forward in time to their adulthood, noting Abel's vocation as a "keeper of sheep" and Cain's as a "worker of the ground" (4:2b). At an appointed time, the brothers appear before Yahweh to engage in an act of worship[4] with an offering corresponding to their respective vocations (4:3–4a). Cain brought Yahweh "of the fruit of the ground [מִפְּרִי הָאֲדָמָה]," which corresponds to his vocation as a farmer. Abel, on the other hand, brought Yahweh "of the firstborn of his flock [מִבְּכֹרוֹת צֹאנוֹ]," which matches his profession as a sheepherder. However, "Yahweh looked with approval [וַיִּשַׁע] toward Abel and his offering, but toward Cain and his offering he looked with disapproval [לֹא שָׁעָה]"[5] (4:4b-5a; author's translation). The chiastic structure underscores the stark contrast in the way Yahweh views the respective worshipers and their gifts. Some commentators have attempted to ground God's rejection of Cain's offering or acceptance of Abel's offering either in the nature of their vocations or their sacrifices (i.e., a grain offering vs. an animal

3. Eve's reference to her firstborn child as "a man [אִישׁ]" rather than "a child [יֶלֶד]" has suggested to some commentators that she may have viewed Cain as the promised "offspring" of the *protoevangelium* (Gen 3:15) or at least the progenitor of that future redeemer. See Luther, *Lectures on Genesis*, 1:249; Aalders, *Genesis*, 118–19; Keil and Delitzsch, *Pentateuch*, 108–9. Following this line of thought, de Boer has suggested that the preposition אֶת be emended to the noun אֹת [אוֹת] and the clause translated, "I have gained a man, the sign of the Lord." *Nederlands theologisch tijdshrift* 31 (1942) 197–212, cited in Wenham, *Genesis 1–15*, 102. Whether Eve's speech at Cain's birth is an evidence of true faith in the divine promise is not beyond doubt. More plausible evidence of Eve's saving faith will appear when she responds to Seth's birth (see below).

4. It is highly likely that the original Israelite reader would have viewed the acts of Cain and Abel as acts of worship. Outside the Garden there is still fellowship with God, but that fellowship is mediated through an altar and special offerings.

5. As Austel observes, "The basic idea of shāʿa^{h} is 'to look at with interest.' It is never a casual or disinterested glance." שָׁעָה (shāʿa^{h}) look at, look to, regard," *TWOT*, 2:944–45.

offering).[6] Herman Gunkel, for example, draws the conclusion, "The narrative maintains that Yahweh loves the shepherd and animal sacrifice, but wants nothing to do with the farmer and fruit offerings." Others have supposed that the basis for God's rejection of Cain's offering lies in the fact that it was bloodless in contrast with Abel's. Robert Candlish asserts, "To appear before God with whatever gifts, without atoning blood, as Cain did—was infidelity."[7] But these interpretations are tenuous. Both the items Cain and Abel bring to Yahweh are designated a מִנְחָה, that is, an offering, gift, or tribute. In the Pentateuch, מִנְחָה designates Jacob's "gift" or "tribute" given to Esau, which consisted of livestock (Gen 32:13ff.) and Jacob's "gift" of agricultural products to the vizier of Egypt (Gen 43:10, 11, 15, 25, 26). The term is also used for an acceptable "grain offering" (Exod 29:41; Lev 2:1ff.; 5:13; 6:7, 8, 13). Outside the Pentateuch, מִנְחָה is used for a gift or tribute that usually corresponded in nature and value to one's social standing (Judg 3:15–18; 2 Sam 8:2, 6; 1 Kgs 4:21 [Heb 5:1]; 10:25). These facts should suffice to demonstrate that Yahweh's displeasure with Cain's act of worship resided neither in his vocation nor in the type of gift he brought. Moreover, careful reading of the text indicates that Abel's devotion to the Lord was authentic and heartfelt; Cain's was not. The use of the personal pronoun הוּא suggests that Abel took *personal interest* in this offering: "*he himself*, or *he, on his part*, brought the offering." Moreover, Abel is said to have brought "the firstborn [מִבְּכֹרוֹת]" from among his flock; whereas, it is not said that Cain brought of the "first-fruits [בִּכּוּרִים]" (see Lev 2:14; 23:17, 20). Moses also draws attention to the fact that Abel's offering included the "fat-portions [וּמֵחֶלְבֵהֶן]" of the firstborn. This may be a hendiadys and could be translated as "the fattest of the firstborn." So Abel brought the Lord *his very best*, and he did so with *personal interest*.[8] Cain's lack of devotion to Yahweh is the first indication that sin has spread from the primordial parents to their offspring.

6. Gunkel, who assigns the Cain and Abel story as well as the Genesis 2 narrative to J (*Genesis*, 43) seems to forget that it was Yahweh who planted a Garden and assigned Adam the task of working and keeping it (Gen 2:15).

7. *Studies in Genesis*, 94.

8. See Waltke, "Cain and His Offering," 363–62. Such a conclusion is consonant with the NT writer's assessment of Abel's offering, namely, that it evidences genuine faith and devotion to God (Heb 11:4) in contrast to Cain's, which manifests an absence of faith and devotion (1 John 3:12).

More troubling, however, is Cain's response to Yahweh's disapproval and admonition. Like his parents, Cain fails to render to Yahweh supreme love and loyalty. But whereas Adam and Eve's response was primarily one of guilt and fear (3:7–10), Cain responds in anger and self-pity (4:5b). There appears to be an intensification of evil in Cain's heart that was not present in his parents' hearts. Yahweh initially responds to Cain by encouraging repentance (4:6–7a).[9] Moreover, he warns Cain against succumbing to sin's enslavement: "if you do not do well (i.e., repent), sin is crouching at the door [לַפֶּתַח חַטָּאת רֹבֵץ]. Its desire is for you, but you must rule over it" (4:7b). This may be an allusion to the Serpent poised to strike and poison Cain, as he poisoned Cain's parents (Gen 3:1, 4–5).[10] Whatever the precise imagery, Cain must master sin, or sin will master him.[11]

Instead of publicly acknowledging his wrong to Yahweh and dealing with his sinful anger,[12] Cain speaks to Abel privately (4:8a),[13] probably

9. The Lord confronts Cain with a series of rhetorical questions: "Why are you angry, and why has your face fallen? If you do well, will you not be accepted?" Just as in God's earlier judicial interrogation of Adam and Eve, these questions were designed not to solicit information but to elicit confession and repentance (see Gen 3:9, 11, 13).

10. Noting the difference in gender agreement between the feminine noun חַטָּאת and the masculine participle רֹבֵץ, Ephraim Speiser attempts to link the participle to the Akkadian word rābiṣum, meaning "demon." In this case, God is warning Cain that sin is a "demon at the door," *Genesis*, 33. One might follow this suggestion and view the "demon at the door" as a reference to Satan, a historical referent that became corrupted over time into a superstitious notion among pagan cultures of benevolent or malevolent "door demons." The verb רֹבֵץ, however, is used elsewhere in Genesis to describe a crouching lion (49:9). And feminine abstract nouns may sometimes take masculine verbs (GKC § 122r; *IBHS* § 6.6b). Thus, the language appears metaphorical, portraying sin as an animal lying in wait to pounce upon its victim.

11. The noun describing sin's "desire" for Cain (i.e., תְּשׁוּקָה) may be used for an appropriate desire (Song 7:10 [Heb 11]). But with sin as the subject in Genesis 4:7, the connotation is negative: sin (personified) *wants possession* of Cain's soul. For the lexical, syntactical, and semantic links between this verse and 3:14a, see Foh, "What Is the Woman's Desire," 376–83.

12. The Bible often warns against sinful anger (Prov 27:4; Eccl 7:9; Eph 4:26, 31) and portrays it as the seed that gives rise to murder (Matt 5:21–26; Jas 1:15).

13. This would explain the seeming laconic reference, וַיֹּאמֶר קַיִן אֶל־הֶבֶל אָחִיו וַיְהִי. Note that the MT does not provide the content of Cain's message to Abel. The LXX supplies the words διέλθωμεν εἰς τὸ πεδίον ("let us pass through into the plain"), and a number of English translations follow suit (NIV, NET, NJB, NLT, CSB). It is possible that the LXX has preserved the original text. But the "omission" preserved in the MT may have been intentional and in turn may have prompted the conflation found in the LXX and other ancient texts (Samaritan Pentateuch, Vulgate, Syriac).

suggesting to his brother that he had something he wanted to communicate to him outside, away from Yahweh's presence. Hence, Cain's deed is premeditated.[14] And when the two brothers pass through "the door" of the sanctuary,[15] Cain conveys to Yahweh and all present that he will not humble himself and acknowledge his sin. Instead, he chooses to align himself with the Serpent and give vent to his enmity against "the woman's seed" (Gen 3:15) by murdering his brother Abel (4:8b). From Adam and Eve's eating of the forbidden fruit sin accelerates to violent fratricide—within one generation!

Next follows the divine inquest. Yahweh confronts Cain and demands, "Where is Abel your brother?" (4:9a).[16] But Cain, unlike his parents, who at least acknowledged their sin (3:12, 13), insolently lies and disclaims responsibility for his brother (4:9b).[17] Therefore, Yahweh issues a charge of wrongdoing,[18] which is followed by a divine curse,[19] paralleling his earlier curse on the Serpent and signaling an extension of the previous curse on the ground (3:17–19; 4:11–12).[20]

14. Briggs sees the enmity between Cain and Abel as a fulfillment of the Genesis 3:15 prophecy and suggests the Serpent will strike the woman's seed "in secret and in treachery, behind the back." *Messianic Prophecy*, 71.

15. Most interpreters overlook the reference to "the door" or take it figuratively and include it as part of the metaphor (i.e., "the door of Cain's heart"). But the fact that Yahweh dialogues with Cain and that Cain later departs from Yahweh's "presence" (4:16) seems to imply that God appeared to Cain and Abel in a theophany, as he did to Adam and Eve in the Garden (3:8–21). Moreover, the common phenomena of sanctuaries or temples throughout the ancient Near East that predate the Sinai instructions for a tent-sanctuary suggest some primeval prototype. If "the door" in Genesis 4:7 implies a literal sanctuary enclosure, then Cain's departure through the door without acknowledging his guilt would have publicly signified his refusal to repent.

16. As noted above, the divine interrogatives are intended to elicit repentance (Gen 3:9, 11, 13; 4:6–7a). "Where is Abel your brother?" carries the same intent.

17. Von Rad perceives the defiant tone in Cain's response when he writes, "Cain gets rid of this difficult question, which graciously offered him opportunity to confess his deed (Zi.), with an impertinent witticism: Shall I shepherd the shepherd? He lies impertinently directly to God's face, [*sic*] is therefore much more hardened than were the first human pair." *Genesis*, 106.

18. "What have you done?" functions here and elsewhere in Genesis as a formal accusation of a crime committed (Gen 3:13; 12:18; 20:9; 26:10; 29:25; 31:26; 44:15).

19. As Ross observes, "The Lord's speech moves instantly from accusation to judgment, as if the insolent answer that Cain had given indicated there would be no confession forthcoming," *Creation & Blessing*, 160.

20. In chapter 3, God directly curses the Serpent (אָרוּר אַתָּה, v. 14) and indirectly curses the man by cursing the ground (אֲרוּרָה הָאֲדָמָה, v. 17). Here God directly curses

Instead of asking for pardon, Cain seeks protection from the consequences of his sin and registers a judicial appeal. Anticipating the potential ramifications of God's curse sanction, namely, the loss of God's protection against an avenger of Abel's death (4:14)[21] Cain complains, "My punishment is greater than I can bear" (4:13).[22] As in the case of

---

Cain (אָרוּר אַתָּה). Waltke concludes, "God now links Cain with the Serpent in the cursed state (3:14)." *Genesis*, 98. The prepositional phrase "from the ground [אֲרוּרָה הָאֲדָמָה]" reminds the reader of the מִן preposition in the curse on the Serpent (3:14). Some argue that the מִן preposition should be understood in the ablative sense, "designating movement *away from* a specified beginning point" (*IBHS* § 11.2.11b). Thus, as God *banished* the Serpent from the other animals, so he *banished* Cain from the fertile soil. See Brichto, *The Problem of "Curse" in the Hebrew Bible*, 82–85. On the other hand, one may interpret the מִן preposition in Genesis 3:14 as a comparative marker (*IBHS* § 11.211e), denoting a *comparison of degree*, i.e., "cursed are you more than" (*IBHS* § 14.4d) or a *comparison of exclusion*, i.e., "cursed are you rather than" (*IBHS* § 14.4e). If Cain's curse is parallel to the Serpent's, then either God has cursed Cain *instead of* the ground or God has cursed Cain *more than* the already cursed ground. The latter option makes better sense here. In any case, God's curse upon Cain is *graver* than his judgment upon Adam and has *intensified* the already existing curse upon mankind in general. See Currid, *A Study Commentary on Genesis*, 1:148; von Rad, *Genesis*, 106; Ross, *Creation & Blessing*, 160.

21. Somehow Cain intuitively anticipates a talionic response (i.e., life for life) from one of his kinsmen. Buis is correct when he notes, "Not only Special Revelation but also the conscience of man is deeply imbued with the conviction that a man will be punished according to his deeds." "Retribution," *ZPEB*, 5:84.

22. The LXX translates the Hebrew עֲוֺנִי with ἡ αἰτία μου, which can refer either to an accusation or verdict of wrong doing (Matt 27:37; Acts 25:28; 28:20) or to the basis or ground of an accusation, i.e., guilt or blameworthiness (Luke 23:4; John 18:38; 19:4, 6; Acts 13:28; 23:28; 28:18). The LXX would seem to favor the latter since it uses the verb ἀφεθῆναί ("to be forgiven") to translate the Hebrew מִנְּשֹׂא, which can mean "to bear" or "to forgive." Similarly, the Vulgate translates the noun with *iniquitas* and the verb with the phrase *ut veniam merear* ("to merit pardon"). Hence, the Douay-Rhiems Bible renders the verse, "My iniquity is greater than that I may deserve pardon." Cassuto supports this interpretation when he asserts that "as a rule" the terms עָוֺן and נשׂא when used together refer to the idea "to forgive iniquity." *From Adam to Noah*, 222. Despite the witness of these early versions and opinion of Cassuto, the majority of modern translators and commentators are correct in interpreting עֲוֺנִי as "punishment" and מִנְּשֹׂא as "to bear." First of all, the Hebrew infinitive is active in contrast to the passive rendering in the LXX. Second, the terms עָוֺן and נשׂא, when used together, do not always or even predominantly mean, "to forgive iniquity." Just as frequently (if not more often) they refer to *the bearing of guilt, responsibility, or punishment* (Exod 28:43; Lev 5:1, 17; 7:18; 17:16; 19:8; 20:17, 19; 22:16; Num 5:31; 14:34; 18:1, 23; 30:16; Ezek 4:4, 5, 6, 10; 18:19, 20; 44:10, 12). Third, nowhere in the surrounding context does Cain appear to reflect genuine contrition and a desire for forgiveness. In light of the fact (1) that Cain defies God's punishment by settling down and building a city (4:16–17), (2) that there appears to be no trace of true religion preserved in Cain's lineage (4:17–24), and (3) that Cain's

Adam and Eve, Yahweh manifests a gracious forbearance and mitigates the punishment. He places Cain under a protective edict by appointing for Cain's advantage an oath-sign (אוֹת)[23] that threatens divinely authorized vengeance on anyone who would take Cain's life (4:13–14). Both the similarity and also the disparity between God's dealings with Adam and his dealings with Cain are significant. In God's primeval curse on the Serpent and on humanity's earthly life and vocation (3:14–19), Adam apparently detects a note of grace that engenders a response of faith despite the reality of the curse (3:20). Following Adam's positive response, God mitigates his curse by providing Adam and Eve with clothing to serve as a covering, indicating a divinely initiated expiation of their guilt (3:21). Unlike his father, Cain senses no mercy in Yahweh's curse and responds with an impenitent grievance (4:13–14). Nevertheless, Yahweh once again mitigates his curse by providing Cain with an oath-bound promise to protect him from the full extent of the punishment he deserves (4:15).[24] In both cases, God shows grace. But Adam's and Cain's responses differ, as does the nature of divine grace extended to each. Adam's response is positive; Cain's is negative. Correspondingly, God's sign to Adam and Eve signifies a grace that operates on a different level than the grace he extends to Cain.[25] The former highlights reconciliation.

descendants manifest his evil recalcitrance to a greater degree (4:23–24), the depiction of Cain entreating God forgiveness is tenuous.

23. Most interpreters identify the אוֹת as a physical mark that Yahweh places on Cain's body in order to visibly identify him. This interpretation has led to speculation about the nature of "the mark." According to a number of lexicographers and commentators, the אוֹת on Cain was some form of bodily tattoo. See Stolz, "אוֹת ʾôt sign," *TLOT*, 1:68; Gunkel, *Genesis*, 46–47; Sarna, *Genesis*, 35; von Rad, *Genesis*,107; Waltke, *Genesis*, 99. However, the noun *sign* need not always refer to something visible. For example, Rahab requests an אוֹת from the Israelite spies (Josh 2:12). And Rahab's "give me a sure sign [וּנְתַתֶּם לִי אוֹת אֱמֶת]" parallels "please swear to me [הִשָּׁבְעוּ־נָא לִי]." The spies respond to Rahab's entreaty for an אוֹת with an oath-bound promise to spare her and her family (Josh 2:14). See Keil and Delitzsch, Joshua, Judges, Ruth, 1 & 2 Samuel," 1:37. This less common meaning for אוֹת would make better sense in Genesis 4:15b. See Kline, "The Oracular Origin of the State," 138–39.

24. Notes Kidner, "God's concern for the innocent (10) is matched only by His care for the sinner. Even the querulous prayer of Cain had contained a germ of entreaty; God's answering pledge, together with His *mark* or *sign* (the same word as in 9:13; 17:11)—not a stigma but a safe-conduct—is almost a covenant, making Him virtually Cain's gōʾēl or protector; *cf.* 2 Samuel 14:14b, AV, RV. It is the utmost that mercy can do for the unrepentant," 76.

25. Theologians have traditionally distinguished these two species of grace as *special grace* and *common grace*. For a fuller development of these two facets of divine grace and their relationship to each other, see Van Til, *Common Grace and the Gospel*.

The latter is intended (1) to leave the door open to reconciliation (Rom 2:4),[26] (2) to teach Adam's posterity that the redemption of the righteous (Abel) and the punishment of the wicked (Cain) are not always meted out in this life, and (3) to serve as a foil against which all may clearly see not merely the continuation of human sin but rather *the progressive degeneracy* of Adam's posterity. For as soon as God communicates his forbearance to Cain, the ungrateful wretch turns on his heel, departs "from the presence of Yahweh, and settle[s] in the land of Nod, east of Eden" (4:16). Hence, Yahweh's goodness serves to highlight the gravity of human sin in its stark ingratitude and proud refusal to acknowledge God's benevolent Lordship (see Rom 1:18–32).

This analysis of Cain's fall into sin highlights both its similarities and its disparities from the original Fall. Table 1 provides a more detailed comparison of these two accounts to help the reader conceptualize the downward trajectory of sin and its effects from Adam to Cain.[27]

As Table 1 demonstrates, human sin not only moves from the first generation of human beings to the second, but there is a marked increase in sin's odious nature. What began as a seed planted within the hearts of the primordial man and woman has taken root in the second generation[28] and grown into an ugly weed of human hubris that will rapidly spread throughout the earth, turning what God intended to be a paradisiacal Garden into a howling wasteland of evil and misery. So begins the spread of sin!

A KINGDOM TO RIVAL GOD'S

In Genesis 4:17, Moses begins a new section[29] highlighting several major developments in the human race that resulted from Cain's exile from

26. "Why does the Lord's anger not burn against Cain? Undoubtedly it did. But though capital punishment was the way God directed Israel to respond to murder cases, it is not always the way God chooses (see, e.g., 2 Sam 11–12). Already we see a God who holds justice in his right hand and mercy in his left." Walton, *Genesis*, 271.

27. The writer has adapted and expanded Fretheim's helpful structural comparison of the narratives of Genesis 3:1–24 and Genesis 4:1–16 in *Creation, Fall and Flood*, 93–94. For a similar but simpler structural comparison, see Westermann, *Genesis 1–11*, 303, and Wenham, *Genesis 1–15*, 99.

28. For a helpful assessment of the primeval narrative's contribution to the doctrine of original or hereditary sin, see Wenham, "Original Sin in Genesis 1–11," 309–28.

29. Genesis 4 can be divided into three sections (4:1–16; 17–24; 25–26), each beginning with the phrase "X knew Y, and she [conceived and] bore Z." Collins, *Genesis 1–4*, 191–92.

Table 1: A Comparison of the Falls Inside and Outside the Garden

The Fall Inside the Garden	The Fall Outside the Garden
1. Context: unhindered fellowship with God inside the Garden (2:4–24)	1. Context: altar-mediated fellowship with God outside the garden (4:2–4)
2. Occasion: a temptation that arises from without—the Serpent (2:25; 3:1)	2. Occasion: a temptation that arises from within—Cain's evil heart (4:5–6)
3. Fall: Satan seduces Eve to violate God's law (3:1–5). The human couple eats the forbidden fruit (3:6).	3. Fall: God urges Cain not to violate his law (4:6–7), but Cain premeditatedly murders Abel (4:8).
4. Inquest: Adam and Eve feel guilt and fear (3:7–8). God confronts them with questions to solicit confession and repentance (3:11–13). They blame-shift yet admit their sin (3:12–13).	4. Inquest: Cain does not feel fear or remorse (4:9). God confronts Cain with questions to solicit confession and repentance (4:6–7, 9–10). Cain lies and defiantly refuses responsibility (4:9).
5. Curse: a direct curse on the Serpent (3:14) but an indirect curse on Adam and Eve (3:16–19)	5. Curse: a direct curse on Cain that exceeds the curse that was directed to ground (3:17–19)
6. Human response: faith and hope in the promise (3:20; 4:25)	6. Human response: self-pity and appeal regarding the punishment (4:13–14)
7. Divine mitigation: God provides a covering for guilt—a symbol of special grace (3:21)	7. Divine mitigation: God pledges protection of life—an indication of common grace (4:15)
8. Expulsion: Adam is driven from inside to outside the Garden to till the ground (3:22–24). Adam accepts his punishment and passes on the knowledge of God to his sons (4:2–4).	8. Expulsion: Cain is driven farther away from the Garden to wander aimlessly (4:11–12). Cain resists his punishment (4:17) and passes on a negative view of the true God (4:17–24).

Eden. These advances in "civilization" bear witness both to the potency of common grace as well as to the escalation of human sin. The first major development is the commencement of human empire-building. Cain fathers Enoch and initiates the process of urbanization.[30] Both biblical data and extra-biblical evidence suggest that Cain's motivation for building the city involved three factors. First, Cain probably put little stock in God's oath-bound protection edict and therefore built a fortified city for protection,[31] one of the primary purposes for city-building in the ancient Near East.[32] Second, since Cain's curse entailed wandering aimlessly as a man without a home (4:12b, 14b),[33] his determination *to settle* (ישׁב) in the land of *Nod* ("Wandering"!) appears to be a human effort to reverse or override the divine curse.[34] Third, Cain names the city after his son,[35] reflecting an effort to secure an enduring name and

30. Technically, the antecedent of "and he was building" could be Enoch, making Cain's son the city builder rather than his father. This reading is favored by Westermann, *Genesis 1–11*, 326–27, and Wenham, *Genesis 1–15*, 111. However, such a reading would require an emendation of the text as the present construction of the text identifies "Enoch" as the son after whom the city is named. Hence, the text favors Cain as the original architect and builder.

31. Hamilton suggests that "Cain's act of city building is an attempt to provide security for himself, a security he is not sure that God's mark guarantees." *Genesis 1–17*, 238.

32. Archaeological data as well as Biblical evidence indicates that many of the ancient cities were characterized by large fortified walls and often built in strategic locations to render the citizens less vulnerable to foreign invaders. Because of migration and territorial boundary disputes, "massive fortifications were constructed, which both defined the boundary between rural and urban space and restricted points of entry." Stone, "The Development of Cities in Ancient Mesopotamia," *CANE*, 1:235–48; See also Mazar, "The Fortifications of Cities in the Ancient Near East," *CANE*, 3:1523–37; Houston, "City," *ZPEB*, 1:873–80; Stambaugh, "Cities," in *ABD*, 1:1031–48. Leviticus 25:31 contrasts smaller villages with "walled" cities. There are also many references to "walls," "towers," and "gates" of cities as features of fortification (Num 13:28; Deut 3:5; Josh 2:5, 15; 6:5; Judg 9:51; 2 Sam 18:33; Neh 3:1–3, 11, 25).

33. The Hebrew expressions— וָנָד and נָע (4:12, 14) are roughly synonymous and may be translated as an hendiadys: "a restless wanderer" (NIV) or "a homeless wanderer" (NET). See Ross, *Creation & Blessing*, 160.

34. Mathews agrees. "Cain's action is in direct violation to the injunction of God that restricted him to the life of a vagabond," *Genesis 1–11:26*, 284–85. Waltke combines the first two of Cain's motivations when he remarks, "The city functions as an anodyne to wandering and alienation and as a protection against human irrationality and retaliation." *Genesis*, 99–100. See also Ross, *Creation & Blessing*, 166–67.

35. The name "Enoch" (חֲנוֹךְ) is probably related to the verb חנך, which often refers to an official ceremony of *inauguration* or *consecration* (Deut 20:5; 1 Kgs 8:63; 2 Chr 7:5).

dynastic succession.[36] Moses indicates that Cain succeeded in this endeavor by providing a genealogical chronicle of Cain's kingly successors culminating with the infamous Lamech (4:18), whose exploits not only reflect the image of his ancestor but whose recorded taunt song testifies that the Cain-tradition lives on in his offspring (4:19–24). It would be wrong to conclude from the narrative that all empire-building is inherently evil. As redemptive history unfolds, the reader will discover that Yahweh's program of empire-building is advanced through the City (i.e., Zion) and the King (i.e., the Son of David). What makes Cain's project sinful is its secular character[37] and prideful aim,[38] both of which will find their fuller expression in the postdiluvian empire-building on the plains of Shinar (11:1–9).[39] As one ancient writer aptly noted, "Children and the building of a city establish one's name, but better than either is the one who finds wisdom" (Sir 40:19a, NRSV). Some within the line of Seth pursued this preferred path of wisdom, developing an empire-building of a different sort—that of re-asserting the interests of Yahweh's Kingdom (4:26b).

See Naudé, "חנך (ḥnk)," *NIDOTTE*, 2:200–01. In light of the basic meaning of the verb, Kidner suggests that Cain's naming of his first son and first city "Enoch" signified his intention to start a new beginning (77). Delitzsch similarly remarks, "The son and the city were together the beginning of a new epoch." *New Commentary on Genesis*, 1:191.

36. Naming a city after oneself or one's son implies ownership and lordship over that city, establishing the legal basis for dynastic succession (Deut 3:14; 2 Sam 5:9; 12:28). See Frick, *City in Ancient Israel*, 41.

37. Here, the writer does not intend "secular" in the absolute sense of describing a civilization without any form of religion. As the apostle Paul notes, even unregenerate humanity can "maintain the outward appearance of religion" (2 Tim 3:5, NET). The "religion" of ungodly culture, however, exchanges "the glory of the immortal God for images resembling mortal man and birds and animals and reptiles" (Rom 1:21–23). And "since they did not think it worthwhile to retain the knowledge of God, he gave them over to a depraved mind [that is, a mind devoid of a saving knowledge of God]" (Rom 1:28, NET). In this sense, Cain's empire-building was *secular*.

38. Ellul captures the spirit of Cain's empire-building well: "In Cain's eyes it is not a beginning again, but a beginning. God's creation is seen as nothing. God did nothing and in no case did he finish anything. Now a start is made, and it is no longer God beginning but man. And thus Cain digs a little deeper the abyss between himself and God." *Meaning of the City*, 6.

39. Kline notes the connection when he writes, "The account of Babel's founding, like that of Cain's city, begins with a reference to expelled mankind wandering in the east (Gen 11:2; cf. 4:16)." *Kingdom Prologue*, 273. Observes Waltke, "The earthly city provides both civilization and protection but culminates in 11:4 in the building of a city that challenges God's supremacy."

The second major development in the human race resulting from Cain's exile involved advances in culture, particularly in the areas of the trades, arts, and sciences. Cain's descendant Lamech fathers three sons, each noted for his contribution to a cultural achievement: Jabel, for his advances in animal breeding (4:20); Jubal, for his contribution to the musical arts (4:21); and Tubal-cain, for his development of metallurgy (4:22). These specific examples of cultural advancement function as a synecdoche, representing cultural development in all other areas of trade, arts, and technology. Moreover, by associating cultural advancement with the descendants of Cain, Moses does not imply that the Sethites or other lines of Adam's progeny failed to make cultural contributions. Rather, his purpose is to highlight the human potential that common grace makes possible even among the ungodly.[40] Yet it must be admitted that the absence of any hint of true religion among the Cainites is conspicuous,[41] especially when contrasted with the one achievement for which the descendants of Seth are noteworthy, namely, the revival of Yahwehism (4:26b).[42]

The third major development in the human race following Cain's exile was the alarming escalation of human hubris and tyrannical ag-

40. Moses "expressly celebrates the remaining benediction on that race, which otherwise would have been deemed void and barren of all good," says Calvin. "Let us then know, that the sons of Cain, though deprived of the Spirit of regeneration, were yet endued with gifts of no despicable kind; just as the experience of all ages teaches us how widely the rays of divine light have shone on unbelieving nations, for the benefit of the present life." *Genesis*, 1:218.

41. Gage notes, "The τέχνη of Cain's descendants is remarkable in its similarity to the skills required to erect the tabernacle in the wilderness. In Jabal they have their tents, but no tent of meeting. In Jubal they have their pipes, but no psalms to sing. In Tubal-cain they have their craftsmen, but no tabernacle to furnish. Such is the nature of urban man (Cf. the τέχνη of Babylon, Rev 18:22)." *Gospel of Genesis*, 59 n. 52. Henry draws the following lesson: "That worldly things are the only things that carnal wicked people set their hearts upon and are most ingenious and industrious about. So it was with the impious race of cursed Cain. Here was a father of shepherds and a father of musicians, but not a father of the faithful. Here was one to teach in brass and iron, but none to teach the good knowledge of the Lord. Here were devices how to be rich, and how to be mighty and how to be merry, but nothing of God." *Commentary on the Whole Bible*, 1:145.

42. As the cultural achievements of the Cainites point to the potential made possible by common grace, so the religious revival among the Sethites points to the redemptive potential made possible by special grace, and it serves to distinguish the "seed of the woman" from the "seed of the Serpent" by a concern to advance what matters most in human culture, namely, true religion.

gression as epitomized in the seventh successor to Cain. Lamech's sin underscores the growth of human pride and violence in two striking ways. First, Lamech apparently originated bigamy (which would later burgeon into polygamy) by taking two wives instead of one (4:19) and thereby violating the sacred institution of monogamous marriage (2:18–24). The narrator does not indicate whether Lamech's action was motivated by an unbridled lust for sexual pleasure or by an effort to increase the likelihood of more offspring.[43] In either case, he oversteps the parameters of the creation ordinances and acts autonomously. Second, Lamech violates the sanctity of human life in a way that exceeds the heinous nature of Cain's murderous deed. Cain killed Abel and attempted to evade responsibility when confronted (4:9). But Lamech artfully gloats about his murderous act (4:23f.).[44] Cain pled for divine leniency and protection (4:13–14), but Lamech assumes Yahweh's authority and with godlike prerogative places himself under imperial immunity (4:24).[45] So the seven-step progression from Cain to Lamech manifests an unmistakable escalation in hubris and violence.[46]

43. Though the barrenness of a man's wife could sometimes lead to the temptation of acquiring another (Gen 16:1–4), this "excuse" is not available to Lamech since the account indicates that both his wives bore him children (4:20–22).

44. Blocher poignantly remarks, "This is the second human poem in the text of Genesis, and what a contrast it makes with the first one, the lover's greeting before the fall (Gen 2:23)! Lamech's poetry oozes hatred. The comparison with Cain's words is instructive, marking human progress on the path of violence. Just as Lamech is more 'civilized,' able to forge weapons with which to deliver his 'seventy-fold' blows, so also he possesses the art of words and of phrases to express brutality." *In the Beginning*, 199. Dempster notes, "The first genealogical list of the Bible (Gen 4:17–24) . . . is an 'anti-genealogy' (Robinson 1986: 600), since it begins with Cain, the brother-killer, and ends with the child killer, Lamech [whose] boastful taunt to his wives at the conclusion of this first family tree reveals a man of titanic arrogance and heartless cruelty." *Dominion and Dynasty*, 70.

45. Lamech's poem parallels Cain's divinely pledged edict of protection with Lamech's autonomously presumed edict of protection. Von Rad appropriately observes, "Lamech's defiant demand reaches into Yahweh's own domain." *Genesis*, 112. Von Rad goes on to suggest that Christ's teaching regarding a seventy-fold forgiveness may have been a conscious retort to Lamech's bold taunt.

46. Several scholars note this progression (or rather degeneration). Von Rad, for example, concludes, "The Song of Lamech is the third section of the primeval history which the narrator emphasizes. It is a story of the increase in sin and the more and more profound disturbance of the original orders of life with which it goes hand in hand. First the Fall, then fratricide, and now the execution of vengeance (which God has reserved for himself!) is claimed by man." *Genesis*, 111–12. Fretheim observes, "Progress in sin

ANOTHER ONE BITES THE DUST

The dreadful taunt of Lamech closes Cain's line,[47] and the narrator transports the reader back in time to the birth of Seth, which marks a renewed hope in God's redemptive promise (4:25).[48] After noting Seth's birth, the birth of Seth's son Enosh, and the revival of Yahwehism (4:26), the narrator parallels Cain's genealogy with a genealogical list beginning with Adam and tracing his lineage through Seth to Noah (5:1–32). Yet in spite of clear parallels,[49] this genealogy differs from the Cainite genealogy in several important ways. First, as already noted, the Genesis 5 genealogy begins with Adam—Cain's does not.[50] This fact not only reminds the reader that Cain has been banished from the primordial family but may also suggest that Adam preserved the true religion and passed it down through Seth and his seed.[51] Second, the genealogy of Genesis 5 provides chronological information regarding the age of the father at the

---

and its effects matches the progress in civilization." "Genesis," 375. Gowan remarks, "[The genealogy of Cain] reveals a streak of increasing violence running alongside all these important human accomplishments. The Song of Lamech completes the Cain story with the return to killing." *From Eden to Babel,* 74.

47. It will be argued below that the narrator resumes the story of Cain's line (as well as Seth's) in Genesis 6:1ff., where he continues to trace the spread of sin and its effects throughout the human race.

48. Eve names the child Seth (שֵׁת), which sounds like the verb שִׁית, which God uses in Genesis 3:15 where he declares, "*I will set* [אָשִׁית] enmity between [the Serpent] and the woman" (author's translation). Then Eve gives her reason for the child's name: "*For Elohim has set for me* [שָׁת־לִי אֱלֹהִים] *another seed* [זֶרַע אַחֵר] in place of Abel whom Cain killed" (Gen 4:25, author's translation and emphasis). Here, Eve appears to allude to the promise of the special זֶרַע in Genesis 3:15. Dempster agrees and remarks, "Immediately after the genealogy, Eve has another 'seed' that replaces his slain brother, Abel (Gen 4:25, 26). In the context, this reference to the replacement of the seed instantly resonates with Genesis 3:15 and represents an implicit hope that Eve has for this child to relieve the earth from the curse imposed on it" (71). Eve's use of the perfect "has appointed" may be interpreted and translated as the precative perfect or "perfect of prayer": "May God appoint for me another seed in place of Abel!" (*IBHS* §30.5.4c–d).

49. Both genealogies are primarily vertical or linear (i.e., connecting an individual to an ancestor) and become horizontal or segmented at the end (i.e., listing several siblings or relatives of a particular ancestor). There is also a similarity between the names of Cain's ancestors and those of Seth. Finally, in each genealogy the narrator gives special treatment to the seventh from Adam.

50. For this reason, the author prefers to view the Genesis 5 narrative as the "Adam-Seth genealogy" rather than the more common "Sethite genealogy."

51. That true religion was revived and passed down through Seth's lineage is clearly indicated in the text (see 4:26; 5:22–24, 28–28). Moreover, the narrator has already highlighted believing responses in Adam (3:20) and Eve (4:25).

time he fathered the specified descendant, the number of years he lived after begetting that offspring, and the total length of his earthly life.[52] The unusually long life spans attributed to the antediluvians in this genealogy have led a number of scholars to see the theological motif of divine blessing and human vitality.[53] Hence, while two murderers bracket Cain's genealogy, emphasizing the motif of premature death, extreme longevity characterizes the Adam-Seth genealogy throughout, emphasizing the theme of fullness of life. Third, while the Cain genealogy features two individuals who inflict death (Cain/Lamech), the Adam-Seth genealogy features an individual who escapes death, namely, Enoch (5:22–24). Finally, the Cain genealogy concludes with an unbeliever (Lamech) whose offspring (Jabal, Jubal, Tubal-cain) merely advance human culture (4:20–22). But the Adam-Seth genealogy concludes with a believer (another Lamech!) whose offspring (Noah) preserves the human race from extinction (5:29; 6:8ff.). These positive features of the Adam-Seth genealogy in contrast with the negative features of the Cainite genealogy have caused a number of scholars to see either a *discontinuation of* or a *disconnect with* the spread of sin theme that has heretofore characterized the primeval narrative since the Fall.[54]

52. The consistent pattern is "When X lived ___ years, he fathered Y. X lived after he fathered Y ___ years and had other sons and daughters. Thus all the days of X were ___ , and he died." Only this genealogy and that in Genesis 11 provide these seemingly unbroken chronological links. For a survey of different approaches to interpreting the chronological information provided in these genealogies and defense of a traditional approach, see Shaw, "The Genealogies of Genesis 5 and 11 and Their Significance for Chronology."

53. Hamilton writes, "The genealogy of this chapter and the transmission of the divine image may be one way in which the writer is stressing his point about the operations of divine grace." *Genesis 1–17*, 256. Mathews argues that one of the theological functions of the genealogy is "to show the perpetuation of the *imago Dei* and blessing (1:26–28)." *Genesis 1–11:26*, 305. Commenting on the chronological data for the antediluvians in the Genesis 5 genealogy, Warfield asserts, "All these items cooperate to make a vivid impression upon us of the vigor and grandeur of humanity in those old days of the world's prime." "Antiquity and Unity of the Human Race," 244.

54. Some conservative scholars, focusing on the amazing longevity of the Sethites, emphasize the theme of God's blessing and grace. Keil, for instance, writes, "In the genealogy of the Cainites no ages are given, since this family, as being cursed by God, had no future history. On the other hand, the family of Sethites, which acknowledged God, began from the time of Enos to call upon the name of the Lord, and was therefore preserved and sustained by God, in order that under the training of mercy and judgment the human race might eventually attain to the great purpose of its creation." *Pentateuch,* 1:120–21. Likewise, Leupold agrees with Luther that the Sethites "were the very greatest

However, a careful reading of Genesis 5 indicates that the narrator has not set aside the motif of sin's spread. Indeed, there are several reasons for viewing the spread of sin as one of the primary themes of this narrative. To begin with, the above-mentioned contrasts between the Cain genealogy and the Adam-Seth genealogy assume an intentionally structured antithetical parallelism, thereby linking this chapter with the preceding narrative. Even a critic such as Walter Brueggemann is forced to admit, "This account follows Genesis 2–4 in the present tradition. Thus, longevity cannot now be attributed to the 'absence of sin.'"[55] Second, the narrative begins by noting that God's conferral of the *imago Dei* on Seth is mediated through Seth's father Adam (5:1–2), in whose likeness Seth was born (5:3). The fact that the divine image is now conferred on humanity *through Adam* suggests that the image is no longer untainted by sin.[56] In the third place, the deafening refrain, "and he died," which reverberates throughout this entire passage (5:5, 8, 11, 14, 17, 20, 27, 31) reminds the reader of God's curse on Adam (2:17; 3:19). The fact

---

heroes who ever came upon earth barring Christ and John the Baptist" and supports this reading by noting that "in point of longevity their strength and natural vigor far excelled that of later generations," concluding that "they represented a less decayed stage of human life." Leupold adds, as a contributing factor to their longevity, his conviction that "here is a race of godly men who lived temperately and sanely." Leupold acknowledges that the deaths of these patriarchs points to "God's justice and wrath against sin," but he believes the message of Genesis 5 is "where sin prevails, grace does the more prevail," *Exposition of Genesis*, 230–36. Thus, these commentators appear to see a *discontinuation* of the spread of sin theme as the reader transitions from Genesis 4 to 5. On the other hand, critical scholars posit a *disconnection* between these chapters. They see "J" (Yahwist) as the author or final redactor behind the Cainite genealogy, whose purpose is to emphasize the theme of sin or crime. The author or final redactor of the Genesis 5 genealogy is "P" (Priestly writer), whose purpose is to emphasize the fulfillment of the creation mandate and divine blessing. See Skinner, *Genesis*, 129; von Rad, *OT Theology*, 1:154–56.

55. *Genesis*, 68.

56. This point is noted by Brueggemann when he observes, "Verse 3 contains an odd ambiguous statement about Seth, the father of humankind. It is not said he is the image of God, but in the image of Adam, who is the image of God. Thus, he is one step removed. This might mean he continues to be the image of God, for the image of God is granted not only to the first human but to all humans. But such an assertion is hedged, for the image of Adam is something less, and marred (cf. Gen. 3). Thus, the text may realistically recognize that Seth and his heirs are a strange, unresolved mixture of the regal image of God and the threatened image of Adam." *Genesis*, 68. Currid agrees and writes, "Seth receives the likeness of God as it has been passed through his father Adam. It is a nature that is twisted, frail, mortal and miserable. The imputation of Adam's nature to his descendants is thus recorded," *Study Commentary on Genesis*, 1:162.

that Moses chooses the Adam-Seth genealogy rather than the Cain genealogy to scatter these "tombstones"[57] underlines the reality that even those among whom true religion may be found do not escape the gravity of the curse.[58] Of course, there is one exception—"Enoch walked with God, and then he disappeared because God took him away" (5:24, NET).[59] Nevertheless, this exception to the rule provides a fourth argument since it only serves to reinforce the rule. In other words, Enoch's extraordinary exemption from death's sting literarily functions to accord *death* pride of place in the narrative's plot.[60] Fifthly, every protracted lifespan *falls short* of the millennial mark, which, as Wenham notes, "is a mere day in the light of God's eternity."[61] So even in his "primeval-prime," man can only attain to a brief moment in the divine reckoning! Sixthly, Lamech's lament at the close of the narrative (5:29) suggests a keen awareness of the growing burden of sin's curse from which humanity desperately needs

57. This is Davis's catchy term for the death notices. *Paradise to Prison*, 106.

58. Murray remarks, "Death. How eloquently this is advertised in Genesis 5! Notwithstanding the longevity of man, he cannot escape the fulfillment of the divine threat, and must prove that the wages of sin is death." "The Fall of Man," 2:72. Clines comments, "No reader of Genesis 5, to take one example, fails to be impressed by the recurrent phrase 'And he died,' which baldly and emphatically concludes the entry for each of these antediluvians. The whole movement of the regular form of these notices is towards death. . . . Their function must be to emphasize a finality about each of these lives, as if to say: through possessed of an excess of vitality by ordinary human standards, these men also die. Thus the thrust of the Genesis 5 genealogy is toward death, even though human life continues." *Theme of the Pentateuch*, 72. Summarizing the primary themes of both the Cain genealogy and the Adam-Seth genealogy, Walton writes, "We see the blessing in generation after generation as people are fruitful and multiplying. But the countertheme resounds in each generation, 'and then he died.' Likewise as people multiply, the sin problem multiplies. The advances in civilization may enhance the ability to procure food, but they do nothing to stem the tide of death and sin. Instead of the blessing resulting in subduing and ruling . . . , it is the curse that is spreading." *Genesis*, 284.

59. The last half of the verse might be literally translated, "and non-[earthly]-existence of him [וְאֵינֶנּוּ] because God removed him [כִּי־לָקַח אֹתוֹ אֱלֹהִים]." That the narrator intended to convey Enoch's supernatural exemption from death is supported contextually by the absence of the typical phrase, "and he died," together with the verb לקח, which is elsewhere used of God's miraculous removal of Elijah from earth into heaven (2 Kgs 2:3, 5, 9). As Hebrews unambiguously asserts, "By faith Enoch was taken up so that he should not see death [τοῦ μὴ ἰδεῖν θάνατον]" (Heb 11:5a).

60. Kidner notes how Enoch's translation "conspicuously breaks the rhythm" of the "reign of death" refrain and views it as "the standing pledge of death's defeat" (80).

61. *Genesis 1–15*, 146. Wenham is probably alluding to the apostle Peter's comment, "With the Lord . . . a thousand years [are] as one day" (2 Pet 3:8).

relief. Finally, the narrative concludes with Noah, the "Rest-Giver," whose calling is to provide deliverance from the curse (5:29).[62]

These observations lead to the conclusion that the Genesis 5 genealogy plays an integral part in advancing the spread of sin motif commenced in the previous chapter. Far from an interruption of or respite from sin's doleful encroachment on human life, the Adam-Seth genealogy reminds the reader that God meant business when he warned Adam not to disobey, and his death-threat was not empty—a point not missed by the apostle Paul (Rom 5:12–14).

THE FLOOD OF HUMAN SIN

In Genesis 6, human sin reaches titanic proportions. Sin matured rapidly from the taking of forbidden fruit (Gen 3:6) to the taking of human life (Gen 4:8). Moreover, Cain's angry and impenitent recalcitrance grew until his seventh successor, Lamech, displayed a defiant disregard for the sanctity of marriage and human life (4:19, 23–24). But Cain-like rebellion does not end with Lamech. The story of Lamechial arrogance and tyranny resumes in Moses's commentary on "the Sons of Elohim" (בְּנֵי־הָאֱלֹהִים) and their infamous offspring, "the Mighty Warriors" (הַגִּבֹּרִים). After the Genesis 5 genealogy, Moses describes the proliferation of humankind in general and the procreation of female offspring in particular (6:1). Then he observes that the בְּנֵי־הָאֱלֹהִים found "the daughters of man" (בְּנוֹת הָאָדָם) to be "attractive [טֹבֹת]" (6:2a). As a result, the בְּנֵי־הָאֱלֹהִים "took to themselves wives from all which they desired" (6:2b, author's translation). The grammatical links between the action described here and human sin in the Garden are unmistakable.[63] Thus, before the reader can reflect on the exact identity of these בְּנֵי־הָאֱלֹהִים and

62. "Linked to the consequences of Gen 2–4," reasons Brueggemann, "it is the task of Noah to end the banishment of the man and woman (3:24) and of Cain (4:16). He is to invert the sorry situation and cause a homecoming. . . . This anticipation of the work of Noah, placed in the mouth of Lamech, is a gospel announcement. . . . In a way more intentional than most of these, our verse places Noah at the turn from death to life. . . . The comfort promised by Noah (v. 29) is to reverse the destiny of living with the consequences of sin" (70). Of course, Noah's deliverance from the curse is only provisional and functions at a typical level pointing to the Greater Noah, Jesus, who will lead his spiritual family through the deluge of divine judgment unto the ultimate new heavens and new earth (Matt 24:37–42; Luke 17:26–37; 1 Pet 3:18–22; 2 Pet 3:5–13).

63. Just as Eve "saw" (ראה) that the fruit was "good" (טוֹב) and so "took" (לקח) "from" (מִן) what her heart desired, likewise these בְּנֵי־הָאֱלֹהִים "saw" (ראה) that the daughters of men were "attractive" (טוֹב) and so "took" (לקח) "from" (מִן) among them any they chose. Eslinger has also noted some of these parallels in "A Contextual Identification of the bene haʾelohim and benoth haʾadam," 65–73.

the precise nature of their deed, he smells again the stench of Eden's first transgression.

The Titans of Sin Identified

After two millennia of debate,[64] three basic interpretations have emerged concerning who the בְּנֵי־הָאֱלֹהִים were and what they did. Some early rabbis, church fathers, and modern interpreters view the "sons of Elohim" as a reference to supernatural beings (angels or demigods), who took human wives, produced semi-divine offspring and thereby fell from their first estate and precipitated God's judgment on the earth.[65] Thus, the resultant sin has both a human and an angelic dimension—a mingling the Bible forbids (Lev 19:19; 20:16; Deut 7:3; 22:9–11). More precisely, the sin involves angels and men transgressing divinely imposed limits, with the latter attempting to attain immortality.[66] A few proponents of this view, sensing the apparent incongruity between a rebellion initiated by angelic beings and a retribution aimed primarily at humans, either attempt to lay the blame chiefly on "the daughters of men" (or their fathers)[67] or suggest a case of demon possession whereby fallen angels

64. For a survey of early interpretations of this passage, see Newman, "The Ancient Exegesis of Genesis 6:2, 4," 13–36; P. S. Alexander, "The Targumim and Early Exegesis of the 'Sons of God' in Genesis 6," 60–71; Wickham, "The Sons of God and the Daughters of Men," 135–47.

65. See *Enoch*, 13–26; *Jubilees*, 43; *Philo*, 2:449–55; Josephus, *Antiquities*, 28; Clement of Alexandria, *Christ the Educator*, 3.2.14, and Ambrose, *On Noah* 4.8, in *ACCS*, 1:124, 126; Brueggemann, *Genesis*, 70–73; Cassuto, *From Adam to Noah*, 291–94; Delitzsch, *A New Commentary on Genesis*, 222–26; Fretheim, *Creation, Fall and Flood*, 105; Merrill, *Everlasting Dominion*, 144–45; von Rad, *Genesis*, 114; Sarna, *Genesis*, 45; Wenham, *Genesis 1–11*, 140–41; Westermann, *Genesis 1–11*, 372. For a thorough defense of this view, see VanGemeren, "Sons of God in Genesis 6:1–4 (An Example of Evangelical Demythologization?)," 320–48.

66. Fretheim remarks, "The strict separation between God's world and man's world had been broken down; the orders of creation had become confused. Evil is not confined to men; it is cosmic in scope." *Creation, Fall, and Flood*, 105. VanGemeren suggests, "Being under God's judgment since the Fall, man made an attempt to circumvent God's plan (*Grenzüberschreitung*) by being enticed to the Satanic scheme of intermarriage with demonic beings with the hope of ultimate prolongation of life." "The Sons of God in Genesis 6:1–4 (An Example of Evangelical Demythologization?)," 347.

67. So Wenham writes, "Here the fault of the daughters of men lies presumably in their consenting to intercourse with 'the sons of the gods.' It ought also to be borne in mind that the girls' fathers would also have been implicated, since, if there was no rape or seduction, their approval to these matches would have been required. The obvious avoidance of any terms suggesting lack of consent makes the girls and their parents

took possession of evil men.[68] A second view, advanced among some of the church fathers[69] and popularized by some of the Reformers,[70] holds that the "sons of God" represent the godly line of Seth and the "daughters of men" represent the sinful line of Cain. Hence, the precise sin in view is that of intermarriage between the righteous and the wicked, resulting in a breakdown of religious beliefs and values, which in turn served to advance the proliferation of evil in the world.[71] Finally, a third position, represented in some Targums[72] and recently refined by modern scholars acquainted with the divine-kingship ideology of the ancient Near East, interprets the "sons of God" as human rulers who arrogantly assume divine prerogatives.[73] None of the three views is totally free of interpretive challenges. Yet, the immediate and larger canonical context interpreted in light of the current archaeological evidence available favors the third view. The בְנֵי־הָאֱלֹהִים are ancient suzerains who engage in unrestrained polygamy (or even rape!?, 6:2b),[74] build royal harems, and exercise des-

---

culpable, the more so when the previous chapter has demonstrated that mankind was breeding successfully on its own." *Genesis, 1–15*, 141.

68. See Delitzsch, *New Commentary on Genesis*, 226; VanGemeren, "Sons of God in Genesis 6:1–4 (An Example of Evangelical Demythologization?)," 348; Waltke, *Genesis*, 117.

69. Ephrem the Syrian, *Commentary on Genesis* 6.3.1., *ACCS*, 1:124; Augustine, *City of God*, 510–14.

70. Luther, *Lectures on Genesis*, 2:7–13; Calvin, *Genesis*, 1:237–40.

71. Modern proponents of this view include Bush, *Notes on Genesis*, 1:116; Currid, *A Study Commentary on Genesis*, 1:173–75; Hamilton, *Genesis 1–17*, 264–65; Hartley, *Genesis*, 95–96; Keil and Delitzsch, *Penteteuch*, 1:127–34; Leupold, *Exposition of Genesis*, 1:249–54; Mathews, *Genesis 1–11:26*, 329–32; Murray, *Principles of Conduct*, 243–49; Payne, *Theology of the Older Testament*, 205–7; Robertson, *Genesis of Sex*, 35–43; Stigers, *Commentary on Genesis*, 97–98; Vos, *Biblical Theology*, 46–49.

72. Targum Onkelos reads, בני רברביא ("the sons of the great ones [i.e., nobles]"), *Onkelos*, 50–51; Targum Neofiti reads, בני דייניא ("the sons of the judges"). *Neofiti*, 71.

73. Note especially Kline, "Divine Kingship and Genesis 6:1–4," 187–204. See Millard, "New Babylonian 'Genesis Story,'" 12; Clines, "Significance of the 'Sons of God' Episode (Genesis 6:1–14) in the Context of the 'Primeval History' (Genesis 1–11)," 42; Walton, "Are the Sons of God in Genesis 6 Angels? No," 184–209; Blocher, *In the Beginning*, 200–203; Ross, *Creation & Blessing*, 181–83; Waltke, *Genesis*, 115–17; Ward, *Foundations in Genesis*, 141–45.

74. The linking of the verbs "they saw" (וַיִּרְאוּ) and "they took" (וַיִּקְחוּ) is found elsewhere in contexts of forced or illicit sex (Gen 34:2; 2 Sam 11:2–4). But the verb לקח can also refer to taking a bride (Gen 4:19; 11:29; 12:19; 20:2, 3; 25:1; 36:2, 6; Exod 34:16). Most likely, the reference is to marriage but not to monogamous marriage. The Hebrew reads, וַיִּקְחוּ לָהֶם נָשִׁים מִכֹּל אֲשֶׁר בָּחָרוּ. This construction may simply mean that *they*

potic tyranny. Their offspring, the הַגִּבֹּרִים,[75] perpetuate their evil, filling the earth with corruption and violence (6:11, 13), and thus earn the epithet, "men of fame [infamy!]" (אַנְשֵׁי הַשֵּׁם) (6:4).[76] The story of Cain and Lamech continues, and its tragic plot thickens.

---

chose any single wife of their liking. In this case the sin, if there is a sin implied, would be indiscriminate marriages based on physical attraction rather than spiritual affinities. On the other hand, the plural נָשִׁים followed by the phrase מִכֹּל אֲשֶׁר בָּחָרוּ may suggest that *they chose each and every bride they wanted*. In favor of the latter, the reader should note the close parallel in Ecclesiastes 6:2, where Qoheleth describes a wealthy man who "lacks nothing of all that he desires" (וְאֵינֶנּוּ חָסֵר לְנַפְשׁוֹ מִכֹּל אֲשֶׁר־יִתְאַוֶּה). The text in Ecclesiastes employs the verb אוה ("desire"), whereas the text in Genesis 6:2 uses בחר ("choose"). The two verbs, however, appear as synonyms in Psalm 132:13. Moreover, the increase in Lamech-like violence (see Gen 6:11, 13) leads the reader to expect a concomitant increase in Lamech-like marital practices, i.e., polygamy (see also Gen 12:10–20; Gen 20:2–7, 17–18). The grammatical and contextual indications combined have led Blenkinsopp to conclude that here we have a description of "titan promiscuity." *The Pentateuch: An Introduction to the First Five Books of the Bible*, 40. See also Kline, "Divine Kingship," 195–96; Kraeling, "The Significance and Origins of Gen. 6:1–4," 197; Westermann, *Genesis 1–11*, 366–68.

75. It is not clear whether the הַנְּפִלִים identified in 6:4a were merely contemporary with the הַגִּבֹּרִים, or whether they were among the offspring of the בְנֵי־הָאֱלֹהִים and therefore numbered with the הַגִּבֹּרִים. Elsewhere in the OT, the same expression is used to describe men of gigantic stature (Num 13:33). It may be that Moses is using the term here to refer to the presence of such "giants" who lived both before and after the Flood, and who were also often employed in the service of those military powers that opposed the people of God (Num 13:33; Deut 1:28; 2:10; 3:11; 9:2; 1 Sam 17:4–7, 47; 2 Sam 21:20–22; 1 Chr 11:23). In this reading, the narrator may be introducing them here not as the offspring but perhaps as the mercenaries of the הַגִּבֹּרִים.

76. Arguments for this position include the following: first, modern archaeological evidence suggests that ancient Near Eastern monarchs were viewed as sons of deities. See especially the works of Engell, *Studies in Divine Kingship in the Ancient Near East*; Frankfort, *Kingship and the* Gods; and Johnson, *Sacral Kingship in Ancient Israel*. Second, the primeval account has already depicted humankind as God's royal vice-regent and son, that is, his image whose kingly commission is to rule over and to subdue the earth (Gen 1:26–28; 5:1–2; Ps 8). This biblical and primeval reality provides the historical root from which later sacral kingship theology developed (of course, in a form corrupted by sinful ideology that tended to deify the human potentate). Third, Scripture elsewhere applies the term אֱלֹהִים to human rulers (Exod 21:6; 22:8, 9, 27 [Heb 7, 8, 28]; 2 Sam 7:14; Pss 2:7; 82:6; John 10:34–35). Fourth, the preceding and subsequent context lends weight to this view. The earlier reference to Lamech, the bigamist tyrant, provides the prototype of this multiplication of Lamech-like rulers who transgress the bounds of monogamous marriage and promote oppression and violence in the earth. Nimrod's empire-building and heaven-assaulting Babel enterprises (10:8–12) also echo the despot-like depiction of the בְנֵי־הָאֱלֹהִים and their offspring, הַגִּבֹּרִים. Moreover, the descriptions of the Pharaoh of Genesis 12 and the Abimelechs of Genesis 20 and 26 depict them as human rulers that were known for their attraction to beautiful women

The Depths of Sin Sounded

How does Yahweh respond to the rising tide of human sin? Moses depicts the divine response in terms of moral assessment, emotional sensation, and penal/remedial action: "Then Yahweh saw that *multiplied* [רַבָּה] was the evil of humanity in the earth *and every* [וְכָל] intention of the thoughts of his heart was *altogether* [רַק] evil *unceasingly* [כָּל־הַיּוֹם]"[77] (6:5, author's translation). This theological assessment of human evil underscores the spread of sin in at least three ways. First, it describes sin's *distributive spread* among humans. Just as people "began

---

and their habit of harem building. Indeed, we find the verbs "to see" (ראה) and "to take" (לקח) in Genesis 12:12, 15. What is more, the concern for an enduring "name" (6:4) is tied to Cain (4:17) and to the Tower builders (11:4) who were empire-builders (compare 10:8–12). Finally, this view is preferred in light of the objections inherent in the other views. Though the phrase "sons of God" could arguably refer to the line of Seth (cf. 5:1ff.), the phrase "daughters of men" does not naturally lend itself to a narrow interpretation of daughters born in the line of Cain. The reference to "mankind" (generic) multiplying in the land and giving birth to "daughters" (6:1) is more naturally interpreted as inclusive of all humanity, not one portion. Furthermore, until now, there has been no clear prohibition against intermarriage among families or clans. Moreover, the clause "they took wives for themselves from any they chose," as noted above, probably refers to polygamy—a theme already introduced in 4:17—rather than to intermarriage. And the fact that the "Serpent's seed" may be found even among the holy family (Gen 4:5–8) seems to render an identification of all those in Seth's line as "godly men" in contrast to the "ungodly men" of Cain's line questionable. Since the Genesis narrative is primarily focusing on the origin, spread, and consequences of *human sin*, it seems unlikely that Moses would introduce fallen angels into the picture. In Genesis 3, the Serpent tempts mankind to sin, and Adam and Eve acquiesce. As a result, *both* the Serpent *and* the humans are cursed and judged. However, here there is only judgment pronounced on man (6:3) as well as animal life under his dominion (6:7). Finally, it should be noted that Scripture elsewhere implies that angels are not given in marriage, do not procreate (Matt 22:30; Mark 12:25; Luke 20:34–36), and therefore are not inclined towards the practice of sexual intercourse (Gen 19). The boundaries of multiplying according to one's "kind" established at creation would also seem to discount this view (compare Gen 1:11, 12, 21, 25; 2:19–20). In sum, the evidence seems to lean in favor of viewing these beings as human despots who viewed themselves and who were viewed by others as semi-divine. Perhaps, as some have suggested, fallen angels did play a part in exerting an unseen influence on these rulers (Jude 6 [?]). However, demon possession is too strong a concept, since in that case the demon takes over the human consciousness. Better to see the "principalities and powers in heavenly places" (Eph 6:12) as working "behind the scenes" exerting an influence on human rulers that in no way suspends the rulers' own consciousness or moral responsibility before God (compare Daniel 10:10–14). See Blocher, *In the Beginning*, 202–3; Ross, *Creation & Blessing*, 182.

77. Literally, "all the day." Most translations appropriately interpret this as an adverbial phrase and render it "continually" (KJV, NAS, NKJ, ESV) or "all the time" (NIV, TNK, NET, CSB).

to multiply [לָרֹב] on the face of the land" (6:1a) so sin commensurately *multiplied* (רַבָּה). Secondly, the verse highlights the *inward spread* of sin. Not merely the actions of humans but their mental conceptions and volitional affections are tainted and inclined towards evil.[78] Moreover, this inward character of sin is *pervasive* (וְכָל־יֵצֶר מַחְשְׁבֹת לִבּוֹ)[79] and *prevailing* (רַק רַע).[80] Thus, Moses affirms the doctrine of total depravity.[81] Thirdly,

78. The Hebrew noun לֵב or its alternate form לֵבָב occurs over 800 times in the OT. In its most basic sense, it refers to *the center* or *core* of a person or thing and is sometimes used contiguously with קֶרֶב, 'inward part' (Prov 14:33; Jer 31:33). *Physiologically*, it may refer to the physical blood-pumping organ (1 Sam 25:37; 2 Kgs 9:24) or to its proximate location, i.e., breast (Exod 28:29; Job 41:24; Nah 2:8). But by far its most frequent use is *psychological*, in which it denotes the *inner* or *essential* nature of God (Ezek 28:2, 6), man (Dan 4:16; 7:4), or beast (Dan 4:16; 5:21). Unlike the English word *heart*, which usually denotes the emotive aspect of man, the Hebrew term can refer to the totality of man's immaterial nature as distinct from his physical nature (Pss 73:26; 84:2; Prov 14:30; 27:19). In some contexts, the לֵב is used for one or more constituent parts of a man's inner nature, standing for the center or seat of the mind (Gen 6:5; Deut 29:4; 1 Kgs 3:12; Eccl 2:1, 15; Song 5:2; Isa 4 4:19), the emotions (Gen 42:28; Deut 28:65; 1 Sam 2:1; Neh 2:2; Hos 11:8), the will (Deut 2:20; Judg 9:3; 1 Chr 22:19; Ps 37:4; Eccl 8:11), or the conscience (1 Sam 24:6; 2 Sam 24:10; Job 27:6). It may also stand for the center of a man's ethical-religious identity, being characterized as basically evil (Gen 6:5; Deut 15:9; Prov 10:20), good (1 Sam 13:14; 2 Kgs 20:3; Ps 32:11), or changed (Deut 30:6; Jer 31:33; Ezek 36:26). The Bible also uses לֵב in reference to the seat of God's spiritual faculties and moral capacity (Gen 6:6; 8:21; Hos 11:8; etc.), reminding us that man was created as God's visible replica (Gen 1:26–27). Thus, sin has affected the very core of man's identity. The Decalogue confirms that the ancient Hebrew conceived of sin as originating within the heart and not merely as an outward action (Exod 20:17).

79. The Hebrew noun יֵצֶר is related to the verb יצר, meaning "to mold or form." Used together with מַחְשָׁבָה (cf. Gen 50:20) and predicated of man's *heart* (לֵב), it refers to "that which is conceived in man's mind and that to which he inclines in his affections" (see 8:21; Deut 31:21; 1 Chr 28:9; 29:18; Prov 15:26).

80. "Altogether evil" is not a denial of *common grace* by which unregenerate men may exhibit certain outward virtues and perform deeds that are beneficial to humanity (see Gen 4:21–22; 20:5; 26:9–11; 45:16; 1 Kgs 21:27–29; 2 Kgs 10:30–31; Rom 2:14). Instead, the phrase serves to underline the stark reality that even the "good" deeds of men are tainted by evil motives. To use the language of Paul, the unregenerate man is under sin's reign (Rom 6:12–14; 8:7–8).

81. By "total depravity" theologians do not intend to denote that every human being manifests the full potential of evil residing in his heart. The many biblical statements that imply gradations of evil and culpability among human beings discount such a notion (Jer 7:26; Matt 11:21–24; 12:45; 26:24; Heb 10:29; 2 Pet 2:20). As Hoekema helpfully clarifies, what is meant is that "(1) the corruption of original sin extends to every aspect of human nature: to one's reason and will as well as to one's appetites and impulses; and (2) there is not present in man by nature [he means *fallen* nature] love to God as the motivating principle of his life." *Created in God's Image*, 150. For other OT passages

6:5 underscores the *durative spread* of sin. That is, as God surveys the human landscape, he does not only see intermittent discreet acts of sin but a *perpetual habit* towards sinful behavior (כָּל־הַיּוֹם). Humankind is thoroughly given over to the sway of evil.[82]

Moses is not content to portray sin's sway by dissecting man's rotten heart but quickly turns to a staggering disclosure of God's broken heart. Using emotionally charged vocabulary, he depicts Yahweh as feeling both *regret* (וַיִּנָּחֶם) for creating humanity and *heart-deep pain* (וַיִּתְעַצֵּב אֶל־לִבּוֹ) because of the rebellion of his images (6:6). In their effort to preserve divine transcendence, some theologians and commentators have emptied the terminology of significance, treating it as anthropopathic metaphor for the incomprehensible God accommodating himself to finite human understanding.[83] But the God Moses portrays is not apathetic to the

---

that confirm the depravity of the human heart, see Deut 31:21; Ps 14:1–3; 51:3–12 [Heb 1–10]; Jer 17:9–10.

82. Vos provides a similar analysis when he writes, "In the strongest terms the extreme wickedness reached at the end of the period is described. The points brought out are *firstly*: the intensity and extent of evil ('great in the earth'); *secondly*: its inwardness ('every imagination of the thoughts of his heart'); *thirdly*: the absolute sway of evil excluding everything good ('only evil'); *fourthly*: the habitual, continuous working of evil ('all the day')." *Biblical Theology*, 50–51. Vriezen says of this text, "A more emphatic statement of the wickedness of the human heart is hardly conceivable." *An Outline of OT Theology*, 210.

83. Calvin, for instance, is quick to assert, "The repentance ["grief," NIV] which is here ascribed to God does not properly belong to him, but has reference to our understanding of him. For since we cannot comprehend him as he is, it is necessary that, for our sake, he should, in a certain sense, transform himself. . . . Certainly God is not sorrowful or sad; but remains for ever like himself in his celestial and happy repose: yet, because it could not otherwise be known how great is God's hatred and detestation of sin, therefore the Spirit accommodates himself to our capacity." *Genesis*, 1:248–49. Two logical inconsistencies appear in Calvin's reasoning. First, he seems willing to allow God the emotions of anger and detestation but not the emotions of regret and sorrow. Second, in Calvin's view God uses descriptive language that, on the one hand, is untrue of God in order to, on the other hand, make known to us what "could not otherwise be known." Modern scholars have also referred to this language of accommodation as *anthropopathism* ("human emotions attributed to God which in fact do not have correspondence with human emotions"). Carson offers a fitting rebuttal to this interpretive approach: "It is no answer to espouse a form of impassibility that denies that God has an emotional life and that insists that all of the biblical evidence to the contrary is nothing more than anthropopathism. The price is too heavy. You may then rest in God's sovereignty, but you can no longer rejoice in his love. You may rejoice only in a linguistic expression that is an accommodation of some reality of which we cannot conceive, couched in the anthropopathism of love. Give me a break. Paul did not pray that his readers might be able to grasp the height and depth and length and breadth of

human condition.[84] On the contrary, in response to man's change from *very good* (1:31) to *very evil* (6:5), Yahweh genuinely feels a mixture of extreme disappointment and anger, which in turn produces a profound heart-felt sorrow, something any reader who has felt the pangs of the curse can to some degree identify with.[85] This exposure of emotional turbulence within the heart of an infinite, eternal, unchangeable God is one of the greatest indicators of the colossal proportions of human sin.[86]

But there is more. The narrator's reference to Yahweh's *seeing* (6:5a; see also 6:11–12) and his *feeling* (6:6; see also 6:7b) the profoundly sinful

---

an anthropopathism and know this anthropopathism that surpasses knowledge (Eph 3:14–21)." *Difficult Doctrine of the Love of God*, 58–59.

84. Observes Fretheim, "Here, God is revealed as one who, from creation on, is open to and affected by the world. The sinful response of humankind has indeed touched God; God is not apathetic. Even more, it indicates that God's judgment is not a detached decision. God is shown to be one who does not, indeed cannot, remove self and feelings from such a momentous judgment regarding the future of the creation; such a decision is not like flicking a switch or sending an impersonal command through a subordinate. God is caught up in the matter; and in some respects will never be the same. And so the judgment is a very personal decision, with all the mixed sorrow and anger that go into the making of decisions that affect the people whom one loves." *Suffering of God: An OT Perspective*, 112. Fretheim's study provides some helpful insights into an otherwise neglected area of study, namely, the exegetical data concerning divine emotivity, particularly, God's emotional responses to human sin and misery. The Process Theology and Open Theism framework into which he works many of his exegetical conclusions, however, seriously flaws his study. For a helpful critique of Fretheim, see Waldron's review, "Suffering of God: An OT Perspective, Terence E. Fretheim," 128–37. For a more biblically and theologically balanced view of the divine emotivity, see Carson, *Difficult Doctrine of the Love of God*, 58–64; Matthew Elliott, *Faithful Feelings*, 105–11; Frame, *Doctrine of God*, 608–16; Nichols, "Emotivity of God," 95–143; Ware, *God's Greater Glory*, 144–55.

85. The verb עצב and its cognates often refer to *deep emotional pain* experienced by humans. It denotes the aroused feelings of brothers whose sister has just been raped (Gen 34:7), a loyal friend who has just learned of his father plans to murder his best friend (1 Sam 20:34), a father who laments the untimely death of a prodigal son (2 Sam 19:3 [Heb 2]), and a wife whose husband has just deserted her (Isa 54:6). Interestingly, the same terms are used to depict the "pain" Adam and Eve must suffer as a result of the curse—a pain including both emotional as well as physical dimensions (3:16, 17). Hence, man's fall into sin brings pain to his Creator's heart as well as to his own.

86. Notes von Rad, "From the first Fall sin had grown like an avalanche; here at a special climax the narrator pauses and interrupts the regular progress of the account. He takes us from the world of complete disorderliness to God and dares to look into God's grieving heart. . . . In daring contrast to what is said about the human heart there follows a word about what takes place in God's heart: grief, affliction, and disappointment in man. Precisely in this way, by reference to the Creator's bewilderment, he has communicated something of the incomprehensibility of this incursion of sin." *Genesis*, 117.

human condition serves as a harbinger of divine action. Thus, God's perception and passion portrayed in 6:5–6 lead *reflexively* to his response of judgment and grace portended in 6:7–8.[87] Because the spread of human sin has reached such extreme proportions, God must now erase the moral filth from off the face of the earth with a universal flood (6:7, 13ff.).[88] After many centuries, his divine forbearance now approaches its limit (6:3).[89] The tidal wave of human hubris brings a deluge of divine

87. Often, the phrase, "and Yahweh saw," portends divine action whether judgment or mercy (see Gen 6:12; 29:31; Exod 2:25; 3:4; 4:31; Deut 32:19; 2 Kgs 14:26; 1 Chr 21:15; 2 Chr 12:7; Isa 59:15–16). As Cassuto notes, "It does not denote sudden perception but the consideration of a state of affairs that had long been in existence, and on account of which a decision has to be taken." *From Adam to Noah*, 302. God's emotions also prompt him to take action (Judg 2:18; Ps 78:58–62; Hos 11:8–9; John 3:16).

88. The Hebrew verb מחה ("to blot out") is repeated three times with reference to the obliterating effects of the Flood (see also 7:4, 23). It is used elsewhere of erasing names from community registrars (Exod 32:32–33), of wiping clean plates (2 Kgs 21:13), and even of washing away sin (Ps 51:1, 9 [Heb 3, 11]; Prov 6:33; Isa 43:25; 44:22; Jer 18:23). Here God does not erase the sin but the sinners!

89. In 6:3 Yahweh responds to the union between the sons of God and the daughters of men as well as their resultant offspring by declaring, "My Spirit shall not contend [or 'abide,' LXX] with man perpetually, since he is flesh. Therefore, his time shall be 120 years." The reference to Yahweh's רוּחַ is likely an allusion to the life-giving Spirit of Elohim earlier introduced in 1:2. But how does one understand the Hebrew verb יָדוֹן? This hapaxlegomena may be related to the verb דִּין, which means "to judge." However, the LXX translates the verb with καταμείνῃ, which means "to remain" (see also the Vulgate, *permanebit*). So the verse may refer either to the Spirit's work of convicting human hearts of sin or to the Spirit's presence among humanity restraining sin and preventing eschatological judgment. In the end, both interpretations end up at roughly the same place: when the Spirit ceases what he is doing (whether contending or abiding among men), judgment and death will ensue. But to what does the 120-year limit refer? Some argue that God has decided to reduce human lifespans and appeal to the decrease in lifespan after the Flood from hundreds of years down to somewhere closer to 120 years towards the end of patriarchal history (e.g., Jacob's 147 years and Joseph's 110 years). After Joseph, the lifespans of God's servants seemed (at least for a time) to remain close to 120 years (Moses's 120 years, Aaron's 123 years, and Joshua's 110 years). Furthermore, this verse is compared to 3:22, where God seeks to prevent man from attaining immortality. See von Rad, *Genesis*, 114; Wenham, *Genesis 1–15*, 141–42; Mathews, *Genesis 1—11:26*, 334–35. More likely, though, God is portending a timeframe for the coming judgment. Nowhere in Genesis does the lifespan of humanity consistently level out to 120 years (see especially 11:10–26). At the time of Moses's writing of Genesis, seventy or eighty years was considered the norm (Ps 90:10). Moreover, it seems preferable to take the time period not as a warning of what will happen *after the Flood* but as a warning of what was *about to happen*: judgment was coming, and humanity had 120 years to repent! Compare Jonah 3:4 and 1 Pet 3:20. See also *Onkelos*, 52–53; Hamilton, Genesis 1–17, 269; Ross, *Creation & Blessing*, 183; Waltke, *Genesis*, 117.

wrath. The worldwide scope of this judgment[90] is another factor that underscores the epidemic spread of human sin. Nor does God's mercy to one family lessen the enormity and extensiveness of humanity's wickedness. Rather God's act of saving grace towards Noah (6:8, 13–21; 8:1, 15–17; 9:1ff.), as in the case of Enoch (5:24), is an exception that only reinforces the rule. Thus, with the broad strokes of human depravity, divine emotivity, and universal judgment, Moses paints a dark portrait of the invasive and pervasive spread of sin.

A NEW BEGINNING SPOILED BY SIN

Yahweh's pained heart is soothed when he smells the aroma of the burnt offerings wafting from Noah's altar (8:20–21a). In response, God pledges never again to destroy the world with a flood but to provide a stable environment wherein he may bring to fruition his redemptive plans for humanity (8:21b–22; 9:1–17). Yet, an ominous note sounds among an otherwise harmonious chorus of divine goodness. Yahweh's covenant promise is made "*even though* [כִּי][91] every inclination of [man's] heart is evil from childhood" (8:21b, NIV). This concessive clause indicates that though the Deluge washed away sinners, it failed to eradicate sin. Regrettably, Noah and his family imported the sin from the world-that-then-was to the world-that-now-is. That tragic reality quickly unfolds.

Noah, portrayed as a New Adam in a New World with a renewed mandate to subdue the earth,[92] becomes the father of viticulture (9:30).

90. Throughout Genesis, God refers indiscriminately to man and animals as the recipients of his judgment (6:7; 7:32), with the only exceptions being Noah, his family, and the animals that enter the ark (6:18–21). Moreover, God speaks of making "an end of *all* flesh" (6:13, emphasis added) and of destroying "*all* flesh in which is the breath of life under heaven. *Everything* that is on the earth shall die" (6:19, emphasis added). Finally, 7:21–22 summarizes the results of God's judgment: "And *all* flesh died that moved on the earth, birds, livestock, beasts, *all* swarming creatures that swarm on the earth, and *all* mankind. *Everything* on the dry land in whose nostrils was the breath of life died" (emphasis added). Moses could not find better language to underscore the universality of God's judgment.

91. Many translations give the כִּי a causal meaning, rendering it "because" or "for" (KJV, DRA, ASV, RSV, NAS, NJB, NRSV). But this does not make sense in the context. Indeed, the previous context indicated that the depraved human heart was *the cause* for worldwide judgment (6:7, 13). The כִּי may also function to introduce a concessive clause, which makes better sense here (see NKJ, NIV, NLT, NET, CSB). See *HS* §§ 448, 530; Joüon, *GBH* § 170b.

92. For the many verbal and thematic parallels between Adam and Noah, see Gage, *Gospel of Genesis*, 7–12; and Tomasino, "History Repeats Itself: the 'Fall' and Noah's Drunkenness," 128–30.

But Noah abuses one of God's gifts to mankind,[93] transgressing the limits of moderation, and becomes intoxicated (9:21a).[94] Worse, drunken Noah disrobes in his tent (9:21b)[95] and provides an occasion for a greater sin. Noah's son Ham *gazes at* (וַיַּרְא) his father's nakedness. Then he tells Shem and Japheth (9:22), who go into their father's tent *not to see* (לֹא רָאוּ) but to cover their father's nakedness (9:23). Since the brothers' covering of Noah parallels Yahweh's covering of Adam and Eve's nakedness (3:21), the reader is led to evaluate their action *positively* and Ham's *negatively*.

93. So "wine" (יַיִן) is portrayed in Gen 14:18; 27:25; Judg 9:13; Deut 14:26; Ps 104:15; Eccl 2:3; 9:7; 10:19; Isa 25:6; 55:1. Nevertheless, like many of God's gifts to humanity, wine may be abused, and its misuse is strongly condemned and sometimes even portrayed as a curse in Scripture (Prov 23:29–35; Isa 5:11–12; 28:1, 7; 56:12; Jer 13:13–14; 25:16; Lam 4:21–22; Ezek 23:28–33; Nah 1:9–10; Hab 2:5, 15–16; 1 Cor 5:11; 6:10; Gal 5:19, 21; Eph 5:18). Not surprisingly, the OT also forbade priests and kings to use wine while acting in the capacity of their office-bearing functions because of its potential to dull the senses and weaken moral judgment (Lev 10:8–11; Prov 31:4–5; Isa 5:22–23). Moreover, the NT also lists intemperance as a disqualifying vice for the pastoral or diaconal office (1 Tim 3:2–3, 8) and discourages believers from the use of wine in situations that would cause a brother to stumble (Rom 14:21).

94. Walter Brown attempts to make a case that Noah did not become intoxicated. He suggests "that in Gen 9:21 שָׁכַר should be translated as 'to be fully content' or 'to be satiated to sleep.'" Brown then concludes, "Noah's action was not negative and despicable; rather, it was positive and commendable." "Noah: Sot or Saint? Genesis 9:20–27," 37. Brown's interpretation, however, is flawed. First, though the verb does not always have negative connotations (Gen 43:34; Song 5:1; Hag 1:6), it more often carries a negative connotation when connected with the use of wine (2 Sam 11:13; Lam 4:21; Isa 29:9; 49:26; Jer 25:27; Nah 3:11). Second, the exposure of Noah's "nakedness" after transgressing the limit related to the "fruit of the vine" (9:21) finds a parallel in the exposure of Adam and Eve's "nakedness" after their transgressing the limit with respect to the "fruit of the Tree" (3:6–7). In both cases "nakedness" functions as an indicator of guilt (see also the connection between a drunkenness that leads to shameful nakedness in Hab 2:15 and Lam 4:21). Third, the controlling presupposition that turns the rudder of Brown's exegesis is the assumption that the narrator's portrait of Noah is that of a "saint" not a "sinner." Brown avers, "Noah is described positively in the strongest possible fashion. . . . From the perspective of character analysis, the positive reading of Gen 9:20–27 is expected" (53). But as will become evident in the subsequent analysis of the patriarchal narratives, even saints still sin. Indeed, by recording the "Fall" of Noah, Moses subtly indicates that Noah himself is not the ultimate "Rest-Giver," that is, "The Seed Par Excellence," who is yet to come.

95. The LXX renders the Hebrew וַיִּתְגַּל as a passive (ἐγυμνώθη), as do a number of English versions: "and he was naked" (KJV, DRA, ASV, NIV, ESV). But the verb appears in the Hithpael theme, which is normally reflexive, not passive (*IBHS* § 26.2; *GBH* § 53i), and the only other place where this verb appears in the Hithpael form is clearly reflexive (Prov 18:2). The translation "and he uncovered himself" is, therefore, preferable (NAU, NIV, CSB).

This is how Noah, once awake and sober, evaluates the actions of his sons (9:24–27). Fundamentally, Ham's sin is an intentional act of contempt accompanied by a mocking disclosure to his brothers—both actions the original audience would interpret as blatant violations of the fifth commandment (Exod 20:12).[96] Whether perverted sexual curiosity prompted Ham to intrude into Noah's private quarters to gaze on his nude body can only be conjectured.[97] Interpretations that construe Ham's deed as a scandalous sexual crime go beyond the textual and contextual data.[98] But keeping in view Noah's public devotion to Yahweh (6:9; 8:20) and his prophetic office as a preacher of righteousness (1 Pet 3:18–20; 2 Pet 2:5), Ham's contempt for his father may also be viewed as contempt for his father's religion and his father's God.[99]

96. Hamilton suggests, "Ham was in the wrong place at the wrong time." *Genesis 1–17*, 322. But this interpretation lessens the gravity of Ham's sin by limiting Ham's crime to his disclosure to his brothers. The antithetical response of Ham's brothers (9:23) and Noah's subsequent curse (9:24–25) suggest that both Ham's *looking* and *telling* were intentional acts of contempt and mockery. See Fretheim, "Genesis," 404; Luther, *Lectures on Genesis*, 2:167; Mathews, *Genesis 1—11:26*; 419–20; Westermann, *Genesis 1–11*, 487–88.

97. Leupold suggests an inordinate voyeurism (1:346).

98. Ham has been accused of either incest (Ham had intercourse with his mother) or homosexuality (Ham committed some sexual act with his father). See Bassett, "Noah's Nakedness and the Curse of Canaan: A Case of Incest?" 232–37; Brueggemann, *Genesis*, 90; Walton, *Genesis*, 346–49. While it is true that the expression "to uncover [another's] nakedness [לְגַלּוֹת עֶרְוָה]" may refer euphemistically to an act of sexual immorality, the expression is normally accompanied by an explanatory clause indicating its function as such (see Lev 18:6ff.; 20:11ff.). Moreover, apparently it is Noah, not Ham, who "uncovers" himself (see note 95 above); Ham only looks on his father's nakedness and informs his brothers. This is further supported by the antithetical parallelism of the action of Ham's brothers—the text does not say they refrained from uncovering their father's nakedness but from merely looking on his nakedness. Furthermore, since the subsequent narrative does not shy away from exposing illicit sexual acts (Gen 19:5, 8–9, 32–36; 34:2; 38:16–18), one would not expect the narrator to veil such an immorality here, if indeed it happened. Accordingly, there is no basis in the text for viewing Ham's sin as a full-blown act of immorality. For a further rebuttal, see Rice, "The Curse That Never Was," 11–13.

99. According to Luther, "[Cain's action] points to a heart that despises not only its parent but also the command of God." He continues, "Ham's deed must be traced back, not to some childish playfulness but to the bitter hatred of Satan, who inflames his members against the church, especially against those who are in the ministry, and makes them constantly watchful, so that they may be on the lookout for anything that can be turned into slander." *Lectures on Genesis*, 2:168. Calvin also suggests this reading when he writes, "We see many such at this day, who most studiously pry into the faults of holy and pious men, in order that without shame they may precipitate themselves into all iniquity; they may even make the faults of other men an occasion of hardening

So a "Cain," an offspring of the Serpent, has been discovered among Noah's family. And as Cain and his descendants inherited Cain's father's (i.e., the Serpent) curse (3:14–15; 4:11–12), so must Canaan and his offspring inherit his father's (i.e., Ham) curse. Thus Noah curses Ham's descendants, the sons of Canaan,[100] consigning their destiny to abject servitude (9:25),[101] while blessing Shem and Japheth, who shall become lords over the Canaanites (9:26–27). Yet, long before the Noachian curse begins to find its initial fulfillment, Ham's contempt for the true religion represented by Noah will grow to mammoth proportions that rival the hubris of the בְּנֵי־הָאֱלֹהִים and their offspring, הַגִּבֹּרִים.

THE KINGDOM OF MAN REBUILT

Following God's reestablishment of the primeval covenant with Noah (6:18) and its mandate to "be fruitful and multiply and fill the earth" (9:1ff.), the narrator describes what at first appears to be mankind's obedient response to that mandate. What is known as the Table of Nations recounts the dispersal of Noah's descendants across the face of the earth after the Flood (9:18–19; 10:1–32).[102] Two individuals from the list of

---

themselves into a contempt for God." *Genesis*, 1:303. Candlish is most explicit: "Foolish, giddy, willful as he might be, who that had not some more malignant end to serve, could find his father as Noah was found, and make the discovery a matter of jest or exultation? But Ham had another quarrel with his father; he hated his religion. He not merely dishonoured him as a parent—he disliked him as a preacher of righteousness." *Studies in Genesis*, 158–59.

100. Literally, Noah declares, "Cursed be Canaan" (אָרוּר כְּנָעַן). Moses has already conspicuously referred to Canaan twice as Ham's son (9:18, 22). This fact suggests that he is providing his Israelite readers the etiological origin of God's soon-to-be-enacted Holy War on the Canaanites. Hence, the curse had primary reference to Ham's descendants who would arise through the line of Canaan and not to Canaan in particular. This interpretation relieves the reader of looking to interpretations that attempt to make Canaan an accomplice in Ham's crime. On the other hand, the primeval narrative has already established the fact that the particular anti-God disposition of a family head (4:4b, 8–9, 13–14) will often be passed on to and through his descendants (4:19, 22–23; 6:1–2, 4–5, 11–13). Perhaps Noah already perceived Ham's evil ungodly traits being replicated in his son. At the very least, he has, through prophetic insight, anticipated the moral decadence of Canaan's distant ancestors. See Kline, *Kingdom Prologue*, 263; and Ronning, "Curse on the Serpent (Genesis 3:15) in Biblical Theology and Hermeneutics," 181.

101. Here we have the juxtaposition of two identical nouns, the first a singular and the second a plural—עֶבֶד עֲבָדִים—a *superlative genitive* (*IBHS* § 9.5.3j), which may be translated, "The lowest of slaves he will be to his brothers" (NIV, NET).

102. For a fuller treatment of the Table of Nations, see Block, "Table of Nations," *ISBE*rev, 4:707–13; Kitchen, *On the Reliability of the OT*, 430–38; Ross, "Table of Nations

descendants as well as activities associated with each are singled out for special attention—Nimrod, a descendant of Ham through Cush (10:6–8a), and Peleg, a descendant of Shem through Eber (10:21–25a). Nimrod, whose name possibly derives from the Hebrew verb "to rebel" (מרד),[103] is associated with an empire-building enterprise that began in the land of Shinar and eventually engulfed much of Mesopotamia (10:10–12). Peleg, whose name derives from the Hebrew verb "to divide" (פלג), is associated with the dividing of the earth (נִפְלְגָה הָאָרֶץ) (10:25b). The somewhat enigmatic references to these two individuals and the activities associated with them are more fully explained in the infamous "Tower of Babel" story (11:1–9). Here the reader discovers that humanity's apparently obedient response to the divinely commissioned dispersal (9:1) was in fact, by and large, reluctant acquiescence to divine judgment.[104]

Most (perhaps all) of Noah's descendants[105] had initially migrated from Ararat to the land of Shinar "where they settled [וַיֵּשְׁבוּ שָׁם]" (11:2,

in Genesis 10—Its Structure," 340–53; idem, "Table of Nations in Genesis 10—Its Content," 22–34; Wiseman, *Peoples of Old Testament Times*, xv-xxi.

103. Hamilton, *Genesis 1–17*, 338; Wenham, *Genesis 1–15*, 222; Sarna, *Genesis*, 73. BDB notes that Wilhelm Gesenius in his *Thesaurus Linguae Hebracae* lists נִמְרֹד as a substantive of מָרַד, *rebel*, but considers this meaning dubious (650). Whatever the ultimate etymological root, the Jews apparently made the connection between the name נִמְרֹד and rebellion. Nimrod is called "a mighty sinner and rebel before the Lord" in *P-Jonathan*, 47. See also *Neofiti*, which calls Nimrod "a giant in sin before the Lord" (82). Likewise, note parashah 37:2–3 in *GR*, 2:38–39.

104. Many scholars have noted the apparent dischronologization of the Table of Nations (10:1–32) and the Tower of Babel (11:1–9) narratives. Some, like Clines, propose a thematic purpose behind the order. *Themes of the Pentateuch*, 74–76; Hamilton, *Genesis 1–17*, 350. Ross, though, is more precise: "The passages are arranged in a manner consistent with Genesis. The broad survey is given first, and then the narrowing and selection or explanation." *Creation & Blessing*, 243. One may compare the panoramic view of creation provided in Genesis 1:1–2:3 with the more selective focus on one segment of that creation, namely, mankind and the Garden in Genesis 2:4–25.

105. The Tower of Babel narrative does not identify the Shinar "settlers." Indefinite terms and expressions are used throughout, such as "they," "them," "people." The most specific reference is found in verse 5: "children of man" [בְּנֵי הָאָדָם.]. "Babelites" may represent one rebellious *cross-section* of postdiluvian humanity, particularly, the descendants of Ham. On the other hand, expressions such as "*the whole earth* [כָּל־הָאָרֶץ] had one language" (11:1) and "the Lord confused the language of *all the earth* [כָּל־הָאָרֶץ]" (11:9) seem to carry universal overtones. Even "the children of man" (בְּנֵי הָאָדָם) may not be an indefinite expression but all-inclusive of postdiluvian humanity. The fact that Abram's family is called out of Ur of the Chaldeans, a city located in Shinar, may indicate that his ancestors were in some way involved in the Babel enter-

author's translation). Not only is the fact of their "settling down" unsettling (in light of the mandate to "fill the earth," 9:1), but the *eastward* (מִקֶּדֶם) location of their colony is troubling also. *Settling in the east* signals a Cain-like movement away from God (see 4:16). These people are up to no good. To be more precise, they are up to "No! God." Like Cain of old they fear impermanence and choose to defy Yahweh's mandate by building a city that will not only provide security but also secure for them a lasting "name" (compare 4:17 with 11:3–4).[106] What is more, these postdiluvian city-builders will outdo Cain. They will construct their own Holy Mountain,[107] their own Eden,[108] and thereby autonomously attempt to "reenter" the sphere from which man had been earlier banished (3:22–24) through their own Gate of God.[109] With a common language[110]

---

prise. Whether or not every human being alive at the time participated in the event, the Babel-event certainly affected the entire human race.

106. Cain fears the destiny of an "aimless wanderer" (4:14), so he settles and builds a city, naming it after his son (4:17). Likewise, the Babel-builders are motivated to "make a name for [themselves], lest [they] be dispersed over the whole earth" (11:4).

107. The מִגְדָּל normally refers to a fortified tower or acropolis (Judg 8:9, 17; 9:46–52; Ps 48:12 [Heb 13); 61:3 [Heb 4]; Ezek 26:9). In Isaiah the מִגְדָּל is a symbol of human power and pride (Isa 2:15; 30:25; 33:18). In a Mesopotamian context, the מִגְדֹּל is the ancient ziggurat (derived from the Akkadian, zaqāru, 'to build high'). Archaeologists have uncovered the remains of several ziggurats in Mesopotamia and discovered them to consist of several narrowing levels or steps with each successive level accessible by a flight of stairs. At the very top of this "man-made mountain" was a shrine where humans communicated with the deity. See Wiseman, "Ziggurat," *ZPEB*, 5:1059–61. For an aerial view of an ancient ziggurat at the city of Ur, see *ANEP*, 233 n. 747.

108. In the center of Eden, the reader will recall, was a huge mountain from which emerged a subterranean stream that flowed into the Garden (which was located on the slopes of Eden), where it forked into the four major rivers of the then-known world (Gen 2:6, 8–9, 10–14; Ezek 28:14, 16). For the significance of the Holy Mountain motif in biblical theology, see Kline, *God, Heaven, and Har Magedon.*

109. The Hebrew presumably derives from the Akkadian bāb-ilu or Babylonian bāb-ilāni, meaning, "gate of god(s)." *HALOT*, 107–08. Most commentators miss the connection between the man-made mountain-temples of Mesopotamia and the primordial Sacred Mountain of Eden. Meredith Kline, however, sees the link and remarks, "In their proud unbelief [the Babel builders] spurned God's promised restoration of the true focus and fullness as an act of saving mercy and grace, purposing in an incipient spirit of antichrist to become themselves the creators of a cosmic focus. . . . So they conspired to erect the mythic sacred mountain of the divine assembly and thus re-create the central axis between earth and heaven." *Kingdom Prologue*, 273.

110. Following the lead of Cyrus Gordon, Hamilton interprets the שָׂפָה אֶחָת as referring to a *lingua franca*, that is, an international language shared by the builders who, in fact, already spoke their own local dialect (לָשׁוֹן, 10:5, 20, 31). *Genesis 1–17*, 350. In this

that facilitates their monumental efforts (11:1), these rebels actually begin to storm the stratosphere with their "stairway to heaven."

But as Jan Fokkelman wryly remarks, "Those who want to ride on clouds must reckon with cloud-bursts; God stands no nonsense."[111] So, even as "the sons of Adam" (בְּנֵי הָאָדָם)[112] toil away in their attempt to scale heaven, Heaven *comes down* (ירד) to investigate their tower-building efforts (11:5).[113] Yahweh is not amused. What he "discovers"[114] is the same alarming grasp for divinity that motivated the primordial couple to take the forbidden fruit—only this time on an international scale

---

view, God did not miraculously create new languages, so to speak, but miraculously disrupted the builders' ability to communicate using the common diplomatic tongue. However, part of the rationale driving this interpretation is the denial by some modern linguists of an *Ursprache* from which all other languages developed. But if the reader interprets the primeval narrative as an accurate reflection of historical events, then certainly Noah and family brought with them on the ark a "mother tongue," and it does not seem unreasonable to suppose that it was this preserved antediluvian tongue that was shared among the initial descendants of Noah and confounded at Babel. Whether dialectal variations of this existed prior to Babel or whether the dialectal variations occurred as a result of Babel and later developed into distinct language groups is uncertain. What is certain is that divine intervention supernaturally affected a linguistic fragmentation among the peoples engaged in this enterprise.

111. *Narrative Art in Genesis*, 41.

112. Moses may simply intend בְּנֵי הָאָדָם generically, as a reference to mankind. More likely, he depicts Yahweh's perception of the folly of this enterprise with a tinge of sarcasm: *will mere mortals scale heaven*!

113. Nearly every commentator catches the irony: man is building "a tower with its top in the heavens," yet Yahweh must actually descend (!) in order to see what man is up to. In the words of Mathews, "The necessary descent of God and the humanness of the enterprise, 'that the men were building,' shows the escapade for what it was—a tiny tower, conceived by a puny plan and attempted by pint-sized people." *Genesis 1—11:26*, 483.

114. Sarna is correct to observe, "This figurative usage ['come down to see'] implies no limitation on God's omnipotence, for the divine 'descent' presupposes prior knowledge of human affairs from on high, and God's subsequent counteraction unqualifiedly exhibits His absolute sovereignty." *Genesis*, 83.

(11:6)![115] Therefore, divine resolve counters human resolve.[116] In a stroke of judgment that is both ironic and talionic, God punishes them with "a name for a name." They lusted for meaning apart from God, but such godless schemes can only end in nonsense.[117] So by divine decree, the coveted "Babel" becomes "Babble"![118] Thus, Yahweh obstructs what they seek to construct by disrupting their ability to communicate (11:7). As a result, the ecumenical effort comes to a screeching halt, and the vertical movement turns horizontal. Formerly linguistically united, the builders now become dialectally fragmented. Dropping trowel and spade, the

115. Some interpreters find no hubris at all in the narrative. Laurin, for example, suggests that "the story . . . is an artful parable about the failure of pagan idolatry to provide the necessary foundation for a continuing culture." "The Tower of Babel Revisited," 143. While this proposal contains an element of truth, the narrator has already shown ungodly culture quite capable of making cultural advancements that are beneficial for all humanity with the help of common grace (4:21–22). Gowan agrees with most commentators who compare the hubris of Babel with that of the Fall but assesses Babel's pride as "a subdued form" of hubris. *When Man Becomes God*, 29. On the contrary, Babel is "the Fall" writ large! As Blocher notes, "The difference between Eden and Babel is that which distinguishes the individual deed and the collective act. . . . Having become a collective enterprise, the sinful project [Babel] takes on the face of totalitarianism, with technology and ideology as its means of realization. If Genesis 3 reveals the religious root of human evil, Genesis 11 shows it in its most logical and perhaps most terrible political expression." *In the Beginning*, 204. Fretheim also notes the pride when he observes, "The towers of Babylonia were an attempt not only to facilitate the descent of the gods to men, but also to force the deity's approach to man into a set mold." *Creation, Fall, and Flood*, 125.

116. Man's double cohortative, "Come, let us make bricks. . . . Come, let us build ourselves a city and a tower" (11:3–4), is matched by God's double cohortative, "Come, let us go down and there [let us] confuse their language" (11:7). For an extensive analysis of both the syntactic and the phonetic symmetry of the narrative, consult Fokkelman's insightful analysis (11–45).

117. As Ellul observes, "Man certainly did not expect his project to take such a turn. He did not anticipate that the name he wanted to make for himself would refer to a place of noncommunication." *Meaning of the City*, 482. Following up on Ellul's observations, Mathews offers an appropriate modern application: "Babel would also be a fitting name for our 'postmodern' world of pluralism, deconstructionism, and therefore 'noncommunication,' which declares the autonomy of text and reader and sets meaning afloat in a sea of uncertainty. Revolt against divine and absolute truth has fated lost humanity to wander aimlessly and alone in a silent, chaotic world." *Genesis 1—11:26*, 482 n. 189.

118. As noted above, *Babel* (בָּבֶל) meant "Gate of God" to the builders. However, Moses employs a wordplay, linking the phonetic sounds of "ba-bel" with "ba-lal" the verb translated *confused* (בָּלַל). Fokkelman notes the stinging irony: "People want a name? Well, they can have it, but how different it will be from the name they had dreamt of. '. . . therefore its name was called Babel, 'Muddle!' This unexpected turn is like a judgment, so biting is its sarcasm." *Narrative Art in Genesis*, 14.

people scatter "over all the face of the earth," just as Yahweh willed it to be (11:8–9).

Now the reader sees the Table of Nations not as a memorial to human fidelity but as a memorial to a divine overruling of human infidelity. Understanding "the division" of Peleg's day (10:25b),[119] he trembles as he recalls the exploits of Nimrod! For "the beginning [רֵאשִׁית] of his kingdom was Babel . . . in the land of Shinar" (10:10). Whether or not Nimrod was the mastermind behind the original Babel venture, the list of city-building projects originating from Babel, spreading through Shinar and extending into northern Mesopotamia,[120] leaves the reader with an ominous impression: Nimrod did not take God's "no" seriously. Defying Yahweh's vision for human decentralization and divine exaltation, Nimrod decided with relentless persistence to revive and rebuild fortified cities and skyscraping towers.[121] In an effort to advance Man's kingdom in place of God's kingdom, he became a postdiluvian version (גִּבֹּר, 10:8) of the tyrannical antediluvian הַגִּבֹּרִים (6:4) well earning the ignominious epithet that became a proverbial saying in Israel, "Like Nimrod a mighty hunter before the LORD" (10:9).[122] So the spirit of Cain lives on. The "seed of the Serpent" strikes again, and thus continues the spread of sin.

At this point it will be helpful to compare recurring patterns that highlight the spread of sin theme. Building on the insights of others[123]

119. The psalmist strengthens the connection by using the same verb from which Peleg's name derives and which depicts the "division." Invoking God's judgment on his enemies, he cries, "Destroy, O Lord, *divide* [פַּלַּג] their tongues" (Ps 55:9a).

120. *Shinar* may refer to the region of Mesopotamia in general (Gen 14:1, 9; Josh 7:21) or just to Babylonia (Dan 1:2). Here, it refers to the southern region of Mesopotamia (10:10), which Moses distinguishes from the northern region of Mesopotamia, later called Assyria (10:11–12; see also Isa 11:11).

121. Modern archaeological endeavors have unearthed numerous ancient fortified cities and ziggurat towers in Mesopotamia. For a helpful survey of the archaeological evidence, see Andre Parrot, *Tower of Babel*.

122. As Waltke remarks, "Ancient Near Eastern kings prided themselves on their hunting prowess. They were not shepherd kings." *Genesis*, 169. Hence, the expression "mighty hunter [גִּבֹּר־צַיִד]" (10:9) should be understood in connection with the narrator's earlier characterization of Nimrod as a "mighty warrior [גִּבֹּר]" (10:8).

123. Von Rad notes the themes of sin, mitigation, and judgment. *Genesis*, 152f. Westermann highlights the pattern of *Vergehen/Schuld* (sin/guilt), *Strafspuch/Beschluß* (judgment-speech/decree), *Strafakt/Strafe* (act of judgment/punishment). "Arten der Erzählung," 47–58. Clines combines the work of these two scholars and proposes the four categories: sin, speech, mitigation, and punishment. *Themes of the Pentateuch*, 68.

and drawing from the observations of this study, the following table illustrates recurrent literary patterns throughout the primeval narrative that lead from sin to judgment:

TABLE 2: Thematic Pattern of Sin—Discovery—Speech—Mitigation—Judgment

	Sin	Discovery	Speech	Mitigation	Judgment
The Fall	3:6	3:8–13	3:14–19	3:21	3:22–24
Cain & Abel	4:8	4:9–10	4:11–12	4:15	4:16
The Flood	6:2, 4–5, 10	6:5–6, 11	6:3, 7, 13–21	6:8, 18–21	7:6–24
Babel	11:4	11:5–6	11:7	10:1–32; 11:[9]10–12:3	11:8–9

As the table above demonstrates, repeated outbreaks of human sin have served as a major theme in the primeval narrative. Indeed, the grave and gargantuan character of human unbelief and pride only becomes more apparent as the story unfolds. But "He who sits in the heavens" will have the last laugh (Ps 2:4). Even as Nimrod and his successors wearied themselves building cities and gaining renown, God quietly bided his time until a descendant of Shem[124] should arise through the line of none other than Peleg (11:10–26)! One who was born in the days when God divided the families of the earth would father an offspring (Abram) through whom a people from "every nation and tribe and language" would someday unite with divine blessing in a City whose Architect is God and under a Name above all other names (Gen 12:1–3; Phil 2:9–10). Where sin abounds, grace shall much more abound! But not all at once. Not quite yet. The saga of sin's spread has been a major theme in primeval history. As the remainder of this study will demonstrate, that theme continues throughout patriarchal history. Genesis is, after all, the beginning, not the end of the story.

Bratcher builds on all three and adds the categories of temptation and discovery, "The Pattern of Sin and Judgment in Genesis 1–11," 225–54. The table above excludes the theme of "temptation," since it is not obvious in the Flood or Babel narratives.

124. *Shem* (שֵׁם) actually means "name." So it would be to "Name's" offspring that Yahweh would promise, "And I will make your name great [וַאֲגַדְּלָה שְׁמֶךָ]" (Gen 12:2).

PART THREE

Sin and the Curse in the Patriarchal Narratives

3

The Spread of Sin among Pagan Societies

The patriarchal narrative emerges out of the context the Babel event, that epitome of human hubris (11:1–9). Yahweh's judgment on the Babel endeavor did not eradicate human sin any more than his worldwide Flood erased antediluvian evil (8:21). Instead, it resulted in the dispersal of sinful people-groups throughout the ancient world. Consequently, the reader finds numerous allusions to the prevalence of sin among ancient societies, including a striking example of aggravated evil that rivals the primeval degeneracy.

ALLUSIONS TO SIN AMONG PAGAN SOCIETIES

Violations of the sanctity of marriage and of human life featured prominently in primeval history. A careful reading of the patriarchal history uncovers several allusions to these same sins. For example, Abraham's and Isaac's use of the "wife-sister" ruse during their respective residencies in Egypt (12:10–20) and Gerar (20:1–18; 26:1, 7) is prompted by the patriarchs' fear that powerful rulers may attempt to satisfy their lust for sex and/or possessions by killing the husband in order to obtain the wife and perhaps gain access to the husband's wealth (12:12–15; 20:2, 11).[1]

1. Ancient Near Eastern societies apparently retained a degree of respect for the legal bond of marriage and, to some degree, a sense of impropriety with respect to the sin of adultery. See Goodfriend, "Adultery," in *ABD*, 1:82–86; Moran, "The Scandal of the 'Great Sin' at Ugarit," 280–81; Rabinowitz, "The 'Great Sin' in Ancient Egyptian Marriages Contracts," 73. Yet that degree of aversion towards the crime of adultery did not stop individuals, especially those in places of power, from devising ways of eliminating the marriage bond via the murder of the woman's husband so that they could obtain her for their harem (2 Sam 11:2–27). The Egyptian story entitled "The Two Brothers" depicts a pharaoh falling in love with a married woman, taking her into his house, and having her husband killed. Although the story is fictional, it probably reflects the cultural practices of that day. Lichtheim, *Ancient Egyptian Literature*, 2:203–11.

Similar examples of polygamous harem-building and political tyranny have already surfaced in the primeval narrative (4:19, 23–24; 6:2, 4–5, 10–11). Hence, what marked the spread of sin in primeval history continues to find expression in patriarchal times.

Genesis 14 depicts a war between four allied Mesopotamian city-states and five allied Palestinian city-states (14:1–2). The cause of this conflict, the reader is told, was the rebellion of the vassal city-states against their suzerain, Chedorlaomer (14:4). The text does not identify the circumstances that gave rise to the inauguration of a suzerain-vassal treaty between the king of Elam and the Palestinian city-states.[2] The narrator neither condones nor condemns explicitly the insurgence. The leading reference to "Amraphel, king of Shinar," however, reminds the reader of the center of postdiluvian pride, empire-building, and tyranny (10:8–12; 11:1–9).[3] One might read the chapter as the "easterners" still attempting to grasp at "renown" (see 11:4) in contrast with Abram who gains "a great name" (see 12:2) by defeating the Mesopotamian armies.[4] Moreover, in celebrating Abram's victory and identifying the defeated armies as Abram's "enemies" whom "God Most High" had "delivered . . . into [Abram's] hand" (14:18–20), Melchizedek provides a negative assessment of the Mesopotamian hegemony.[5] These observations would probably remind the Israelites of the oppressive conditions under which they lived and served their Egyptian overlords (Exod 1:11–14; 2:23; 6:6, 9; 13:3, 14; 20:2; Deut 5:6; 6:12; 26:5–7). They also remind the modern

2. On the historicity of this account, see Kitchen, *On the Reliability of the OT*, 319–23; Wenham, *Genesis 1–15*, 318–20.

3. Although Chedorlaomer, not Amraphel, is presented as the leader of the eastern alliance, the narrator gives the latter prominence by prefacing the account, "In the days of Amraphel king of Shinar" (14:1). By dating the events within the reign of "Shinar's" king, Moses is likely reminding the reader that the empire-building hubris of the former Babel (11:1–9) is still at work. See Sailhamer, "Genesis," 121–22.

4. As Roop remarks, "No foreign king can exercise power against the blessing of God, as Pharaoh discovered by accident (12:10–20; cf. Num 22–24)." *Genesis*, 107. Abram's successful raid parallels the later exploits of Gideon (Judg 7) and of David (1 Sam 30).

5. A few scholars correctly see Abram's defeat of the Mesopotamian kings and Melchizedek's blessing speech as an allusion to the Abrahamic promise, namely, that God would "curse" those who "dishonored" Abram (Gen 12:3). Fretheim, "Genesis," 442; Ross, *Creation & Blessing*, 294; Hamilton, *Genesis 1–17*, 410–11. Hamilton, however, does not include Sodom's king under that curse, but see discussion in chapter 4.

reader that political tyranny and forced servitude were common in the ancient Near Eastern context of Genesis.[6]

Another violation of the sacred marriage-bond among pagan societies can be inferred from Sarai's proposal and Abram's acquiescence to use Hagar as a surrogate mother to provide the needed heir (16:1–4). The Israelite reader was well aware that such a practice found sanction neither in Mosaic law nor in primeval revelation[7] but in the customs of their pagan neighbors. Ancient Near Eastern societies allowed for or sometimes required a barren wife to give her husband a slave girl as concubine to bear children in her place. For example, a Nuzi text dating to the early second millennium BC reads, "If Gilimnimu (the bride) will not bear children, Gilimnimu shall take a woman of N/Lullu land (whence the choicest slaves were obtained) as a wife for Shennima (the bridegroom)."[8] Although the practice was probably not fueled mainly by lust, it did serve to enhance one's economic potential and insure the likelihood of familial succession, two blessings coveted by human societies since primeval times (Gen 1:28; 9:1, 7) but pursued in disregard of God's revealed norm (Gen 2:23–24).

Other violations of the sanctity of marriage are motivated by lust. When Jacob returns to Canaan, he settles with his family in the city of Shechem (Gen 33:18–20). There, Shechem, a city magistrate, "seized

6. Allusions to the social institution of slavery are found throughout the patriarchal narrative (Gen 12:16; 15:13; 20:14, 17; 21:10; 24:35; 30:43; 32:5; 37:26–28, 36; 39:1, 19–20; 44:16; 47:19, 21, 25). Although some slaves were treated well (e.g., 39:1–6; Exod 21:5–6; Deut 15:16–17), slavery as such was not the ideal for human society (Lev 25:39–40; cf. Phlm 8–22) but a by-product of human sin (see especially Gen 37:26–28, 36). For further discussion of the nature and institution of slavery in the ancient Near East and the OT, see Dandamavev, "Slavery (ANE)," "Slavery (OT)," in *ABD*, 6:58–65; Rupprecht, "Slave, Slavery," *ZPEB*, 5:453–60.

7. According to the earliest revelation, humans were to obtain offspring through the institution and covenant of marriage, which was to be monogamous in character (Gen 1:18–24; Mal 2:14; Matt 19:4–6; Mark 10:6–9).

8. Gordon, "Biblical Customs and the Nuzu Tablets," 3. A text in the Hammurabi Code also alludes to this practice and reads, "When a seignior [i.e., a free man] married a heirodule [priestess] and she gave a female slave to her husband and she has then borne children, if later that female slave has claimed equality with her mistress because she bore children, her mistress may not sell her; she may mark her with the slave-mark and count her among the slaves." "The Code of Hammurabi," *ANET*, 172. See also Speiser, *Genesis*, 120–21; idem, "New Kirkuk Documents Relating to Family Laws," 31–32; Frymer-Kensky, "Patriarchal Family Relationship and Near Eastern Law," 209–14.

[Dinah, Jacob's daughter,] and lay with her and humiliated her" (34:1–2). The verb rendered "humiliated" (וַיְעַנֶּהָ) refers in this context to forced sex (Judg 19:24; 20:5; 2 Sam 13:12, 14, 22, 32; Lam 5:11),[9] which the narrator appropriately interprets as a violation of moral law (34:7).[10] Moses further highlights Shechem's sensual appetite with the language of infatuation,[11] which relentlessly drives him to secure Dinah as a wife whatever the cost.[12] One should note the parallel between Shechem's

9. *HALOT* defines the verb in the Piel as "to rape a woman" (1:853). Betchel argues that Shechem's act with Dinah was a case of consensual sex, noting that the verb may simply refer to the social stigma of premarital sex and highlighting what she sees as the narrator's positive assessment of Shechem and the Shechemites. "What If Dinah Is Not Raped? (Genesis 34)," 19–36. But the reader should interpret the narrator's "positive" assessment of the Shechemites only in terms relative to the treacherous and murderous actions of Jacob's sons. In reality, Shechem and his people are not honorable; they just happen to be a little less guilty than Simeon and Levi (see Chapter 7 of this study). Moreover, the vocabulary used in 34:2 is clearly employed elsewhere for acts of forced sex (2 Sam 13:12, 14, 22, 32; Judg 19:24; 20:5; Lam 5:11).

10. The Hebrew term translated "an outrageous thing" [נְבָלָה] often refers to sexual immorality (Deut 22:21; Judg 19:23–24; 20:6, 10; 2 Sam 13:12; Isa 9:16; Jer 29:23). When used together with the clause "for such a thing must not be done [וְכֵן לֹא יֵעָשֶׂה]," it underscores the gravity of the sin (2 Sam 13:12).

11. "And his soul was drawn to Dinah. . . . He loved the young woman and spoke tenderly to her" (34:3). Shechem's father declares to Jacob, "The soul of my son longs for your daughter" (34:8). Later the narrator tells us that Shechem agreed to the marital terms offered by Jacob's sons "because he delighted in Jacob's daughter" (34:19). Some, like Fretheim, interpret this repetition as an indication of Shechem's "integrity" and "the sincerity of his desire for this marriage." "Genesis," 578–79. Shechem's initial act of rape and his subsequent withholding of the real reason from his countrymen for complying with the rite of circumcision (34:20–24), however, do not suggest a noble character and motivations. Although this language of romantic desire may describe noble love and affection, it may also be used to describe sensual lust or short-lived desire (2 Sam 13:1, 4, 15; Deut 21:11–14), which is likely the intended meaning here. Moreover, the reader should not miss the fact that Shechem's act is a reversal of the creation order. From the beginning, God ordained that marriage should precede sexual intimacy (Gen 2:23–24). Shechem, however, has sex with Dinah. Then he requests her hand in marriage (34:2–4, 8–12). Caspi alludes to this reversal when he compares the verbs of verse 2—"took, lay, defiled"—with the verbs of verse 3 that follow—"clave, loved, spake," "The Story of the Rape of Dinah," 33.

12. First, he insists that his father, "Get [him] this girl for [his] wife" (34:4), which finds a parallel in Samson's sensually driven demand on his parents (Judg 14:2, 3). Then Shechem pleads with Dinah's father and brothers, "Let me find favor in your eyes, and whatever you say to me I will give. Ask me for as great a bride price and gift as you will, and I will give whatever you say to me. Only give me the young woman to be my wife" (34:11–12). Finally, he (along with his father) entices the men of Shechem to consent to the condition of circumcision in order to secure the object of his desire (34:20–24).

behavior and that of the בְּנֵי־הָאֱלֹהִים in Genesis 6:1–2. In both cases, men of power take advantage of the weaker sex in order to gratify their own lust. Also notable is the narrator's description of Shechem as "the most honored of all his father's house" (34:19). While this description may simply reflect Shechem's prominent influence in the community,[13] it may also serve as a comment on his moral character.[14] If this latter reading is correct, then the account serves as a sad commentary on the moral state of the Shechemites since their most "honorable" citizen is driven by sexual appetite rather than moral principle. Moses later alludes to the same kind of moral laxity in Egyptian society. Only in this case, a married woman lusts after a young man and attempts to allure him into an adulterous relationship (Gen 39:7–11).[15] Whereas the primeval narrative introduced the male abuse of females, the patriarchal narrative continues that theme and adds a role reversal to show that the violation of the sanctity of marriage is being perpetrated by both sexes.

Perhaps the most significant allusion to the spread of sin in pagan society is found in Genesis 15. Yahweh appears to Abram in a dream and predicts a four hundred year sojourn in Egypt for the patriarch's descendents prior to their taking possession of the Promised Land (15:12–13). The detour is predicated on the portended judgment against two pagan societies, the Egyptians and the Canaanites (15:14, 16). Moses's readers

---

Some place a noble spin on Shechem's actions. But Ross is more correct when he remarks, "Shechem was a rather stormy fellow—no savior-faire. He simply wanted the girl and would pay for her. But this attempt to pay her price only signified to the brothers that he was treating their sister like a prostitute (v. 31)," *Creation & Blessing*, 573–74.

13. So the New English Translation (NET) translates the clause parenthetically: "Now he was more important than anyone in his father's household."

14. The Hebrew word translated "honored" appears in the Niphal and may refer to dignity of character (Deut 28:58; 1 Sam 9:6; 22:14; 1 Chr 4:9; see also Sir 10:20). A few commentators apply this sense to the narrator's description of Shechem, but they take the commendation seriously and construe his character positively. Skinner, 420; Fretheim, "Genesis," 578–79. It is better to interpret the "commendation" of Shechem as relative to the others who belonged to the Shechemite community and therefore as a satirical commentary on the morally degraded situation into which Jacob had placed his family.

15. According to the narrator, Potiphar's wife "cast her eyes on Joseph" and repeatedly entreated him to lie with her (39:7, 10, 12). One should note the parallel with the Akkadian version of the Gilgamesh Epic where the goddess Ishtar begins to lust after Gilgamesh: "When Gilgamesh had put on his tiara/Glorious Ishtar raised an eye at the beauty of Gilgamesh/'Come, Gilgamesh, be thou (my) lover!'" Tablet VI, lines 5–7 of "Gilgamesh Epic," in *ANET*, 83.

were well acquainted with the sins of the former and were given plenty of warnings concerning the debaucheries of the latter (Lev 18:1–30; Deut 9:4–5).[16] Of special note is the causal clause which brings 15:16 to a conclusion: "for the iniquity of the Amorites[17] is not yet complete [כִּי לֹא־שָׁלֵם עֲוֹן הָאֱמֹרִי עַד־הֵנָּה]." The picture portrayed is that of collective societal sins increasing and mounting to the point where God can no longer extend forbearance.[18] This ominous portrait finds analogy in the primeval history (6:3, 5–7, 11–13) and serves to continue the "spread of sin" theme.

SODOM AND GOMORRAH: EXTREME SOCIETAL DEPRAVITY

While Canaanite society had another four hundred years before its collective depravity would tax the limit of divine forbearance, there was one region on the edge of Canaan's borders whose sin was so great that divine judgment could not tarry. The reader is first introduced to the "cities of the plain" as the place where Lot, Abram's nephew, chose to settle (13:10–12). The narrative highlights the ominous nature of Lot's choice in several ways. First, Lot "lifted up his eyes and saw that the Jordan Valley was well-watered everywhere like the garden of the Lord, like the land of Egypt, in the direction of Zoar" (13:10). The casting of one's eyes in the direction of Eden and Egypt's fertile bread-baskets (Gen 2:9; Deut 11:10) reminds the Israelite reader of Eve's fateful choice (Gen 3:6) as well as the wilderness generation's constant yearning to return to Egypt (Exod 16:3; Num 11:5; 21:5; Acts 7:39). The fertility of these regions was relatively more predictable because they were fed by large rivers (Gen 2:6, 10–14; Isa 23:3; Jer 2:18; 46:7–8; Nah 3:8).[19] On the other

16. In Leviticus 18:3, God prefaces his prohibitions against a catalog of sexual sins with the indictment, "You shall not do as they do in the land of Egypt, where you lived, and you shall not do as they do in the land of Canaan, to which I am bringing you. You shall not walk in their statutes."

17. Waltke correctly notes that "Amorites" here serves as a synecdoche for all the tribes of Canaan. *Genesis*, 244.

18. Appropriately, the NET renders the clause, "for the sin of the Amorites has not yet reached its limit." Hamilton observes, "This last half of the verse articulates the idea that the fixing of times is conditioned not on necessity but on morality. This commentary on the immorality of the indigenous population of Canaan also establishes Joshua's invasion as an act of justice rather than of aggression." *Genesis 1–17*, 436.

19. Nevertheless, the fertility of these regions was not beyond the reach of God's hand of judgment. The narrator is aware that his readers know the region of Sodom

hand, Canaan's hill country depended largely on rainfall (Deut 11:11), which was less predictable.[20] Sadly, Lot walks by sight,[21] whereas Abram walks by faith (Gen 12:1–3). Secondly, the narrator highlights the fact that Lot "journeyed east" (Gen 13:11–12). Elsewhere in Genesis, eastward travel usually signals movement away from God's blessing (Gen 3:24; 4:16; 11:2; 25:6).[22] Numbers 34:1–12 includes part of the Jordan valley within the Promised Land. Here, however, Moses contrasts "the cities of the valley" with the "land of Canaan" (13:12), implying that this region stood just outside the Promised Land. Lot's departure from the Promised Land together with the comment that he and Abraham "separated from each other" indicates a departure from the sphere (Canaan) and divinely appointed agent (Abram) of blessing (12:1–3). Finally, Lot's fateful decision is underscored when he is said to have "moved his tent as far as Sodom" (13:12).[23]

---

and Gomorrah was no longer fertile in their day. Therefore, he makes a parenthetical comment, "This was before the Lord destroyed Sodom and Gomorrah." Likewise, Eden's Garden perished with the Flood, and Egypt's Nile suffered various judgments of God (Exod 7:17–25; 8: Isa 19:4–8; Ezek 30:12; Zech 10:11).

20. According to Oded Borowski, "Conditions for agriculture in the Near East, and especially in Israel, are not very favorable. Many hardships have been encountered by the farmer, and these include lack of sufficient amount of water and soil. The terrain in most cases is uneven and rocky, and very few natural water sources are available; thus, farming in biblical times depended heavily on rain (Deut 12:11 [*sic*]) and on the ability of the farmer to clear and prepare the land (Josh 17:17–18; Isa 5:2)." Borowski, "Agriculture," in *ABD*, 1:96. Of course, rainfall was less predictable from a *human* standpoint. In reality, God promised to insure the needed rainfall on the condition that Israel remained faithful to the covenant (Deut 11:14; 28:12) and threatened to withhold the rain should Israel prove unfaithful (Deut 11:17; 28:22, 24), which it often did (1 Kgs 8:35; 17:1, 7; 2 Kgs 8:1; 2 Chr 6:26; 7:13–14; Isa 5:6; Jer 14:1–4; Amos 4:7–8; Hag 1:10–11).

21. "Dazzled by the surface appearance of prosperity, he pays no heed to the moral depravity of his future neighbors." Sarna, *Genesis*, 99.

22. Jacob's journey eastward to Paddan-aram may be an exception (Gen 28:1ff.). Yet, this exception reinforces the rule since only God's providential care overrules evil for good (Gen 28:15; 31:6–9, 24, 29) and eventually reverses his steps westward again to the Land of Promise (31:11–13; 32:1–2; 33:18–20; 35:1).

23. The Hebrew preposition translated "as far as" [עד] when spatial usually denotes close proximity or arrival at a geographical location (Gen 11:31; Deut 2:23). Hence, it is possible that Lot did not merely settle outside the city limits but within the city walls. The later narrative makes it clear that Lot eventually moved into the city.

Sin Cities

Moses piles up modifiers to stress the depravity of the Sodomites and the peril of Lot's future.[24] He utilizes a hendiadys to distinguish these people from ordinary sinners.[25] He adds the adverb מְאֹד, which is best translated here "exceedingly." Moreover, he describes them as sinners "against the Lord [לַיהוָה]" (13:13). The Hebrew phrase לַיהוָה often connotes God's presence and elsewhere in Genesis is always associated with acts of worship directed towards God (4:3; 8:20; 12:7, 8; 13:18; 24:26, 48, 52; 25:21). Instead of worshiping in God's presence, the Sodomites boldfacedly sin in God's presence.[26] This depiction of the Sodomites is comparable to the description of rampant evil and human hubris in antediluvian (6:1–6, 10–11) and postdiluvian society (10:8–9; 11:2–4, 6).[27]

Further characteristics of Sodom and Gomorrah may be inferred from Genesis 14. The Mesopotamian overlords defeat the Jordanian forces in battle, spoil the cities of the plain, and take their citizens captive, including Lot (14:8–12). When Abram learns that the Jordanian cities have been overthrown, spoiled, and their inhabitants taken captive, his chief concern is for his nephew (14:13–14), which may be Moses's way of highlighting the patriarch's disrespect for the twin cities as a whole. Abram musters his trained warriors and Canaanite allies, routs the invading forces, and rescues his nephew along with the people of the cities and their possessions (14:14–16). One might expect that such a life-threatening experience followed by a miraculous deliverance would move a people to self-examination, humility, repentance, and gratitude.[28]

24. Ross remarks, "Few passages in Genesis describe the wickedness of a people so strongly." *Creation & Blessing*, 287. Wenham observes, "The rare phraseology implies the extreme seriousness of Sodom's sin. Thus obliquely the future fate of the city is indicated and the folly of Lot's choice is underlined." *Genesis 1–15*, 298.

25. The phrase רָעִים וְחַטָּאִים is literally "evil ones and sinners." But the first substantive probably functions adjectively to modify "sinners"; hence, "evil sinners."

26. Hamilton appropriately notes that this indictment against the Sodomites extends Yahweh's moral jurisdiction beyond the boundaries of Canaan. *Genesis 1–17*, 394. As Genesis and the rest of the OT make clear, Yahweh, unlike the regional deities of pagan nations, is Lord and Judge of all the earth (Gen 6:7ff.; 11:5–9; 18:25).

27. Janzen remarks, "If Babel typifies the city-state form of human condition in contrast to which Abraham and Sarah are called to found a new community, Sodom and Gomorrah appear in their story as a continuing contrast to what that new community is to be." *Abraham and All the Families of the Earth*, 57.

28. So notes Luther: "[The Sodomites] should have been reminded by this lashing, as well as by this blessing, that they ought to refrain from sin and live a holy life." *Lectures on Genesis*, 2:380.

Sodom's king (as representative of the people), however, appears to respond coldly to the patriarch (14:17) in contrast to the warm response given by the King of Salem (14:18–19).[29] If Salem's king is said explicitly to have "blessed" Abram and his God, one may infer that Sodom's king implicitly "dishonors" Abram and his God, a response that prepares the way for divine judgment (see 12:3).[30]

Divine Visitation

The time of Sodom's visitation comes in chapter 18. The Angel of Yahweh with two other angels visits Abraham (18:1–8) to announce the imminent conception of the promised offspring (18:9–15), as well as to inform his favored patriarch of Sodom's great sin and impending peril (18:16–19). The narrator underscores the magnitude of Sodom's degeneracy and the imminency of divine judgment in several ways. To begin with, Yahweh gives his present assessment: "The outcry" (זְעָקָה)[31] against Sodom and Gomorrah is great and their sin is "very grave" (כָּבְדָה מְאֹד)

29. Hartley suggests the king of Sodom's "coming so far with empty hands is evidence that he was displeased with Abram." *Genesis*, 149. Mathews develops this negative response further by contrasting it with the response of Salem's king: "the king of Sodom's welcome to Abram contrasts the beneficent action taken by the king of Salem. . . . The king of Sodom 'came out' (yāṣā') to meet Abram (v. 17), but Melchizedek 'brought out' (yāṣā') food (v. 18) and offered a blessing (vv. 19–20)" *Genesis 11:27—50:26*, 145–46. Waltke also observes, "[The King of Sodom's] unnatural lack of gratitude and preoccupation with the spoils of war provides an index of Sodom's wickedness." *Genesis*, 232.

30. While a number of commentators note the connection between Abram's defeat of the Mesopotamian kings and God's promise to "curse" those who "dishonor" Abram (12:3), this writer was unable to locate any writer who made the connection between the king of Sodom's refusal to "bless" Abram (in contrast with Melchizedek) and God's subsequent "curse" on the cities of the valley. Some might suggest that the king of Sodom's apparently generous offer of the booty (14:21) qualifies as an expression of goodwill and an official "blessing" conferred on the patriarch. However, the stark contrast with Melchizedek and Abraham's subsequent refusal of the king of Sodom's offer insinuate something less than gratitude and goodwill behind the Sodomite king's presence and proposition. At a redemptive-historical level, God's threat to "curse" those who "dishonor" Abraham refers to those who fail to align themselves in covenant with Abraham's God. But this theological meaning is developed pictorially in the many historical occasions where the patriarch's pagan neighbors suffer divine judgment because they sin, wittingly or unwittingly, against the patriarch.

31. The Hebrew noun may refer to a desperate plea for help (Isa 65:13; Jer 18:22; 20:16; 48:4, 34; 51:54) or a plaintiff cry for justice (Job 16:18; Prov 21:13; Neh 5:6; 9:9; cf. the verbal form in Gen 4:10; 24:34; Exod 2:23). The latter sense is intended here, and the subjects of the complaint are left unidentified.

(18:20).[32] Second, Yahweh announces his plan to investigate the situation (18:21). This divine inquest resembles God's dealings with human sin in primeval history, where he follows the sin by an investigation of the crime (Gen 3:8–13; 4:9–10; 6:5–6; 11:5–6). Third, Abraham's intercession for the city serves to underscore its irredeemable condition (18:22–33). Abraham entreats Yahweh to withhold judgment for the sake of the righteous who may dwell in the city. The patriarch's prayer is no doubt based on the supposition that God is just and would not bring forth such catastrophic judgment prematurely, that is, while a sufficient amount of righteous citizens inhabited the city. Abraham begins with fifty and continues to reduce the number as he takes the hint, either from Yahweh's tone of voice or from the fact that Yahweh does not recall his angels, that such an amount of righteous citizens does not exist (18:24–31). When he reaches ten, the patriarch goes no further (18:32–33). The reader is not told why the patriarch ceased at ten persons. Maybe Abraham has deduced that a number less than ten is not sufficient to stay divine judgment. Or perhaps he stops out of fear of discovering that even his nephew has assimilated into the debauched culture and apostatized from the faith. Whatever Abraham's reason for cutting short the intercession, the reader is left with a striking confirmation of God's preliminary assessment (18:20)[33] and the indelible impression that things do not bode well for the cities of the plain.

When the two angels arrive in Sodom, their initial plan is to lodge in the town square. Lot, however, strongly urges[34] them to come under his roof for food and lodging (19:1–3). Some view Lot's action as "aggressive" hospitality.[35] But Lot's insistence betrays a concern for the visitors' safety and suggests his knowledge of an inhospitable environment with-

32. According to Waltke and O'Connor, the combination of the verb and the adverb yield the emphatic "egregiously serious." *IBHS* § 39.3.4g.

33. Janzen has perceptively noted that Abraham's diminishing numbers correspond with God's estimation of the magnitude of Sodom's sin (18:20) when he writes, "One should note how Abraham's concern for a remnant, in shrinking from fifty eventually to ten, mirrors in reverse God's concern over the expanding mass of wickedness (vv. 20–21: 'great . . . very grave . . . altogether')," *Abraham and All the Families of the Earth*, 60.

34. The Hebrew verb translated "pressed . . . strongly" [פצר] often means "to entreat intensely." It can also denote physical coercion, as later in this context (19:9).

35. Hamilton writes, "Here Lot actually outdoes his uncle in his show of welcome to the newcomers." *Genesis 18–50*, 32.

in the city walls.[36] The subsequent context confirms this interpretation when the reader finds a host of Sodomite men from every age group and social status[37] surrounding Lot's house, demanding that he hand over the visitors for the purpose of sexual gratification (19:5). Lot entreats his fellow citizens to desist from their intentions, which he assesses as evil (אַל־נָא אַחַי תָּרֵעוּ) (19:6–7). Ironically, he offers his own two virgin daughters as substitutes (19:8), which highlights the weakening influence Sodom's immoral culture has had on Lot's integrity and natural affection.[38] The men of Sodom reject Lot's offer, further intensifying the degeneracy of their lust,[39] and they threaten to "deal worse [נָרַע] with [Lot] than with [the visitors]" (19:9). The shocking implication is that they now intend to abuse Lot sexually.[40] Before the Flood, men sought to gratify their lust by taking from among the daughters of men "any they chose" (6:1–2). Now matters have further degenerated to the point of men forcibly raping any [man!] they choose.[41] Thankfully for Lot, the

36. Kidner perceptively remarks, "Lot's alarm in 3a reveals that he knew his Sodom." *Genesis*, 134. This interpretation of Lot's action finds further support by comparing it to the parallel account in Judges 19 where a citizen of Gibeah finds a young man and his concubine lodging in the town square (v. 15, 17) and, like Lot, graciously invites them to lodge in his home with the added warning, "Only, do not spend the night in the square" (v. 2). The particle רַק (*only*) introduces a strong contrastive clause and emphasizes the intensity of his warning (see Gen 19:8; 24:8).

37. The phrase מִנַּעַר וְעַד־זָקֵן כָּל־הָעָם מִקָּצֶה does not necessarily mean that the entire male population of the city was actually present at Lot's house since that would include Lot's "sons-in-law" (19:14). More likely, the narrator is using an idiom that conveys the sense that every age group and strata of Sodom's society had been infected with the immoral and violent character that was about to be displayed.

38. Fretheim observes, "Lot's reply (v. 8) borders on the incredible. Interestingly, he thinks that the men of Sodom would be satisfied with heterosexual abuse (as in Judges 19–20, where it is condemned). The offer of his daughters to be abused 'as you please' provides but another example of the depravity of Sodom." "Genesis," 1:474.

39. According to Mosaic law, the rape of virgin women and acts of homosexuality were crimes punishable by death (Deut 22:25–27; Lev 20:13). The latter, however, is referred to twice as an "abomination [תּוֹעֵבָה]" to God (Lev 18:22, 29; 20:13), marking it as a greater perversion of human sexuality. Notes Gordis, "It is difficult to see how the clear indication in both Genesis [ch. 19] and Judges [ch. 19] that homosexuality is worse than rape can be ignored." "Homosexuality and the Homosexual," 250, n. 10. Actually, the case of Sodom involved a combination: homosexuality and rape!

40. This is confirmed by their use of the same verb רעע (v. 9) that Lot had just used to describe their intended action against his visitors (v. 7).

41. Some modern writers have attempted to avoid this text's negative portrayal of the sin of homosexuality. A few, like Doyle, have argued that the sin of the Sodomites has nothing to do with sexuality but rather with a proud demand to "know" God in

angels rescue him from the would-be rapists, draw him into the house, and shut the door (19:10), a gesture that reminds the reader of Yahweh's shutting the door of the ark behind Noah just prior to judgment (7:16). Then the angels inflict the Sodomite intruders with "blindness" which prevents them from finding the house entrance (19:11).[42]

The angels' judicial inquiry has confirmed the charges filed against the twin cities (18:21). Consequently, they warn Lot of impending judgment and order him to gather his family and prepare for escape (19:12–13), just as Yahweh warned Noah of the coming Flood and provided a way of escape (6:13–21). Having unsuccessfully attempted to persuade his betrothed sons-in-law (19:14), Lot himself hesitates, so that the angels must virtually drag Lot, his wife, and two daughters out of the city (19:15–17). The angel's urgency and intensity of warning[43] portend the sweeping magnitude of judgment about to overtake the cit-

---

one's own terms. 84–100. This interpretation not only conflicts with Lot's understanding of their intentions (see 19:7–8), but it also contradicts the NT's own assessment of their action as "sexual immorality" (ἐκπορνεύσασαι) and the pursuit of "unnatural desire" (ἀπελθοῦσαι ὀπίσω σαρκὸς ἑτέρας), i.e., homosexuality (Jude 7; see also Rom 1:26–27). Others have alleged that the text condemns non-consensual homosexuality (i.e., rape) rather than homosexuality per se. See Helminiak, *What the Bible Really Says About Homosexuality*, 45–47. The fact that the Sodomite's sin was intended nonconsensual homosexuality, however, does not in itself condone consensual homosexual acts, which the original Israelite reader knew were explicitly condemned by God (Lev 18:22; 20:13). Still others try to draw attention away from the sexual nature of Sodom's sin by focusing on its sin of "inhospitality." Boswell, for example, asserts, "A sexual element, if at all present, was probably intended only as the concrete expression of the Sodomites' lack of hospitality." *Christianity, Social Tolerance, and Homosexuality*, 97. Janzen likewise avers, "It is clear from a comparison of 19:1–3 with 18:1–8 that the test of Sodom turns on the question of hospitality." *Abraham and All the Families of the Earth*, 61. But one may acknowledge a lack of hospitality while still noting that the depth of Sodom's degeneracy is expressed in a combination of sexual immorality and violent aggression, both of which are evils that the primeval narrative has already highlighted (Gen 4:19, 23–24; 6:1–2, 5, 11, 13). For a comprehensive treatment of the biblical view of homosexuality as treated in Genesis and elsewhere in Scripture, see Bahnsen, *Homosexuality: A Biblical View*.

42. As Hamilton suggests, the "blindness" here may not have been a total inability to see but rather a kind of optical confusion that prevented the Sodomites from locating the door. *Genesis 18–50*, 37–38. Physiologically, they could still "see," but what they were seeing was not in accordance with reality (see 2 Kgs 6:18–20).

43. The fact that the angels will tolerate no lingering and that the only avenue of escape is to remove oneself from close proximity to the cities demonstrate that the judgment will be catastrophic because the iniquity of Sodom and Gomorrah has, to use the imagery of Genesis 15:16, "reached its limit" (NET).

ies (19:24–29), which in turn serves to link the iniquity of Sodom and Gomorrah with that of the antediluvians before the Flood (Gen 5–7).[44]

In conclusion, the reader should not miss the analogous literary structure that this narrative shares with several of the sin narratives in primeval history:

Table 3: Thematic Pattern of Sin—Discovery—Speech—Mitigation—Judgment

	Sin	Discovery	Speech	Mitigation	Judgment
The Fall	3:6	3:8–13	3:14–19	3:21	3:22–24
Cain & Abel	4:8	4:9–10	4:11–12	4:15	4:16
The Flood	6:2, 4–5, 10	6:5–6, 11	6:3, 7, 13–21	6:8, 18ff.	7:6–24
Babel	11:4	11:5–6	11:7	11:27—12:3	11:8–9
Sodom	13:13; 19:4–9	18:21–22; 19:1–3	18:17–23; 19:13	18:23–32; 19:12, 15–22	19:24–29

This resemblance of literary structure and theme in turn informs the reader that the narrator has not ended his "great hamartiology"[45] at Genesis 11, as many scholars have concluded. Indeed, the account of Sodom and Gomorrah together with the many scattered allusions to human sin in pagan society confirms that the spread of sin continues to be a major theme in the Genesis narrative.

44. Chapter 8 of this study will further explore the nature and magnitude of this judgment. Here it will suffice to note that the judgment consisted of no mere famine or series of plagues but an absolute annihilation of the cities, obliterating all life, including humans, animals, and even plants (19:25–26). Such absolute destruction of life finds parallels with the Flood judgment (6:7, 13, 17; 7:21–23).

45. Von Rad, *OT Theology*, 1:154.

4

The Spread of Sin in the First Generation of Patriarchs

THE PREVIOUS CHAPTER SURVEYED the spread of sin among pagan societies as recorded in the patriarchal narrative. That allusions to sin among peoples wholly or partially deprived of redemptive revelation[1] should appear in the patriarchal accounts is not surprising. The reader has already witnessed the epidemic spread of sin among human societies in the primeval narrative (Gen 4–11). A shift in focus from humanity in general to the "righteous seed" in particular should occasion a stark contrast between light and darkness, bringing the sin of pagan society into greater relief. The expected contrast, however, is often lacking. While the patriarchal family does at times exhibit virtues that strongly contrast with their pagan neighbors, they more often reflect an unspiritual conformity to the worldly values and practices around them. This fact supports the thesis that the spread of sin continues to function as a major theme throughout the remaining chapters of Genesis. Indeed, the examples of sin among the patriarchs serve to intensify and magnify sin's sway over Adam's posterity. Not even the covenant community can completely escape the gravity of the Fall and its effects. This study focuses on four generational segments: sin in the generations of Abraham, Isaac, Jacob, and the sons of Israel.[2] The present chapter highlights expressions

1. Speaking of pagan nations in general, Paul describes them in Romans 2:12 as "without law" [ἀνόμως], meaning that they did not have access, as did the Jewish nation, to redemptive revelation. Paul's assertion, however, should not be interpreted in an absolute sense. As pagan nations and individuals came into contact with the covenant community, they were often exposed in varying degrees to special revelation (Gen 20:3–7; 21:22–23; 23:6; 41:1ff.; 47:10; Exod 5, 7–12, 14; Num 22–24; Josh 2:8–11; Dan 2:1ff.; 3:24–30; 4:1ff.; 5:5ff.; Jonah 3:4–9).

2. This "generational" division is not to be confused with the *toledot* structuring followed by commentators such as Waltke, *Genesis*, 7–9.

of sin in the first generation of the patriarchal family (Abraham, Sarah, and Lot).

ABRAM'S FALSE START

Yahweh commands Abram to depart from his homeland and journey to a land God would show him (12:1), having promised the patriarch an offspring, a name, and great blessing for him and the families of the earth (12:2–3). Abram sets out for Canaan, according to 12:4–5, with his wife and nephew and upon arrival expresses his devotion to Yahweh with altars (12:6–8). In these instances of altar-building, Abram not only espouses Yahweh as his God, but he stakes claim to the respective regions of Canaan, evidencing faith in the promissory grant of territory. It seems the patriarch is off to a good start. Not surprisingly, commentators are quick to commend him. Nahum Sarna describes his response as an "unwavering obedience to the divine will."[3] John Currid remarks, "There is no sense of hesitation or lingering—he does as God bids."[4] Victor Hamilton lauds him as "a paragon of faith and obedience."[5]

But a careful reading of the larger context suggests that Abram's apparently "good start" needs to be qualified. To begin with, God's command that Abram travel to Canaan (12:1) was initially issued while the patriarch was still residing in Ur. This is suggested by Genesis 11:31: "Terah took Abram his son and Lot the son of Haran, his grandson, and Sarai his daughter-in-law, his son Abram's wife, and they went forth together from Ur of the Chaldeans *to go into the land of Canaan*" (emphasis added).[6] What prompted Terah to leave Ur and set off for Canaan? The narrator hints at two possible reasons: Haran's death (11:28) and Sarai's barrenness (11:30). Terah may have felt compelled to leave Ur and journey to Canaan in order to appease deity since both barrenness and premature death in the ancient Near East were often viewed as divine judgments (Gen 20:17–18; 30:2; 38:7, 10; Exod 20:12; 23:26; Lev 26:9;

3. Sarna, *Genesis*, 90.

4. Currid, *Study Commentary on Genesis*, 1:254.

5. *Genesis 1–17*, 376. Luther also sees Abram as "an outstanding example of faith." *Lectures on Genesis*, 2:268. R. Kent Hughes is also guilty of lionizing Abram. *Genesis: Beginning and Blessing*, 179–80, 182–88.

6. Accordingly, a number of English versions translate the Hebrew וַיֹּאמֶר in 12:1 as a pluperfect: "Now the Lord *had said* unto Abram" (KJV; see also NKJ, NIV, NLT). Yet the call in 12:1 may have been a reiteration of an earlier call.

Deut 4:26, 40; 7:14; 25:15; 28:4, 11; Job 20:11, 22; Ps 21:4; Prov 3:16). But for Terah to arrive at such a conclusion would have required a previously revealed divine directive for such a journey. So God must have spoken to the family while they still lived in Ur.

The plausibility of such a reading is confirmed in Acts 7:2–4, where Stephen, an early Christian martyr, argues that God's call to Abram came originally in Ur (Acts 7:2–3). A reconstruction of events suggests that after (and perhaps partly because of) Haran's death and Sarai's barrenness, Abram was able to convince his father, Terah, to heed God's directive and depart for the Promised Land. Terah at first followed his son's urging (11:31a) but later stopped short of Canaan and settled in Haran (11:31b; Acts 7:4a). Rather than heeding God's command unhesitatingly, Abram chose to remain with his father in Haran. It was only after his father's death that Abram finally followed through (12:4–9) on his earlier commitment (11:31a; Acts 7:4a). Instead of providing a paradigm of immediate and unqualified obedience to the divine call, Abram's behavior is more reminiscent of the man who put off following Christ in order to remain home and "bury [his] father" (Matt 8:21; Luke 9:59).[7] This is not to deny that genuine faith may have prompted Abram's initial departure from Ur towards Canaan or the certainty that real faith motivated his eventual trek to Canaan from Haran.[8] Genuine faith, however, may co-

7. The would-be disciple's request, "Lord, let me first go and bury my father," should not be read as a sincere desire to keep the fifth-commandment but as an indication of a covetous heart, a violation the tenth-commandment. In other words, the man's father was most likely still alive, and the son did not want to risk losing his family inheritance by placing allegiance to Christ above his family. Perhaps Abram, like the hesitant disciple, wished to wait around in Haran for his father's inheritance. As the subsequent narrative indicates, the patriarch did at times struggle with an inordinate desire for worldly riches (cf. 12:13).

8. Without question the writer of Hebrews uses Abraham's response to the divine call to leave homeland and sojourn to Canaan as a paradigm of genuine faith (11:8–9). What is uncertain is whether the writer is referring to Abram's initial departure from Ur or his later departure from Haran. The text itself is indecisive, though most commentators tie the reference to God's initial call in Ur. See Bruce, *The Epistle to the Hebrews*, 294–96; Philip Hughes, *A Commentary on the Epistle to the Hebrews*, 466; Westcott, *The Epistle to the Hebrews*, 358–59. These writers often acknowledge two stages in Abraham's call: one in Ur and the other in Haran—alleging the first to be indefinite in terms of disclosed location and the second to be specific, i.e., "go to Canaan." But this interpretation ignores the obvious fact that Abram's family was already on its way to Canaan (Gen 11:31). The indefinite expressions, "to the land that I will show you" (אֶל־הָאָרֶץ אֲשֶׁר אַרְאֶךָּ) (Gen 12:1) and "not knowing where he was going" (μὴ ἐπιστάμενος ποῦ ἔρχεται) (Heb 11:8), need not be interpreted absolutely but relatively. God told Abraham where to go

exist with remaining doubts and unbelief, especially in its early stages of maturity (cf. Mark 9:24).[9] This realization should caution the reader or teacher against making too much out of Abram's exemplary obedience[10] and serve to shift the focus to God's faithfulness instead. Such an approach is more consistent with Stephen's reading of the text, which highlights the divine agency in Abram's move,[11] thereby shifting the weight of praise from Abram to God (Acts 7:4b).

ABRAM'S MORAL DETOUR

As noted above, Abram eventually obeys the divine commission (12:4–6), and the reader finds the patriarch laying claim to the Promised Land by building altars as he sojourns within its boundaries (12:7–8).[12] Abram's next move, however, does not end with an altar. As he "journeyed on, still going toward the Negeb" (12:9), he encounters a "famine in the land" (12:10a). The scarcity of food prompts him to leave Canaan and relocate to Egypt,[13] a land less affected by famines because of the Nile River's steady water supply (cf. Deut 11:10). On his way to Egypt, Abram anticipates the possibility that his wife's physical beauty may provoke the lust

(i.e., Canaan), and he would further reveal the layout of that land once the patriarch arrived (i.e., "show" that Abram might "know").

9. See the helpful observations of Boice, *Genesis*, 441.

10. Philo makes this mistake when he excessively eulogizes Abram's response to God's initial call: "But Abraham, the moment he was bidden, departed with a few or even alone, and his emigration was one of soul rather than body, for the heavenly love overpowered his desire for mortal things. And so taking no thought for anything, either for his fellow-clansmen, or wardsmen, or schoolmates, or comrades, or blood relations on father's or mother's side, or country, or ancestral customs, or community of nurture or home life, all of them ties possessing a power to allure and attract which it is hard to throw off, he followed a free and unfettered impulse and departed with all speed from Chaldea, a land at that time blessed by fortune and at the height of its prosperity, and migrated to Haran." *Philo*, 6:37–39.

11. Stephen declares, "And after his father died, God *removed* (μετῴκισεν) him from there into this land in which you are now living." The Greek verb is causative and is later used in the same discourse for God's *deportation* of Israel to Babylon (Acts 7:43). The noun form (μετοικεσία) is used in Matthew 1:12 for Israel's *deportation* to Babylon. The point of comparison is not to construe God's relocating Abram to Canaan as a form of punishment but to underscore the divine agency in Abram's relocation.

12. See Greidanus, *Preaching Christ from Genesis*, 154; Kline, *Kingdom Prologue*, 374.

13. While the term *sojourn* (גּוּר) does not necessarily connote permanence, it may suggest plans for an extended residency (see Gen 21:23, 34; 26:3; 47:4).

of unruly Egyptian officials, one of whom could have Abram murdered to obtain Sarai for his harem (Gen 12:11–12).[14]

The Wife-Sister Ruse

In light of this potential scenario, Abram concocts a plan to escape harm by means of deception. Abram's ploy is to present Sarai, his wife, as if she were his sister (12:13).[15] For this to work, Sarai will, of course, have to comply. So he tells her the plan, underscoring the need for it: "See now, I know that you are a beautiful woman" (12:11, NAU). As Thomas Lambdin argues, the tandem interjectory particles "see now" (הִנֵּה־נָא) are probably logical in meaning and indicate that this remark "is a logical consequence, either of an immediately preceding statement or of the general situation in which it is uttered."[16] Thus, Abram frames his request to Sarai in the form of a logical necessity arising out of the exigencies of their circumstances.[17] When the couple enters Egypt, Abram's suspicions prove true. Soon the royal court officials laud Sarai's beauty before Pharaoh, and the Egyptian monarch does not waste time acquiring Abram's "sister" for his royal harem (12:14–15). Moreover, not only do the Egyptians spare his life, as Abram had hoped, but Pharaoh also rewards Sarai's "brother" with a healthy dowry (12:16). Yahweh, however, brings judgment on Pharaoh and his household for taking Abram's wife (12:17). The Egyptian king, in turn, rebukes the patriarch, restores his wife, and banishes him from Egypt (12:18–20).

14. That such a scenario was plausible in the ancient Near East, note Gen 6:1–3; 1 Sam 8:11–18; 2 Sam 11. See also the ancient Egyptian story entitled, *The Two Brothers*, which depicts an Egyptian Pharaoh falling in love with a married woman, taking her into his house, and having her husband killed. Lichtheim, *Ancient Egyptian Literature*, 2:203–11.

15. This narrative begins the first of three "wife-sister" stories, two of which pertain to Abraham (12:9–20; 20:1–18) and one of which involves Abraham's son Isaac (Gen 26:1–11). Modern scholars such as Speiser argue that these three separate stories actually reflect one original story (oral folklore) that was repeated and expanded. *Genesis*, 91. For a defense of their integrity and historicity, see T. D. Alexander, *Abraham in the Negev*, 32–51. For a helpful table comparing similarities as well as differences among the three accounts, see Ross, *Creation & Blessing*, 271.

16. Lambdin, *Introduction to Biblical Hebrew*, 170. See also *IBHS* § 34.7.

17. Interestingly, Sarah will use this same device in Genesis 16 when she tempts Abraham to take Hagar as concubine (see below).

Attempts to Defend Abram

The interpreter must struggle with the question of whether Abram's ruse should be classified as sinful or as justifiable. According to a claim Abram later makes, his proposed "deception" did not entail a complete falsehood. Sarai, he alleges, was "[his] sister, the daughter of [his] father though not the daughter of [his] mother" (Gen 20:12). Abram's claim is not verified elsewhere. Nevertheless, whatever her blood-ties to the patriarch, Sarai was Abram's legal wife, as the narrator repeatedly underscores throughout the narrative (12:11, 14, 15, 17, 20). Some commentators believe the circumstances facing Abram obliged him to deceive. Martin Luther, for example, does not excuse Abram exposing his wife to danger, but he is willing to justify Abram's deception. According to Luther, Abram is "full of faith" and believes God can protect him and Sarai from danger, but the patriarch decides that "God must not be put to the test."[18] While not justifying Abram's actions completely, Calvin defends his basic motivation and the uprightness of his character.[19] More recently, Ephraim Speiser

18. Luther imagines Abram reasoning with Sarai as follows: "Therefore, my dear Sarah, do not say that I am your husband; say that I am your brother. Thus I shall remain alive through your favor. But as for you, do not have any doubt. You will experience the help of the Lord, so that nothing dishonorable may befall you; and I shall also help you in this regard as much as I am able, with prayers before the true God, who has promised that He will be merciful." *Lectures on Genesis,* 2:294. Luther then confesses his predisposition in reading the text when he writes, "Because Scripture often presents Abraham to us as a believing father and a perfect model of faith, I prefer to decide in favor of the opinion that here, too, his great faith is revealed rather than either that he sinned or that his faith succumbed in the trial." Ibid. Luther appears to be following Augustine's interpretation of this event as presented in the latter's "Reply to Faustus the Manichean," Book XII, 33–40, trans. R. Stothert, *NPNF*, 4:285–88.

19. Writes Calvin, "While he reflected that the hope of salvation was centered in himself, that he was the fountain of the Church of God, that unless he lived, the benediction promised to him, and to his seed, was vain; he did not estimate his own life according to the private affection of the flesh; but inasmuch as he did not wish the effect of the divine vocation to perish through his death, he was so affected with concern for the preservation of his own life, that he overlooked every thing besides. . . . But in devising this indirect method, by which he subjected his wife to the peril of adultery, he seemed to be by no means excusable. . . . Hence it follows, that Abram's end was right, but he erred in the way itself. *Genesis*, 1:359–60. One might use Calvin's defense of Abram to defend or minimize the sin of Adam and Eve. God ultimately desired Adam and Eve to acquire the knowledge of good and evil (i.e., wisdom) and the consequent higher-life. Following Calvin's line of thought, one might construe the primordial couple' taking of the fruit simply as "thoughtlessness in catching at unlawful means" and "swerving from the word." In other words, they had the right goal but went about achieving it in the wrong way. Yet God did not treat their sin lightly, and likewise it seems unadvisable

has sought to justify Abram's actions on different grounds. Appealing to an ancient Hurrian custom, Speiser infers that Abram was attempting to provide Sarai with a greater level of social status and protection. Since later Jewish interpreters were unaware of this custom, Speiser argues, the interpretation of Abram's action as a "half-truth" or "outright deception" is anachronistic.[20]

Abram's Ruse Censured

A more natural reading of the text suggests less than noble motivations behind Abram's scheme and condemns his deception as sinful. Since, in Abram's mind, going to Egypt would mean the inevitable and irresistible forfeiture of his wife, Abram likely envisioned two possible scenarios. (1) The Egyptians would be attracted to Sarai, learn that she was married to Abram, murder him in order to sever the legal ties, and take Sarai as wife. (2) Even with his deceptive scheme in place, the Egyptians would be attracted to Sarai, think that she was Abram's sister, negotiate with him for her hand in marriage (as was customary), enrich him with a significant dowry, and take Sarai as wife. In both cases, his wife would be

---

to minimize the gravity of Abram's sin. Besides, if Abram's faith were really fixed in the primeval promise, then it would be the seed of the woman he would be concerned to protect over and above his own self-preservation.

20. *Genesis*, 92–93; idem, "The Wife-Sister Motif in the Patriarchal Narratives," 15–28. Speiser's thesis has been questioned by a number of scholars who have examined the Nuzi texts more carefully. It appears that the "sisterhood contracts" were made not primarily to protect the women but that the women might actually be given away in exchange for a bride's dowry. As Longman notes, "The original family must have been hard-pressed for money, and so the buyer bought the rights to sell her so he could get a larger future compensation, while the seller got an infusion of money right away." *How to Read Genesis*, 94. Jordan appears to follow Speiser's interpretation (though he makes no reference to Speiser). According to Jordan, "Abram knew that if he were killed Sarai's protection would be gone. Abram deceived Pharaoh by telling the Egyptians nothing more than that Sarai was his sister and not that she was also his wife. Abram counted on the common law of the ancient near east to protect Sarai, because any man desiring her would have to negotiate with her brother, and thus Abram would be able to forestall any marriage." *Primeval Saints*, 89. Jordan's comment about the common law of the ancient Near East appears to find some biblical support in the account of Abraham's servant Eliezar negotiating Rebekah's betrothal to Isaac through the mediation of Rebekah's brother Laban (Gen 24:29–33, 50, 53, 55, 59–60; cf. 34:11–17). Extrabiblical sources also bear witness to the custom of an elder brother negotiating his sister's marriage. See van Seters, *Abraham in History and Tradition*, 77; Selman, "Comparative Customs and the Patriarchal Age," 119, 122, 138. Nevertheless, Speiser's and Jordan's claim that Abram used this custom to protect his wife is nowhere found in the text.

forfeit. In the second scenario, however, at least he would escape harm and even obtain some compensation for his loss. Moreover, Abram would be free to obtain a new wife, one that might bear him the promised seed, which Sarai's barren womb had as yet failed to yield. The outcome looks bleak for Sarai but promising for Abram.

This reading definitely casts a dark shadow over Abram's moral character. Yet there are several indications in the immediate and larger context of the text that support this more negative reading. To begin with, the narrator identifies two motivations behind Abram's ruse. First, Abram commands Sarai to pose as his sister "that it may go well [יִיטַב] with me [לִי] because of you" (12:13).[21] Not only is Abram's concern self-directed (לִי), but the verb he employs (יטב) is used in 12:16 to characterize Pharaoh's dowry gift: "and for her sake he dealt well [הֵיטִיב] with Abram; and he had sheep, oxen, male donkeys, male servants, female servants, female donkeys, and camels." Abram may have had such material benefit in mind when he urged Sarai to comply with his scheme.[22] Second, Abram implores Sarai to pose as his sister "that my life may be spared for your sake." Once again, Abram's concern is self-directed. According to some interpreters, this was only a means to a greater end (i.e., that he might be around to protect Sarai). But Abram makes no mention of protecting Sarai. He seems only concerned or primarily concerned about his own welfare even at the expense of a female family member whom he was obligated as male head to protect. James Jordan argues that the Egyptian Pharaoh should be viewed as a "tyrant" and that he "took Sarai without permission."[23] But Pharaoh's bestowal of gifts that Abram willingly accepted suggests otherwise.[24] Moreover, one cannot but note the contrast between Abram's passively allowing of Pharaoh to

21. Sarna points to a parallel expression in Jeremiah 38:20 and argues that the second clause explains the first, i.e., "that it may go well with me" is equivalent to "that my life may be spared." *Genesis*, 95. But the expression "that it may go well [אֲשֶׁר יִיטַב]" is used elsewhere in the Pentateuch to refer to more than the mere extension of one's life; it includes various temporal blessings such as fruitfulness and material wealth (Deut 6:3, 18).

22. The ambiguity of his wording may serve to cloak his full intentions from Sarai.

23. Jordan, *Primeval Saints*, 89.

24. As Baldwin notes, "As a foreigner in search for food Abram was aware that he had no rights in Egypt, and he feared for his life. In particular he was aware that the Pharaohs were always interested in adding beautiful women to their harem, and that they paid handsomely for the privilege." *Message of Genesis 12–50*, 38.

"take" Sarah versus his proactive reaction to the Mesopotamian forces that "took" Lot (14:14). One may also compare Abram's actions to Adam leaving Eve to fend for herself against the Serpent (Gen 3:2–6) or to Lot's unhesitating willingness to hand over his daughters to the men of Sodom for sexual abuse in order to protect the male visitors in his home (Gen 19:8). Both betray a disregard for the weaker sex and a lack of familial loyalty and affection. Worse, both Abram and Lot evidence that they have been influenced by the pagan culture around them that tended to accord women a lower social status and in some cases treated them merely as objects of sexual gratification. The reader should also note that Abram's notion of what would "be good for [him]" is not based on a word from God.[25] Rather, Abram's assessment of what would "be good" (טוֹב) for him parallels Eve's autonomous assessment of the tree of knowledge (Gen 3:6). He is seeking "the blessing" but leaning on his own understanding to obtain it (Prov 3:5–6).

Second, Pharaoh clearly interprets Abram's actions as morally wrong. His summons of the patriarch and rhetorical question indicate a formal charge of transgression (Gen 3:13; 4:10; 20:9; 26:10; 29:25; 31:26; 44:15) leveled against the patriarch, and Abram makes no attempt to answer the charge.[26] Furthermore, once Pharaoh discovers the truth, he insists on referring to Sarai as Abram's "wife" (12:18–19).[27] The narrator sides with Pharaoh and makes a point of identifying Sarai as Abram's "wife" (12:11, 14, 15, 17, 20).[28]

25. Elsewhere in the Pentateuch, the Israelites are commanded to obey God's word in order that "it may go well" with them (Deut 4:40; 5:16, 33; 6:3, 18; 12:28), clearly linking their prosperity with their fidelity to the divine command.

26. Later, when Abram commits this same sin a second time, he does attempt to justify his actions (Gen 20), but his excuses are lame (see below).

27. As Wenham observes, "All three wife-sister stories in Genesis (chs. 12, 20, 26) have in common that the foreign monarch is more concerned about morality than is the patriarch." *Genesis 1–15*, 291. One might also note that Pharaoh restores Sarai, refuses to punish Abram for his misdeed, and allows the patriarch to leave Egypt unscathed with the huge dowry gift. While Pharaoh's kindness is probably not motivated by pure virtue, it does reflect a fear of Yahweh that the patriarch himself surprisingly seemed to lack. In contrast with Pharaoh, Abram's actions seem motivated more by the fear of men than by the fear of God.

28. Although many English versions translate הָאִשָּׁה "woman" in 12:14–15 (KJV, NAU, ESV), the noun can be rendered "wife" (NET) and the article functions as a possessive (cf. Exod 2:2; 21:4; Num 5:18–30). See *HS* § 86; *IBHS* § 13.5.1e.

Third, God's plagues upon Pharaoh and his household and his providential conferral of riches on the patriarch should not be read as an endorsement of Abram's actions. God's action against Pharaoh was to protect Sarai, who would become the mother of the promised offspring; his blessing Abram with riches underscores not Abram's merit but God's unmerited favor to his chosen.

Finally, Abram's departure from Canaan to Egypt signals a drift away from a state of trust and devotion to Yahweh and serves as an indicator of spiritual declension. The famine was probably God's way of testing the patriarch's faith and patience.[29] At this point, Abram lacked spiritual maturity and failed the test. His move to Egypt is made without divine warrant and contradicts God's previous directive (12:1). Viewed in connection with God's subsequent warning to Isaac in the days of famine (Gen 26:1–2), Abram has stepped outside God's revealed will and thereby placed himself (and the promise) into the sphere of temptation and danger.[30] Thankfully, though, the patriarch appears to have recognized his error. His returning to the former altar in Canaan (13:3–4a), reengaging in worship (13:4b), and displaying a less opportunistic disposition (13:9) suggest repentance and spiritual recovery.

In light of these considerations, the reader cannot view Abram's detour to Egypt in a positive light.[31] Nor can one take a neutral position,

29. Such testing is common place in Genesis (Gen 2:16–17; 22:1ff.; 32:1–32; 42:15–16, 28) and the Bible (Exod 16:4; 20:20; Deut 8:16; Judg 2:22; 2 Chr 32:21; Matt 4:1–11; Luke 4:1–13; Heb 3:8; Jas 1:2ff.). Famine is not only an effect of God's curse upon the earth (Gen 3:17–19), but it also occurs frequently in Genesis (26:1; 42:5, 19, 33; 43:1; 45:6, 11; 47:4) and elsewhere (Ruth 1:1; 2 Sam 21:1; 2 Sam 23:13; 1 Kgs 8:37–39; 1 Kgs 18:2; 2 Kgs 4:38; etc.) as a God-appointed means to test his people's loyalty.

30. Some commentators draw parallels between this account and Jacob's sojourn in Egypt from which, four hundred years later, he returns to Canaan with much spoil. See, for example, Mathews, *Genesis 11:27–50:26*, 123; Ross, *Creaion & Blessing*, 273. Such a parallel suggests a more positive reading of Abram's sojourn. While there may be some intentional analogies between the two incidents, it seems precarious to read too much into these parallels. God commanded Jacob to go to Egypt, where he and his family would be preserved under Joseph's care. There is no such command to Abram.

31. Visotzky goes too far when he portrays Abram as "pimping his wife": "Abraham knows only too well the horror Pharaoh and the Egyptians have of taking another man's wife, and that they would pay a high price for an attractive woman, but an even larger sum of hush money to quiet the scandal of adultery." *Genesis of Ethics*, 27. See also Garland and Garland's comparison of Abram to "an ancient sex trader." *Flawed Families of the Bible*, 23. There is no evidence of a second payment of "hush money" or indication that Abram's scheming had such as a goal. More on target is Baldwin's assessment: "With a brutal disregard for Sarai, and a total lapse from faith in his Lord, Abram resorted to

as does John Walton when he argues, "The text offers no moralizing lesson from Abram's action of identifying Sarai as his sister. It does not say why he does it, nor does it condemn or approve. The Bible is not trying to teach us how to act or how not to act by Abram's example."[32] In contrast to Walton's reluctance to "moralize," the NT writers do exactly that (1 Cor 10:1–13; Heb 11:4–40; Jas 5:11, 17–18; 1 Pet 3:1–5)!

LOT'S SPIRITUAL DECLINE

The analysis of sin's spread among the patriarchal community will shift its focus to Abram's nephew Lot. The fact that Lot accompanied Abram and Sarai to Canaan, leaving his uncle Nahor and family behind in Haran (12:5), suggests that at some level he shared the faith of Abraham in the divine promise (12:1–2).[33] The next reference to Lot finds him returning to Canaan from Egypt with his uncle (13:1). But unlike Abram, who shows signs of moral improvement following the Egypt fiasco, Lot begins a steady process of spiritual decline that undermines his reputation and places him and his family in great jeopardy.

The Signs of Selfish Greed

The narrator begins the chronicle of Lot's demise by noting that he, along with Abram, had materially profited from the detour to Egypt

---

deceit in order to save his own skin. Sarai was in fact his half-sister as well as his wife (20:12), so while it was not altogether a lie to pass her off as his sister, it was a deliberate deception, intended to enable him to escape danger and incidentally to enrich himself. But it was a despicable ruse, and one which might have endangered the birth of his promised son." *Message of Genesis 12–50*, 38.

32. *Genesis*, 398. When commenting on the second wife-sister account, Walton seems finally to see some clear fault with Abraham's behavior when he notes, "Instead of being the righteous one bringing grace and deliverance to the nations, Abraham nearly brings destruction to the innocent (= same word as righteous)." But then, perhaps sensing a contradiction with his basic anti-moralizing approach, he adds, "While this may not intend to criticize Abraham, it shows that God is able to carry out his blessing program even when Abraham cannot see how it will be done." *Genesis*, 499.

33. Although one cannot determine for certain when Lot became a genuine believer, the NT unmistakably portrays him as a regenerate man. Jesus seems to imply this fact when he parallels Lot with Noah, God's righteous servant (Luke 17:26–29). Peter, however, places the question beyond doubt when he identifies Lot as a "righteous" man whose heart "was greatly distressed by the sensual conduct of the wicked [i.e., the inhabitants of Sodom]" (2 Pet 2:7).

(13:5).[34] Their increased population of livestock makes living in close proximity difficult (13:6) and results in strife between their herdsmen (13:7a). The narrator's passing mention that "at that time the Canaanites and the Perizzites were dwelling in the land" (13:7b) may serve further to underscore the limited amount of ideal grazing tracts available to the patriarchs,[35] though the ultimate cause of the strife appears to have been motivated in part by selfish greed. In other words, the problem was not insufficient space per se but rather what parcel of land belonged to whom.[36] The reader might expect Lot to end the strife by simply deferring to his uncle Abram, who was the elder of the two and as such should have had the preferable grazing land. Yet Lot remains silent. The thought of showing deference to his uncle does not seem to occur to him. Consequently, Abram must initiate the conflict resolution. He proposes a magnanimous solution: "Separate yourself from me. If you take the left hand, then I will go to the right, or if you take the right hand, then I will go to the left" (13:8b). Such deference and generosity coming from a man who was previously willing to sell off his wife for self-preservation and material gain serves as a further indication of his repentance and of

34. Sarna suggests that the narrator's mention of Lot *after* delineating Abram's possessions and *after* highlighting his return to the worship of Yahweh (13:2–3) "hints at a degree of estrangement" that had already begun (97). See also Mathews, *Genesis 11:27—50:26*, 130.

35. A few commentators have suggested that the reference to the indigenous population serves to provide the reason why Abram suggested a resolution to the strife. The patriarch did not want family infighting to create a bad testimony before his pagan neighbors. Bush, *Notes on Genesis*, 1:213; Leupold, *Exposition of Genesis*, 434–35. While Abram does underscore the inappropriateness of kinsmen strife (13:8), he does not explicitly express concern over the patriarchal family's testimony before their pagan neighbors. Instead, he offers a solution that seeks to address the source of the strife, namely, what part of the land shall each man and his herds occupy (13:9).

36. Subsequent references in the patriarchal narrative imply that there was plenty of space within Canaan's borders for the patriarchs to live among their neighbors (Gen 14:13; 21:22–24, 30–34; 23:3–20; 33:19–20; 34:10, 21). Note also Abram's remark to Lot, "Is not the whole land before you?" (13:9a). "The irony," notes Hamilton, "is that Abram and Lot seem to be able to share the land with the Canaanites and Perizzites, for these peoples were also occupying or 'dwelling' (yōšēḇ) in the land, but there is not enough room for Abram and Lot 'to dwell' (lāšeḇeṯ) adjacently." *Genesis 1–17*, 391. Although at times there were disputes over the land (Gen 21:25; 26:6–33), even these disputes appear to have been motivated by envy (26:14) rather than by cramped quarters. Hence, it is likely that the strife between Abraham and Lot's herdsmen was not merely a complaint about cramped quarters but an argument over who had rights to the best pasturelands.

a forward step in spiritual growth. The incident in Egypt does not appear, however, to have had a positive affect upon Lot. On the contrary, his uncle's prior motivation, "that it may go well with me" (12:13), appears to be driving Lot's affections at this point. For as soon as Abram's offer is delivered, Lot wastes no time relocating to the more fertile Jordan Valley (13:10–13).

The reader should note several features in the narrator's depiction of Lot's fateful choice. That Lot's gaze seems to have moved first in the direction of the well-watered valley suggests that he had already been nursing a desire to move in that direction. Lot's casting of his eyes toward an Eden/Egyptian-like breadbasket (Gen 2:9; 11:10) is reminiscent of Eve's craving for the forbidden fruit (Gen 3:6) and Israel's lusting for the fleshpots of Egypt (Exod 16:3; Num 11:5; 21:5; Acts 7:39). Hence, Lot's choice is cast in the form of a grasping for something outside the will of God. This point is further underscored by the fact that the region Lot chose took him in an easterly direction (13:11), which elsewhere in Genesis usually signifies a movement away from God (3:23–24; 4:16; 11:2).[37] Indeed, it appears that Lot chose to live just outside the borders of the Promised Land (13:12),[38] separating himself from the divinely appointed *sphere* (Canaan) and *agent* (Abram) of redemptive blessing (12:2–3).[39] Finally, the narrator portends the peril of Lot's choice with two editorial comments inserted into the narrative: (1) the parenthetical qualifier that the region of Lot's choosing could no longer (in the days of Moses) be characterized as fertile because of divine judgment (13:10b) serves as an ill omen for Lot's future; (2) the supplemental description of Lot's new neighbors, the Sodomites (13:13), foretells the basis for God's eventual destruction of Lot's new abode. Lot is headed for trouble!

37. This is noted by Stordalen when he observes, "In the movement from 'Eden to Nod' . . . east is constantly associated with the negative. Adam is moved from the Garden Eden (2:8, 15) to a position east of the garden (3:24), apparently still in Eden. Cain is driven out to the east of Eden (4:16). Easterly cities like Nimrud (10:8–12) and Babylon (11:1–9) house unfavourable incidents. And indeed, when the tide turns and the Promised Land is again focused, the movement goes from the south-east to the west (11:31—12:9). Clearly, in Genesis 1–11 movement towards the east is unfavourable." *Echoes of Eden*, 267–68.

38. At least part of the Jordan Valley lay within the borders of the Promised Land according to Numbers 34:1–12. However, the narrator's contrast between "the land of Canaan" and "the cities of the valley," together with the locative phrase "as far as Sodom [עַד־סְדֹם]" (13:12) suggests a departure from the Promised Land.

39. See Helyer, "Abraham's Eight Crises," 45–47.

Too Attached to Sodom

The next reference to Lot comes in the fourteenth chapter where his status has changed from a semi-nomadic neighbor of Sodom (13:12) to a city-dweller, having taken up permanent residence within Sodom's precincts (14:12).[40] After the Mesopotamian armies defeat the Jordanian alliance (14:1–10), they spoil the cities of Sodom and Gomorrah of both people and property (14:11–12). Once Abram learns of his nephew's capture, he musters his own warriors as well as his Canaanite allies and successfully routes the Mesopotamian forces, recovering the spoil, including "his kinsman Lot with his possessions" (14:13–16). But Lot's ending is not as happy as it may first appear. Chapter 14 concludes with Abram refusing any reward from Sodom's king, not "a thread or a sandal strap or anything" of the Sodomite spoil. Some commentators read Abram's action as a conventional form of ancient Near Eastern etiquette.[41] However, Abram's added explanation, "Lest you should say, 'I have made Abram rich,'" suggests more than mere politeness as a motivation for the patriarch's refusal. To understand properly Abram's response to the seemingly generous offer one should not miss the contrast between Sodom's king and Salem's king, as well as Abram's respective responses. Salem's king meets Abram with a feast and "blesses" him as victor (14:18–20). Sodom's king, on the other hand, praises neither Abram nor his God. Abram pays tribute to Melchizedek, in whom he recognizes a spiritual affinity (14:20b), but refuses to accept the "gift" from Sodom's king. Indeed, he appears to have made a prior oath to Yahweh not to

40. In 13:12, Moses informs the reader that "Lot settled among the cities of the valley and moved his tent as far as Sodom." The Hebrew preposition translated "as far as" (עַד) may denote either close proximity or arrival at a geographical location. Thus, it is possible that Lot was already within the city walls. Nevertheless, the verb translated "moved his tent [וַיֶּאֱהַל]" suggests that he still maintained sojourner status (Isa 13:20) and had not yet become a permanent resident of the city. But here the narrator describes Lot as "dwelling in Sodom [יֹשֵׁב בִּסְדֹם]," thereby indicating a more settled residency.

41. Hamilton, for example, cites a text from Ugarit in which a vassal offers his Hittite suzerain a gift in lieu of the latter's deliverance of the former from his enemies. The Hittite emperor replies to the vassal using language roughly parallel to that of Abram: "Suppiluliuma, the Great King, saw the loyalty of Niqmaddu, and as far as what belongs to Ugarit . . . Suppiluliuma, the Great King, will not touch anything, be it a straw or splinter." *Genesis 1–17*, 414. To chalk this down as merely "royal etiquette" is conjectural at best. Suzerains regularly accepted gifts from vassals, and there may have been other factors prompting the Hittite king's response. It may be that he wanted to maintain his position as the supreme benefactor, leaving the vassal indebted to him and not the reverse.

accept such an offer should it be extended (14:22–24).[42] In light of these contrasts, the narrator encourages the reader to suspect the motives behind the king of Sodom's offer. It is likely that the Sodomite king was attempting to place himself in the role of Abram's benefactor, thereby making the patriarch indebted to his generosity.[43] Abram wisely declines the offer of spoil, desiring to be indebted to Yahweh alone, "Possessor of heaven and earth" (14:22–24).

Interpreters note the positive light in which this narrative places Abram.[44] But they miss the narrative's implications for Lot. Not only had Lot been the beneficiary of his uncle's daring deliverance; he probably witnessed Abram's bold refusal to align himself with Sodom's king or to defile himself with Sodom's riches (14:22–24). In Egypt, Lot had seen his uncle succumb to the temptation of riches obtained outside the will of God (12:13). Now he sees his uncle affirm his trust in God alone as his benefactor. Here is Lot's opportunity to realign himself with the God-appointed agent of blessing (12:3) and to return to the Promised Land.

42. Some modern commentators see the verses about Melchizedek as a later interpolation into the narrative. They base their suspicion on two factors: (1) The narrative would flow naturally from verse 17 to verse 21 were this section (vv. 18–20) removed, and (2) the appearance of Melchizedek is too sudden and unanticipated. Hamilton concedes, "Few, if any, studies have attempted to integrate exegetically the Melchizedek episode with the larger narrative." *Genesis 1–17*, 408–9 n. 4. However, Sailhamer notes that the grammatical structure of verses 17 and 18 is not unusual in unified narratives. He argues that the Melchizedek section (vv. 18–20) is necessary to provide background information to Abram's response to the king of Sodom (vv. 21–24). "Thus," remarks Sailhamer, "a contrast is established between Abraham's response to the king of Salem and his response to the king of Sodom. The response to the one is positive, but to the other it is negative." "Genesis," 122–23.

43. Observes Kline, "Since the prerogative of determining the disposition of a vassal's battle spoils belonged to his suzerain, Abraham did not permit the king of Sodom to assume that role (Gen 14:21–24). For Abraham to accept the king's offer to act as benefactor (cf. Luke 22:25) would have been a contradiction of his oath of allegiance to the Lord God." *Kingdom Prologue*, 312. Waltke reasons in a similar vein when he writes, "What is wrong with the king of Sodom's proposal is his audacity and attitude. The victor, not a defeated king, has the right to stipulate the disposition of the spoils of war. Moreover, the king's attitude is deceitful and begrudging. He does not greet Abraham with joy and gladness. Abraham anticipates that, were he to accept the offer, the king of Sodom would claim that he disadvantaged himself to order for Abraham to be advantaged." *Genesis*, 235.

44. Of note is the contrast between Abram's refusal to accept riches from Sodom's king and his allowance of riches from Pharaoh in Genesis 12. Perhaps Abram sees his own prior folly in seeking prosperity outside the Promised Land (Gen 12) mirrored in Lot's folly (Gen 13), and so he refuses to make the same mistake again (Gen 14).

Lot's silence and Abram's subsequent reference to his steward Eliezer of Damascus as the only qualified heir of his estate (15:2) suggest that Abram's nephew did not attempt to reunite with his uncle.[45] Instead, he followed his earthly possessions back to Sodom, which the narrative later confirms (19:1ff.).

The Double-Minded Man

The reader next encounters Lot "sitting in the gate of Sodom" (19:1).[46] Lot's prompt and insistent hospitality mirrors that of his uncle's in the preceding narrative (18:1–8). Lot's act of kindness, Abram's intercessory prayer (18:23–32), and the angel's subsequent deliverance (19:15–22) confirm Lot as a genuine believer (Luke 17:28–29; 2 Pet 2:5–8).[47] Nevertheless, there are clear indications in the text that Lot's conscience had become calloused and his moral values conditioned by his societal surroundings. Although he commendably attempts to protect his visitors from homosexual rape (19:3–7), he compromisingly offers his own virgin daughters in the place of his visitors in order to appease the raging lust of his fellow Sodomites (19:8). Some have attempted to justify or at least minimize Lot's crime by emphasizing the importance of hospitality in the ancient Near East and by stressing the host's responsibility to protect his visitors at all costs.[48] But the narrator gives no indication that Lot's willingness

45. See Helyer, "The Separation of Abram and Lot: Its Significance in the Patriarchal Narratives," 77–88.

46. Besides a means of protection, the city gates were often the place in which the local magistrates presided in order to conduct civil affairs and judicial hearings (Gen 23:10, 18; Deut 21:19; 22:15; 25:7; Ruth 4:1; 2 Sam 19:8; 1 Kgs 22:10; Jer 38:7; Prov 31:23). Hence, Lot's official "seat" at Sodom's gate indicates that he occupied some position of prominence in the city. Abram's deliverance of Sodom's citizens from the Mesopotamian armies may have facilitated Lot's promotion. Yet, as the subsequent narrative demonstrates, the Sodomites esteem for Lot was superficial or short-lived.

47. The apocryphal book Wisdom refers to Lot as a "righteous man," comparing him with other pious OT believers (10:4–13; 19:17).

48. Mathews, for example, remarks, "The thought of Lot as a 'righteous man' confounds the contemporary reader, for his action against his daughters indicates otherwise. But the author of Genesis would have us evaluate Lot in terms of his conduct toward the traveling strangers. Lot commits a grievous sin by subjecting his two daughters to sexual predators, but we miss the author's chief point if we read Lot's checkered character solely in terms of his mistreatment of his daughters." *Genesis 11:27—50:26*, 232. Mathews is correct when he encourages the reader to include Lot's act of hospitality into any overall assessment of his character. The proper treatment of strangers was stressed in Mosaic legislation (Exod 22:21 [Heb 20]; Lev 19:33–34; Deut 10:19). Nevertheless,

to have his virgin daughters raped in order to protect his guests is justifiable. The Mosaic law elsewhere condemns rape (Deut 22:25–27) and forbids a father from forcing his daughter into prostitution (Lev 19:29). So while the narrative may reflect the premium ancient Near Eastern society accorded hospitality, it also depicts the general debasement of women among these cultures.

Lot's character does not improve as the narrative continues. The angelic visitors command him to gather his family and flee from the city to escape divine judgment (14:12–13). Lot attempts to save his sons-in-law, who, ironically, may have been betrothed to the very daughters Lot had been prepared to deliver over to be raped.[49] But Lot's tarnished testimony has undermined his moral authority, and his sons-in-law do not take him seriously (19:14). The angels issue a final warning, urging Lot to escape with his wife and two daughters (19:15). "But he lingered" (וַיִּתְמַהְמָהּ)" (19:16a). The Hebrew verb stem emphasizes both a reflexive and repetitive action.[50] This action exposes Lot's moral "Achilles' heel." He has grown too fond of Sodom and its worldly goods. As a result, only

---

Lot's mistreatment of his daughters should receive equal if not greater emphasis for at least three reasons. First, it continues the theme of sinful self-preservation at the expense of even family members. We have already seen this theme in Abram's willingness to sacrifice Sarai so that his life might be spared (12:13). Similarly, Lot could have offered himself as a substitute for his visitors, since it was a male victim, not a female victim that the Sodomites desired (19:5, 9). But Lot is unwilling to lay down his own life to spare his daughters. Second, Lot's poor treatment of his daughters repeats the theme of the debasement of women by men as objects of sexual gratification (see Gen 6:1–2; 12:11–15; 34:1–2; 38:15–18). Third, the narrator ends the story with an ironic twist—Lot's own daughters whom he offered for sexual abuse end up abusing him sexually (Gen 19:31–36). Thus, the author's own denouement to the narrative highlights Lot's sin rather than minimizes it. Mathews provides a better assessment of the story when he later writes of Lot's misdeed, "For a moment it is Sodom that has taken up residence in Lot's soul." *Genesis 11:27—50:26*, 237.

49. Literally, the Hebrew text reads, "And he spoke to his sons-in-law, the ones who were to marry his daughters [וַיְדַבֵּר אֶל־חֲתָנָיו לֹקְחֵי בְנֹתָיו]." It is possible that the daughters in view were not the same ones Lot had just offered for the sexual gratification of the Sodomite men. However, the fact that the two virgin daughters introduced in 19:8 provide the only identifiable antecedent in the text and the fact that the angels only rescue "his two daughters" render it likely that the very daughters Lot offered to the Sodomites were the same ones he had already promised to others for marriage. This fact serves to aggravate Lot's sin.

50. The verb is in the Hithpalpel stem and is reflexive-iterative in meaning. See *HS* §152.

divine intervention can save Lot from the doom of Sodom (19:16b–17).[51] The tenacity of the world's hold on Lot's heart is further seen in his entreaty that the angels allow him to take refuge in the nearby city of Zoar rather than to escape to the hills as instructed (19:18–20). Zoar, though smaller than Sodom, represents a final opportunity for Lot to remain in the plains of Jordan where he has staked his future hopes. The angel grants his request though Lot soon realizes that the moral state of this city is not much different from Sodom's, and fear of divine judgment drives him to take residence in the hill country (19:30). Lot had left the hill country for the plains with great possessions (13:5–6), but he returns to the hill country a widower (19:26) and virtually empty handed to live in a cave with his two daughters.[52]

Had the narrative ended here, Lot's story would be sad enough. Lot's former sins, however, come back to haunt him. The very daughters Lot was willing to allow the men of Sodom to rape in effect rape their father in order to obtain offspring (19:35).[53] The reader should not miss the parallels with the story of Noah and his sons. God rescued both Noah and Lot, along with their families, from a cataclysmic judgment (6:7, 13, 17; 7:4, 21–23; 19:13, 17, 24–29). Both Noah and Lot become drunk with wine sometime after their deliverance (9:21; 19:33, 35). In both cases, the "nakedness" of Noah and Lot is exploited by their offspring (9:22; 19:33, 35).[54] The result, in both cases, is a line of cursed descendants (9:24–25;

51. Lot's attachment to Sodom and his double-minded response to God's command to flee impending judgment have led the expositor Alexander Whyte to characterize him as "the father of all such as are scarcely saved." *Bible Characters*, 81.

52. As in the case when Abraham rescued his nephew from his Mesopotamian captors, Lot had the opportunity to forsake Sodom and return to his father-in-law, the God-appointed agent for blessing. But once again, Lot refused to reconcile himself with his uncle. Perhaps Lot struggled with facing the shame of his life-choices. Duguid notes Lot's lamentable end and writes, "The problem of Lot's prosperity had been radically dissolved by God; like the Prodigal Son, he now had literally nothing to stand in the way of his return home. . . . Yet even after Lot finally did abandon the plain and leave the halfway house of Zoar behind, and return to the mountains, he still did not seek out the one person in whom blessing could have been found: Abraham. . . . So he ended his days in misery and depravity, a sorry shell of what he once was." *Promise and Reality*, 106.

53. Duguid astutely observes, "You can take Lot and his daughters out of Sodom, but it's a lot harder to take Sodom out of them. Living alone with his daughters hardly led to renewed righteousness." *Promise and Reality*, 105.

54. Although the term for "nakedness," עֶרְוָה, does not occur in the Lot narrative, later Mosaic legislation describes the acts of sexual immorality, including incest, in terms of "uncovering another's nakedness" (Lev 18:6ff.; 20:11ff.; Deut 22:30; 27:20).

19:37–38). One should mark the dissimilarities as well. First, while both men may be characterized as "righteous" (Gen 6:8–9; 12:5; 19:1–3, 14; cf. 2 Pet 2:7–8), Noah's moral character shines brighter than Lot's.[55] In fact, the reader is almost tempted to think the angels should have left Lot to perish along with the Sodomites. Second, Noah complied with the divine directives related to the coming judgment and God's appointed method of escape (6:22; 7:5, 13–16). But Lot's response was half-hearted and inconsistent (19:16, 18–22). Third, the narrator implicates Noah once for an immoderate use of wine (9:21), whereas he depicts Lot becoming intoxicated twice (19:33, 35). Fourth, one of Noah's son's disrespectfully gazed upon his father's nakedness and mockingly disclosed his father's shame to his brothers (9:22). But Lot's two daughters did not merely gaze on their father's nakedness; they engaged in incestuous intercourse with him (19:33, 35)! Fifth, Noah cursed his son's offspring in moral indignation (9:24–25). There is no indication, however, that Lot pronounced a curse on his daughter's offspring, though the Scriptures elsewhere indicate that God marked them as a cursed people (Num 21:25–30; 23:7—24:19; 2 Sam 8:2, 12; 2 Chr 20:22–23; Neh 13:23; Isa 1 5:1—16:14; Jer 9:25–26; 48:1–46; Ezek 25:8–11; Amos 2:1–3), even assigning them a judgment likened to that of Sodom and Gomorrah (Zeph 2:8–11).[56]

In summary, Lot's spiritual decline not only serves to continue the spread of sin motif in the patriarchal narrative; it actually amplifies sin's spread. In primeval history, the righteous servant whom God saves along with his family from cataclysmic judgment proves vulnerable to sin (9:21) but still stands in contrast to his perverse generation (6:8–9). Yet

55. One would expect the opposite, seeing that Lot probably had access to a greater amount of special revelation than did Noah.

56. God's curse upon certain people groups in general does not preclude the possibility of his mercy shown to individuals from among those people groups. Although the Canaanites as a whole fell under God's curse, Rahab trusted in the Lord and was shown mercy (Josh 2:8–14; 6:17). Similarly, Ruth the Moabitess chose to identify herself with the people of God and was privileged to be included within the ancestral line of Messiah (Ruth 1:16–17; 4:13–22). While cursing a nation for its wickedness, God may yet leave the door open for repentance and blessing for those who turn to him. Thus, after portending judgment upon Moab and Ammon, Yahweh adds, "But in the latter days I will restore [their] fortunes" (Jer 48:47; 49:6). Commenting on this statement, Keil remarks, "This infliction of judgment, however, on the Moabites [and Ammonites], is not to prove a complete annihilation of them. At the end of the days, i.e., in the Messianic times . . . there is in store for them a turn in their fortunes, or a restoration." *Jeremiah, Lamentations*, 2:234.

the righteous servant whom God delivers from calamitous judgment in patriarchal history is hardly distinguishable from his morally depraved neighbors (19:8). Thus, Hamilton's thesis that "Genesis moves [the reader] progressively from generation (chs. 1–2), to degeneration (chs. 3–11), to regeneration (chs. 12–50)"[57] is at best superficial and does not reflect the exegetical data of the patriarchal narrative. The picture is complex. While shining examples of faith and piety appear in the patriarchal narrative (12:4–8; 14:22–24; 15:6; 22:1–14; etc.), as in the primeval narrative (4:4, 26; 5:22–24; 6:8–9), examples of shameful sin are not hard to find, even among the patriarchal family.

THE "FALL" OF ABRAM AND SARAI

As noted earlier, Abram retraced his steps from Egypt back to Canaan, showing signs of repentance and reformation. The attraction of material possessions does not seem to have the same hold on him (13:8–9; 14:22–24) as it did before (12:13). He also appears willing to place his life at risk in order to protect a relative (14:14–15), whereas in Egypt self-preservation appeared as his dominant motivation (12:12–13). And when God reassures him that he will have an heir and multitudinous descendents from his own loins (15:4–5), Abram responds with the same genuine faith that first prompted his trek to the Promised Land (15:5; cf. Rom 4:1–3, 18–22; Heb 11:8–9).

I Believe—Help My Unbelief!

It would be a mistake, however, to paint Abram's faith in too rosy a hue. The exercise of faith does not preclude lingering pockets of unbelief (Matt 28:17; Mark 9:24). Hence, after Abram rejects the tempting offer of material enrichment from Sodom's king, God appears to him in a vision and declares, "Fear not, I am your shield;[58] your reward shall be very

57. Hamilton, *Genesis 1–17*, 11.

58. The English phrase "your shield" translates the Hebrew מָגֵן לָךְ, which some versions render metaphorically as "protector" (VUL, DRA, NLT). Nevertheless, following Michel Dahood's comparative analysis of Hebrew and Ugaritic words ("Hebrew-Ugaritic Lexicography iv," 414; "Northwest Semitic Notes on Genesis," 78), some scholars have suggested emending māḡēn, "Shield," to māḡān, "Benefactor." See Hamilton, *Genesis 1–17*, 419. This reading seems to fit the context better. Abram has just declined the king of Sodom's offer to be the patriarch's benefactor and sworn fidelity to Yahweh as his supreme Suzerain, the one who is "Possessor of heaven and earth" (14:22–23). Moreover, God's subsequent promise, "your reward shall be very great," corresponds more to the

great" (15:1). The admonition against "fear" does not refer primarily to the dread induced by a vision of deity but to circumstances in Abram's life that were giving rise to anxiety. Abram identifies these circumstances as the lack of an heir (15:2–3) and an inheritance (15:8). God addresses the patriarch's fears by reiterating the promises of an offspring (15:4–5) and inheritance (15:7). While Abram responds in faith to this promise (15:6), his faith seems to demand more than a bare word. The appeal "Oh, Lord God, how am I to know I shall possess it?" (15:8) suggests that Abram's faith needed greater assurance. Accordingly, God condescends to his weakness and places himself under a self-maledictory oath (15:9–21; Heb 6:13–18). Thus, the accent of chapter 15 falls on God's faithfulness rather than on Abram's faith.[59]

Taking the Forbidden Fruit

Genesis 16 strikingly confirms that Abram's faith was yet immature. Subsequent to God's promise of an heir and inheritance,[60] Abram and Sarai are still faced with the nagging problem of Sarai's barren womb (16:1a). Sarai finally proposes a common-sense solution.[61] She offers

---

role of *benefactor* than of *protector*. Writes Kline, "The imagery of Genesis 15:1 is that of the Great King honoring Abraham's notable exhibition of compliance with covenant duty by the reward of a special grant that would more than make up for whatever enrichment he had foregone at the hands of the king of Sodom for the sake of faithfulness to Yahweh, his Lord." *Kingdom Prologue*, 324.

59. This observation is critical to a proper interpretation of Genesis 15:6. According to a traditional Protestant reading of the text, Abram's faith is passive or receptive in character and the focus is on *Yahweh's faithfulness*. Some modern evangelicals, however, are parting company with the Reformation tradition of *sola fide* and interpreting Abram's faith in the active sense as *faithfulness* or *conformity to the covenant*. Garlington, for examples, writes, "The point of Genesis 15:6, as taken up by Romans 4, is that Abraham was regarded as a righteous, that is, covenant keeping, person when he continued to place his trust in God's promise of a seed." Garlington then defines Abraham's faith as "fidelity to God" and equates his divinely reckoned "righteousness" as "conformity to the covenant relationship," that is, "faithful obedience." "Imputation or Union with Christ? A Response to John Piper," 49, 52. For a rebuttal and critique of Garlington's interpretation, see Piper, "A Response to Don Garlington on Imputation," 121–29; and Waldron, *Faith, Obedience, and Justification*, 185–223.

60. The opening clause is disjunctive, indicating a new narrative. That chapter 16 follows temporally is supported by the fact that Abram makes no mention of Ishmael as a potential heir in chapter 15.

61. Recall Lambdin's observation: "Behold, now [הִנֵּה־נָא]" indicate that the address they punctuate "is a logical consequence, either of an immediately preceding statement or of the general situation in which it is uttered." *Introduction to Biblical Hebrew*, 170.

Abram her Egyptian maidservant Hagar as a concubine, so that the couple might obtain a child through her (16:1b–2a). Abram acquiesces, takes Hagar "as a wife," and Hagar conceives (16:2b–4a). Unfortunately, the pregnancy does not bring the anticipated happiness Sarai had hoped for but rather contempt, jealousy, and strife, which in turn prompt Hagar to run away (16:4b–6). But at Yahweh's prompting, Hagar returns and bears Abram a son whom he names "Ishmael" (16:7–16).

Ancient Near Eastern societies placed a high premium on bearing children, particularly male progeny. Not surprisingly, the practice of a barren wife offering her husband a female servant to serve as surrogate mother was practiced and even legislated in the ancient Near East.[62] These facts have led some commentators to absolve one or both Abram and Sarai of any wrongdoing. Hamilton, for example, is "inclined to think that Sarai's action was obligatory, and that no ignominy was attached to such a procedure" because of "the indispensability of (male) progeny to perpetuate the family line."[63] Luther concedes that the couple gave in to temptation, but he quickly defends their motives.[64] The strongest defense of the couple's action comes from a rabbinical commentary on the text which equates Sarai's words, "Go in to my servant" (16:2), with "the voice of the Holy Spirit" to which Abram hearkened in obedience to the Lord.[65]

There are good reasons for questioning these attempts to minimize or deny sin on the part of Sarai and Abram. First, a common pattern in

---

Just as her husband, Abram, had logically deduced from the potentially life-threatening circumstances in Egypt the "necessity" for the wife-sister ruse, so Sarai now reasons from the circumstances of her chronic barrenness the "necessity" for a surrogate mother. Both parties lean more on common sense than on God's word.

62. *ANET*, 172; Speiser, "New Kirkuk Documents," 31–32; Gordon, "Biblical Customs," 3; Frymer-Kensky, 209–14.

63. Hamilton, *Genesis 1–17*, 445.

64. According to Luther, Abram is not motivated by lust but by the future prospect of worldwide redemption through the promised seed. The patriarch does not doubt that "a descendant would come from his own body," but he questions Sarai's fertility. Luther then insists that Sarai "does not abandon her faith; nor does she doubt the promise." Knowing that God loves her, "she willingly concedes the glory of fertility to her maid. Thus the virtue of this woman is extraordinary in every respect." *Lectures on Genesis*, 3:43–44.

65. "It was to the voice of the holy spirit, in line with the following verse, 'Now therefore hearken to the voice of the words of the Lord' (1 Sam 15:1)." Parashah 45:2 in *GR*, 2:147.

Genesis is that of divine testing following a divine blessing or promise of blessing. God tested Adam after blessing him (compare 2:16–17; 3:1–5 with 1:28; 2:8–9, 15).[66] God tested Abram with a famine after promising him an offspring and an inheritance (compare 12:9 with 12:1–3). God would later test the patriarch by asking him to sacrifice the very son of promise with which God had just blessed him (compare 22:1ff. with 21:1–7). These and other examples should lead the reader to look for a test following God's promise in chapter 15. The opening statement regarding Sarai's continued barrenness sets the stage for such a test.

Second, the narrator persistently underscores and emphasizes the legal relationship of Sarai and Abram in a way that almost seems superfluous. Moses does not merely indicate that Sarai took Hagar and gave her to Abram as wife; he makes the point to say, "Sarai, *Abram's wife*, took Hagar . . . and she gave her to Abram *her husband* as wife" [emphasis added] (16:3). Indeed, the narrator not only underscores the existing legal relationship between Abram and Sarai, but he also highlights a new legal relationship that is forged. Abram does not merely have sexual relations with Hagar, but she actually becomes his "wife" (16:3b). Of course, in one sense the formalization of this relationship makes it less detestable since it technically removes Abram's act from the realm of adultery. Nevertheless, if the reader takes seriously the monogamous pattern already established at creation (Gen 2:23–24) and carefully notes the negative implications and consequences that result from polygamous relationships as reflected in the Genesis narrative (Gen 16:4–6; 29:30–31; 30:15), then he will interpret the introduction of a second wife as outside the scope of God's original "good" intention for humanity and as a recipe for trouble.[67]

Third, the narrator underscores the fact that Hagar was the *Egyptian* slave who belonged to Sarai (16:1, 3). That Hagar was from Egypt would

66. After commissioning Adam to be fruitful and subdue the earth, God tests Adam's loyalty by introducing a prohibition against taking from the tree of the knowledge of good and evil (Gen 2:16–17). Theologians have correctly viewed this as a kind of "probation" (i.e., test), though they have sometimes disagreed as to the exact nature of this probation. The reader should view the Serpent's temptation that follows not merely in terms of a satanic enticement to evil but as a divinely imposed ordeal to test Adam and Eve's loyalty. Divine testing is always the opposite side of temptation's coin (see Job 1, 2; Matt 4:1–11; Mark 1:12–13; Luke 4:1–13; 2 Cor 10:7–9; 1 Pet 5:6–11).

67. The introduction of a concubinal and bigamous relationship into a formerly monogamous marriage resulted in hatred and strife (16:4–6), which are commonly portrayed in Genesis as the fruits of sin (Gen 4:2–10, 17; 6:5–8; 27, etc.).

have likely provoked a degree of detestation in the mind of the original Israelite reader. How could the father of the Israelite nation stoop so low as to marry a woman from among those outside the covenant! Furthermore, the fact that she was an Egyptian servant-girl may suggest that she was part of the spoil Abram gleaned from his sinful ruse in Egypt several years earlier (12:16). Hence, Abram's earlier sin will come back to haunt him, and the chosen family will have to reap something of what they have sown.

Fourth, the narrator may intend the parenthetical time referent, "after they had dwelt in the land of Canaan ten years," to help the reader to place this event along the patriarchal timeline. On the other hand, Moses may have inserted this phrase to suggest that Sarai (and Abram) had reached the end of their patience—the number ten indicating "completeness"[68]—and thus they decided to take matters into their own hands. If this is the author's purpose, then he may be comparing the patriarchal couple to the primeval couple. In both cases, the humans refused to be content with God's time-clock and took matters into their own hands. Since patience is essential to genuine faith in God's word, the lack of patience is a sure sign that faith is either absent or immature.

Fifth, the parallel between the action of the patriarchal couple and the sin of the primeval couple is evident in the language chosen by the narrator to depict Sarai and Abram's deed. Sarai "took" (וַתִּקַּח) Hagar, like Eve "took" (וַתִּקַּח) the fruit of the forbidden tree, and she "gave" (וַתִּתֵּן) Hagar to Abram, as Eve "gave" (וַתִּתֵּן) the fruit to Adam (compare 3:6 with 16:3). Furthermore, as Adam "listened to the voice of [his] wife [שָׁמַעְתָּ לְקוֹל אִשְׁתֶּךָ]" (3:17), so Abram "listened to the voice of Sarah [וַיִּשְׁמַע אַבְרָם לְקוֹל שָׂרָי]" (16:2). These linguistic parallels have led Werner Berg to the conclusion that "Gen 16, 1–6 ist tatsächlich die Erzählung von einem Sündenfall."[69]

Sixth, Sarai and Abram experience a degree of alienation from each other prompted by the guilt of their sin and as a result engage in a degree of blame-shifting (16:5–6), which is reminiscent of Adam and Eve's

68. One may recall the ten words of creative fiat (Gen 1:3, 6, 9, 11, 14, 20, 24, 26, 28, 29), the ten commandments (Exod 20:3–17), the ten plagues upon Egypt (Exod 7–11), the ten times Laban changed Jacob's wages (Gen 31:7, 41), the ten times God tested Israel in the wilderness (Num 14:22), and many other examples of "ten" in Scripture (1 Sam 1:8; Neh 4:12; Job 19:3; Eccl 7:19; Rev 2:10).

69. Translation: "Gen 16:1–6 is actually the story of a Fall." Berg, "Der Sündenfall Abrahams und Saras nach Gen 16, 1–6," 8. See also Sailhamer, "Genesis," 134.

alienation and attempts to shift responsibility in the Garden (3:12–13).[70] Sarai's appeal to Yahweh to act as advocate between her and her husband suggests that a moral offense has been committed. Of course, one might deduce from Sarai's appeal that the wrong committed (at least in her eyes) is nothing more than Hagar's unfair treatment of her and (perhaps) Abram's hesitancy to punish Hagar. It is possible, however, that the narrator wants the reader to see more here. Technically, Sarah calls on the Lord to render a judicial decision between her and Abram, assuming she is in the right.[71] Yet ironically, Sarai's appeal may actually serve to condemn both parties, just as both parties were found guilty in the Garden (Gen 3:16–19).

Seventh, the sinfulness of this action is also indicated by the fact that the welfare of the "seed," which is alive in Hagar's womb, is not a concern in their deliberations regarding what to do with Hagar. The verb translated "mistreat" (וַתְּעַנֶּהָ) is in the Piel and commonly refers to physical violence or oppression. Hence, Sarai does not seem to be concerned about the possibility of bringing harm to the unborn child through afflicting the mother. Moreover, by allowing his wife to do to Hagar "whatever seems good in [Sarai's] eyes," Abram appears to manifest a diminished concern for the offspring Hagar bears. The hasty and inconsiderate actions of both Abram and Sarai towards Hagar evidence a guilty conscience and serve as self-indictments that their attempt to realize God's promise through a concubine was a mistake.

Eighth, when Yahweh finally steps in as Advocate, he acts primarily on behalf of Hagar, not on behalf of Abram and Sarai (16:7–14). God's sympathy for Hagar serves as a further indictment on the patriarchal couple. This does not imply that Hagar was justified in showing contempt to her mistress. It simply indicates that she herself was not the ultimate cause of the problem and that her role in this incident is primarily that of victim, not perpetrator.[72]

Ninth, after Ishmael, the child of Sarai and Abram's own engineering, is born (16:15–16), God makes it clear to Abram (now Abraham) that Ishmael is not the promised seed and insists that the seed will come through Sarah (17:15–21). That God's rejection of Ishmael sequentially

70. Berg, "Der Sündenfall Abrahams und Saras nach Gen 16, 1–6," 11–12.

71. Her plea, יִשְׁפֹּט יְהוָה בֵּינִי וּבֵינֶיךָ employs language used elsewhere when a plaintiff invokes Yahweh to settle a legal dispute (Judg 11:27; 1 Sam 24:12, 15).

72. Gordon, "Hagar: A Throw-Away Character Among the Matriarchs?" 271–77.

follows Ishmael's birth serves as an indication that he has rejected Sarai and Abram's attempt to advance the promise. Hence, Sarai and Abram's scheme, like Eve and Adam's fig leaves (3:7), will not do. God himself must bring about redemption in his own way and timing.

In light of the foregoing evidence, Genesis 16 highlights a major lapse in Abram and Sarai's faith. Moreover, the narrator describes their sin in language reminiscent of Adam and Eve's apostasy from the Lord. This fact provides another reason for seeing a continuation of the spread of sin motif in the patriarchal narratives. The echo of that first transgression can be heard not only as far as Babel but continues to reverberate in the patriarchal narratives.

OLD SINS DIE HARD

Approximately fourteen years after Abram and Sarai's lapse, God renews his pledge of an offspring and an inheritance, institutes circumcision as a covenant sign, and changes the patriarchal couple's names to emphasize the certainty and magnitude of his promised blessing (17:1–21). After a brief time, the Lord reappears as the Angel of Yahweh with two angelic escorts and guarantees that Sarah will give birth to a child within a year (18:1–10). Despite these divinely appointed tokens of assurance, Abraham and Sarah still vacillate between faith and doubt, particularly in light of their advanced age and the seeming impossibility of conception (17:17–18; 18:11–13).[73]

73. Abraham and Sarah's struggle with unbelief is reflected in their response of "laughter" to the divine promise. Some commentators have attempted to interpret Abraham's laughter in terms of overwhelming joy at the good news of a son, even linking the event with Jesus's assertion, "Abraham rejoiced that he would see my day. He saw it and was glad" (John 8:56). The exegetical data, however, does not support such an interpretation. First, Abraham's laughter is followed by an expression of incredulity, "Shall Sarah, who is ninety years old, bear a child?" (17:17b). Second, he requests an alternative to God's plan, "Oh, that Ishmael might live before you!" (17:18), suggesting that he views God's promise as unrealistic and frankly impossible, at least from a human standpoint. Third, Abraham's laughter is paralleled later by Sarah's (18:12), which in turn is censured by Yahweh's rebuke, "Is anything too hard for the Lord?" (18:13–14). That Sarah tries to deny her laughter proves that she felt the guilt of a sinful response (18:15a). Hence, the patriarchal couple's laughter must not be construed in terms of *believing joy* but rather *incredulous surprise*. God's assigning the name "Isaac" (יִצְחָק; "he laughs") to the promised offspring serves as a constant reminder to the couple of their initial stumbling at the promise. Thankfully, neither Abraham nor Sarah allowed their initial doubt to harden into a fixed cynical unbelief. The fact that Abraham followed through with the commanded rite of circumcision (17:22–27; Rom 4:19–21) demonstrates that he was

Déjà Vu

Abraham's remaining doubts about the certainty of the promise become evident when he migrates from Hebron to Gerar (Gen 20:1).[74] As the narrative of chapter 20 unfolds, the reader experiences déjà vu when he finds Abraham resurrecting the wife-sister ruse he employed twenty-five years earlier in Egypt. The patriarch unhesitatingly identifies Sarah as his sister (20:2a), thereby making her available to become another man's wife. Abimelech, king of Gerar, takes advantage of the opportunity and, like Pharaoh before, unwittingly gets more than he bargained for (20:2b). Sarah's beauty is not said to be the cause or motivation for Abimelech's action.[75] In this case, the motivation was probably political.[76] It is not clear whether Abimelech gave Abraham a dowry gift prior to obtaining Sarah. The subsequent narrative, however, indicates that Abraham comes away, once again, financially well off as a result of this ploy (20:16).

Abram's Ruse Censured (Again!)

How should the reader assess this second ruse? One might attempt to argue, as in the case of Abraham's earlier ploy in Egypt, that the patriarch was ultimately trying to protect his wife by employing a legitimate form

---

willing to take God at his word though the promise seemed incredible. Sarah also overcame her initial doubts and trusted the promise (Heb 11:11).

74. The move does not appear to have been prompted by a famine as Abraham's earlier detour to Egypt and Isaac's later sojourn in Gerar were prompted (12:10; 26:1). More likely, Abraham was so saddened by the distant sight of Sodom's destruction (19:27–28) and perhaps the uncertain outcome of his nephew Lot that he felt compelled to move further away from that area.

75. Prior narrative indications make her about ninety years old at this time (17:17) and in her own words, "worn out" (18:11–13).

76. As Walton observes, "Rulers did not see marriage as a means of fulfilling their lust for a woman (though that may occasionally be the case), but often as a means of fulfilling their lust for power. Their harems were filled with those whom they had married to cement political alliances." *Genesis*, 397. Similarly, Baldwin remarks, "Abraham intended to stay there only a short time, but his status as a tribal leader, with a large household, flocks and herds, meant that he did not go unnoticed. Moreover his reputation as a military leader had gone ahead of him, and in the world of his day he may well have had princely status. Such families entered into solemn agreements promising mutual support, and often cemented such treaties by intermarriage. But Abraham was at a disadvantage in this respect, having no daughters." *Message of Genesis 12–50*, 82. See also the extrabiblical examples advanced by Hoffmeier in "Wives' Tales of Genesis 12, 20 & 26 and the Covenants at Beer-Sheba," 81–99.

of "half-truth" telling.[77] Or one might argue that the references to God's judgment on the king's household and threat against his life (20:3, 6–7, 17–18) together with the patriarch's defense (20:11–13) and his divine commission to pray for the pagan king (20:7, 17) combine to exonerate Abraham from any wrongdoing. There are, however, several indications in the text that prevent the reader from letting the patriarch "off the hook" that easily.

First, had the protection of Sarah been chief in Abraham's mind, he would have avoided a scheme that had previously proven unsuccessful. Or, once the ruse proved unsuccessful in Gerar, Abraham would have refused Abimelech's request to add Sarah to his royal harem. The reader should recall that by this time Abraham had successfully defeated and rescued his nephew Lot from *four* Mesopotamian armies (14:33–16)! Abimelech's subsequent desire to make a covenant with Abraham (21:22–34) suggests that the patriarch still possessed a contingency of capable fighting men at his disposal. Abraham, however, neither calls on his fighting men to rescue Sarah (as he did for Lot) from the king of Gerar nor calls on the Lord for deliverance. Instead, the narrative portrays him has a passive bystander.

Second, the narrator portrays Abimelech in a role similar to that of Abraham in chapter 18, where the latter is interceding on behalf of Sodom and Gomorrah. In that chapter, Abraham reminds God that as the "Judge of all the earth," he must do what is right, namely, he must not destroy the righteous (18:23–25). Abimelech's plaintiff prayer is analogous: "Lord, will you kill an innocent people?" (20:4).[78] It seems likely that

77. Consistent with his interpretation of Abraham's earlier ploy, Jordan writes, "Abraham knew that there was no real fear of God in the land of Philistia (Gen 20:11), and Abimelech's actions proved it. In order to protect themselves when they went into a pagan land, Abraham and Sarah would point to their brother-sister relationship rather than their husband-wife relationship (Gen 20:2, 12). This was because in the ancient cultures the brother was the sister's especial protector, and no one would have laid a hand on Sarah without seeking Abraham's permission. That Abimelech seized Sarah showed that he did not respect either God or custom." *Primeval Saints*, 69. But the narrator does indicate that "the fear of God" was in that place—at least to a greater degree than Abraham assumed (20:8). Moreover, there is no hint in the text that Abraham was trying to hinder another man from taking Sarah as wife. On the contrary, Abraham's action opened the door for Abimelech's action, just as it had done for Pharaoh before. Consequently, it seems preferable to read this account in light of Abraham's earlier ruse. Once again, he himself fell prey to the fear of man (20:11) and resurrected the very same ploy which had proven so "successful" before.

78. Notes Wenham, "God had been prepared to spare a whole town for the sake of just ten righteous (18:31) people in her. Should he now kill one righteous man, who rep-

Moses intends to highlight Abraham's inconsistency here. In Genesis 18, Abraham stood on high moral ground. But here in Genesis 20, Abraham is really the one who deserves divine judgment with Abimelech, the pagan, being portrayed as relatively morally superior.

Third, Abimelech defends himself by appealing to "the integrity of [his] heart" or purity of motive (1 Kgs 9:4; Pss 78:72; 101:2; cf. Job 1:1, 8; 2:3), and "the innocence of [his] hands" or outward action that is above reproach (Ps 26:6; 73:13; cf. Hos 8:5). God accepts Abimelech's defense as valid (20:5) though he takes credit for preventing the adulterous affair from happening[79] and demands that the king restore Sarah to her legal husband (20:6–7). Abimelech could have returned Sarah privately and avoided public embarrassment. But as Hamilton notes, "His willingness to be open and tell the truth contrasts with Abraham and his subterfuge."[80] One should also note the promptness of Abimelech's obedience (20:8). Moreover, the narrator reveals that Abraham's guiding assumption, namely, that there was "no fear of God in this place" (20:11), was unfounded. Abimelech and his servants had more conscience and sense of moral decency than Abraham had anticipated.[81] Moses's point is not to elevate the morality of pagan culture but to highlight the lack of morality even among God's chosen.

Fourth, Abimelech, like Pharaoh before him, files a juridical complaint against the patriarch and accuses him of a moral transgression

---

resents a nation? Given our knowledge of God's attitude declared in chap. 18, Abimelek's prayer seems guaranteed to succeed." *Genesis 16–50*, 71.

79. How did God providentially prevent the king from initiating a conjugal relationship with Sarah? Mathews offers a plausible suggestion when he conjectures that God smote Abimelech with some kind of plague that hindered him from having intercourse with Sarah or with his wife and other concubines. *Genesis 11:27—50:26*, 252.

80 Hamilton, *Genesis 18–50*, 67.

81. There is irony in this passage. Abraham engages in a bit of deception because he "fears" that there is not sufficient "fear of God" in the land to keep him and Sarah safe. In fact, it is Abraham who does not sufficiently "fear God" to keep Sarah protected. Thus the narrator very subtly highlights the patriarch's ongoing weakness and his need for further testing. Such testing will come in chapters 21 and 22, when Abraham will have to send away and sacrifice his two sons, motivated by the "fear of God." Note also the similarity between Abraham's unfair and inaccurate assessment of the people of Gerar and Jonah's assessment of the pagan sailors and the people of Nineveh (Jonah 1:10; 3:5–9). Just as Jonah was wrong about the Ninevites, so Abraham was wrong about the Gerarites, since, as it turns out, they really did fear God (20:8).

(20:9).[82] But Abraham's defense is lame. His appeal to an assumed[83] absence of the fear of God has been invalidated (20:11). The men of Gerar seemed to possess more fear of God than did God's own prophet (20:8)! Abraham's claim that Sarah was his half-sister (20:12) might be true, though neither the narrator nor God confirms his claim.[84] The primeval narrative, however, indicates that the husband-wife relationship is to take priority over familial blood-tie relationships (Gen 2:23–24). Certainly, a consanguineous relationship cannot annul a marital covenant in which the husband has vowed to protect and cherish his wife (Eph 5:25–28; 1 Pet 3:7). Since Abraham's motive for highlighting Sarah's sibling relationship to him was for his protection rather than hers, he cannot be excused. Perhaps sensing the weakness of his defense, Abraham adds some background information to solicit sympathy from the pagan king. His ruse was necessitated by the fact that "God [had] caused [him] to wander from [his] father's house" (20:13). The verb translated "caused to wander" (הִתְעוּ) is a Hiphil causative and sometimes connotes an aimless wandering without purpose or guidance (Gen 21:14; 37:15). Hence, this statement may be a subtle case of blame-shifting, i.e., "God is the one who placed me into this dilemma," which is comparable to Adam's blame-shifting in the Garden (Gen 3:12). Even more troubling is Abraham's use of the plural verb with the nominal אֱלֹהִים, which normally calls for a *numeric plural* meaning, "gods," rather than the *honorific plural*, "God." If

82. Once again we have the rhetorical question that usually functions in Genesis as a judicial accusation: "What have you done to us?" meaning "You have done wrong to us" (see Gen 3:13; 4:10; 12:18; 26:10; 29:25; 31:26; 44:15). This is followed with plainer language: "You have done to me things that ought not to be done." For a fuller discussion of this juridical terminology, see Bruckner, *Implied Law in the Abraham Narrative*, 76–198.

83. Some scholars suggest the passage be emended to read something like "I observed worthlessness [emending רַק to רֵיק], namely, there was no fear of God in this place." Thus, it would be a statement of fact rather than a mere supposition. Dahood, "Abraham's Reply in Genesis 20,11," 90–91. The narrative, however, discounts any empirical evidence that would support such an "observation." Hence, Dahood's proposed emendation, like Abraham's assumption, is groundless.

84. When Moses introduces Terah's family, he identifies three sons born to Terah: Abram, Nahor, and Haran (11:27). The last of these died in Ur (11:28). Later, the two remaining brothers marry. Abram married Sarai; Nahor married "Milcah, the daughter of Haran" (11:29). Apparently, Nahor married his niece. If this is true, then Abraham's claim would seem plausible since intermarriage within certain bounds of consanguinity took place within his family. Nevertheless, it is noteworthy that the narrator himself does not link Sarai to Terah's family line, as he does Milcah.

this is Abraham's intent, then he is guilty not only of blame-shifting but also of religious compromise, adopting the polytheistic worldview of the Philistine king as an attempt to cloak his exclusive (and possibly offensive) monotheism.[85] Whether or not Abraham was actually attempting to shift the blame on deity and minimize religious differences by adopting polytheistic language, one thing is certain—neither the narrator nor God nor Abimelech takes Abraham's claim seriously.[86]

In conclusion, Abraham's use of the wife-sister ruse again only aggravates his blameworthiness[87] and serves to highlight both the reality as well as the tenacity of remaining sin in the heart of a believer. Despite the fact that Abraham had aligned himself with Yahweh and committed himself to a life of faith, he was at times ensnared by remaining sin (Heb 12:1). Indeed, his failure illustrates the lamentable truth that certain sins do not easily go away, and the true believer may "once more strike his foot against the same stone."[88] Sin has not only spread to *all* mankind but

85. Kidner observes, "The confession is marred by an attempt to shift the blame, Adam-like, in 13, which reads literally '. . . when (the) gods caused me to wander . . .' It is the language and very wry attitude of the pagan; one man of the world might be speaking to another." 138–39. Mathews also comments, "Abimelech's polytheism may explain why the patriarch uses the plural verb 'wander' (hitʾû) with God (*Elohim*) rather than the customary singular. If this is not a simple grammatical accommodation, Abraham reaches an all-time religious low by granting such a concession to the pagan king." *Genesis 11:27—50:26*, 257–58. Duguid remarks, "Abraham made his divine call to go to the Promised Land sound like nothing more than the aimless wandering of a refugee. Instead of witnessing to Abimelech about God's enduring faithfulness to him over the past twenty-five years, he talked like one pagan to another. Instead of speaking of God's goodness to him, in spite of his own failures, he talked as if his future lay in the hands of blind Fate." *Promise and Reality*, 115. On the other hand, the plural verb may be an anomaly (see Gen 35:7).

86. The narrator repeatedly refers to Sarah as Abraham's "wife" (20:2, 14, 18). God himself views Sarah's relationship to Abraham primarily as "wife" (20:3, 7). Abimelech's prompt restoration of Sarah to Abraham indicates that he assumed the divine viewpoint. The king's later allusion to Abraham as Sarah's "brother" (20:16) should be understood sarcastically and rendered in quotation marks (see NET). Even Abraham cannot avoid referring to Sarah as his "wife" in his confession (20:11, 12).

87. As Simeon remarks, "The repetition of so heinous a crime, after such a warning and such a deliverance [Pharaoh's rebuke and God's deliverance], increased its malignity an hundred-fold." *Expository Outlines on the Whole Bible*, 1:165.

88. Calvin, *Genesis*, 1:521. Likewise Henry remarks, "Note, It is possible that a good man may, not only fall into sin, but relapse into the same sin, through the surprise and strength of temptation and infirmity of the flesh." *Commentary on the Whole Bible*, 1:128. Thomas makes a similar observation: "The continuance and power of the evil nature in believers are among the most patent and potent facts of universal spiritual

it has become so deeply entrenched that even the righteous cannot easily escape its grip.[89] Indeed, the next chapter will demonstrate not only that a general tendency towards sin is passed on from parent to child but also that specific character flaws can be reproduced in the offspring.

experience. That the 'infection doth remain in the regenerate' is as certain as it is sad and serious." *Genesis*, 178.

89. Of course, the portrayal of Abraham is not entirely negative. After Abraham's relapse in Gerar, he not only shows signs of spiritual recovery, but he also evidences amazing spiritual maturity when he willingly "sacrifices" first Ishmael (21:8–14) then Isaac (Gen 22:1–10) in obedient response to God's command. These acts of obedience to the divine command demonstrate the reality of Abraham's faith and prompt God's high commendation of the patriarch (22:12, 15–20; 26:5). But these high points in the patriarch's spiritual walk do not necessarily imply that he had broken completely free from the power of sin. In fact, the reader is introduced to Abraham's other concubine-wife, Keturah, at the close of his life (25:1–11). It is likely that Abraham married Keturah after his union with Hagar and after God's promise of Isaac's birth in chapter 17 since he never suggests her sons as alternatives to Ishmael or Isaac. But the fact Keturah is also identified as one of Abraham's "concubines" (25:6) suggests that Abraham married Keturah while Sarah was still alive, in which case the verb should be translated as pluperfect—"Now Abraham *had married* another a wife whose name was Keturah" (25:1). Isaac's identification as Abraham's "only son" in chapter 22, which can mean a *special* child (Prov 4:3) but more often means a *lone* child (Judg 11:34; Jer 6:26; Amos 8:10; Zech 12:10), may further suggest that Abraham married and fathered sons through Keturah sometime *after* Isaac's birth but *before* Sarah's death. If this is so, then the patriarch may have continued to struggle with doubts about the fulfillment of God's promise that he would become "the father of a multitude of nations." Having just learned that his brother Nahor had obtained a total of twelve children through polygamy (Gen 22:20–24), Abraham may have decided once again to "lend God a hand" by taking another concubine (in addition to Hagar, who was now gone) that he might obtain more sons. That nations came from Abraham through Keturah does not serve as God's endorsement of the union. It only serves, once again, to highlight God's determination to bless his chosen people *despite their sin and lack of faith.*

5

The Spread of Sin in the Second Generation of Patriarchs

In spite of their many sins and failures, Abraham and Sarah persevere in faith till the end of their lives (23:1–20; 25:7–8; 2; Heb 11:13–16). At this point, the analysis shifts from the sins of the first generation to focus on the sins of the second generation of the patriarchal community (Ishmael, Isaac, and Rebekah), where the traits of the fathers are replicated in the children, sometimes with more tragic results.

ISHMAEL'S MOCKING UNBELIEF

Despite Abraham's relapse in Gerar, God kept his word and blessed the patriarchal couple with the long-awaited son of promise (21:1–2). In keeping with God's earlier directive (17:19), Abraham named the child Isaac (יִצְחָק) meaning "he laughs" (21:3). This name would serve not only to mark the child as a source of the couple's joy (21:6) but also to remind them of their former incredulity (17:17–18; 18:12–15). Abraham and Sarah had laughed in disbelief at the prospect of a "promise-child" in their old age (17:17; 18:12–17). Regrettably, their failure to take God's promise seriously would find intensified expression in the mocking laughter of Abraham's firstborn son. Ishmael's contempt for the promised child was first openly expressed at the celebration held on the day of Isaac's weaning (21:8).[1] On this festive occasion, "Sarah saw the son of Hagar the Egyptian, whom she had borne to Abraham, laughing" (21:9), and as a result Sarah demanded that Abraham banish Hagar and Ishmael from the chosen family (21:10). Abraham is displeased with Sarah's demand (21:11), and the reader is initially tempted to share Abraham's feelings

1. Most commentators estimate the age of weaning to be around three years old. That would make Ishmael about seventeen years old by this time.

until he finds God siding with Sarah and commanding the patriarch to do his wife's bidding (21:12–13).[2]

A proper understanding of this incident centers on the nature of Ishmael's "laughter" (21:9). The Hebrew participle מְצַחֵק, translated by the English Standard Version as "laughing," is related etymologically to Isaac's name and to the joyful laughter of which Sarah speaks earlier in the passage (21:6). In light of this, some interpreters think that Ishmael was innocently playing with Isaac and that Sarah became sinfully jealous. According to Skinner, "It is the spectacle of the two young children playing together, innocent of social distinctions, that excites Sarah's maternal jealousy and prompts her cruel demand."[3] But Sarah's strong reaction (21:10) and God's endorsement of her call for banishment (21:12) suggest a negative understanding of the word. That the verb in its Piel form sometimes carries sexual connotations (26:8; 39:14, 17) has led Jonathan Kirsh to the conclusion that Ishmael was sexually abusing his little brother.[4] But the Piel form may also be used in the

2. Ironically, Abraham listened to Sarah's voice in taking Hagar when God did not want him to follow her scheme (16:2). Now Abraham does not want to listen to her request to banish Hagar and Ishmael when God in fact does want him to do as she says.

3. Skinner, *Genesis*, 322. See also Speiser, *Genesis*, 155; von Rad, *Genesis*, 232; Westermann, *Genesis 12–36*, 339. Most of these interpreters appeal to the LXX, which adds the phrase "with Isaac her son [μετὰ Ισαακ τοῦ υἱοῦ αὐτῆς]." Visotzky also interprets Ishmael's actions as innocent but attempts to import several senses of the word into this single context: "It is Ishmael, not Sarah, who spends hours playing (*metzaheq*) with him. It is Ishmael who laughs (*metzaheq*) with him and can get him to laugh. It is Ishmael who hugs and fondles (*metzaheq*) baby Isaac (*yitzhaq*). Yet the feelings Sarah's dour presence engender [*sic*] are no laughing matter. Ishmael worries that Sarah will go back to hitting them—Hagar, himself, and now his baby Isaac, too." *The Genesis of Ethics*, 89. It is highly doubtful that Moses intended to convey as much semantic range in the word as Visotzky seems to find. Donald Carson identifies this linguistic fallacy as an "unwarranted adoption of an expanded semantic field." See *Exegetical Fallacies*, 62.

4. After reviewing the traditional interpretations of the text, Kirsh asserts, "What the translators are reluctant to let us know is that another meaning of ṯ'sahaḵ is 'fondle' and that the original Hebrew text of the Bible may indicate that what Sarah actually saw was some sort of sex play between Ishmael and his little brother." "What Did Sarah See?" 108. Kirsh reasons, "Unless we regard Sarah as so jealous of her son's birthright that she would literally kill for him—or as an out-and-out paranoid, as one Bible scholar has suggested—then we must look for a more plausible explanation for her punishing rage than the mockery of a younger sibling by his older brother. . . . Ishmael is taking liberty with his little brother that his stepmother finds too shocking to tolerate." "What Did Sarah See?" 110.

sense of foolish jesting or mockery (19:14; 39:14, 17).[5] In favor of this meaning is Paul's allusion to this text in Galatians 4:29, where he says, "He who was born according to the flesh [Ishmael] persecuted him who was born according to the Spirit [Isaac]." The Greek word translated "persecuted" (ἐδίωκεν) does not carry sexual connotations, but it does include the idea of mockery or contempt. Moreover, Sarah's reaction to Ishmael to some degree parallels her earlier reaction to Hagar when the latter "looked with contempt upon her mistress" (16:4b), suggesting that Hagar and Ishmael's deeds can be viewed as somewhat analogous. Ronning has suggested that Ishmael's mocking of Isaac may have taken the form of accusing the child of being born of Abimelech rather than of Abraham, denying his legitimacy as heir to the promise.[6] Whether the accusation took this form is uncertain. But it does appear that the narrator intends to contrast Sarah's call for celebrative laughter (21:6) with Ishmael's display of contemptuous laughter (21:9).[7] Paul's use of this text to contrast the responses of faith in the promise and opposition to the promise implies that Ishmael's "laughing" should be understood

5. In Genesis 19:14, Lot's son-in-laws interpret his warnings to flee the city as "jesting," which the LXX appropriately translates with γελοιάζειν. The LXX translators interpret Potiphar's wife to be accusing Joseph of *mockery* when they employ the Greek ἐμπαίζειν to translate the Hebrew (39:14, 17).

6. Ronning, "The Curse on the Serpent (Genesis 3:15) in Biblical Theology and Hermeneutics," 188.

7. Sarah exclaims, "God has made laughter for me [צְחֹק עָשָׂה לִי אֱלֹהִים]; everyone who hears will laugh over me [כָּל־הַשֹּׁמֵעַ יִצְחַק־לִי]." Steinmetz argues that we should interpret the laughter to which Sarah refers in parallel to Ishmael's laughter later in the chapter, which Sarah condemns. Writes Steinmetz, "That Ishmael's laughter be seen as a mocking of Isaac and his special status as Sarah's son is suggested also by Sarah's expectation that all who 'hear' (hashomeʾa) will laugh (21:6). While many translations suggest that the laughter will be joyous—'will laugh with me'—laughter until this point has been mocking or disbelieving. Ishmael, whose name includes the word 'to hear,' is the one who now laughs, and it seems reasonable to conclude that, like Hagar and as Sarah anticipates, he laughs at Sarah and Isaac." *From Father to Son*, 169–70, n. 34. If this is the case, then Sarah is expressing *anxiety* rather than *joy*. It seems preferable, however, to follow most translations and interpreters in understanding Sarah's reference to laughter in a positive sense, though Steinmetz's interpretation of Ishmael's mocking laughter is correct and may hint at a double entendre. Sarah is overjoyed at the birth of Isaac. The birth of this child, which once occasioned *disbelieving laughter*, now occasions *believing joy*. Sarah expects that "everyone who hears will laugh [with joy]" over her. Yet, her hope is frustrated when Ishmael turns the laughter of celebration (21:8) into the laughter of mockery (21:9). Hence, Sarah's prediction comes true but not in the way she intended.

as a rejection of Isaac's role in God's redemptive plan.[8] Sadly, what began as the laughter of incredulity in the parents (17:17; 18:12–17) became the laughter of scornful unbelief in the son (21:9). As God's rejection of Cain led the latter to nurse malice against his brother (4:5b–8), so God's rejection of Ishmael as the promised seed led Hagar's son to despise his brother (21:9).[9] The divinely endorsed banishment of Hagar and Ishmael may have prevented Isaac's fate from becoming that of Abel.[10] Yet the enmity that was sown in the Garden of Eden is bearing its fruit not only in primeval history but in patriarchal history as well.

LIKE FATHER, LIKE SON

Aside from the allusion to Isaac at his birth and the weaning party, Moses's initial descriptions of Isaac are generally positive.[11] He appears to have picked up all his father's good traits and avoided his negative ones.[12] But

8. As Ross notes, "In Genesis 21, then, the 'laughter' [v. 6] was the response of faith to the promise of God, but the 'mockery' [v. 9] signified the response of unbelief in God's plan that Isaac should be heir. The story illustrates the truth that faith and unbelief are incompatible. That which trifles with God's work must be removed so that the faith can prosper under God's blessing." *Creation & Blessing*, 380. See also Aalders, *Genesis*, 2:36.

9. Ishmael's violent character was predicted by the angel of Yahweh: "He shall be a wild donkey of a man [i.e., untamable]/his hand shall be against everyone /and everyone's hand shall be against him/and he shall dwell over against all his kinsmen" (16:12). Some English translations follow the LXX and translate the last clause, "And he shall dwell in the presence of all his brethren" (KJV, NKJ). But the Hebrew עַל-פְּנֵי may also mean that he will dwell "opposite" his brothers (VUL, ESV). Since the first half of the verse portrays him as a hostile man and in light of the fact that he actually dwelt south of Palestine between Havilah and Shur, the translation "opposite" or "over against" makes better sense. The point may be that Ishmael chose to have nothing to do with his kinsmen because of his hostility towards them. See also Genesis 25:18b.

10. Ryken depicts Abraham's banishment of Hagar and Ishmael at Sarah's insistence as a case of expediency rather than faith. *Words of Delight*, 69. In this case, however, Abraham is acting in faith and obedience, as he will when Yahweh commands him to sacrifice Isaac (Gen 22:1–2).

11. Isaac is initially portrayed as a submissive son (22:6–10), a contemplative man (24:63), a prayerful husband (25:21), and a believing heir of the promise (26:1–6).

12. The narrator does hint at potential weakness in Isaac when he notes that Isaac preferred the firstborn Esau above Jacob on the basis of Isaac's appetite for wild game (25:28). But the tragic ramifications of Isaac's preference for Esau are not fully revealed until later in the narrative (27:1ff.). For now, Isaac appears to have made a better start than Abraham. As Duguid remarks, "It looks as if the moral of the story would be that the children have learned their lesson from the sins of their father. But immediately after he had received from the Lord a renewal of the covenant made with this father and imitated his father's faith in the covenant-keeping God, Isaac proceeded to imitate also

the reader's hopes in Isaac are dashed when the latter repeats the same "wife-sister" ruse in Gerar that his father had employed over sixty years earlier in the same territory (20:1ff.) and over eighty-five years earlier in Egypt (12:9ff.).[13] Based on the assumption that the Gerarites would murder him on account of Rebekah "because she was attractive in appearance," Isaac informs them, "She is my sister" (26:7). In this case, the pagan king does not attempt to take Rebekah as wife, but he does catch Isaac and Rebekah engaging in behavior that discloses their spousal relationship (26:8).[14] In moral outrage, Abimelech summons Isaac, demands

---

his father's propensity for fudging." *Relentless Grace*, 18. Ronning also notes the initial promise and disappointing turn in Isaac's life: "Isaac is modeled after his father, and thus, as the new Adam. He receives the promises of Abraham (Gen 26:3–4; 24), and he calls on the name of the Lord (Gen 26:25). In one respect he acts better than Abraham; when Rebekah is barren for 20 years, his only response is prayer, rather than adoption of the 'Hagar solution' (Gen 25:21). He thus avoids the 'fall' of Abraham described in Genesis 16. But if all the attention paid to this special child before his birth creates an expectation that he would exceed his father in holiness and righteousness, this expectation is not fulfilled." "Curse on the Serpent (Genesis 3:15) in Biblical Theology and Hermeneutics," 198.

13. Mathews notes at least three ways in which the narrator underscores the continuity of this story with the two previous incidents in Abraham's life: (1) The chapter casts Isaac in the image of Abraham, whose name is mentioned no less than seven times (vv. 3, 5, 15, 18[2x], 24[2x]). (2) The passage identifies the divine promises made to Isaac as the same ones made to Abraham (vv. 3–5, 24; cf. 12:1–3). Mathews notes, "Both explicitly and implicitly in the chapter, the author shows that Isaac's advancement resulted from divine benevolence, not human merit." *Genesis 11:27—50:26*, 396. (3) Chapter 26 continues two central themes that characterize the patriarchs: the reversals of conflicts and the inventions of trickery. *Genesis 11:27—50:26*, 396–97. The similarities between these three accounts have led some scholars to conjecture three versions arising out of one actual event (or fictitious legend). See Gunkel, *Genesis*, 168–73, 218–25, 293–96; Speiser, *Genesis*, 91; Westermann, *Genesis 12–36*, 161–62, 318–20, 423–24. The dissimilarities between these otherwise similar episodes, however, provide good reason to maintain the integrity of each story. What one finds here is not a literary refashioning of a single event but a historical repetition of a particular sin twice in the father and once in the son. Human experience provides abundant examples of sins repeating themselves in the lives of individuals as well as their offspring.

14. Abimelech looks out a window and sees Isaac and Rebecca engaging in an action conveyed by a verb whose root is the same from which Isaac's own name is derived (צחק). Hence, the ESV translates the text "[he] saw Isaac laughing with Rebekah his wife." But mutual laughter hardly seems to be a distinctive mark of a marital relationship (cf. Gen 19:14; 21:9). The verb is used elsewhere in the Piel theme to refer to *amusement* or *entertainment* (Judg 16:25). This may also be the meaning in Exodus 32:6, where after making sacrifices to Yahweh (via the golden calf) the people of Israel "sat down to eat and drink and rose up *to play* [i.e., to amuse themselves]." Some have understood sexual connotations here and inferred sexual immorality or debauchery. The use of the word

a reason for the ruse and then condemns it, underscoring the potential evil it could have caused (26:9–10). Finally, the Philistine king issues a death-sentence warning against anyone who might harm Isaac or his wife (26:11).

Attempts to Defend Isaac

Commentators come to Isaac's defense, as they did for Abraham. After reviewing Augustine's three categories of "lies,"[15] Martin Luther classifies Isaac's deception as an "obliging lie" and writes, "Accordingly, one asks whether what Isaac does is a sin. I answer that it is not a sin. No, it is an obliging lie by which he guarded against being killed by those among whom he was staying if he said that Rebecca was his wife."[16] Calvin is less inclined to excuse Isaac than Luther, but he still stops short of calling Isaac's ruse a sinful act of deception.[17] James Jordan, on the other hand,

in 39:17 might imply sexual connotations but may simply refer to a mockery, which in that context happened to be associated with alleged sexual activity. Nevertheless, it seems fairly certain that the "play" in which Isaac and Rebekah were engaged was in some way conjugal in nature, at least sufficiently enough to give Abimelech warrant to draw his conclusion about their *real* relationship. Perhaps, it was analogous to what we call in modern English sexual "foreplay." Some translations attempt to capture this sense by translating the verb "caressing" (NAS, NIV, NLT, NET, CSB), "fondling" (RSV, NAB, TNK), or less explicitly, "showing endearment" (NKJ).

15. Namely, a harmful lie (which is a violation of the ninth commandment), an obliging lie (in which one seeks to protect life), and a playful lie or jest. *Lectures on Genesis*, 5:40–41.

16. Ibid., 5:41. Interestingly, after removing Isaac's deception from the category of sin, Luther makes a somewhat confusing concession: "Yet it is a weakness of faith, because he did not make an open and firm confession and did not despise death. For that would have been a splendid and truly heroic virtue and firmness. But God wanted him to be weak, in order that there might be an example which teaches the church that God is not offended, whether you confess firmly, which is heroic, or are weak; for He overlooks this and leaves it unnoticed. And from this we see that we have a gracious God who can forgive and wink at our weaknesses and forgive our sins, provided that we do not lie harmfully." So on the one hand, Isaac did not technically sin, but on the other hand, his "weakness" serves to highlight God's grace and forgiveness.

17. Calvin remarks, "On this point [Isaac] ought to have avoided rather than imitated his father's fault; for no doubt he well remembered that the chastity of his mother had twice been put in great danger; and although she had been wonderfully rescued by the hand of God, yet both she and her husband paid the penalty of their distrust: therefore, the negligence of Isaac is inexcusable, in that he now strikes his foot against the same stone. He does not in express terms deny his wife; but he is to be blamed, first, because, for the sake of preserving his life, he resorts to an evasion *not far removed from a lie*; and secondly, because, in absolving his wife from conjugal fidelity, he exposes her

goes farther than Luther or Calvin and praises Isaac's action. He reasons that since the Serpent used deception against Eve while Adam did nothing to protect her, Isaac is justified in using deception against a tyrant like Abimelech in order to protect his wife.[18] Interestingly, after legitimizing Isaac's deception, Jordan still finds it necessary to justify Isaac's calling Rebekah his "sister" by positing a kind of "sister-by-adoption" concept. He appeals to passages in the Song of Solomon where the bridegroom refers to his lover as his "sister" (4:9, 10, 12; 5:1, 2) and to Genesis 24:59–60, where Rebekah's entire family refer to her as their "sister." Says Jordan, "The most important aspect of the leaving and cleaving was not that Rebekah was getting a husband but that she was getting a new brother." Accordingly, Jordan reasons,

> By saying that Rebekah was his sister, Isaac put himself in the best possible position to protect them both. On the one hand, Isaac would be safe. There would be no reason for anyone to kill him in order to get Rebekah, because no one would know they were married. On the other hand, Rebekah would also be safe. Suitors wishing to win her hand would have to negotiate with her brother, and he could put them off indefinitely. God's covenant would be safe, for Isaac would live to preach and perpetuate it.[19]

Isaac's Ruse Censured

In contrast with these valiant attempts to salvage Isaac's character, the narrator attempts no defense. On the contrary, several factors in the passage indict Isaac rather than exonerate him. First, Isaac did not have recourse to the "half-truth" defense, as his father apparently did. Sarah may

---

to prostitution: but he aggravates his fault, principally (as I have said) in not taking warning from domestic examples, but voluntarily casting his wife into manifest danger," [emphasis added] *Genesis*, 2:61.

18. In Jordan's own words, "The basic means for dealing with tyrants in Genesis, and the rest of Scripture, is through deception. The reason for this goes back to the garden. The Serpent tricked Eve through deception (Gen 3:13; 2 Cor 11:3; 1 Tim 2:14) while Adam stood by and failed to protect her. Accordingly, a theme emerges later in Scripture wherein the Serpent attacks the bride and the husband must attempt to protect her. In each case it is the intention of the Serpent to use the bride to raise up his own seed. In each case deception is used against the Serpent as God acts to protect the bride." Jordan then justifies the use of deception against "the Serpent" as an application of the *lex talionis*: "an eye for an eye, a tooth for a tooth, a deception for a deception [!]." *Primeval Saints*, 86.

19. Ibid., 90–91.

have been Abraham's half-sister as well as his wife (20:12), but Rebekah was Isaac's cousin (24:15, 24, 27). Although ethnic and even covenantal kinship may give rise to a kind of brother-sister relationship, such a relationship cannot nullify or trump one's legal marital status. Rebekah was Isaac's wife plain and clear, as Moses and Abimelech take pains to note (26:7, 8, 9, 10, 11). Second, the narrator indicates that this charade continued for "a long time" (אָרְכוּ־לוֹ שָׁם הַיָּמִים; literally, "the days were long for him there"). This phrase has the effect of nullifying Isaac's prior fears. Much time had elapsed, yet no one had attempted to take Rebekah from him. Third, the narrator depicts this Abimelech in much the same light as he has previously portrayed the former Abimelech and Pharaoh whom Isaac's father had deceived. The Philistine king summons Isaac to appear before him to give account of his deceptive scheme. The king's opening words, "Behold [הִנֵּה], certainly [אַךְ] she is your wife!" (NAU) serve to underscore his impassioned indignation,[20] as does his exclamatory question, "How then could you say, 'She is my sister'?" (26:9).[21] Abimelech then highlights the gravity of Isaac's crime by issuing a formal charge of transgression[22] and by pointing out the potential harm that may have resulted from the deceitful ploy (26:10).[23] The king's death-threat against anyone who "touches" (הַנֹּגֵעַ) the couple (26:11) reminds the reader of God's death-threat issued to Adam should Adam take the forbidden fruit (2:16–17; 3:2–3).[24] The fact that this warning is not motivated by divine threats or punishments, which motivated the former kings (12:17; 20:3–7, 17), heightens the reader's admiration for this Abimelech's moral sensitivity. As Mathews observes, "The king acted out of an inherent fear

20. The adverb אַךְ functions as an asseverative here and is intensified by interjectory הִנֵּה. See Snaith, "The meaning of Hebrew ᵓak," 221–25.

21. According to Gesenius, "Astonishment or indignation at something which has happened is introduced by אֵיךְ *how* (likewise originally interrogative) with the perfect." GKC § 148a. See also *IBHS* § 18.4d.

22. Compare Gen 3:13; 4:10; 20:9; 26:10; 29:25; 31:26; 44:15.

23. The reality of potential injury that could have befallen Rebekah, the king, and the citizens of Gerar clearly removes Isaac's deception from the category of an "obliging lie" since it would have brought harm to others.

24. He does not merely warn his people that they will suffer divine justice if they injure Isaac or Rebecca. Rather, he threatens to be God's instrument of punishment. As an aside, Abimelech's use of the same language as the Genesis 2:17 death-threat, along with the prohibition not to "touch" the patriarchal couple, supports the view that Eve's so-called "addition" to the divine prohibition—"neither shall you touch it" (3:3)—was not really a sinful addition but just a further explication of God's full intent.

of divine retribution for offending his moral conscience."[25] Finally, one should note that Isaac's defense is an appeal to self-preservation (26:9).[26] As in the case of the father, so in the case of the son—their lack of the fear of God and their inordinate fear of man fails to provide the expected contrast between moral light and moral darkness as they interact with the pagan world around them. Abraham could not escape the gravity of remaining sin; his son can do no better. Rather than stemming the rising tide of sin portrayed in primeval history, the patriarchal family is dragged along in its current.

ISAAC'S POOR TASTE

Isaac's preferential affection for his firstborn, Esau, over his second-born, Jacob, on account of the Esau's hunting and culinary skills surfaced earlier as a potential weakness in Isaac's character (25:28). But the disastrous fruits of this parental favoritism do not ripen until later when Isaac is old and blind.[27] Despite Esau's lack of fitness to serve as heir to the promise (25:29–34; 26:34–35), Isaac follows personal preference and societal convention and decides to confer the blessing on Esau rather than on Jacob (27:1–4). Rebekah, however, overhears her husband's plans (27:5) and devises a counter-strategy. Taking advantage of her husband's blindness and the window of time in which Esau is hunting game, she summons Jacob and orders him to disguise himself as Esau so that he can obtain the blessing that Rebekah believes rightly belongs to Jacob (27:6–10). Although initially hesitant (27:11–13), Jacob complies with his mother's scheme and pulls off the "great exchange" (27:14–29). No

25. *Genesis 11:27—50:26*, 407. Baldwin is also impressed by this and notes, "What is striking is the high standard of morality in Gerar, and the severity of the punishment decreed there for taking another man's wife. Nothing less than the death penalty was exacted." *Message of Genesis 12–50*, 109.

26. Duguid aptly remarks, "The pronouns are precisely the problem: he was thinking only of himself, not of the damage his actions might do to others. The possibility that others might be taken in by his subterfuge and bring guilt upon themselves by taking Rebekah as a wife apparently never crossed his mind. Equally, he apparently never considered the possibility that this Abimelech, presumably a descendant of the Abimelech with whom his father had dealings in Genesis 20, might turn out to be an honorable and God-fearing man. He neglected the possibility that God could work for good even in the lives of pagans around him." *Relentless Grace*, 20.

27. A comparison of various texts (Gen 29:18, 21, 27; 30:25; 45:6; 46:46; 47:9) suggests that Isaac is now 137 years old; the twins, Esau and Jacob, would be 77 years old (25:26). See Keil and Delitzsch, *Pentateuch*, 1:273–74.

sooner has Jacob departed than Esau enters his father's tent with "the delicious food" in hand ready to receive the blessing (27:30–31). Within moments Isaac and Esau come to the shocking conclusion that Jacob has come "deceitfully" and "taken away [Esau's] blessing" (27:33–36). Defrauded of his coveted double-portion, Esau is enraged and plots to kill Jacob (27:37–41). Once again Rebekah's ear intercepts the plot, and she devises a plan to send Jacob to her kinsmen in Haran, primarily for protection (27:42–45) and secondarily for a wife (27:46–47). In response to Rebekah's promptings, Isaac summons Jacob, reiterates the blessing, and sends him away (28:1–5). The narrative section concludes where it began (26:34–35) with a reference to Esau's choice of wives that are outside the bounds of God's elect community (28:6–9).

Fixing the Blame

Scholars agree that this story constitutes one of the most intriguing and artful narratives in the Bible.[28] The concern of this study is to assess the moral behavior of the patriarchal family members portrayed. Undeniably, the text describes scheming and deceiving. But who is to blame? A few commentators caution against attempting to answer that question. Gunkel, for instance, argues that during the period in which this account was depicted "morality and religion were not yet closely linked in the way we now consider self-evident." He avers, "The god originally discussed in these legends is not the majestic Yahweh, the lawgiver of the ten commandments, but a much more primitive figure, a god who protects his darling and his tribe in all his doings, even the devious ones."[29] Gunkel then chides theologians who "have futilely sought to mold the narrative into a moral tale" and suggests the reader view

28. Whyte writes, "A more powerful and a more fruitful chapter for the sacred ends of tragedy was never written than the tragical chapter of Isaac's deathbed." *Bible Characters*, 102–3. Thomas remarks, "Nowhere, perhaps, is the real character of the Bible more evident than in this chapter. The story is given in all its naked simplicity, and, although no precise moral is pointed, the incidents carry their own solemn lesson to every reader." *Genesis*, 248. Gibson observes, "The story of the filching of Esau's blessing is one of Genesis' best known and is another masterpiece of Hebrew narrative art." *Genesis*, 2:151.

29. *Genesis*, 301. Earlier, Gunkel remarks, "The content of the narrative is and remains, therefore, that a deceit finally comes to a fortunate end. The rascal Jacob truly gains the blessing, Esau draws the short end, with no moral guilt, and the hearers are the fortunate heirs of the deceiver." Ibid., 300.

the story as a comic account of "amusing, successful pranks."[30] Similarly, Brueggemann judges that

> the narrator seems unaware of the incongruity that may appear to us: a blessing gotten by deception! While that may be a problem for us, we do better to stay inside the story itself, to perceive that the narrative is simply that way (as is life itself). . . . This is not a spiritual treatise on morality. It is, rather, a memory of how faith moves in the rawness of experience. We must leave it at that.[31]

Although he does not deny the presence of immoral behavior in the text, John Walton directs the reader's attention away from making moral judgments about the human actors of the narrative by asserting,

> This narrative is not about good or bad parenting. . . . The intention of the passage is not to warn readers against despising those benefits they are born with (as Esau did) or to admonish against exploiting someone's needs to our own advantage (as Jacob did), though undoubtedly those lessons would be constructive.[32]

30. Ibid., 300–301. Of course, Gunkel concedes that modern moral sensibilities are rightly offended by these immoral acts of deceit. But he argues that the modern reader "should also have enough respect for antiquity not to paint over these old legends with modern colors." Ibid., 301. A few interpreters take this reasoning a step further. They believe the narrator portrays a world in which humans are pawns of "fate" or "providence." The conclusion of the matter, according to Speiser, is that "all the actors in this piece are but tools of fate which—purposeful though it must be—can itself be neither deciphered nor side-stepped by man." *Genesis,* 213. In a similar vein, von Rad believes the narrator "intends to awaken in the reader a feeling of sympathetic suffering for those who are caught up mysteriously in such a monstrous act of God and are almost destroyed in it." *Genesis,* 280–81. So it turns out, according to these commentators, that God is the real villain!

31. *Genesis*, 229.

32. *Genesis*, 557. In his introduction to Genesis, Walton discourages the reader from moralizing the text (36–37). Concerning the narratives, he asserts that "moral guidance is not transparent, so it is not likely that this is the primary purpose" (37). Walton advocates instead that the student read Genesis as "covenant history," which has as its primary purpose the revelation of God's character and plan for humanity (37–39). While Walton is correct to stress the narrative's function as a revelation of divine character and purpose, he too easily dismisses the legitimate moral lessons intended by the narrator. That a good narrator need not state such moral lessons in explicit language is noted by Fokkelman, who wisely comments, "As a true artist our narrator does not need to moralize within the story or add a clumsy ending such as: 'the moral of all this is as follows . . .' or, 'actually, it is my intention to show all that . . .' As an adult narrator he assumes our adultness, leaving much to our imagination and remaining reticent about making value judgments himself. He presents the events to us in great detail, he tells us what they smell of (of the field, 27:27) and what colour they are (the red man falls for

In contrast, the majority of commentators are correct in assessing the moral behavior of the biblical characters and in drawing moral lessons for modern readers. Although many interpreters are inclined to place blame on some of the characters while exonerating others, a careful reading of the narrative in its immediate and larger context rules in favor of those commentators who find fault with all four parties: father, mother, and both sons.[33] This part of the analysis will focus first on the sins of Isaac and then on those of Rebekah. The next chapter will address the sins of their sons, Esau and Jacob.

Attempts to Defend Isaac

Not everyone agrees that Isaac bears any guilt. Speiser depicts Isaac and Esau as the helpless victims of a deceptive ruse.[34] Although the unfolding of providence and later revelation interpret the famous birth-oracle in Jacob's favor (compare 25:23 with Mal 1:2–3; Rom 9:11–13), its meaning was initially ambiguous.[35] Martin Luther apparently senses this ambigu-

---

red, 25:30), and there his story ends. We are left to our own discernment by this knotty and subtle narrative style which displays distance and commitment." This, according to Fokkelman, does not mean the stories are amoral. "By no means. We are certainly challenged to sharpen and show our moral discernment when we answer such questions as whether Jacob's and Rebekah's actions please God? But we should understand that in biblical (and other) narrative art 'the moral' is indissolubly interwoven with the words and actions of the characters, just as our own actions always have moral implications, even if we are innocent of writing moral-theological tracts. The characters, the people acting are shown to us 'only' by means of what they say and do, but this is no reason the characterizations should be less clear; on the contrary, this is the most effective means available to the artist for he knows that the qualities, the charisma of 'his' people leave an unforgettable impression if they have been made concrete." *Narrative Art in Genesis*, 115–16.

33. Regarding the question of who is to blame in this narrative, Duguid remarks, "All are to blame; no one emerges from this saga with credit, except God, whose good purposes endure in spite of the worst efforts of men." *Relentless Grace*, 35. Ross agrees and comments, "In fact, all the participants were at fault." *Creation & Blessing*, 471. Waltke also attaches guilt to every actor: "The speech and actions of this scene's peculiar characters glaringly display their flaws: misguided and violent Esau, sensuous and weak Isaac, deceptive and manipulative Rebekah, and opportunistic and unprincipled Jacob." *Genesis*, 374.

34. According to Speiser, "The author himself, by dealing so sensitively with the hapless plight in which Isaac and Esau find themselves through no fault of their own (cf. especially vss. 33–38), demonstrates beyond any doubt that his personal sympathies are with the victims." *Genesis*, 211.

35. The last part of the oracle reads, וְרַב יַעֲבֹד צָעִיר. The Septuagint, Targum of Onkelos, the Vulgate and many English translations follow the Hebrew word order,

ity when he writes, "I incline toward the pious thought that there was a friendly and kindly disagreement about the meaning of the prophecy."[36] But a careful reading of the text reveals several ways in which Isaac's behavior was culpable.

Isaac's Deed Censured

First, even if the meaning of the birth-oracle was not immediately clear to Isaac, he had plenty of time to reflect on its intent in light of his sons' subsequent character development and behavior. It is likely that Isaac knew of Esau's profanation of the family birthright (25:29–34).[37] Moreover, Moses prefaces the blessing conferral narrative by mentioning Esau's bigamous union with Canaanite women (26:34) and expressly notifies the reader that these pagan women "made life bitter for Isaac and Rebekah" (26:35).[38] No doubt much of the parental grief arose from the idolatrous and ungodly behavior these women introduced into the patriarchal family,[39] as well as their disappointment in their son's lack of discernment and sensitivity to family conventions.[40] It is also possible

taking Esau as the subject and Jacob as the object (KJV, NAU, NIV, NET, ESV, etc.). But Hebrew syntax allows the writer to shift the object forward in the sentence for emphasis (*IBHS* § 10.1c). Had Moses desired to remove all ambiguity, he could have placed the accusative particle (אֵת) before Jacob's name. But he did not. Therefore, the meaning of prophecy was initially obscure. For an extensive argument demonstrating the oracle's ambiguity, which most interpreters miss, see Allis, "The Birth-Oracle to Rebekah (Gen xxv. 23)," 97–117.

36. *Lectures on Genesis*, 5:101. Luther goes on to observe, "Friendly mistakes of this kind occur every day between spouses." Ibid., 5:102. Isaac, according to Luther, was simply adhering to "the rule" of primogenitor, while Rebekah viewed the case as an exception to the rule. Ibid., 5:104–6.

37. While the account does not explicitly mention the parents, it is difficult to suppose that Jacob would keep the transaction a secret.

38. The Hebrew reads, וַתִּהְיֶיןָ מֹרַת רוּחַ לְיִצְחָק וּלְרִבְקָה. The phrase מֹרַת רוּחַ is only found here, but it probably conveys an idea similar to that conveyed by passages such as 1 Samuel 1:10, where Hannah's barrenness caused her "bitterness of soul [מָרַת נָפֶשׁ]," and Job 7:11, where suffering Job complains of "my bitterness of soul [בְּמַר נַפְשִׁי]." Deep distress and anguish lie at the root of these expressions.

39. This may be inferred from God's earlier depiction of the growing ungodliness of Canaanite society (15:16) and the many warnings God later gives to Israel concerning the idolatrous and ungodly influence of Canaan's inhabitants (Lev 18:3ff.; Num 33:51–56; Judg 1:21—2:5).

40. Notes Fokkelman, "We see that in the domain of morals Esau is rather easygoing—he ignores the usage of semi-nomads—because he has no sense of the special task of his family under the sign of the blessing." *Narrative Art in Genesis*, 106.

that some of the "bitterness of spirit" with which Isaac struggled betrayed feelings of regret that he had failed to do for Esau what Abraham had done for him, namely, provide his son with a suitable wife. Indeed, Isaac's failure to provide his son with a proper mate not only underscores his failure as a parent[41] but serves to heighten the folly of his plans to bestow the blessing on a son who has legally attached himself to a people under God's curse (Gen 9:25; 15:16).[42] The reader, therefore, is not surprised to find Isaac plotting the blessing conferral to his older son in the secrecy of his tent without (so he thinks) the awareness of Rebekah or Jacob (21:1). Such stealthy proceedings suggest an uneasy conscience.[43]

41. Other commentators highlight Isaac's failure as a father. Wenham observes, "Abraham had arranged his marriage to Rebekah. Why had not Isaac done the same for Esau and Jacob? Throughout Genesis, Isaac is portrayed as rather passive. Indeed, in the previous chapter, his quiet peaceable nature in avoiding confrontation with the Philistines was implicitly applauded, and he was rewarded by a reaffirmation of the promises and great prosperity. Here, however, his virtue has become a vice; his quiet patience has become lethargy." *Genesis 16–50*, 215. So too Steinmetz points out, "[Esau's] marriage also indicates that Isaac has not assumed the role of a father; unlike Abraham, he has not made sure that his son take [*sic*] a non-Canaanite wife. These two verses, then, subtly encapsulate the problem which the ensuing narrative develops and tries to solve, Isaac's inability to be a father to his son." *From Father to Son*, 97.

42. At the time of Isaac's proposal to bless Esau, the latter had been married for thirty-seven years to pagan women (26:34). In light of the sufficient time Isaac had to assess the meaning of birth-oracle in connection with Esau's bigamous marriage, which, like sale of his birthright, served to reveal his profane character, Allis remarks, "While we have a right to stress the ambiguity of the language of the birth-oracle as explaining at least in part the determination of Isaac to bless Esau, we must also recognize that Isaac was not, and was not intended to be, wholly dependent upon the language of the oracle for a guide in his conduct. Isaac had a commentary upon that prophecy in the events of many years which had elapsed since the oracle was uttered. . . . If the prophecy was obscure, it was all the more important that he should study carefully God's providential dealings in the hopes of finding a clue to its solution. Did he do so? The answer seems to be clear. He did not. Had he done so he must have realized that to pass on the blessing of his father Abraham to a son with two Hittite wives and sons who were half-Hittite would be an act of disloyalty, a grievous sin." "The Birth-Oracle to Rebekah (Gen. xxv. 23)," 116.

43. Other commentators note the incongruity in Isaac's secrecy. Observes Wenham, "Elsewhere in the OT, it is normal for a dying man to summon all his close male relatives and to bless them publicly and in this way to organize the succession (cf. Gen. 49; 50:24–25). It is, to say the least, irregular for Isaac to summon merely one of his sons, especially since Jacob and Esau were twins. It raises questions: Why is Isaac prepared to break with convention? Why does he want to bless Esau and not Jacob, since both were entitled to some blessing (cf. vv. 34, 38)?" *Genesis 16–50*, 206. Likewise remarks Duguid, "[Isaac] was seeking to circumvent God's word in favor of his desires and preferences. Otherwise why was there such a need for stealth on his part? Why was this transaction

Second, the sympathetic portrait of a poor old blind man whose feeble mind is exploited by his wife and younger son does not correspond to Moses's description of Isaac in the passage. True, his eyesight is gone (27:1).[44] But his other senses are acute,[45] and his mind is calculating and alert. When Jacob enters the tent with the meal in hand, Isaac quickly calculates the statistical improbability that his son could return so quickly on his errand (27:20a). Isaac is willing to accept Jacob's appeal to a "special act of providence" (27:20b), but he proceeds to implement a battery of tests designed to confirm "Esau's" identity (27:21–27a). Only after careful and thoughtful investigation does Isaac confer the blessing (27:27b–29).[46] As Terence Fretheim notes, "Interpreters often adjudge

---

going to be done in secret, in the bedroom, instead of in front of the whole family? The transfer of the blessing should surely have been part of a devotional service in front of the whole household, not one parent craftily stealing a march on the other!" *Relentless Grace*, 38–39.

44. Literally, the text reads, "his eyes were dim of seeing," which elsewhere is clearly associated with blindness (1 Sam 3:2; Zech 11:17). Isaac's obvious dependence on his other senses proves that he is unable to see. Moreover, the narrative requires absolute blindness for Rebekah and Isaac's scheme to succeed.

45. Isaac employs touch (27:21–23), hearing (27:22), taste (27:25), and smell (27:27). Some have judged two other senses of Isaac's to be defective since he is unable to distinguish goat hair from human hair (27:22–23) or goat meat from venison (27:27). See Hamilton, *Genesis 18–50*, 217; Duguid, *Relentless Grace*, 33. Only Isaac's senses of hearing and smell appear to function properly. Yet the narrator himself likens Esau's hairy skin to the goat skins (27:23), and Isaac's failure to discern the difference between Jacob's dish and Esau's is due to the similarity in taste and texture between goat meat and venison, as well as Rebekah's culinary ability to mimic the flavor of Esau's cooked venison. Only Jacob's inability to imitate Esau's voice raised questions in Isaac's mind.

46. "So he blessed him [וַיְבָרְכֵהוּ]" (27:23b) may appear to contradict this conclusion since it appears to place the blessing *before* Isaac tasted his son's meat and smelled his son's garment. But the statement in 27:23b should not be interpreted as describing a completed action. Instead, the *waw* consecutive imperfect probably carries an ingressive sense here, i.e., "so he began to bless him" (*IBHS* § 33.3.1a). The idea conveyed is that of Isaac commencing the blessing only to stop in midstream, as it were, and introduce further tests to confirm "Esau's" identity. In this way, the narrator heightens the suspense of the narrative. See Ross, *Creation & Blessing*, 478; Speiser, *Genesis*, 209; Waltke, *Genesis*, 379. Keil and Delitzsch have suggested the clause be interpreted proleptically. *The Pentateuch*, 275. Wenham seems to favor the simple idea of "greeting" for verse 23. *Genesis 16–50*, 209. But both of these alternatives would spoil the growing tension in the narrative (i.e., Will Jacob pull it off?), which is not relieved until verse 30: "As soon as Isaac finished blessing Jacob, when Jacob had scarcely gone out from the presence of Isaac his father, Esau his brother came in from hunting."

Isaac's behavior to be naïve, even bumbling, yet the repeated questions and ritual delays reveal that he pursues his suspicions carefully."[47]

Third, Isaac's reaction once Jacob's trickery is uncovered betrays an awakened realization that God has exposed his private scheme to bless Esau contrary to the divinely revealed oracle (25:23). When Esau returns with the cooked game and asks for the blessing (27:30–31), Isaac stutters in confusion: "Who are you?" (27:32a). The moment Isaac is convinced that this is the real Esau, he "tremble[s] very violently"[48] and alludes to the impostor, Jacob, who has preceded Esau and received the blessing, adding the emphatic clause, "Yes, and he shall be blessed" (27:33). Isaac's terror-stricken shock, legitimization of the blessing conferral to Jacob, and refusal to reverse the rite in Esau's favor (27:35, 37) converge to portray Isaac as a man who has come to the realization that God has exposed his own folly and overturned his ill-founded plan. Thankfully, Isaac's submission to God's reversal of his plan (27:33), his reiteration of the Abrahamic blessing to Jacob (28:1, 3–4), and his assumption of the fatherly responsibility to guide Jacob in the taking of a proper bride (28:1b–2, 5) serve together as signs of repentance.[49]

47. "Genesis," 535. Visotzky reads far too much guile into Isaac's actions when he depicts Isaac as fully aware of Rebekah and Jacob's scheme all along and as using it to his own advantage. According to Visotzky, "Isaac was very satisfied with his little ruse. He enjoyed toying with Jacob, asking him again and again, 'Which one are you?' Did Jacob have no sense of shame that he could lie like that to his father? Was the blessing so essential? Hadn't he already cheated Esau out of the birthright? Isaac knew of all this and more, but it was better to pretend to blindness. With dim eyes he could accomplish all he wished to for his boys and leave Rebecca with the illusion that she had the upper hand." *The Genesis of Ethics*, 152. But Visotzky's read makes no sense out of Isaac's emotional shock at the discovery of Jacob's deception (27:33)—unless, of course, Isaac was just faking it, which is highly unlikely.

48. The Hebrew clause consists of the finite verb "to tremble [וַיֶּחֱרַד]" followed by the cognate noun "trembling [חֲרָדָה]," which in turn is followed by the adjective "great [גְּדֹלָה]" and an intensified adverb "unto the utmost [עַד־מְאֹד]." As Wenham observes, "Hebrew can hardly express Isaac's panic more graphically." *Genesis 16–50*, 211.

49. Several scholars catch the implication. Kidner writes, "Isaac's *yea, and he shall be blessed* expresses more than mere belief that the spoken word is self-fulfilling: he knows he has been fighting against God, as Esau has, and he accepts defeat." *Genesis*, 156. Leupold comments, "Isaac sees how God's providence checked him in his unwise and wicked enterprise. From this point onward there is no longer any unclearness as to what God wanted in reference to the two sons. Therefore, the brief but conclusive, 'yea, blessed shall he be.' But his trembling was caused by seeing the hand of God in what transpired." *Exposition of Genesis*, 753. Calvin observes, "Here now again the faith which had been smothered in the breast of the holy man shines forth and omits fresh sparks;

Finally, the narrator provides another clear indication of Isaac's moral failure in this passage. Six times "the delicious food" (מַטְעַמִּים) is mentioned in the text (27:4, 7, 9, 14, 17, 31). Most telling is Isaac's appended phrase "such as I love [כַּאֲשֶׁר אָהַבְתִּי]" (27:4), repeated with slight variation by Rebekah, "such as he loves [כַּאֲשֶׁר אָהֵב]" (27:9) and the narrator, "such as his father loved [כַּאֲשֶׁר אָהֵב אָבִיו]" (27:14). The narrator has already related Isaac's preferential affection for Esau to the fact that Isaac "ate of [Esau's] game" (25:28).[50] What then appeared as a peccadillo now appears as a sensual passion! Isaac's preference for Esau is governed not by a consideration of his son's moral or spiritual qualities but by an acquired taste for his culinary creations.[51] Isaac's physical blindness thus becomes a metaphor for his spiritual blindness.[52] Or as Wenham tersely remarks, "Isaac's sensuality is more powerful than his theology."[53]

In conclusion, not only does Isaac resemble his father in Abraham's initial preference of the child of sight over the child of faith (17:17–18; 21:11), but he also bears some resemblance to Lot and Noah, both of whose offspring uncovered their "nakedness" or shame (Gen 9:21–22; 19:8, 31–38). And Isaac's lust for that which "was good for food" prompt-

for there is no doubt that his fear springs from faith. . . . For unless he had thought that God was the director of his act, what should have hindered him from alleging his ignorance as an excuse and from becoming enraged against Jacob, who had stolen in upon him by fraud and by unjustifiable arts? But although covered with shame on account of the error he had committed, he nevertheless, with a collected mind, ratifies the benediction which he had pronounced; and I do not doubt that he then, as one awaking, began to recall to memory the oracle to which he had not been sufficiently attentive." *Genesis*, 2:93–94.

50. Alter perceptively remarks, "Isaac's preference for Esau is given a causal explanation so specific that it verges on satire: he loves the older twin because of his own fondness for game. Rebekah's love for Jacob is contrastively stated without explanation. Presumably, this would suggest that her affection is not dependent on a merely material convenience that the son might provide her, that it is more justly grounded preference." *Art of Biblical Narrative,* 44.

51. Similarly, Ross observes, "The significant point in this section is the motivation for giving the blessing—a tasty meal." *Creation & Blessing,* 476. Whyte marks this as Isaac's defining weakness: "When I read Isaac's whole history over again, with my eye upon the object, it becomes as clear as a sunbeam to me that what envy was to Cain, and what wine was to Noah, and what lewdness was to Ham, and what wealth was to Lot, and what pride and impatience were to Sarah—all that, venison and savoury meat were to Isaac." *Bible Characters*, 97. Hamilton notes, "If Isaac's eyesight and memory are failing, his appetite is not." *Genesis 18–50*, 213.

52. See Sarna, *Genesis*, 190.

53. Wemham, *Genesis 16–50*, 206.

ed him to place his own autonomous preference above God's just as did his first parents, Adam and Eve (Gen 3:6). So the "son of promise" proves less than promising as his life unfolds and his indwelling sin gets the upper hand.[54]

REBEKAH'S RECKLESS HASTE

Having exposed Isaac's "poor taste," that is, his fleshly motivated rejection of God's revealed preference, the analysis will now focus on Rebekah's moral character and behavior. The reader's first introduction to Rebekah is quite positive. She manifests inward qualities that correspond to her outward beauty (24:16; 26:7): she is polite, considerate (24:18–20, 25), and submissive (24:58). When perplexed about the unusual nature of her pregnancy, she "went to inquire of the Lord" (25:22), which commends her as a woman of prayer and piety. Her preference for Jacob (25:28) may indicate an accurate perception of Esau's profane character (25:29–34). Thus, the narrator initially casts Rebekah, as he did Isaac, in the likeness of a virtuous person.

But as in the case of Isaac, Rebekah's preferential attachment to one son over the other develops into a character weakness. And just as the blessing-conferral incident reveals Isaac's dark side, it likewise serves to bring out the worst in Rebekah. For no sooner does Rebekah learn of her husband's intent to bless Esau (27:5), than she quickly conspires with her favorite son, Jacob, to overturn her husband's plans with deceitful cunning (27:6–13). When she learns of Esau's murderous intention (27:42), she feigns a primary concern for Jacob's need for a wife from within her own ethnic community while cloaking from Isaac her real concern for Jacob's personal safety (27:46). So the initially polite, considerate, and submissive young woman has apparently developed into an indecorous and manipulating woman of intrigue.

54. Whyte's concluding words in his biographical sketch of Isaac are a bit too strong, but they do capture the tragedy of Isaac's spiritual decline: "The patriarch Isaac presents but a pale appearance as he stands planted between two so stately and so impressive personages as his father Abraham on the one hand, and his son Jacob on the other hand. . . . And indeed, as we follow out the sad declension of Isaac's character to the end, it is forced upon us that it would have been well for Isaac, and for all connected with Isaac, that Abraham's uplifted hand had not been arrested by the angel of the Lord. Had Isaac died on his father's altar, an immense impression for good would have been made on all who ever heard of his submission and devotion." *Bible Characters*, 93–94.

Attempts to Defend Rebekah

Not all commentators agree with this assessment. Chrysostom speaks of Rebekah's actions as exemplifying ideal maternal love.[55] Calvin admits that Rebekah's stratagem was "not without fault; for although she could not guide her husband by salutary counsel, yet it was not a legitimate method of acting, to circumvent him by such deceit." But Calvin turns around and construes Rebekah's deceitful scheme as an act of faith.[56] Luther cannot justify Rebekah's deception as an "obliging lie," as he does with Abraham's and Isaac's "wife-sister" ruses. On the contrary, Luther concludes, "This is great rashness and boldness coupled with extraordinary deception and very great harm, for this lie is not playful or obliging but is decidedly harmful."[57] Yet what Luther gives with one hand he takes back with the other, conjecturing that Rebekah did not act on her own initiative. Rather, Luther speculates that she had received prophetic revelation through Abraham's ancestor Eber.[58] He then reasons that Rebekah

55. Reflecting on Rebekah's actions, Chrysostom writes, "See a mother's affection, or rather God's designs: He it was who prompted her to make plans and made sure all turned out well." Then commenting on Rebekah's response to Jacob's fear of being discovered, he queries, "So what does Rebekah do, this extraordinary woman of great affection? Since she was not concocting this only out of her own thinking but was also implementing the prediction from on high, she took every care to banish fear from the child and instill courage so as to bring off the plan. Instead of promising him that he would be able to deceive his father and elude detection, what did she say? 'Let the curse on you fall on me, child; just heed my word, and go and fetch it for me.' 'Even if anything like this should happen,' she is saying, 'you personally will suffer no harm. So don't be afraid: Take heart, "heed my word," and do what I advise you.' This really is a mother's love, readily accepting everything for her child's sake." "Homilies on Genesis 53.3," *ACCS*, 2:169.

56. Writes Calvin, "Now if we consider farther, whence arose this great desire to bestir herself; her extraordinary faith will on the other hand appear. For, as she did not hesitate to provoke her husband against herself, to light up implacable enmity between the brothers, to expose her beloved son Jacob to the danger of immediate death, and to disturb the whole family; this certainly flowed from no other source than her faith." *Genesis*, 2:84–85. Even Calvin's editor is constrained to file a caveat against Calvin's interpretation: "This is a dangerous position, however it may be modified or explained" Ibid., 2:85 n. 1.

57. *Lectures on Genesis*, 5:110.

58. According to Luther, "[Rebekah] often came to Eber and complained that Isaac was unwilling to depart from the rule and to bless Jacob. Then she heard Eber say: 'Do whatever you can to deceive him and to seize the right of primogeniture. Leave nothing untried, for faith is not without the Word.' Therefore, she undoubtedly listened to the spoken Word and pondered it in her heart. Otherwise she would not have had the courage to attempt this." Ibid., 5:111.

and Jacob were acting in obedience to the First Table of the Law, though they were violating the Second Table of the Law. He concludes,

> The law and rule ordained that Esau was the firstborn; but God, with His First Table, made the transfer. Indeed, He changed that law and decreed as follows: "Esau I did not want; Jacob I did want." Hence Rebecca and Jacob *did not sin*. No, *they acted in a godly and saintly manner*. They had every right to despoil Esau and to deprive him of that fief of primogeniture [emphasis added].[59]

As further justification for Rebekah's deception, Luther adds, "Thus in their wars the saints frequently deceived their enemies, but those are lies one is permitted to use in the service of God against the devil and the enemies of God."[60] Hence, what the narrator depicts as a family feud, Luther likens to all-out warfare! Jordan is not far behind Luther in his assessment of the situation. He refers to Isaac as "a tyrant," and he argues that tyrants must be overcome by means of deception. Therefore, faithful and courageous Rebekah steps up to the plate. Having observed Esau's profane life and Jacob's godly life, she cannot allow her husband to move forward with his plan to thwart the will of God. Therefore, "[Rebekah] determined to do something about it (Gen 27:1–5)," and in her actions, Jordan notes,

> We see again that it is the woman who tricks the serpent, eye for eye and tooth for tooth. Even more importantly, we see that Rebekah was willing to die for the covenant. She offers her life and all her happiness to secure God's will. In her willingness to die Rebekah is nothing less than a picture of Jesus Himself.[61]

Rebekah's Act Censured

The reader may be tempted to sympathize with Rebekah, especially in light of the fact that the opinion of women in ancient Near Eastern societies was sometimes ignored or underappreciated. But faithfulness to the text and to the overall teaching of Scripture compels a censure of her ac-

59. Ibid., 5:115–16.

60. Ibid., 5:150. Luther even compares Rebekah's deceitful tactic to Christ's incarnation: "For He came into the world clothed in flesh and was cast into the water like a hook. After biting Him, the devil was suddenly pulled back out of the water by God, thrown on dry land, and crushed." Ibid., 5:150–51.

61. *Primeval Saints*, 92–96.

tions. To begin with, the conflict Rebekah faced in chapter 27 was but the outgrowth of the prenatal conflict she faced in chapter 25: two offspring struggling for preeminence (25:22–23). There, Rebekah "went to inquire of the Lord" (25:22b). Here, Rebekah consults only her own wisdom (27:6–13). In doing so, Rebekah behaves much like Eve who attempted to bring God's plan for humanity to realization apart from the divinely revealed will (2:16–17; 3:6). As a result, one cannot concur with Calvin's depiction of Rebekah's deed as an example of "extraordinary faith."[62]

Second, Rebekah's indignant thwarting of Isaac's plan followed by her rash willingness to suffer God's curse for her deception disclose a degree of hypocrisy and irreverence on her part. When telling Jacob of Isaac's plan to bless Esau, Rebekah adds a phrase to Isaac's speech, which he himself likely omitted. She says, "I heard your father speak to your brother Esau, 'Bring me game and prepare for me delicious food, that I may eat it and bless you *before the Lord* before I die [emphasis added]" (27:6–7). Commentators are correct to note that the phrase "before the Lord" (לִפְנֵי יְהוָה) adds solemnity to the event.[63] Isaac probably excluded it because of an uneasy conscience. Rebekah, however, adds the phrase to impress on Jacob's mind the gravity of his father's sin in acting contrary to the divine oracle as well as Jacob's legal ownership of the birthright. Her addition has the same impact as saying, "How dare your father carry this out in God's presence!"[64] But Rebekah's very disgust with her husband's departure from God's will condemns her own willingness to conspire deceitfully with her son "before the Lord" whose "eyes are in every place, keeping watch on the evil and the good" (Prov 15:3). What is more, when Jacob correctly cautions his mother against the sacrilegious nature of her plan (27:11–12), Rebekah rashly responds by calling for God's curse to fall on her should her son be discovered. On the one hand, Rebekah expects Isaac to handle Yahweh's covenant blessing with care.

62. Rather, as Calvin's own editor is compelled to remark in a footnote, "True faith never leads to sin. It was the mixture, not to say the predominance of unbelief, which caused Rebekah, instead of waiting for the fulfillment of God's promises in his own way, to plot and to execute a scheme of imposture, which involved herself and her family in perpetual disquietude. What Calvin calls zeal, he ought to have called rashness and something worse." *Genesis*, 2:85 n. 1.

63. Leupold, *Exposition of Genesis*, 740; Wenham, *Genesis 16–50*, 206.

64. The phrase is often used in the Pentateuch to reflect the reality of or engender a consciousness of God's special presence (Gen 17:1; 18:22; Exod 6:12, 22; 16:9, 33; 27:21; 28:12, 29, 35, 38; 29:11, 23, 24, 25, 26, 42; 30:8, 16; 34:34; Lev 1:3, 5, 11, etc.).

On the other hand, she treats God's covenant curse lightly, and in doing so, takes the name of God in vain.

Third, Rebekah's deceptive plot must be categorized as a "harmful lie," even as Luther is forced to concede.[65] She encourages her son Jacob to deceive and exploit his blind father, an act that the light of nature (Rom 1:28–32) and Mosaic legislation clearly condemn (Exod 20:12; 21:17; Lev 19:14; 20:9; Deut 5:16; 27:18; Prov 20:20). Jacob himself seems to sense the impropriety of his mother's scheme and to fear the harmful consequences that may ensue (27:11–12). Yet if Isaac's love for the field and wild game had a lasting influence on the proclivities of his favorite son, Rebekah's knack for deceit and manipulation left its mark on her darling Jacob. Moreover, Rebekah not only exposes Jacob to Isaac's potential curse, she also makes him vulnerable to Esau's murderous wrath (27:41). Providentially, God's common grace restrains Esau long enough for Rebekah to arrange a way of escape for Jacob (27:43–46). Nevertheless, her ruse nearly costs her both sons in a day, as she herself admits (27:45). And though she prevents a family homicide, she only aggravates the preexisting tension within the family by betraying her husband's trust (Prov 31:11) and by increasing the distance between her two sons (Ps 133:1). Finally, she herself has to suffer as a result of her deceitful ploy. What she hoped would be a brief absence followed by a joyful reunion between mother and son (27:44–45)[66] turns out to be a twenty-year separation (29:18, 30; 31:38) that ends with Rebekah dying before her beloved son ever makes it home (49:31).[67] Although dark providences cannot always be interpreted with certainty, it is difficult not to see God's chastening hand responding to Rebekah's lack of patience and trust.[68] In spite of her cunning, there was definitely a sense in which she actually was "bereft of [her sons] in one day" (27:45). Rebekah is

65. *Lectures on Genesis*, 5:110.

66. The clause, "and stay with him a while [וְיָשַׁבְתָּ עִמּוֹ יָמִים אֲחָדִים]," literally, "and remain with him a few days" clearly anticipates a brief stay.

67. Although Jacob returned in time to see his father Isaac alive (35:7), there is no mention of his mother Rebekah, which strongly suggests that she had died before he returned. Apparently, Rebekah's nurse, Deborah, did survive her mistress and traveled with Jacob until she died (38:5).

68. God's dealing with her husband's parents in making them wait for Isaac's birth and in disapproving their own attempts to "force" his plan should have served as a guide and motivation to Rebekah, fostering complete trust in God's ability to overrule evil for good. It will cost the patriarchal family many more trials before they learn this lesson (50:20).

never explicitly commended elsewhere in the canon of Scripture for her faith or virtue.[69]

69. This point is noted by Toppin, who offers an overall negative assessment of her deed: "What Rebekah did to her son Esau meant she wanted nothing more to do with him. What she did to her son Jacob, leading him in an act of deceit was evil. What she did to her husband was dishonorable. And, what she did before God was downright sinful. There had to be some deep-seated reasons, beyond the scope of this book, why she did the things she did. Now I understand why Rebekah's name is not mentioned in scripture as a woman of virtue, and I hope she repented." *Biblical Patriarchs and Their Legacy of Family Dysfunctions*, 64. The fact that Rebekah's deceitful plot was wrong and harmful, as well as the absence of any explicit commendation of her faith or character elsewhere in Scripture, need not imply that she was an unbeliever. First, as we have seen, even the patriarchs who are explicitly commended for their faith and obedience could in weaker moments fall into sinful practices. Second, Peter's reference to "the holy women of old who hoped in God . . . by submitting to their husbands" may have included Rebekah, who at least earlier in her life did submit to Isaac in frightening situations (26:6–8) as Sarah did to Abraham (12:11–13; 20:2, 12–13). Third, the list of the patriarchs who "died in faith" (Heb 11:8–22) need not be read as exhaustive. That Sarah is mentioned but not Rebekah, Leah, or Rachel need not imply that the latter were not believers any more than Judah's exclusion deprives him a rightful place among those who died in faith.

6

The Spread of Sin in the Third Generation of Patriarchs

Old Testament scholar William LaSor was so disappointed in the patriarchal second generation that he omitted a chapter on Isaac from his Bible character studies, explaining, "Isaac is hardly worth a chapter of his own in this book: he committed the sins of his father Abraham, he made no advances on the faith of that father, and he was, all in all, a rather colorless personality."[1] This chapter will demonstrate that Isaac and Rebekah's sons (Esau and Jacob) do not prove any more successful in containing the spread of sin. In fact, the parental favoritism, sibling rivalry, and deceptive scheming that characterized the former generations are even more pronounced in the third generation.[2]

1. *Great Personalities*, 31.

2. Space will not permit an extended analysis of the sins of Jacob's uncle Laban or of Jacob's two wives, Leah and Rachel. The narrator portrays Leah primarily as a victim rather than a perpetrator of evil, though her envy of Rachel's favored place in Jacob's affections prompts her to an unhealthy rivalry and sinful deeds (30:9). Rachel in turn envies Leah because Leah's womb is fertile while Rachel's is barren (29:31—30:1). This jealousy also leads Rachel to sin by offering Jacob her maidservant as a surrogate mother (30:3–4). Moreover, Rachel stole and deceitfully hid her father's household gods (31:19, 34–35), the consequences of which proved tragic (compare 31:32 with 35:2–4, 16–20). For an extended analysis of the rivalry between Leah and Rachel, see the following: Dresner, "Rachel and Leah: Sibling Tragedy or the Triumph of Piety and Compassion?" 161–81; Garland and Garland, *Flawed Families of the Bible*, 47–69; Fokkelman, *Narrative Art in Genesis*, 130–41. For an examination of Rachel's theft of her father's household gods and its consequences, see Tucker, "Jacob's Terrible Burden," 145–58. As for Laban, Jacob's nemesis, his opportunist ambitions and deceptive ploys serve largely as God's whip to chasten Jacob and as a foil against which God's providential care of Jacob is highlighted. For a careful analysis of Laban's sinful intrigues, see Daube and Yaron, "Jacob's Reception by Laban," 60–62; Fishbane, *Biblical Text and Texture*, 53–62; Fokkelman, *Narrative Art in Genesis*, 123–30, 141–96; Friedman, "Deception for Deception," 131–44; Sherwood, *"Had Not God Been On My Side"*; Michael J. Williams, *Deception in Genesis*, 19–21.

ESAU'S RELIGIOUS DEFECTION

Moses introduces the reader to the firstborn of Isaac and Rebekah's twins, Esau, who is characterized by unusually dense and reddish body hair (25:25).[3] As the boy develops into manhood, he exhibits the inclinations and skill of a hunter (אִישׁ יֹדֵעַ צַיִד), that is, an outdoorsman (אִישׁ שָׂדֶה) (25:27a).[4] While these physical, temperamental, and vocational descriptions are intrinsically amoral, they may associate Esau with somewhat infamous characters the original reader was probably familiar with. For instance, the despotic empire-builder Nimrod was described as "a mighty hunter [גִּבּוֹר צַיִד] before the Lord" (Gen 10:9). Moses's audience may have been familiar with the Babylonian Gilgamesh epic and its brutish character Enkidu, whose body is described as "shaggy with hair" and who is clothed "like Sumuqan" (the god of cattle). At first, Enkidu lives like the wild animals, feeding on grass. But after he has sexual intercourse with a young maiden, he becomes "human" and begins to hunt wild beasts.[5] Noting the apparent connection between the two characters, Vawter remarks, "Hairiness or shagginess seems to have been *eo ipso* a mark of incivility."[6] This conclusion, as it applies to Esau, seems viable when the reader compares the contrastive description of Jacob (25:27b).[7]

3. The text actually reads, "And the first [i.e., Esau] came out reddish all over, as with a hairy cloak [וַיֵּצֵא הָרִאשׁוֹן אַדְמוֹנִי כֻּלּוֹ כְּאַדֶּרֶת שֵׂעָר]." The Hebrew adjective אַדְמוֹנִי signifies a "reddish-brown" coloring and is used to describe David's complexion (1 Sam 16:12; 17:42). Here, the כְּ preposition expresses identity (*HALOT*, 453–54; *GBH* § 133g) and ties the descriptive coloring to Esau's thick bodily hair, which is likened to a "furry cloak" (see Zech 13:4).

4. Note that the second description stands in apposition to the first. Esau's skill and preoccupation with hunting earned him the epithet "man of the field," translated variously as "a husbandman" (DRA, following the Vulgate: *homo agricola*), "dwelling in the country" (LXE, translating the LXX: ἄγροικος), "a man of the open country" (NIV, NJB), "a man who lived in the open" (NAB), or "an outdoorsman" (NLT, CSB).

5. "The Epic of Gilgamesh," *ANET*, 72–77.

6. Vawter, *On Genesis*, 288.

7. Jacob is described as "a sophisticated man [אִישׁ תָּם] who lives in tents" (author's translation). Most English versions translate the adjective תָּם (literally, "complete" or "whole") as "quiet" (ASV, NIV, NRS, NLT, ESV, CSB), "plain," (GNV, KJV, DRA), "mild" (NKJ; TNK), or "peaceable" (NAS). Not only do these renderings lack lexical support, they fail to correlate with Jacob's character as developed throughout the subsequent narrative. The translation "sophisticated" will be defended below.

Esau Sells His Birthright

It soon becomes apparent in the narrative that Esau's bestial qualities also characterize his spiritual interests (or lack thereof). The narrator recounts the incident when Esau returns from the field famished and entreats Jacob for a serving of stew to satisfy his hunger (25:29–30).[8] Jacob demands Esau's "birthright" (בְּכֹרָה) in exchange (25:31). Unhesitatingly, Esau provides Jacob with an oath-bound promise to sell his birthright for the meal (25:31–33). After consuming the stew, Esau goes on his way, and the narrator concludes, "Thus Esau despised his birthright" (25:34). The Hebrew verb translated "despised" (בזה) means "to treat lightly or to view with contempt that which is important or holy."[9] Elsewhere the verb refers to an attitude or action directed toward another person (1 Sam 10:27; 17:42; 2 Sam 6:6), God's name (Mal 1:6), God's words (Num 15:1; 2 Sam 12:9), or God's covenant (Ezek 16:59; 17:16, 18, 19). In the cases where God's name, word, or covenant is the object of this verb, a form of *religious defection* or *apostasy* is usually in view. Not surprisingly, the writer of Hebrews alludes to this incident and to Esau's actions when warning his Christian readers to avoid religious apostasy: "See that no one is *covenantally unfaithful or profane as was Esau* [πόρνος η' βέβηλος ὡς 'Ησαῦ], who for a single meal gave away his birthright" (Heb 12:16; author's translation).[10]

8. Both the narrator and Esau describe his condition as עָיֵף (25:29–30). This adjective normally refers to physical exhaustion (Deut 25:18; Judg 8:4; 2 Sam 16:14; Isa 28:12; 46:10). Nevertheless, the term is often used in contexts describing those who are faint with hunger and/or thirst (Job 22:7; 1 Sam 14:28; 2 Sam 17:29; Isa 29:8).

9. Grisanti, "בזה (*Bzh*)," *NIDOTTE*, 1:628–30; Waltke, "בָּזָה (bāzāʰ) *to despise, disdain, hold in contempt*," *TWOT*, 1:98–99.

10. Nearly all translations and a good number of commentaries interpret the Greek πόρνος as referring to *sexual immorality*. Since the incident in Genesis alluded to by the author of Hebrews does not explicitly refer to sexual immorality, some punctuate the text so that Esau's action is connected only to the second vice, i.e., βέβηλος (KJV, DRA, ASV, NIV, NIV, NJB). The following commentators also take this approach: Bruce, *The Epistle to the Hebrews*, 367, n. 367; E. Elliott, "Esau," 44–45; Owen, *Epistle to the Hebrews*, 7:295; Westcott, *The Epistle to the Hebrews*, 407. These commentators frequently point to the use of πόρνος in Hebrews 13:4, which clearly refers to sexual immorality and to the disjunctive nature of the Greek conjunction ἤ, "or." On the other hand, Philip Hughes agrees that πόρνος is referring to sexual immorality but argues that the author had Esau's polygamous marriage in his purview (*A Commentary on the Epistle to the Hebrews*, 540). There are, however, good reasons for interpreting πόρνος *metaphorically* as a reference to covenantal unfaithfulness or apostasy. First, this warning is the third in a series of warnings beginning with ἐπισκοποῦντες μή τις, "[See to it] that no one

While these assessments of Esau's actions may at first seem excessively critical, a careful reading of the passage justifies them. To begin with, the reader should keep in mind the significance and value of the family birthright. In the ancient Near Eastern milieu, primogeniture normally entailed a double portion of the family inheritance (Deut 21:15–17) and often the position of leadership within the clan or, in the case of royalty, dynastic succession (2 Chr 21:3).[11] Within the context of the "chosen family," it was generally expected that the בְּכוֹר would assume the privilege and responsibility of carrying forward God's redemptive purposes to "all the families of the earth" (Gen 4:1; 9:10; 12:3; 15:2; 17:18; 27:4; 48:13, 17–18). Of course, God sometimes broke with convention and chose a son other than the firstborn to be heir and mediator of his promised blessing (Gen 4:4, 25; 17:19; 21:12; 25:23; 49:8–10; 1 Sam 16:6–13). But this fact does not nullify the universally recognized privilege and value of primogeniture since exceptions to a general rule

. . ." (Heb 12:15–16). Since the first two admonitions are clearly referring to apostasy (note especially the language of the second admonition which is drawn from Deuteronomy 29:18–20, a passage dealing with covenant infidelity), then it seems likely that the third admonition is referring to apostasy. Second, the larger context of Hebrews is concerned largely with the danger of apostasy (Heb 3:12; 4:1, 11; 6:4–6; 10:26–31) and the description of Esau being rejected by God and falling short of repentance (Heb 12:17) corresponds to that concern. Third, the conjunction ἢ does not always relate opposite or opposing alternatives, such as "white or black" (Matt 5:36). Sometimes it may connect closely related alternatives (Matt 5:17; Rom 1:21; 8:35; 1 Cor 5:10, 11; 13:1; 14:6, 23, 24, 37; 2 Cor 9:7; Eph 5:3, 4, 5, 5:27; 1 Thess 2:19; Titus 1:6; Heb 2:6; Jas 1:17; 4:11; 1 Pet 1:18). See Wallace, *Greek Grammar Beyond the Basics*, 672. Note especially how Paul parallels Πορνεία δὲ καὶ ἀκαθαρσία (Eph 5:3) with πόρνος ἢ ἀκάθαρτος (Eph 5:5), suggesting that ἢ may sometimes function to introduce an appositional description. For these reasons, it seems preferable to understand Esau's example as illustrating *both* πόρνος *and* βέβηλος, which, when taken together, describe religious apostasy. See Buchanan, *To the Hebrews*, 219–20; Lane, *Hebrews 9–13*, 439, 454–55. Ellingworth incorporates both viewpoints when he argues that "πόρνος is probably to be taken primarily in a literal sense, as elsewhere in the Greek Bible, but with OT overtones of πορνεία as unfaithfulness to God, which is the author of Hebrews' ultimate concern." *The Epistle to the Hebrews*, 665.

11. J. M. Wilson and R. K. Harrison define the בְּכֹרָה as "the right belonging to the firstborn son, whether the offspring of a legal wife or a concubine. Such a person ultimately became the head of the family, the line being continued through him. As firstborn he inherited a double portion of the paternal estate." "Birthright," *ISBE*, 1:515. According to 1 Chronicles 5:2, the "birthright" was not always inseparably connected with rulership: "though Judah became strong among his brothers and a chief came from him [וּלְנָגִיד], yet the birthright belonged to Joseph [וְהַבְּכֹרָה לְיוֹסֵף]." The double portion of the inheritance appears to be the most essential component entailed in the birthright.

often serve to highlight and validate that rule. So Esau's בְּכֹרָה entailed a privilege and responsibility not to be treated lightly.

However, treating his birthright lightly is precisely what Esau did. And this act of contempt is what Moses portrays with pungent force. First, he invites the reader to compare a firstborn's birthright to a mere bowl of lentil stew, expecting the reader not to miss the enormous disparity between the two.[12] Second, he contrasts Esau's preference for the bowl of stew over the birthright with vivid language, bordering on hyperbole. Esau does not merely wish to eat some of Jacob's stew, but he pleads, "Let me gulp down [הַלְעִיטֵנִי נָא] some of this red red stuff" (25:30).[13] Indeed, Esau complains that he is on the brink of death[14] and reasons that the potential future benefits of his birthright have no value to satisfy his immediate need (25:32).[15] When called on to solemnize his decision with an oath, Esau readily acquiesces (25:33) and thereby commits sacrilege (Exod 20:7; Lev 5:4; Deut 5:11). Finally, the four successive verbs that complete the transaction, וַיֹּאכַל וַיֵּשְׁתְּ וַיָּקָם וַיֵּלַךְ (25:34a),[16] betray a conspicuous absence of any mental or moral reflection on his deed. There is no second thought or twinge of conscience! Although the

12. The writer to the Hebrews highlights this disparity when he portrays Esau as exchanging his birthright for "a single meal" (βρώσεως μιᾶς) (12:16).

13. This is Robert Alter's translation. *Genesis*, 129. Elsewhere Alter suggests the somewhat humorous rendering, "let me cram my maw." *The Art of Biblical Narrative*, 44. The Hiphil imperative of לעט only occurs here. The Qal is used in Psalm 57:4 [Heb 5] to describe lions "devouring" their prey. According to Alter, the verb is used in post-biblical rabbinical literature to describe the feeding of animals. Not surprisingly, Skinner terms this "a coarse expression suggesting bestial voracity" (361, n. 30). Speiser comments, "Esau is depicted as an uncouth glutton." *Genesis*, 195.

14. Literally, he exclaims, "Look, I am going to die [הִנֵּה אָנֹכִי הוֹלֵךְ לָמוּת]!" Such language resembles English hyperboles such as "I'm starving to death" or "I'm dying of thirst." Such exaggerated language only serves to cheapen Esau's pretended distress.

15. Whyte aptly captures the essence of Esau's reasoning: "The covenant promises made to his fathers had no interest, they had no existence even, to Esau. They can take the promises who care for them; as for Esau, a bird in the hand is worth two in the bush." Thus, Whyte summarizes Esau's character in the following poignant terms: "All the time, an animal more than a man. All the time, all body and no soul. All the time, a profane person, who failed of the grace of God." *Bible Characters*, 100.

16. Mathews compares Esau's rapid, unhesitating deed with "the verbal staccato describing the first couple's disobedience." *Genesis 11:27—50:26*, 394–95. Fretheim notes, "Five verbs depict the moment: ate, drank, rose, departed, and despised. The last verb specifies the narrator's judgment that more is at stake than a lapse in judgment. Although not justifying Jacob's actions, that final verb demonstrates that Esau bears responsibility for what happens here." "Genesis," 522.

reader knows that Esau is a genuine human made in God's image, he can hardly distinguish him from a mere beast of the field in terms of Esau's spiritual sensitivity or interests.[17]

As if to add insult to injury, Esau takes two wives from the local Canaanite population when he is forty years old (26:34), an action that finds its prototype in Lamech of old (Gen 4:19). The original Israelite reader would have been disappointed with Esau's choice, recalling Yahweh's many warnings concerning the idolatrous and immoral influence of the Canaanite peoples (Exod 23:32–33; 34:12–16; Deut 7:1–5). He would also recall Abraham's insistence that Isaac marry within the family clan and not take a wife from the Canaanite population (24:2–4).[18] The absence of parental involvement in Esau's decision not only reflects a lack of proactive leadership on Isaac's part but also implies that Esau married without his parents' consent.[19] This conclusion appears to be confirmed by the narrator's remark that Esau's wives "made life bitter for Isaac and Rebekah" (26:35).[20] Fokkelman summarizes the tragedy of Esau's action: "We see that in the domain of morals Esau is rather easy-going—he ignores the usage of semi-nomads—because he has no sense

17. Nearly all interpreters censure Esau's behavior here. Visotzky seems to be an exception and offers the following somewhat positive spin on the account: "As for Esau, he knows his survival skills are intact. Forget the birthright, he's hungry now. Why wait around for the old man to die? He's not looking to get rich and he is not eager to inherit; he likes having Pops alive and sharing meals with him. Enough of intrigue, investment, hanging around the tents. If Jacob needs the birthright so much, Esau doesn't mind. Let him have it if it makes him happy. He is as generous and easy of spirit as a man of the fields. Hell, he is a man of the fields. Jacob can have what he wants, Esau will still eat venison." *Genesis of Ethics*, 138–39.

18. Wenham remarks, "When Abraham's intense concern that Isaac should on no account marry a Canaanite is recalled, it is somewhat unexpected that Esau should marry two." *Genesis 16–50*, 205.

19. Hamilton agrees and summarizes Esau's culpability as follows: "Esau's errors are threefold: He has contracted the marriage himself, thus bypassing his parents; he married exogamously rather than endogamously; he has gone against the honor of his clan group by intermarrying with the native women." *Genesis 18–50*, 210.

20. It is important to note that both Isaac and Rebekah were unhappy with Esau's choice of two Canaanite wives. They both knew from experience the importance of marrying within the scope of kinship, where some trace of the true religion might be found. Furthermore, their own commitment to a monogamous relationship probably accentuated their disappointment in their son's choice of a bigamous relationship. Strangely, Isaac is grieved at Esau's action, yet he later decides to confer the blessing on Esau despite Esau's unworthy character.

of the special task of his family under the sign of the blessing."[21] Once again, Esau shows his irreligious character.

Esau Loses the Blessing

But Esau's defection from the faith of his fathers is sealed several years later on the day when his brother Jacob deceitfully steals the blessing (27:1–40). Interestingly, some commentators appear to view Esau solely as a victim and absolve him of any blame. According to Speiser, "The author himself, by dealing so sensitively with the hapless plight in which Isaac and Esau find themselves *through no fault of their own* [emphasis added] . . . demonstrates beyond any doubt that his personal sympathies are with the victims."[22] Sarna agrees: "There is no doubt where the author's sympathy lies. Esau is the innocent victim of a cruel ruse."[23] Similarly, Visotzky's empathies are with Esau:

> Esau cries for his own loss of innocence here. He cries for the loss of his father, who appears to be an all-too-willing party to this deception. He cries for the lack of a mother's love. He cries as he realizes that whatever blessing he may wrest from his father, it is time to leave home, it is no longer his.[24]

Several considerations, however, constrain the reader to judge otherwise. First of all, the secrecy of Isaac's plan of blessing conferral and Esau's willingness to comply suggest that both parties were operating with a less than clear conscience. Even if Isaac is unaware that Esau had bartered his birthright for a bowl of stew (which is unlikely), Esau remembers what he had done. Although the בְּכֹרָה and the בְּרָכָה were technically distinct (cf. 27:36), the general assumption was that the possessor of the former was to inherit the latter. Yet Esau acts upon his father's announcement without any hesitation or reservations about defrauding Jacob.[25] This is not to absolve Jacob of any blame in selfishly encouraging his brother to despise the birthright. But it is to note that Esau is

21. *Narrative Art in Genesis*, 106.

22. Ibid., 211.

23. Ibid., 193.

24. *Genesis of Ethics*, 148. Smalley and Trent follow a similar line of reasoning. The "blessing" for which Esau craved, they reason, was essentially "encouragement, love, and acceptance from [his] parents." *Blessing*, 15.

25. Extrabiblical evidence attests to the legality of a firstborn selling his inheritance rights to a younger brother. See Gordon, "Biblical Customs," 5.

accomplice to his father's foul scheme, as Jacob will be accomplice to his mother's deceptive plot.

Second, when Esau discovers that Jacob has tricked him out of the blessing, he shows neither remorse for his wrong nor concern for God's plan. Instead, he equates Jacob's thievery of the blessing with Jacob's obtaining of the birthright (27:36b).[26] Yet Jacob obtained the birthright with Esau's full consent (25:32–34). Esau is quick to pick up on Jacob's character flaw—drawing an appropriate connection between his brother's name and his deed (27:36a). But it does not occur to Esau that his own name may be a wordplay on his own character.[27] Certainly, his preference for a bowl of stew above the family birthright lifts his character no higher than that of a beast of the field. In keeping with his brutish nature, Esau now bawls like a wild animal, begging his father for some residual material blessing (27:34–38), just as he had earlier begged his brother for a bowl of stew (25:30, 32). Isaac appears to have recognized his own error and penitently submitted to God's overruling providence (27:33, 37, 39–40),[28] But Esau manifests no signs of repentance or recognition of God's plan at work. Justifiably, the author of Hebrews concludes that Esau "found no occasion for repentance, though he sought the blessing with tears" (12:17; author's translation).[29]

26. He uses the same Hebrew verb (לָקַח) to describe both actions.

27. While the etymology of עֵשָׂו is uncertain, Esau's parents clearly chose his name because of the sound-association with the noun שֵׂעָר, "hair." (25:25). As noted above, the people of the ancient Near East appear to have associated "hairiness" with brutish qualities or habits.

28. See the analysis in Chapter 5.

29. The Greek text in Hebrews reads, μετανοίας γὰρ τόπον οὐχ εὗρεν καίπερ μετὰ δακρύων ἐκζητήσας αὐτήν. Two important exegetical questions arise from the author's language in this verse. First, what was it that Esau sought with tears? The pronoun "it [αὐτήν]" is a feminine singular and may take either "repentance [μετανοίας]" or "the blessing [τὴν εὐλογίαν]" as its antecedent. A few translators or interpreters have argued that "repentance" is the antecedent (NEB: "he found no way open for second thoughts, although he strove, to the point of tears, to find one"; see Ellingworth, *The Epistle to the Hebrews*, 668. But most commentators take "the blessing" as the antecedent. See Bruce, *The Epistle to the Hebrews,* 368; Lane, *Hebrews 9–13*, 440; Owen, *Epistle to the Hebrews*, 7:303, especially in light of the narrative in Genesis, which portrays Esau as weeping *for the blessing* (27:34, 36, 38). Lane also points out that μετανοίας is in the genitive and dependent on the masculine noun τόπον; hence, the expected pronoun would be the masculine αὐτὸν rather than αὐτήν (440). Second what is the nature and referent of the repentance for which Esau found "no occasion"? Some interpreters understand the "repentance" for which Esau sought to be a reference to a "change of mind" *in Isaac.* See John Brown, *Hebrews*, 642; Buchanan, *To the Hebrews,* 220; Owen, Ibid., 7:303, 304–5;

Third, Esau's final response to Jacob's trickery and his father's refusal to reverse the blessing further reveals his true character. In light of Esau's persistent demand, "bless me, even me also" (27:38), Isaac pronounces a subordinate blessing on Esau (27:39–40), confirming the irrevocability of his preeminent blessing on Jacob (27:27–29).[30] Esau reacts in mal-

cf. ASV, which reads, "for he found no place for a change of mind *in his father*"). This interpretation is consistent with the context of Genesis since Esau sought to no avail to persuade Isaac to reverse his decision (Gen 27:33b–40). But other commentators argue that "the repentance" in view cannot be Isaac's. Moffatt asserts that an additional phrase "of his father [τοῦ πατρὸς]" would have been necessary to give that sense. *Epistle to the Hebrews*, 212. Lane also notes that "the phrase [μετανοίας ... τόπον] is a stereotyped one in Jewish circles and always has reference to repentance in a religious sense (e.g., Wis 12:10; 4 Ezra 7:82; 9:12; 2 Apoc. Bar. 85:12; 2 Enoch 62;2; cf. 1 Clem 7:5; 2 Clem 8:2; Tatian, To the Greeks, 15). . . . The pastoral concern with the significance of repentance in Hebrews (cf. 6:1, 4–6) is decisive in determining the nuance of μετάνοια here." *Hebrews 9–13*, 440. For these reasons, it seems preferable to make Esau the subject of "repentance" and interpret the word with its normal religious-ethical connotations. Philip Hughes helpfully summarizes the author of Hebrew's point and application: "The moment of contempt for his birthright had consequences which could not be reversed. He lost, irretrievably, the blessing of the firstborn in an earthly lineage; but those whom our author is addressing are in danger of forfeiting their place in 'the assembly of the firstborn who are enrolled in heaven' (v. 23 below). . . . It was his loss, not his profanity, that he mourned. How much less will there be escape from judgment for those who are contemptuous of the great salvation they have tasted in Christ Jesus (Heb 2:1–3)! Esau continues as a cautionary example of the impossibility of restoring again to repentance those who have rebelliously sinned against the light (cf. Heb 6:4ff.)." *Commentary on the Epistle to the Hebrews*, 541.

30. The language of Isaac's "blessing" on Esau might be interpreted as an anti-blessing or curse. Whereas the preposition in Jacob's blessing was intended as a partitive marker (*IBHS* § 11.2.11e), indicating *the content* of Jacob's blessing (i.e., "May God give you *of* the dew of heaven and *of* the fatness of the earth."), the preposition in Esau's anti-blessing may function as an ablative of separation (*IBHS* § 11.2.11b, indicating Esau's *separation from* fertility (i.e., "Behold, *away from* the fatness of the earth shall your dwelling be, and *away from* the dew of heaven on high."). Consequently, Fokkelman remarks, "Here the ambiguous meaning of the preposition *min* has been made use of: 'part of' (v. 28) becomes 'far away from' (v. 39). The chiasmus visualizes that the contrast is maximal. A cruel joke, this verse! The second line (v. 40) assures Esau, that he will have as hard a life as Ishmael who has also been driven aside (Gen 16:12), and makes it painfully clear to him that the matter has to stop at the oracle: serve you shall!" *Narrative Art in Genesis*, 111. Moreover, Isaac's declaration "and you shall serve your brother" clearly parallels the language of Noah's curse on Canaan (Gen 9:25, 27). Thus, Kidner writes, "So Isaac pronounces over Esau the appropriate destiny of the 'profane person': the freedom to live unblessed (39) and untamed (40)" (157). The author of Hebrews, however, asserts, "By faith Isaac invoked future blessings on Jacob and Esau" (11:20). So at some level, Isaac's prophetic declaration regarding Esau's future must be viewed as a "blessing." One might argue that Isaac's "blessing" when directed towards Esau was intended euphemistically

ice toward Jacob (וַיִּשְׂטֹם עֵשָׂו אֶת־יַעֲקֹב)[31] and plots to murder him once Isaac has died (27:41). One should not miss the parallels between Esau's rivalry with Jacob and Cain's rivalry with Abel (Gen 4:1–16). In both cases, God prefers the younger brother above the older brother (4:4b–5a; 25:23). Moreover, Esau's destiny, like Cain's, is away from the earth's fertility (4:12; 27:39). The elder brother's response to God's preference for the younger is nearly identical. Cain becomes angry, hates Abel, and kills him (4:5b–6, 8). Esau becomes angry, hates Jacob, and plots to kill him (27:41). In Abel's death and Jacob's escape, God's overruling providence plays the decisive role.

Therefore, in light of Esau's complicity in Isaac's plot, his lack of personal remorse, his disregard for God's redemptive program, and his Cain-like reaction to God's preference for his brother, the reader is compelled to find Esau guilty of sinning against his family and against God. Not only does he show contempt for the covenant promise, but he also plots to destroy its divinely appointed mediator. These facts conspire to reveal Esau as the epitome of an irreligious man and an irrecoverable apostate (Heb 12:16–17).[32] They also serve to demonstrate that the

---

as a curse (see 1 Kgs 21:10, 13; Job 1:5, 11; 2:5, 9). But the author of Hebrews uses one and the same verb to describe Isaac's actions towards both sons. The best solution, it seems, is to view Esau's "blessing" as a kind of *subordinate* blessing that is distinguished from the *ultimate* blessing tied to the promise (Gen 12:2–3). This reading is supported by the fact that the author of Hebrews lists Jacob before Esau, indicating that Jacob received the preeminent blessing tied to the promise. Furthermore, Jacob's deathbed-oracle consisted in his "blessing each [of his sons] with the blessing suitable to him" (49:28). Yet some of his "blessings" included "curses" (see 49:3–7)! So the reader may view Isaac's declaration regarding Esau's future as a "blessing," which fell short of *the* blessing par excellence and which paradoxically contained elements of anti-blessing or curse. This reading explains Esau's subsequent response of murderous anger (27:41). For a similar approach, see Waltke, *An OT Theology*, 326.

31. The psalmist uses שׂטם to describe the animosity his enemies feel towards him (Ps 55:3 [Heb 4]). After their father's death, Joseph's brothers worry that he may be nursing bitter feelings of שׂטם towards them for selling him into slavery (49:23; 50:15). Prolonged suffering tempts Job to the mistaken conclusion that God viewed him with שׂטם (Job 16:9; 30:31). These usages have led Baloian to conclude that the verb שׂטם "has the sense of strong hostility." "שׂטם (śṭm) *NIDOTTE*, 3:1230–31.

32. This last point may be disputed in light of the fact that Esau later reconciles with Jacob and appears to manifest a generous and kind disposition toward his brother (33:4–16). Many commentators make much of Esau's "change of heart." Arnold, for instance, remarks, "The great surprise (and relief!) of the narrative is that Esau too is a different man than he was twenty years before." *Encountering the Book of Geneis*, 134. Peter Williams asserts, "Esau was a changed man, he was no longer the vengeful, bitter brother Jacob had left twenty years before. He was kind and considerate and satisfied

"great harmartiology in Gen. III-XI" where "sin broke in and spread as an avalanche"[33] is still at work in the patriarchal narratives, despite the

---

with what he had. . . . It seems God had been working in Esau's life as well as Jacob's. We ought never to feel that anyone's life is beyond the power of God to change it for the better." *From Eden to Egypt*, 183–84. Luther pushes the optimism a step further and asserts, "It is also likely that in the end Esau was saved." *Lectures in Genesis*, 6:166. Jordan agrees and attributes Esau's change of heart to Rebekah's prayer, which, he thinks, was symbolized in her deceptive ploy in snatching the blessing for Jacob! *Primeval Saints*, 104. Several factors, however, suggest a less optimistic reading of Esau's "change of heart." First, Esau's intention in intercepting Jacob appears to have been initially hostile. The Hebrew phrase translated, "he is coming to meet you [הֹלֵךְ לִקְרָאתְךָ]" often connotes hostile intent (1 Sam 23:28; 1 Kgs 20:27; 2 Kgs 23:29). The fact Esau has mustered four-hundred men, which was the approximate size of a standard militia (Gen 14:14; 1 Sam 22:2, 25:13; 30:10, 17), further supports an unfriendly reading of Esau's action, which Jacob appropriately interprets (32:7–12). Second, Esau's transition from a hostile to a friendly and even affectionate posture may be accounted for on the basis of the extravagant tribute that Jacob shrewdly presented to him (32:13–20), as well as the vassal-like demeanor Jacob demonstrated towards him (33:3). As Vawter notes, "Bowing to the ground seven times is not an invention of Genesis to heighten the impression of Jacob's subservience but was a conventional mark of fealty attested to by the Amarna letters." *On Genesis*, 353; cf. *ANET*, 483–85. So Jacob's gift to Esau, which Jacob actually portrays as a kind of restitution of "the blessing" that he had taken from Esau (33:11), and Jacob's humble posture serve to soften Esau's initially aggressive intent and stir up the remnants of natural affection in him (33:4). The fact that Esau initially refuses Jacob's gift and claims to have plenty (33:9) need not be interpreted as a complete change from a materialistic mindset to a magnanimous goodwill. More likely, Esau's refusal was simply part of common ancient Near Eastern etiquette and by no means implied that he was uninterested in Jacob's gift (see Gen 23:3–16). Third, though Jacob demonstrates a penitent attitude towards his brother, Esau fails to reciprocate. Furthermore, and most importantly, Esau still manifests no signs of interest in God's covenant program, which would have been evidenced by his assuming a posture of subservience towards Jacob, the one whom Yahweh had appointed as the covenant mediator (Gen 12:3; 25:23; 27:29, 40). As Leupold perceptively remarks, "One thing surely stands in the way of regarding Esau as a man who had come to the true faith. Had his faith accepted what the Lord had ordained, he would have held to Jacob as possessor of the divine promise. His failure to do this seems to indicate that the true spiritual values were not grasped or understood by him. This prevents his being classed as a man of faith." *Exposition of Genesis*, 898. See also the assessment of Duguid, *Relentless Grace*, 123; and Waltke, *Genesis*, 453. Leupold concedes, incorrectly, that Esau may have become a believer later in life. Ibid., 898. Since the author of Hebrews likens Esau to the kind of apostate whose condition is irremediable (Heb 12:16–17), it is unlikely he would have interpreted Esau's reconciliation with Jacob or the later inclusion of his genealogy in Genesis as indicative of repentance. In light of these considerations, it seems doubtful that Esau is presently numbered among "the spirits of the righteous made perfect" (Heb 12:23b). It is also worth noting that Moses never portrays Esau as praying to God or calling on the name of the Lord. Nor is Esau the recipient of direct revelation as are the other patriarchs.

33. von Rad, *OT Theology*, 1:154, 168.

greater light and privileges of this latter period. Indeed, right here within the patriarchal community the reader encounters a man whose moral character resembles Cain, Lamech, and antediluvians of old of whom it was said, "every intention of the thoughts of [their] heart was only evil continually" (Gen 6:5).

JACOB'S LEGACY OF INTRIGUE

Something unusual characterized the birth of Isaac and Rebekah's twins. As the first child, Esau, emerged from Rebekah's womb, the second child, Jacob, was "grasping the heel" (אֹחֶזֶת בַּעֲקֵב) of Esau with his hand. Hence, the "heel-grabber" was named Jacob [יַעֲקֹב] (Gen 25:26). As the two boys grew, so grew the gap between their respective temperamental and vocational proclivities. In contrast with Esau, Jacob became, literally, "a complete man who dwelled in tents [אִישׁ תָּם יֹשֵׁב אֹהָלִים]" (25:27b; author's translation). The interpretive crux of this description centers on the Hebrew adjective תָּם. Normally, this term carries ethical overtones and is used to characterize a man of moral integrity.[34] Noting the common moral usage of this adjective, Evans argues that the narrator depicts Jacob as an "innocent man." To support this interpretation, Evans attempts to harmonize the apparent discrepancy between this positive description and the many apparently devious actions of Jacob in the later narratives. He then concludes, "From beginning to end, the stories about Jacob can be read as the narrator's imaginative effort to maintain Jacob's innocence—to be consistent with his opening characterization of Jacob as an ʾîsh tām."[35]

34. For example, both the author of the book of Job and God describe Job as "a blameless [תָּם] and upright man, who fears God and turns away from evil" (Job 1:1, 8; 2:3). By associating תָּם with other positive ethical descriptions, the author clearly highlights its positive moral overtones. Later in the narrative, Bildad assures Job, "Behold, God will not reject a blameless man [תָּם], nor take the hand of evildoers [מְרֵעִים]" (Job 8:20). The antithetical parallelism of "blameless man" with "evildoers" once again confirms the ethical usage of תָּם. And this moral usage of תָּם is found in other texts as well (Job 9:20, 22; Pss 36:37; 50:23; 64:5; Prov 10:29; 29:10).

35. "The Patriarch Jacob: An 'Innocent Man,'" 121–30 [esp. 129]. Jordan essential agrees with Evan's reading and asserts, "The Bible presents Jacob as a righteous man even in the womb and as a mature believer for his entire life: a 'perfect' man." *Primeval Saints*, 112. Hamilton examines other possibilities but decides to throw in his lot with Evans, *Genesis 18–50*, 181–82. Fretheim concedes that the adjective's moral sense may be appropriate "at this point in [Jacob's] life." "Genesis," 521. Alter translates the term "simple" but in a note suggests that the author may intend the moral idea of "inno-

But a perusal of translations and commentaries reveals little support for Evans's thesis.[36] A few scholars, noting the antithetical parallelism of 25:27, depict a "domestic,"[37] "orderly,"[38] or "civilized"[39] Jacob, as opposed to an outdoorsy, undisciplined, or uncivilized Esau. Calvin agrees that the descriptions of Esau and Jacob are antithetical, but he thinks Moses commends Esau's potential as a "courageous man" and censures Jacob's initial traits as an "indolent" man, "addicted to domestic leisure."[40] A more contextually nuanced reading will view the descriptions of Esau and Jacob as antithetical at one level, yet as parallel at another. The antithetical character of אִישׁ שָׂדֶה and יֹשֵׁב אֹהָלִים suggests a corresponding antithesis between אִישׁ יֹדֵעַ צַיִד and אִישׁ תָּם. By themselves, the epithets "a man of the field" and "one who lives in "tents" are morally neutral. Nevertheless, just as Moses probably intended his original readers to perceive a hint of moral weakness in his description of Esau, he is likely preparing the reader for the unfolding of Jacob's character flaw by the phrase אִישׁ תָּם. In this case, Jacob's "completeness" does not refer to "moral wholeness" but rather to the completeness of Jacob's mental acumen and social adeptness.[41] The English term "sophisticated" comes close to

cence" as irony. *Genesis*, 128. Mathews also suggests a double entendre that conveys irony. *Genesis 11:27—50:26*, 391.

36. English translations suggest ideas like "quiet" (ASV, NIV, NRSV, NLT, ESV, CSB), "plain," (KJV, DRA), "mild" (NKJ; TNK), or "peaceable" (NAS). The LXX renders the Hebrew ἄπλαστος, which the Vulgate follows with *simplex*, corresponding roughly to the English "plain" or "simple." Only Luther's German translation (1545) gives the Hebrew term its common ethical sense by rendering the clause *Jakob aber ein frommer Mann*. As far as commentators go, Luther, consistent with his translation of the verse, describes Jacob as "forthright and irreproachable," also allegorizing Jacob's tent-dwelling as referring to his frequenting "a house of God," namely, "a church." *Lectures on Genesis*, 4:378–86. Most commentators follow the English translations and interpret the term in a morally neutral sense. See Driver, *Book of Genesis*, 247; Gibson, *Genesis*, 2:137; Hartley, *Genesis*, 236; Roop, *Genesis*, 170; Sarna, *Genesis*, 180–81; Speiser, *Genesis*, 193–95; Stigers, *Commentary on Genesis*, 210; Wenham, *Genesis 16–50*, 171, 177.

37. Aalders, *Genesis*, 81; Keil and Delitzsch, *Pentateuch*, 268.

38. Skinner, *Genesis*, 361; von Rad, *Genesis*, 266.

39. Ross, *Creation & Blessing*, 448; Waltke, *Genesis*, 362; Westermann, *Genesis 12–36*, 415.

40. Calvin, *Genesis*, 2:49.

41. Fokkelman appears to suggest something close to this when he writes, "Whereas the rough man of nature, Esau, does not know how to control himself at crucial moments and forgets his dignity (25:31!), Jacob, the cattle-breeder, calculating and cute as he is, works at one purpose for all he is worth, to become the blessed one who takes the

capturing the narrator's intent.[42] Intrinsically, the description is morally ambiguous. But just as the "shrewd" (עָרוּם) Serpent might employ his cunning for good (Prov 12:16, 23; 13:16; 14:8, 15, 18; 22:8; 27:12) or evil (Job 5:12; 15:5), so the "sophisticated" (תָּם) Jacob might use his mental acumen and personal ambition for good or ill.[43] That Jacob's תָּם often took a turn for the worse is borne out in the ensuing narratives.

Jacob Snatches Esau's Birthright

Regarding Jacob's obtaining of Esau's birthright, Evans avers, "Nothing in the narrative suggests that Jacob did not act within his legal and moral rights."[44] Hamilton argues, "The author or narrator of 25:27–34 never condemns Jacob for his modus operandi."[45] According to Luther, Jacob somehow knew "by the voice of God" that he was the true heir of the birthright and "did well by watching for all opportunities to obtain the primogeniture that belonged to him."[46] Similarly, Calvin praises Jacob

---

first place. . . . This singleness of purpose constitutes Jacob's 'integrity,' his 'being a man of character.' Thus it looks like the only mysterious adjective in the Story of Jacob describes his personality most tersely." *Narrative Art in Genesis*, 91.

42. The term "sophisticated" captures the basic lexical idea of "wholeness," in this case describing a man who is mentally and socially complete. Furthermore, this rendering best corresponds with Jacob's character as one who has acquired a knowledge about the ways of the world, who is self-confident, and who is not easily deceived (except by others with equal or greater sophistication!). Walton also favors this rendering. *Genesis*, 550.

43. Kidner also notes the potential for good or bad in this quality: "The Hebrew tām which has a suggestion of 'sound' or 'solid,' the level-headed quality that made Jacob, at his best, toughly dependable, and at his worst a formidably cool opponent" (152). Janzen has also captured the implied impending moral weaknesses of Esau and Jacob. Keeping in mind the original reader's familiarity with the bestial Enkidu in the Gilgamesh Epic, Janzen writes, "Esau is the 'natural' man. He is not morally inferior, for his life does not really move in the moral realm at all. . . . Jacob is not a 'natural' man, but one poised before the complexities of human interaction with their opportunities for moral uprightness or deviance, spiritual integrity or alienation." *Abraham and All the Families of the Earth*, 97.

44. "Patriarch Jacob: An 'Innocent Man,'" 125.

45. *Genesis 18–50*, 186.

46. *Lectures on Genesis*, 4:395. Luther seems to equivocate when, on the one hand, he excuses Isaac's plan to bless Esau on account of the ambiguity of the birth-oracle (see *Lectures on Genesis*, 5:101–2) but then, on the other hand, he excuses Jacob's scheme to obtain the birthright from Esau on account of the apparent perspicuity of the oracle—clear at least to Rebekah and Jacob!

for self-denial of earthly things (i.e., he allowed Esau to have the stew) and his aspiration for heavenly things (i.e., he desired the birthright).[47]

Notwithstanding these positive appraisals and the absence of any explicit censure of Jacob's action, there are good reasons for finding fault with Jacob's "modus operandi." To begin with, the narrator's explicit censure of Esau should not be read as an endorsement of Jacob's actions. For, as Ronning observes, "The concluding editorial comment . . . implies that the story is not so much about Jacob's virtue, but about Esau's lack of it."[48] Furthermore, a skillful narrator does not clutter his story with too many obvious moralizations but allows the reader to assess for himself the actor's moral character on the basis of what he says and does.[49] In the present case, the narrator has just introduced Esau as the "dull-witted" brother who cares only about earthly things. Jacob, on the other hand, is the mentally astute and personally ambitious man. While not condemning entirely Jacob's aspirations for the birthright, the sensitive reader can detect a lack of faith and patience in God's providence, as well as a lack of brotherly concern for Esau's spiritual welfare. Whereas both Jacob's parents resorted to prayer when they perceived obstacles to the future (25:21, 22), there is no mention of Jacob praying to God for the realization of his perceived destiny (25:23). Only Jacob's clever cunning comes into view. What is more, Jacob's insistence that Esau seal the transaction "effective today!" (כַיּוֹם) betrays an impatience[50] that reminds the reader of Adam and Eve hastily grasping at wisdom (Gen 3:6) or of Abraham and Sarah impatiently generating the offspring (Gen 16:1–4)—things

47. *Genesis*, 2:50–55.

48. "Curse on the Serpent (Genesis 3:15) in Biblical Theology and Hermeneutics," 201.

49. With this basic axiom in view, the reader does not need the narrator to act as his tutor and draw the moral lesson for him. On the contrary, the narrator invites the reader to assess the actor's speech and actions in the light of the overall worldview in which the story is set. Moreover, the narrator will often provide hints to guide the reader's assessment. See also Fokkelman, *Narrative Art in Genesis*, 115–16.

50. Wenham contrasts Jacob's curt demand, "Sell me your birthright" (25:31) with Esau's more polite request, "Please let me have a swallow of some of that red stuff there" (25:31; NAU). *Genesis 16–50*, 177–78. It seems preferable, however, to interpret Esau's use of the particle נָא not as a precative but simply as an intensification of the imperative, adding a sense of urgency and importance (cf. Gen 22:2). The NIV captures the idea well when it translates Esau's request, "Quick, let me have some of that red stew!" Esau is not trying to be socially polite (which does not fit his brutish character). He, like Jacob, wants what he wants *now*!

God intended each couple to attain in due time and in the divinely appointed way. Finally, Jacob appears just as calloused in taking the birthright, as Esau appears in selling it (25:34). The reader is left with the distinct impression that Jacob had just done to his neighbor (even his own brother) something he would not have wanted his neighbor to do to him (Lev 19:19; Matt 7:12).[51] Nor is the narrator as silent about his opinion of Jacob's action as some interpreters allege. Indeed, Moses frequently betrays his moral judgment against wrongful behavior by noting the age-old law of retribution. Hence, the stone Jacob rolled onto Esau in order to obtain the בְּכֹרָה came rolling back onto him (29:23–26)![52] Consequently, the careful reader will agree with most commentators who appreciate Jacob's ambition to play a part in God's program of blessing but who cannot approve of his modus operandi.[53]

51. Fretheim catches this lack of goodwill on the part of Jacob. After noting the author's explicit censure of Esau, Fretheim writes, "The author, on the other hand, presents Jacob as a clever and opportunistic individual, who knows what he wants. He takes advantage of a brother in need (of which Esau is later rightly critical, 27:36) and his hospitality to his brother contrasts with both Abraham and Lot (chaps. 18–19)" "Genesis," 522.

52. Friedman captures the irony well when he observes, "The man who took away the firstborn privilege of his brother has now suffered because of the firstborn privilege of his beloved's [i.e., Rachel's] sister." "Deception for Deception," 134. Chapter 8 will examine the consequences of Jacob's deception more fully.

53. Leupold writes, "[Jacob's] eagerness was commendable. His choice of means in arriving at the desired end was not always above reproach. He felt he had to help the good Lord along occasionally. He was not fully confident in God's methods for arriving at the goal. He felt the need of occasionally inserting a bit of assistance of his own. Such an attitude was one of mistrust: confidence in human ingenuity rather than divine dependability—in one word—unbelief" (712). Similarly, Ross draws the following moral from the story: "those who earnestly desire spiritual possessions must not seek to attain them through base means." *Creation & Blessing*, 452. Alter arrives at a similar assessment when he observes, "Jacob is a man who thinks about the future. . . . This qualifies him as a suitable bearer of the birthright: historical destiny does not just happen; you have to know how to make it happen, how to keep your eye on the distant horizon of present events. But this quality of wary calculation does not necessarily make Jacob more appealing as a character, and, indeed, may even raise some moral questions about him. The contrast in this scene between the impetuous, miserably famished Esau and the shrewdly businesslike Jacob may not be entirely to Jacob's advantage, and the episode is surely a little troubling in light of the quality of 'innocence' which the narrator has just fastened as an epithet to the younger twin." *Art of Biblical Narrative*, 45.

Jacob Snatches Esau's Blessing

Apparently, Jacob's legal acquisition of the birthright did not alter his father's intention to pass on the Abrahamic blessing to his favorite son (27:1–4). Fortunate (?) for Jacob, though, his mother intercepted the plot and relayed it to him along with a deceptive scheme of her own to secure the blessing for her favorite son (27:5–13). Jacob goes along with her ruse, disguises himself as Esau, and snatches the blessing from his father before Esau returns (27:14–30). Earlier analyses brought Isaac, Rekekah, and Esau before the bar of justice and found each one guilty. Now it is time to assess Jacob's part in this ruse.

Jacob has his advocates. Evans shifts all responsibility to Rebekah and treats Jacob as the reluctant victim who gets caught up in his mother's lie.[54] Jordan depicts Jacob's trickery of Isaac and Esau as a wrestling match of faith.[55] Augustine reinterprets Isaac's negative assessment of Jacob's action (27:35) by arguing for a figurative meaning for Isaac's words.[56] Luther defends Jacob by insisting that Jacob was giving preference to the First Table of the Law (i.e., honoring God's oracle) over the Second Table of the Law (i.e., honoring his father's wish).[57] Calvin acknowledges that Jacob sinned but, to the reader's surprise, alleges that Jacob's sin was not the fact that he went along with his mother's deceitful plot but that he hesitated at the outset, which, according to Calvin, evidenced a lack of faith![58]

54. Evans is quick to assert, "It is Rebekah who is responsible for concocting this act of deception," and to note, "Jacob is reluctant to go along with the ruse," "Patriarch Jacob: An 'Innocent Man,'" 125–27.

55. *Primeval Saints*, 107–8.

56. According to Augustine, "The reason it says 'He came with guile' is that what was being done had a figurative sense. Isaac, after all, would not have confirmed the blessing on a guileful, deceitful man who more justly would deserve a curse. *So it wasn't a case of real guile*, especially since *he did not in fact lie* when he said, 'I am your elder son Esau.' For that one had already made a bargain with his brother and sold him his rights as firstborn. So he told his father that he had what he had bought from his brother; what that one had lost had passed to this one. The title of firstborn had not been eliminated from Isaac's household. The title of firstborn was still here—but not with the one who had sold it. Where else was it but with the younger brother? Because he knew the symbolic mystery in all this, Isaac confirmed the blessing and said to this other son, 'What am I to do for you?' He answered, 'Bless me too, father; you do not only have one blessing.' But Isaac knew of only one" (emphasis added). *Sermon 4.23*, in *ACCS*, 2:178–79.

57. *Lectures on Genesis*, 5:113–17.

58. *Genesis*, 2:85–86.

Once again, the textual data will not let Jacob off the hook. First, Jacob's initial objection to his mother's plan arises not out of moral but merely penal concerns. Jacob is not concerned with moral integrity, as his future son Joseph will be in a later narrative (39:9). He is fearful of the injury that he may incur from his father's curse (27:11–12). Once his mother dispenses with that concern, Jacob is ready to move ahead with the plan (27:13–17) despite the fact that he has acknowledged the immoral nature of that act (27:12).[59]

Second, Jacob plainly lies to his blind father in several ways. He verbally identifies himself as Esau at least twice (27:19, 24).[60] Then, when his father questions the unusual swiftness of his return with game, Jacob deceitfully claims that his father's God has providentially prospered his errand (27:20). By making such a false claim, Jacob not only violates the Second Table of the Law—"you shall not bear false witness against your neighbor" (Exod 20:16)—but he also violates the First Table of the Law—"you shall not take the name of the Lord your God in vain" (Exod 20:7).[61] So Luther's defense of Jacob is invalidated. In addition to verbal lies, Jacob employs other forms of deceptive disguise to approximate the feel of Esau's skin, the smell of Esau's garments, and the taste of Esau's cooking (27:22–23, 25, 27). Although Jacob was not the mastermind behind this deceptive scheme, he was certainly a willing accomplice. And the fact that Jacob took advantage of a father (Exod 20:12; Lev 19:3) who was blind (Lev 19:4; Deut 27:18) only aggravates his culpability.

59. The verb תעע occurs here in the Pilpel theme and in 2 Chronicles 36:13 in the Hithpalpel theme where it describes the Israelites' *repeatedly* and *habitually* scoffing at God's prophets. Both of these themes can convey habitual action, thereby denoting the moral character and not just the action of the subject. See Powell, "תעע (t^{cc})," in *NIDOTTE*, 4:320–21.

60. Isaac's repeated request for a confirmation of "Esau's" identity and Jacob's repeated affirmation deepen the suspense and aggravate Jacob's guilt for the deception.

61. Other commentators have picked up on the aggravated nature of Jacob's offense. Hamilton writes, "The low point in Jacob's conversation with his father is his statement that he is back so quickly because God just put the game in front of him. Here is an appeal to deity in order to cover up duplicity." *Genesis 18–50*, 220. Ross observes, "The first lie was enough to deceive, but the second was blasphemy." *Creation & Blessing*, 478. Duguid remarks, "Jacob played the situation like a consummate professional, proving that he was the smooth brother in every sense of the word. He was not only willing to lie outright to his father, answering his question 'Are you really my son, Esau?' with a boldfaced 'I am' (Gen 27:24). He was even willing to invoke God's name in his dissembling, answering Isaac's query as to how he had been able to return so rapidly with this affirmation: 'The Lord your God gave me success' (Gen 27:20)." *Relentless Grace*, 34.

Third, Isaac passes negative judgment on Jacob's action. Isaac accuses Jacob of coming "deceitfully [בְּמִרְמָה]" (27:35).[62] The reader should recall that Isaac has just realized that his own scheming has been uncovered and overruled by God (27:33). Isaac finally apprehends the true meaning of the birth-oracle, and he knows that it was ultimately God who thwarted his plans to bless Esau and "tricked" him into conferring the blessing irrevocably on Jacob. So in labeling Jacob's ruse as deceitful, Isaac is condemning not *the result* but *the manner* in which Jacob has obtained the blessing. That the narrator himself agrees with Isaac's assessment is once again demonstrated when he highlights the "poetic justice" Jacob suffers for his own deception (29:25; 37:31–34).

Fourth, Jacob's deed creates circumstances that force him to depart from the Promised Land. Earlier, the parallel between Esau's rivalry with Jacob and Cain's rivalry with Abel (Gen 4:1–16) was noted. But in this case, Esau's expulsion from the place of God's special presence, unlike Cain's, is delayed. On the other hand, Jacob is forced eastward into exile, a movement that normally has negative connotations in Genesis (3:24; 4:16; 11:2; 25:6). True, Yahweh promises to protect Jacob and bring him back to the Land of Promise (28:15). Nevertheless, the hardships Jacob suffers during his sojourn in Haran are comparable to the Israelites' afflictions in Egypt. At the very least, one may conclude Abraham's method of obtaining a wife for Isaac (Gen 24:1–67) is to be preferred above the method Jacob is forced to follow.

In summary, Jacob's method of obtaining the blessing from his father is not commendable.[63] Perhaps there was a seed of forward-looking faith in Jacob's ambition, as some commentators have suggested, but at this stage in the narrative, Jacob's תָּם more closely resembles the subtlety of the shrewd Serpent (3:1) than the innocence of the nude primeval parents (2:25). Indeed, in attacking his brother's heel (27:36) in order to

62. The Hebrew noun מִרְמָה is always used elsewhere in a negative sense, never positively (Gen 34:13; Ps 24:4; Isa 53:9). Hence, in Isaac's estimation, Jacob has acted sinfully and treacherously against Esau and against his father. Apparently some rabbis were not comfortable with Isaac's assessment and therefore attempted to reinterpret the text. One Targum reads 27:35 as "Your brother came with wisdom [*bḥwkmh*] and received [*wqbyl*] your blessing." Onkelos, 165 nn. 11–12. Similarly, another Rabbi asserts, "[Jacob] came with the wisdom of his knowledge of the Torah." *GR*, 2:413.

63. For an objective but brief evaluation of this and other deceptive acts in Genesis, see Michael Williams, *Deception in Genesis*, 14–29.

advance God's program, Jacob has unwittingly employed the Serpent's tactics rather than God's (Gen 3:15).[64]

JACOB'S DYSFUNCTIONAL FAMILY

To escape Esau's wrath and to find a suitable wife, Jacob must flee to Haran where his extended family resides (27:42—28:5). Because Jacob is the chosen one (25:23), God promises to protect him during his sojourn (28:15), but such protection does not translate into a trouble-free life. Uncle Laban tricks Jacob into marrying his firstborn Leah rather than Rachel whom Jacob desired (29:18–26) and requires Jacob to work an additional seven years to acquire Rachel as wife (29:27–30). Pressured by his affection for Rachel and resolve not to be deprived of his desire, Jacob agrees to Laban's terms (29:28). The result is a bigamous marriage to sisters in which Jacob "loved Rachel more than Leah" (29:29–30).

Jacob's Polygamy

Most commentators tend to sympathize with Jacob and his wives at this point in the narrative since their unhappy marriage and the rivalry it spawned are traced to the opportunistic deceit of a greedy uncle and unloving father. Certainly, Laban's sins feature largely in this narrative,[65] and some sympathy for Jacob and his two wives is in order. Both Jacob and his wives, however, commit acts that have been censured in the previous narrative and condemned by the Mosaic law. In the first place, the original Israelite audience would not have viewed Jacob's polygamous marriage to two sisters positively. He would have inferred from the creation account (Gen 2:23–24), the negatively portrayed polygamous marriages in primeval history (Gen 4:19; 6:1–2), and the examples of the previous

64. "[The woman's offspring] shall bruise [the Serpent's] head, and [the Serpent] shall bruise his heel [עָקֵב]." Jacob's [יַעֲקֹב] behavior towards Esau and towards his father may indicate that he was not yet a true believer at this time. In that case, he was acting as a genuine "offspring of the Serpent." But even a genuine believer may adopt the Serpent's tactics without fully realizing his error. Thus when Peter urged Jesus to sidestep the cross (Matt 16:22), Jesus rebuked him saying, "Get behind me, Satan!" (Matt 16:23).

65. Although Laban is technically a member of the second generation of the extended patriarchal family, most of his sinful deeds are narrated in connection with the third generation. Nevertheless, his proclivity towards material gain suggests itself as early as Genesis 24:29–31, where he eagerly welcomes Abraham's servant who has expressed in interest in procuring Laban's sister as a wife for Isaac and is prepared to offer a healthy מֹהַר for her hand (24:10, 53).

patriarchs[66] that monogamy was God's norm and that polygamy was to be avoided. What is more, the idea of a man simultaneously marrying two sisters would have been detestable to Moses's original audience (Lev 18:18).[67] Of course, Jacob's guilt is somewhat mitigated by the fact that he married Leah unaware, thinking she was Rachel (29:22–25). Yet the text does not suggest that Jacob was legally or morally obligated to work another seven years for Rachel. Perhaps Jacob could have successfully annulled the marriage on the basis of Laban's breach of contract.[68] Or he could have acknowledged God's own hand behind the ruse, as his father Isaac had been forced to acknowledge (27:33, 37, 39–40), accepting *the firstborn* (הַבְּכִירָה) as an appropriate complement for the one who by his own deceitful cunning had obtained *firstborn status* (בְּכֹרָה) (25:31–34). But Jacob's preferential affection for Rachel overruled (29:18), and he willingly entered into a relationship that would breed the same kind of sibling rivalry that he had known at home.[69]

66. Abraham's example upheld the principle of monogamy both positively and negatively. The many years that Abraham remained in a monogamous relationship with Sarah despite her barrenness demonstrate a conscientious commitment to the ideal of monogamy on his part. When he finally does succumb to the temptation of taking of Hagar as wife, the narrator portrays the decision negatively. Isaac's exclusive commitment to Rebekah despite her 20 years of barrenness also bears witness to an awareness of monogamy as God's ideal standard for marriage.

67. A few, such as Kaiser and Murray, have suggested that the phrase in Leviticus 18:18, וְאִשָּׁה אֶל־אֲחֹתָהּ לֹא תִקָּח לִצְרֹר, should be translated, "You shall not take one wife to another to be a rival wife" on the basis of similar expressions elsewhere in the OT (Exod 26:3, 5, 6, 17; Ezek 1:9, 23; 2:13; see also the analogous phrase, אִישׁ אֶל־אָחִיו [Gen 42:21, 28; Exod 10:23; 16:15; 25:20; 37:9; Num 14:4; Isa 8:18; Jer 13:14; 23:35; 25:26; Ezek 24; 23], which does not necessarily connote siblings). If this translation is correct, then we have an explicit prohibition against polygamy in the Mosaic legislation. See Kaiser, *Toward OT Ethics*, 185–86; Murray, *Principles of Conduct*, 251–56. Most commentators, however, understand this verse to be a prohibition against a particular species of polygamy, namely, a man marrying sibling wives while both are living (e.g., Jacob's marriage of Leah and Rachel). See R. Laird Harris, "Leviticus," 599; Keil and Delitzsch, *The Pentateuch*, 416; Ross, *Holiness to the Lord*, 345. The Mosaic law may have tolerated and circumscribed the abuses of polygamy "because of [the Israelites'] hardness of heart," though "from the beginning it was not so" (Matt 19:8). For more on polygamy in the OT, see Hesselgrave, "Polygamy," *BDCE*, 514–15; Toon, "Polygamy," *EBCE*, 314.

68. As Fokkelman points out, Laban is careful not to mention verbally Rachel's name when agreeing to Jacob's terms. *Narrative Art in Genesis*, 127–29. Nevertheless, Jacob's terms clearly identified Rachel as the "wage" for his seven-years of work. Laban, therefore, clearly breached contract.

69. When Esau and Jacob "struggled [וַיִּתְרֹצֲצוּ]" in their mother's womb, they portended the one-upmanship that would characterize most of their relationship outside

Even if the reader feels inclined to judge Jacob lightly for taking Rachel in addition to Leah, he will find it more difficult to justify Jacob's compliance with Rachel's plan to obtain children and Leah's counterplan to obtain more children through their respective concubines, Bilhah and Zilpah (30:3–13). The wives' desire to bear children for Jacob is commendable. But their tactic mirrors Sarah's attempt to fulfill the primeval mandate (16:1–6), and Jacob is just as blameworthy as Abraham for listening to the voice of his wives.[70] Indeed, if, as Werner Berg has observed, "Gen 16, 1–6 ist tatsächlich die Erzählung von einem Sündenfall,"[71] then Genesis 30:3–13 may be viewed as *die Erzählung von einem Doppelsündenfall.*

Jacob's Favoritism

In addition to Jacob's violation of the sanctity of marriage, his preferential treatment of his spouses and later their children calls for further reflection. Moses first highlights Jacob's preference for Rachel over Leah with the comparative clause וַיֶּאֱהַב גַּם־אֶת־רָחֵל מִלֵּאָה (29:30).[72] Then he notes that "the Lord saw that Leah was hated [וַיַּרְא יְהוָה כִּי־שְׂנוּאָה לֵאָה]" (29:31). The juxtaposition of these statements reminds the reader that the Hebrew verb שׂנא does not always denote a strong emotional aversion. Oftentimes, the verb simply denotes the choice of one person or object in preference to another.[73] Nevertheless, the ensuing narrative suggests

---

the womb. So too, Leah and Rachel play their own game of one-upmanship that also stems from activity (or the lack thereof) in the womb (29:31—30:24).

70. The language in the two accounts is nearly identical. First, Sarah entreated Abraham to *go into her maid* (בֹּא־נָא אֶל־שִׁפְחָתִי) that *she might build a family through her* (אוּלַי אִבָּנֶה מִמֶּנָּה) (Gen 16:2). Rachel too entreated Jacob to *go into her* maid (בֹּא אֵלֶיהָ) in order that *she may also build a family through her* (וְאִבָּנֶה גַם־אָנֹכִי מִמֶּנָּה) (30:3). Sarah *gave* (וַתִּתֵּן) *her maidservant* (שִׁפְחָתָהּ) to Abraham *as wife* (לְאִשָּׁה) (16:3). Likewise, Rachel and Leah each *gave* (וַתִּתֵּן) *her* respective *maidservant* (שִׁפְחָתָהּ) to Jacob *as wife* (לְאִשָּׁה) (30:4, 9). And just as Abraham complied and *went into Hagar* (וַיָּבֹא אֶל־הָגָר) (16:4), so too Jacob complied and *went into* each of his wives' maidservants (וַיָּבֹא אֵלֶיהָ) (30:4).

71. "Der Sündenfall Abrahams und Saras nach Gen 16, 1–6," 8.

72. The comparison is indicated by the *min* preposition prefixed to Leah's name. See *IBHS* § 11.2.11e; 14.4d.

73. In English, "to hate" often signifies strong emotional aversion as in "to loathe or detest." The semantic range in Hebrew, however, is broader. Often the term simply denotes the lack of preference for one person or object in favor of another. The classic example is found in Malachi 1:2–3, where God declares to the returned exiles, "'Is not Esau Jacob's brother?' declares the Lord. 'Yet I have loved Jacob, but Esau I have hated.'"

that Jacob's "love" for Rachel and "hatred" of Leah was not merely a matter of preferential status.[74] It is likely that Jacob conveyed some degree of *negative* emotional overtones towards Leah.[75] In other words, Jacob failed to convey both the warm affection and the proactive kindness to Leah that an ideal husband ought to show towards his wife (Prov 15:18, 19; Eccl 9:9; Eph 5:25–33).[76] Several factors serve to underscore Jacob's failure.

First, God's displaying preferential treatment towards Leah in "seeing"[77] that she was unloved and granting her womb fruitfulness in contrast to Rachel's barrenness suggests that God sympathized with Leah and disapproved of the way her husband was treating her.[78] In a similar way, God shows his disapproval of Laban's maltreatment of Jacob by materially blessing the patriarch in spite of Laban's attempts to renege on his original commitment and repeatedly alter the contract (30:38–43, 31:6–13). God will also demonstrate his disapproval of the mistreatment Joseph suffers at the hands of his brothers (37:18–28), Potiphar's wife (39:7–20), and Pharaoh's chief cupbearer (40:23) by prospering Joseph in each situation following the maltreatment (39:2–6; 39:21–23; 41:9–45).

The sense is not that God felt strong affection for Jacob and an opposing aversion toward Esau. Rather, as the apostle Paul correctly interprets the text, God chose Jacob as the heir of the covenant and rejected Esau *irrespective of the merit of either* (Rom 9:10–13). In light of this, the New English Translation's rendering of Malachi 1:2b–3a, "yet I chose Jacob and rejected Esau," is preferable.

74. Von Rad views the language "was hated" as mere legal terminology, which is reflected in Deuteronomy 21:15ff. *Genesis*, 294.

75. Currid agrees and notes, "It is not merely that Jacob loves Leah less than Rachel, but he apparently does not love her at all." *A Study Commentary on Genesis*, 2:87.

76. It must be conceded that Jacob was in a difficult position. God instituted marriage to be monogamous and by its very nature such a relationship calls for an exclusive kind of love that does not mix well with intruders. This is one of the primary themes of the Song of Solomon; see Tanner, "The Message of the Song of Songs," 143–62. Nevertheless, as the ensuing arguments will demonstrate, once bound to Leah in marriage Jacob was obligated to demonstrate to her some degree of genuine affection and kindness though he still may have struggled with a more natural inclination to prefer Rachel.

77. Elsewhere, Scripture speaks of God "seeing" the afflictions of the weak and oppressed and coming to their defense (Gen 16:13–14; 31:42; Exod 2:25; 4:31; Deut 26:7).

78. Trible is correct when she observes that "this pericope does not contrast the favor of God for Leah with disfavor for Rachel. It says only that 'Rachel was barren,' not that Yahweh had closed her womb. In other words, Yahweh is not punishing Rachel but rather blessing Leah, the rejected wife." *God and the Rhetoric of Sexuality*, 34–35.

In light of these examples, one may conclude that God's preferential blessing of Leah's womb is a censure of Jacob's unloving treatment of Leah.[79]

Second, Leah's naming of her first four children calls attention to Jacob's unloving treatment.[80] Reuben is so named[81] because, says Leah, "the Lord has looked upon my affliction" (29:32). The term "affliction" (עֳנִי) refers to a situation of misery or oppression.[82] Interestingly, Leah interprets Jacob's maltreatment of her with the same word that Jacob later uses to describe Laban's mistreatment of him (31:42). Seeing no change in Jacob after the first son, Leah names her second son Simeon to express her conviction that "the Lord has heard that I am hated [כִּי־שְׂנוּאָה אָנֹכִי]" (29:33).[83] Leah bears Levi and expresses her hope that "now this time my husband will be attached to me [עַתָּה הַפַּעַם יִלָּוֶה אִישִׁי אֵלַי]"

79. Gibson agrees, noting, "There is an implied rebuke in this to Jacob—if he was minded to hear it—for his blatant favouring of Rachel." *Genesis*, 2:182. Stigers compares Jacob's unfair favoritism to the very injustice he himself had suffered from his father Isaac: "Let it be seen also that Jacob followed his father's footsteps, in preferring someone other than God's choice, but God gave approval to the elder, again a manner of divine rebuke and retribution. But in his preference, Jacob caused strife, as did his father. Love had blinded his eyes." *Commentary on Genesis*, 234. Aalders is basically right when he remarks, "To compensate for the lack of love showed for Leah, God blessed her with fertility while Rachel remained childless. In this we see both the mercy and the righteousness of God. His mercy was evident because Leah was certainly not without guilt with respect to this unhappy relationship. God's righteousness was evident in that Jacob certainly was not justified in making Leah unhappy after he had accepted her as his wife." *Genesis*, 2:116. That Leah was a sinner and that any display of God's goodness to her was an act of mercy is a truism. But there is no indication at this point in the narrative that Leah was actively contributing to the unrest in the home. At this point, she is rightly portrayed as the victim. Nevertheless, she will later stumble in her rivalry with Rachel when she foolishly offers Jacob her maidservant as wife, a move that only exacerbates the tension in the family.

80. There is a sense in which all the names Leah and Rachel give their respective sons testify directly or indirectly to a tension in the home. As Dresner points out, "These names clearly express the motherhood-love tension, with Rachel possessing Jacob's love but seeking motherhood, and Leah possessing motherhood but seeking Jacob's love." "Rachel and Leah," 165.

81. Reuben [רְאוּבֵן] means, "See, a son."

82. *HALOT*, 856. Hagar uses the term to describe Sarah's harsh dealings with her (16:11). Joseph will use that term to depict the suffering he endured in Egypt prior to his exaltation (41:56). Moses frequently employs the term to portray the Israelites' affliction in Egypt (Exod 3:7, 17; 4:31; Deut 16:3; 26:7).

83. Simeon [שִׁמְעוֹן] resembles the verb שָׁמַע, "he has heard."

(29:34), implying that Jacob has been detached.[84] By the time her fourth child (whom she names Judah[85]) is born, Leah no longer seeks fulfillment in her husband's love but strives to find her joy in Yahweh.[86] Hence, Leah's naming of her first four sons bears witness against Jacob's unloving disposition towards his first wife.

Third, later in the narrative Rachel asks Leah for some of the mandrakes her son has gleaned from the field (30:14). Leah retorts bitterly, "Is it a small matter that you have taken away my husband? Would you take away my son's mandrakes also?" (30:15a). Leah's response seems to imply that her sister had managed to monopolize much of Jacob's time and affection. Of course, this does not mean Rachel was wholly to blame. Apparently, Jacob preferred spending his free time with Rachel and as a result often neglected Leah. This fact seems to be confirmed when Rachel replies to Leah's brusque retort, "Then he may lie with you tonight in exchange for your son's mandrakes" (30:15b). Rachel does not deny Leah's charge but agrees with it. Rachel, however, is desperate for children, and perhaps an aphrodisiac may increase her fertility. So she is willing to barter with her sister and lend Jacob for hire. Desperate for her husband's attention, Leah willingly pays the price and greets Jacob coming in from the fields with the language of commerce, "You must come[87] in to me, for I have definitely hired you [כִּי שָׂכֹר שְׂכַרְתִּיךָ][88] with my son's mandrakes" (30:16; author's translation). At one level, the reader feels sympathy for Jacob who is being treated like a piece of merchandise

84. The key verb, לוה, resembles the name Levi [לֵוִי] and means, "to join." It is frequently used in prophetic literature to refer to the remnant of Israel and the Gentiles who join themselves in covenant to Yahweh and his people (Isa 14:1; 56:3, 6; Jer 50:5; Zech 2:11 [Heb 15]). By implication, Jacob was refusing to live with Leah in a way appropriate to the covenant of marriage.

85. יְהוּדָה means, "praised."

86. "This time I will praise the Lord," declares Leah. One praises what one highly prizes. Up to this point, Leah had highly valued and coveted her husband's love. But when she eventually realized that she might never find a special place in Jacob's heart, she turned her attention to the God who shows special favor to the widow (Deut 14:29; 16:11; 24:19; 26:13; 1 Tim 5:4, 5; Jas 1:27).

87. The verb translated "you must come" is a simple Qal imperfect [תָּבוֹא], which in this context carries an obligatory force similar to an imperative. See *IBHS* § 31.4g.

88. Note that the finite "I have hired you [שְׂכַרְתִּיךָ]" is preceded by the infinitive absolute שָׂכֹר, which serves to intensify the meaning of the main verb (*IBHS* § 35.3.1b-f), hence the rendering, "I have definitely hired you." Many English translations miss this strengthening of the verb (DRA, NAB, NIV, NLT, NET, ESV, CSB), but a few capture it (KJV, ASV, NAS, NKJ).

to be sold and bought.[89] But at another level, the reader remembers that Jacob is partly to blame for neglecting Leah and thereby reducing her to desperate measures in order to obtain that which should have been hers by right. Sadly, the child who is born as a result of Leah's purchase testifies by name that Leah's attempt to buy her husband's love was unsuccessful. She only managed to buy another child (30:17–18).[90]

Fourth, Jacob's inequitable treatment of his wives spills over into his relationship with their respective offspring. When Jacob becomes aware of Laban's disfavor, he summons both his wives to apprise them of his plan to return to Canaan (31:1–13). For the first time, Moses portrays Jacob speaking to Leah (31:5ff.). That Jacob consults both wives and that both wives agree with his plan (31:14–16) gives the reader some hope that a degree of mutual love and harmony has been achieved in the home. But later in the narrative, when Jacob must face Esau, he divides the wives and their children into three successive ranks for protection, giving preference to Rachel and her son Joseph (33:1–2). Some commentators display ambivalence towards Jacob's arrangement of his wives and children.[91] But most agree that Jacob's placing Rachel and Joseph

89. Actually, as our analysis will demonstrate in chapter 8, the degrading treatment of Jacob as a mere servant for hire by Laban and by Laban's daughters serves as a major motif in this section of the narrative and highlights the consequences of Jacob's former sins.

90. Issachar (יִשָּׂשכָר) resembles the Hebrew verb "to pay" or "give wages" and may mean something like "there is payment." Hence, the son, not the husband's love, was what Leah received from the "commercial transaction." Fokkelman underscores the unhappy climate that characterizes the home as a result of Jacob's preferential treatment of Rachel and the consequent wifely rivalry: "The family's life is rotten and broken by the dehumanizing atmosphere of SERVICE-WAGES. Things have come so far that the enslaved and oppressed wife must 'hire' (*skr*) her husband to have intercourse, but it does not bring her the loving communication which gives recognition." *Narrative Art in Genesis*, 137.

91. Sarna believes that Jacob's "act is solely a matter of arranging mothers with their respective children for formal presentation to Esau," but he makes no comment on the significance of the order (229). Wenham suggests the possibility of preferential treatment but remains noncommittal (*Genesis 16–50*, 298). Luther (*Lectures in Genesis*, 6:160) and Fokkelman (*Narrative Art in Genesis*, 223) acknowledge the successive ordering of the wives and children, but they obscure its significance by emphasizing Jacob's sacrificial willingness to go before his family members. In some cases, commentators just ignore the reference to Jacob's dividing of his wives and children. See Baldwin, *Message of Genesis 12–50*, 140–41; Kidner, *Genesis*, 171. One suspects that optimism regarding Jacob's character change at Penuel (32:22–32) makes commentators hesitant to point out his fault at this stage of the narrative.

behind Leah and her children betrays preferential treatment.[92] As later rabbinical commentary suggests, "Last is best."[93] Jacob's division of the family here probably influenced its later near disintegration.[94]

This interpretation of Jacob's action is confirmed when his favoritism for Joseph grows to extravagant proportions after Rachel's death (35:16–20). In language that mirrors Jacob's preference for Rachel above Leah (29:30), the narrator informs the reader, "Now Israel loved Joseph more than any other of his sons [וְיִשְׂרָאֵל אָהַב אֶת־יוֹסֵף מִכָּל־בָּנָיו]" (37:3a). As a reason for Jacob's preferential treatment of Joseph, Moses appends the phrase, "because he was the son of his old age [כִּי־בֶן־זְקֻנִים הוּא לוֹ]" (37:3b). This statement puzzles some commentators.[95] The meaning is obtained by noting that Isaac is twice called "the son of [Abraham's] old age" (21:2, 7). The context suggests that Isaac's "untimely" birth made him a kind of "miracle child." Jacob probably viewed the births of Joseph and Benjamin as unique, not only because of his advanced age but also because of the general barrenness of Rachel's womb. Hence, Jacob now has two reasons to show partiality towards Joseph—he is the son of his favorite wife and one of his two "miracle children."[96] In order to broad-

92. The following commentators argue that Rachel and Joseph are placed last in order to increase their likelihood of escape should a battle ensue. Calvin, *Genesis*, 2:205–6; Currid, *Study Commentary on Genesis*, 2:140; Gibson, *Genesis*, 2:208; Janzen, *Abraham and All the Families of the Earth*, 132–33; Leupold, *Exposition of Genesis*, 885–86; Mathews, *Genesis 11:27—50:26*, 565–66; Ross, *Creation & Blessing*, 564; von Rad, *Genesis*, 327. Other commentators believe Jacob's order of wives and children reflects the way in which he desired to present them to Esau, giving the highest honor to Rachel and Joseph. Aalders, *Genesis*, 2:148; Fretheim, "Genesis," 571; Hamilton, *Genesis 18–50*, 342–43; Hartley, *Genesis*, 288.

93. Parashah 78:8 in *GR*, 3:128.

94. This is suggested by Visotzky when he remarks, "In this moment, Jacob determines Joseph's fate with his brothers and plants the seed of Simeon and Levi's lethal protectiveness of their sister." *Genesis of Ethics*, 189.

95. Sarna points out that Joseph was the final son born in Paddan-aram. *Genesis*, 255. Thus, Jacob would have been approximately ninety-nine years old when Joseph was born. But that fact by itself does not seem to account for Jacob's preferential treatment unless it serves as an indirect allusion to the fact that Joseph was *Rachel's son*, whose womb God opened last when Jacob was older. The fact that Benjamin was actually Jacob's last son has prompted some to suspect different sources behind the text imperfectly harmonized. See Janzen, *Abraham and All the Families of the Earth*, 149. Actually, a similar expression is used for Benjamin in 44:20. So both sons are referred to as the sons of Jacob's old age.

96. This interpretation makes sense out of Jacob's special favoritism toward both Joseph and later Benjamin (42:36, 38). Mathews also suggests this interpretation when

cast his preference for Joseph above his other sons, Jacob has a special garment tailored for Joseph to distinguish him from his brothers (37:3c). So Jacob's preference for Rachel has now been transferred to Rachel's firstborn son, Joseph, and will later be transferred to Benjamin (42:36, 38), when Joseph is thought to be dead.[97]

Some commentators find no fault with Jacob's favoritism towards Joseph. Claus Westermann follows Gunkel and argues that the original Israelite reader would have viewed an elderly father's preference for his youngest son quite natural and innocent. "Thus," writes Westermann, "if we try to apply our own moral yardsticks to judge Jacob's favoritism, we will end up misinterpreting this story from the very outset."[98] Luther commends Jacob for his partiality towards Joseph and asserts, "I also would have loved such a son more than the rest, even if he had not been the firstborn, inasmuch as he showed himself obedient and compliant in all things."[99] Others endeavor to mitigate Jacob's guilt by laying the primary blame for his undue favoritism towards Rachel, which spilled over on her sons, at Laban's feet.[100]

Yet, to whatever degree the reader may sympathize with Jacob, he cannot condone the blatant and extravagant proportions of Jacob's

---

he notes that "like Sarah, who valued Isaac as the miracle child of answered prayer, Rachel's children received Jacob's special protection." *Genesis 11:27—50:26*, 689.

97. Noting Jacob's persistent partiality as seen in his overly protective posture towards Benjamin (42:38), Bryan Smith remarks, "Addicted to the same poison that divided his family two decades ago, Jacob is presented as one who has grown older but not wiser." "The Presentation of Judah in Genesis 37–50 and Its Implications for the Narrative's Structure and Thematic Unity," 247–48.

98. Westermann continues, "The storyteller's perspective of Jacob's favoritism is utterly free of criticism; his intention is to present it merely as one special—and fateful—instance in human relations." *Joseph: Eleven Bible Studies on Genesis*, 4–5. See also *idem*, *Genesis 37–50*, 36–37; Gunkel, *Genesis*, 389–90. For similar reasons, Calvin too finds no fault with Jacob's preference or ground for the brother's envy. *Genesis*, 2:258–59.

99. *Lectures on Genesis*, 6:320. Jordan also justifies Jacob's special treatment of Joseph as a just reward for the latter's faithful service. *Primeval Saints*, 117. Bush follows the Babylonian Targum that reads, "for he was a wise son to him," and writes, "Certain it is, that Joseph was very wise in his early years; and it is not less certain that a wise son makes a fond as well as a glad father." *Notes on Genesis*, 2:222. See also *Onkelos*, 215 n. 1.

100. Notes Fokkelman, "[Laban] has sown poison in the inner circle by giving Jacob two daughters as wives and by following the natural order, elder before younger. . . . Instead of offering harmony the circle of family-life becomes a pit of snakes. Hatred weighs heavy on Leah, envy poisons her's and Rachel's married lives." *Narrative Art in Genesis*, 131.

favoritism and the ongoing familial disunity such partiality was perpetuating. Laban certainly deserves some of the blame, but Fretheim is correct when he notes, "While Laban's deception set up the conflict in the first place, Jacob perpetuates it."[101] Moreover, the parallel description of Jacob's preferential love for Rachel above Leah (29:30) and his preferential love for Rachel's son above Leah's and the concubines' sons (37:3) suggests to the reader that God would have shared a sympathy towards Joseph's brothers similar to that which he felt towards Leah (29:31). The God who compassionately "saw that Leah was hated" also witnessed the rejection of Leah's children (and those of the concubines) with the same empathy.[102] Furthermore, Moses's original audience was warned against the evils of a kind of parental partiality very similar to that found in Jacob's treatment of Leah and Rachel (Deut 21:15–17).[103] Finally, the reader recalls the imprudence of Isaac and Rebekah's favoritism and the resultant family discord (25:28; 27:1–45), and he wonders why Jacob did not learn from his parents' mistakes and break the cycle of sinful behavior.[104]

101. Fretheim, "Genesis," 554.

102. That God would sympathize with Joseph's disfavored brothers does not condone their malicious attitude and murderous actions against Joseph.

103. This passage need not imply Jacob was wrong in withholding the double portion from Reuben and conferring it on Joseph (via Ephraim and Manasseh) (Gen 48). It is possible for a son to disqualify himself for an inheritance, as a number of verses indicate (Gen 25:34; 26:34; 49:4–7; Deut 21:18–21; Prov 17:2). Nevertheless, it does teach that the conferral of the double portion must not be based merely on a father's partiality for a particular wife or son. See Craigie, *Book of Deuteronomy*, 282–83; Merrill, *Deuteronomy*, 292–94. McConville is correct to see the connection between this passage and the story of Jacob, but he is wrong to conclude that Jacob's final actions of conferring the double portion on Joseph rather than Reuben "runs counter to the law of Deuteronomy." *Deuteronomy*, 330.

104. Mathews writes, "Jacob's partiality for Rachel and for her two sons doomed his family to the same strife he had experienced in his father's household." *Genesis 11:27—50:26*, 689. Hamilton remarks, "Surely [Jacob] was aware of the potential for friction in a family where parental favoritism was blatant. He knew personally the schism that results from such tactics. Nevertheless, he proceeds to make it clear to all his preferential concern for Joseph." *Genesis 18–50*, 407. With a degree of surprise, Whyte queries, "Can Jacob have forgotten the sea of trouble into which his father's favourtism, and his mother's indulgence, cast both themselves and their children? The woeful harvest of all that long past folly is still making both Jacob's life and many other lives as bitter as death to this day; and yet here is Jacob poisoning the whole of his family life also, and spoiling Joseph, just as Isaac and Rebekah had spoiled and poisoned their own and their children's lives when Jacob and Esau were still their children." *Bible Characters*, 117.

Or perhaps the reader does not wonder. After all, he has surveyed three generations of the patriarchal community and found the sins of the parents frequently repeated in the children—often with intensified expression and aggravated effects! So that "avalanche" of sin that begins in primeval history continues to spread beyond the hubris of Babel and into the patriarchal history, where it wreaks havoc even among God's chosen people, one generation after another.

7

The Spread of Sin in the Fourth Generation of Patriarchs

THE PREVIOUS CHAPTERS HAVE demonstrated that the spread of sin has contaminated the patriarchal community. Indeed, the reader has noted a downhill trend as he has transitioned from the first to the second and third generations. Moses turns the spotlight upon the fourth generation of the patriarchal community at 37:2 where the final תֹּלְדוֹת section of Genesis begins: "These are the family records of Jacob" (CSB). Nevertheless, he begins his transition to the fourth generation as early as Genesis 34 by highlighting certain character and behavioral flaws among some of Jacob's children, portending future troubles for the patriarchal family and preparing the reader for the main plot of Genesis 37–50.[1] With Abraham's great grandchildren, sin reaches a crescendo, echoing some of the raucous clamor of moral corruption previously heard in primeval history.

1. According to Janzen, in Genesis 34 "the action begins to pass to the next generation. . . . If the story of Jacob is of a deeply divided person who has finally 'come to himself' (32:28) and has begun to use that name [i.e., 'Israel'] for himself (33:20), this passage [ch. 34] raises in an ominous way the question as to how effectively this newly affirmed identity will pass on to his descendants." *Abraham and All the Families of the Earth*, 136. Waltke also shows a connection between chapters 34–35 and the Judah-Joseph story in chapters 37–50 when he writes, "Behind the foregrounded plot of Jacob's fortunes and misfortunes in connection with each site of his itinerary lies a subplot concerning Jacob's successor. The genealogy inserted in this scene [35:22b–26] presents the twelve sons in the order of their primogeniture rights of succession. In Scene 1 [34:1–31], Simeon and Levi, Leah's second and third sons, disqualify themselves by their cruel rashness. In this scene [35:22a] Reuben disqualifies himself by his high-handed debauchery. Accordingly, either Judah, son of Leah, or Joseph, the firstborn of Rachel, is next in line." *Genesis*, 476.

THE RAPE OF SHECHEM

Jacob's rupture with Laban (31:1–55), reconciliation with Esau (32:1—33:16), and return to Canaan (33:17ff.) leave the reader hopeful that the remaining pages of patriarchal narrative will portray a brighter and happier future for the chosen family. Not long after the patriarch fords the Jordan, however, he makes the improvident decision to stop short of Bethel and to reside several years near the Canaanite city of Shechem (33:18–20).[2] In the course of time, Jacob's daughter Dinah is raped (34:1–2), and Jacob's sons Simeon and Levi retaliate against the entire city with deception, murder, and pillage (34:7, 13–17, 25–29). As a result, Jacob and his family are forced to flee from the scene of the crime out of fear of reprisal from neighboring Canaanite cities (34:30—35:5).

Fixing the Blame

Many commentators and scholars label Genesis 34 "The Rape of Dinah" or something similar.[3] But such characterization is misleading. To begin with, the narrator takes only two verses to depict Dinah's rape (34:1–2) but dedicates the remaining twenty-nine verses to describe the aftermath, which includes Dinah's victimizer negotiating with her family for her hand in marriage (34:3–12), a seemingly peaceful agreement (34:13–24) that turns out to be a cruel ruse leading to a bloody massacre (34:25–26), unrestrained looting (34:37–29), and a heated altercation between Jacob and his sons (34:30–31). Obviously, Moses is more concerned with the events following Dinah's rape than with the rape itself. Most important,

2. The narrator notes that Jacob "came safely" to the Land of Canaan (33:18a) in order to highlight the fulfillment of God's promise to protect Jacob so that he might return in peace (Gen 28:21). Rather than pushing forward to fulfill his vow in Bethel, however, Jacob stops short and settles in the vicinity of the city of Shechem (33:18b). This decision on Jacob's part resembles Lot's decision to settle before the city of Sodom, and it will result, unfortunately, in similar consequences for Jacob and his family. Yet, Jacob's compromise was mitigated by the fact that he did carry through on his vow *partially*. He had promised that if God would bring him safely back to the land of his fathers, "then the Lord shall be my God" (Gen 28:21). Now he keeps that promise by calling God not merely "the Fear of Isaac" but his own God, "El-Elohe-Israel" (33:20).

3. See Caspi, "Story of the Rape of Dinah," 25–45; Fretheim, "Genesis," 574; Hartley, *Genesis*, 291; von Rad, *Genesis*, 329; Speiser, *Genesis*, 262; Sternberg, *Poetics of Biblical Language*, 445; Peter Williams, *From Eden to Egypt*, 186. Arnold refers to it as "The Violation of Dinah." *Encountering the Book of Genesis*, 135; Hamilton calls Genesis 34 "The Humbling of Dinah." *Genesis 18–50*, 351; Sarna, "The Ravishing of Dinah." *Genesis*, 233; Skinner, "The Outrage on Dinah." *Genesis*, 417.

the characterization of the narrative as "The Rape of Dinah" slants the reader's moral assessment in favor of Dinah and her family and against the Shechemites. Accordingly, the reader is tempted to view the patriarchal family primarily as the victim of immoral intrusions from their surrounding pagan neighbors.[4]

In reality, the chapter is not primarily intended to highlight the sin of pagan society but to expose sin in the patriarchal community. This is not to minimize Shechem's sexual abuse of Dinah or his townsmen's opportunistic motives for tribal integration with Jacob's family.[5] It should, however, remind the reader of a pattern sometimes seen in earlier patriarchal narratives. At times Moses portrays the pagans with whom the patriarchs come into contact as less blameworthy than the patriarchs themselves.[6] Chapter 34 is a case in point. The Shechemites behave badly, but the family of Jacob behaves worse. The real question for debate concerns which of Jacob's family members is primarily to blame—Dinah, Jacob, or Jacob's sons, particularly Simeon and Levi?

Some early Jewish commentators attempt to lay much of the blame at Dinah's feet. The Genesis Rabbah compares the verb describing Dinah's excursion (וַתֵּצֵא דִינָה) into Shechem (34:1) with the verb describing her mother Leah's actions when the latter "went out [וַתֵּצֵא לֵאָה] to meet [Jacob]" (Gen 30:16a). Since Leah's purpose was to inform Jacob that she had hired him for intercourse (30:16b), the rabbis reason, "she went out all made up to meet him, just like a whore. That is why it is written, 'And Dinah, daughter of Leah, whom she had borne to Jacob,

4. According to Philo, Dinah represents "Virtue"; Shechem and the Shechemites represent everything that is opposed to virtue; Simeon and Levi represent "the champions who stand ready to repel such profane and impure ways of thinking." *Philo*, 5:241–47. The apocryphal books Judith (9:2–4) and Jubilees (30:1–26) laud Simeon and Levi for the zeal against the evil and profane Gentiles. See *Judith*, 123; *Jubilees*, 178–84. A fourth-century AD rabbinical commentary on Genesis justifies Simeon and Levi's deceitful answer to Shechem and even portrays Jacob as joining together with his sons in the slaughter. Parashah 80:8, 10, in *GR*, 3:152, 155. Kessler interprets the primary point of this story as a direct polemic against intermarriage with the Canaanites and as an indirect indictment against the evils of Canaanite culture. "Genesis 34—An Interpretation," 3–8.

5. Chapter 3 of this study has addressed these sins.

6. In particular, the reader should recall Abraham's moral conduct contrasted with the Egypt's pharaoh (12:10–20) and later with Gerar's Abimelech (20:1–18), as well as Isaac's behavior unfavorably compared with a later ruler of Gerar (26:6–11).

went out.'"[7] The modern Jewish commentator Nahum Sarna agrees that the verb in this context probably connotes "coquettish and promiscuous behavior" and notes, "Girls of a marriageable age would not normally leave a rural encampment to go unchaperoned into an alien city."[8] The verb יצא, however, is used elsewhere with a woman as its subject without sexual connotations (Judg 4:18, 22; Ruth 1:7; 2 Sam 6:20; 2 Kgs 4:21, 37; 8:3), and there are no clear indications in the text that Dinah was up to no good. Dinah's solo venture into a pagan city may betray a degree of naïveté,[9] but the language of 34:2 represents her as a victim of sexual abuse. Dinah is not the focus of Moses's censure.

Many commentators portray Jacob as the real loser in this episode. His settlement and purchase of land near Shechem (33:18–19) is construed as opportunistic greed.[10] He is also accused of parental neglect and a lack of concern for Dinah's protection (34:1).[11] Moreover, Jacob's silence at the news of Dinah's rape (34:5) and his deference to Dinah's

7. Parashah 80 in Neusner (3:146).

8. *Genesis*, 233. Sarna also observes that elsewhere in Genesis and in postbiblical literature references to "the daughters of the land" convey "undertones of disapproval." Ibid., 233, 367, ch. 34 n. 3.

9. Most commentators agree that her action was imprudent. Calvin, *Genesis*, 2:218; Leupold, *Exposition of Genesis*, 898; Wenham, *Genesis 16–50*, 310; Peter Williams, *From Eden to Egypt*, 187. An underlying psychological need and motivation is suggested by David and Diana Garland when they write, "[Dinah's] own family life had long been dominated by the extended battle between her mother, Leah, and her stepmother, Rachel, for Jacob's attention and their competitive trying to produce the most baby boys. Who wouldn't want to escape the tension and loneliness that must have characterized life for a daughter in this household?" *Flawed Families of the Bible*, 76–77. Of course, such factors do not excuse Dinah's lack of prudence though they may help the reader to sympathize with her need for love and attention.

10. Currid writes, "Shechem at the time was a large and important Canaanite town; Jacob, as a semi-nomad, must have been drawn to the urban centre for obvious reasons, such as social advantages, trade, and so forth. His attempt to settle, however, has dire consequences." *Study Commentary on Genesis*, 2:148. He also notes Jacob's silence at the news of Dinah's rape and raises the question, "Is he reluctant to confront the people of Shechem, with whom he has recently made a deal?" Ibid., 2:149. Arnold candidly asserts, "The entire account is also a subtle condemnation of Jacob. He has delayed in his journey to Bethel, presumably because of the tempting benefits of trade with the Shechemites (34:10)." *Encountering the Book of Genesis*, 135–36.

11. Commenting on Dinah's solo venture, Garland and Garland query, "Where was Jacob? Had no one warned her against going out alone? Had Daddy ignored the admonishment to parents to know where your children are at all times and to know who is with them? Was she as unloved and neglected by Jacob as Leah had been?" *Flawed Families of the Bible*, 77.

brothers in the negotiations over her future (34:13–17) are interpreted as signs of pathetic passivity and moral indifference.[12] When Jacob finally does speak out against Simeon and Levi's retaliation against the Shechemites (34:30), he is perceived as a coward whose primary concern is self-preservation.[13] And since the narrator appears to allow Simeon and Levi the final word (34:31), his judgment is presumed to be against Jacob and his sympathies with Jacob's sons.[14] As a result, Wenham concludes,

12. Steinmetz writes, "Jacob, both after the rape of Dinah and after Reuven sleeps with Bilhah, remains passive (34:5; 35:22); he allows his sons to take control." *From Father to Son*, 112. Sternberg's criticism is stronger: "Jacob's response is conspicuous by its absence. He 'kept still' (*hekherish*). In the Bible's usage, this verb often has the pejorative connotations of inertness or neglect (e.g., 2 Sam 19:11; Hab 1:13; Esth 4:14). But our context charges the verb with its maximal sense of a double omission: both to act and to speak. Jacob certainly stirred no finger before the arrival of his sons." Commenting further, Sternberg opines that "the do-nothing ending 'and Jacob kept still until they came' lets us down with a vengeance; and who if not Jacob is to blame for the anticlimax?" *Poetics of Biblical Language*, 448–49. Following Sternberg's lead, Wenham adds, "Jacob was never fond of his first wife, Leah, and it seems that his coldness spilled over to her six sons and her daughter Dinah. So he took no action about her rape and abduction, whereas her brothers were incensed by it." *Genesis 16–50*, 317.

13. Noting the many first-person pronouns in Jacob's response, Thomas asserts, "Jacob-like, the patriarch looks at the matter solely from this own point of view. . . . Could anything be feebler or more unworthy? No blame for the sin committed, only for the danger involved." *Genesis*, 324. Hamilton suggests, "[Jacob's] concerns are tactical and strategic, rather than ethical (as in 49:5–7). He is without the resources to oppose a united force; Jacob has been reduced to a position of vulnerability." *Genesis 18–50*, 371. The strongest rebuke comes from Sternberg: "Jacob breaks his long silence only to reveal himself as the tale's least sympathetic character. The cowardice betrayed (not for the first time, but never so perceptibly as vis-à-vis the boldest of his sons) is less damning than the immorality. If Jacob reproached the pair for the massacre or the abuse of the rite of circumcision or even the breach of contract, he would gain a measure of understanding and support from the reader. But he does not even remotely protest against any of these offenses." *Poetics of Biblical Language*, 473.

14. Sarna compares Simeon and Levi's rhetorical question—"Should he deal with our sister as with a harlot?"—to God's final question in the Book of Jonah (4:11) and concludes, "As with the Book of Jonah, the closing rhetorical question provides an irresistible argument. The women of Israel are not to be regarded as objects of abuse. They cannot be dishonored with impunity" (238). Sternberg argues, "Whatever its force elsewhere, therefore, Jacob's argument sounds shabby in the Bible's court of conscience. The ending rubs in the point by having his wordy and terror-driven onslaught countered by Simeon and Levi's proud and epigrammatic 'Should he treat our sister like a harlot?' The voice of egocentricity and self-preservation finds itself opposed by the voice of idealism. Damn the consequence, they say, and their response vibrates with the sense of injury that drove them to seek redress in the sword." *Poetics of Biblical Language*, 474. Sternberg and Wenham even suggest that the brother's rhetorical question should

"Undoubtedly, the heroes of this story, though they are the villains of the Joseph story, are Dinah's brothers, particularly Simeon and Levi."[15]

There are, however, several factors that mitigate Jacob's guilt in this affair and heighten the culpability of Jacob's sons, especially Simeon and Levi. Jacob's decision to prolong his residence near Shechem rather than returning to Bethel and then to his father at Hebron may have been unwise.[16] Yet to attribute greed and opportunism as Jacob's primary motives exceeds and even contradicts the contextual data. There is no indication that the purchase of land within the territory of Canaan was forbidden to the patriarchs (see Gen 23:3–20). Moreover, the text indicates that Jacob genuinely worshipped God while at Shechem (33:20).[17]

The charge that Jacob was guilty of parental neglect and showed no concern for Dinah's protection may contain an element of truth. Unquestionably, Jacob's favoritism for Rachel and his lack of love for Leah (29:30–31) spilled over into his relationship to the wives' respective children (see 33:2; 37:3). It seems reasonable to conjecture that Dinah may have keenly sensed a lack of fatherly affection, which may have

---

be read not only as a retort *to* Jacob *about* Shechem but also as an accusation *against* their father: "Will he [Jacob] treat our sister like a harlot?" "He who twiddles his thumbs about the rape and deems the gifts fair compensation," writes Sternberg, "is as guilty of making a whore of Dinah as the rapist and giver himself." Ibid., 475. "To do nothing about the rape and then to be willing to accept gifts after the event," contends Wenham, "is to act like a pimp." *Genesis 16–50*, 317.

15. Wenham, *Genesis 16–50*, 319. In favor of his reading, Wenham also compares Simeon and Levi's behavior to Phinehas, a descendant of Levi, who was commended for godly zeal when he slew a fellow Israelite and a Midianite princess for brazenly committing fornication in the midst of Israel's camp (Num 25:6–15).

16. Jacob's decision to encamp near Shechem bears some resemblance to Lot's decision to pitch his tent near Sodom (13:10–13). In the case of Lot, however, there are clear indications of a motivation for material gain as well as a conspicuous absence of acts of piety. In the case of Jacob, no indication is given that his purchase of land near Shechem was motivated by greed and his altar-building follows the pattern of Abraham rather than that of Lot. Yet, it cannot be denied that his decision to settle so close to a pagan city had negative consequences for his family.

17. Kidner views Jacob's altar-building at Shechem as a pious façade for disobedience (172). But as noted earlier, Jacob's altar building and his naming God "El-Elohe-Israel" represent an advance in religious maturity. He no longer refers to God as the God of his fathers but as his own God. Moreover, the reader should note that chapter 34 is bracketed by accounts in which Jacob is building altars to God (33:20; 35:1–7). One may read chapter 34 as a period of backsliding from which Jacob recovers in chapter 35. Or he may interpret the altars before and after Shechem as indicating that Jacob was endeavoring to walk with God during his residence in Shechem; his children were not.

prompted her to look for such affection in inappropriate places (34:1). But it is unclear whether Jacob approved of her venturing alone into the city. Such a conclusion is purely conjectural.

Admittedly, Jacob's reaction to the news of Dinah's abuse at first seems inordinately passive and indifferent (34:5), especially when contrasted with the brothers' fiery indignation (34:7). But silence need not imply the absence of righteous indignation; it may indicate prudent restraint (Prov 14:29; 15:18; 16:32; 19:11; James 1:19).[18] Indeed, Solomon may have been thinking of the contrast between Jacob and his sons in Genesis 34 when he penned the words: "Whoever is slow to anger is better than the mighty, and he who rules his spirit than he who takes a city" (Prov 16:32). Holding one's peace may also be an indication of hope that God will provide a solution.[19] Furthermore, Moses explicitly limits the duration of Jacob's silence with the phrase "until [the broth-

18. In Numbers 12:1–2, Aaron and Miriam murmur against Moses, and the reader is told, "And the Lord heard it [וַיִּשְׁמַע יְהוָה]" (12:2b)—the same language used to depict Jacob's initial reaction to the news of Dinah's rape: "And Jacob heard that he had defiled his daughter [וְיַעֲקֹב שָׁמַע כִּי טִמֵּא אֶת־דִּינָה בִתּוֹ]" (Gen 34:5a). Only later does the reader learn that the murmurings had angered Yahweh (Num 12:9). In Isaiah 42:14a, God describes his response to the nation of Israel's long history of sin and infidelity in terms of moral restraint: "For a long time I have held my peace; I have kept still and restrained myself." The phrase "I have kept still [אַחֲרִישׁ]" translates the same verb depicting Jacob's response (וְהֶחֱרִשׁ יַעֲקֹב) (34:5b). A few interpreters read Jacob's silence in this positive light. Calvin interprets Jacob's silence as an indication of overwhelming grief—"he was so oppressed with insupportable grief, that he held his peace"—but Calvin's editor suggests a better reading: "Or, he might be restrained by prudence from imparting his feelings to others, lest making them public, he should expose himself to danger before he was prepared to meet it. At all events, it was wise to restrain the expression of his indignation, till he was surrounded by those who might help him with their counsel, or attempt the rescue of his daughter from the hands of her violator." *Genesis,* 2:220 n. 1.

19. The verb used to describe Jacob's remaining silent [וְהֶחֱרִשׁ יַעֲקֹב] is used in Moses's words to Israel: "The Lord will fight for you, and you have only to be silent [וְאַתֶּם תַּחֲרִישׁוּן]" (Exod 14:14). This seems to be Luther's interpretation of Jacob's silence: "Jacob himself, smitten with great sorrow, kept silent. For he found no remedy or consolation. He is not even able to think of avenging the injury inflicted by a very powerful lord. Accordingly, he does nothing. He does not make complaints to the perpetrator of the crime, nor does he approve the deed. But he is silent and patiently enduring, waiting for counsel and a remedy from the Lord." *Lectures on Genesis*, 6:196. Similarly, Fretheim comments, "The author understands this reticence positively (cf. v. 30). In the verses enclosing chap. 34 (33:20; 35:1–4), Jacob focuses properly on the God who has made promises to him. One can best assess Jacob's attitude in chap. 34 as one of prudence and care, informed by the worship of God and in view of a future in the land of promise that is in some jeopardy." "Genesis," 578.

ers] came home" (34:5b, NIV). Jacob's decision to wait until Dinah's brothers arrived before responding to Hamor and Shechem's proposal is consistent with the customs of those days in which a woman's marriage was negotiated with her brothers as well as her father.[20] Finally, Jacob's silence during the negotiations and willingness to accept the terms offered by Dinah's brothers may simply indicate that he was persuaded by the reasonableness of their argument. According to ancient Near Eastern custom and Mosaic law, a man who took sexual advantage of a virgin was obligated to offer to marry her and pay a bride-price stipulated by the woman's father and/or brothers (see Exod 22:16–17 [Heb 15–16]; Deut 22:28–29).[21] Hamor and Shechem were apparently following this custom (34:4–6, 8–12), but Jacob's sons rightly objected to the prospect of assimilation with the Hivites (34:14), insisting instead that the Hivites adopt the covenant sign of Abraham and become, as it were, "Israelites" (34:15–17).[22] On the surface, this proposal would not only (to some

20. According to Genesis 24:29–51, Rebekah's brother Laban played a key role in the negotiation of her marriage to Isaac. On ancient Near East parallels, see van Seters, *Abraham in History and Tradition*, 77, and Selman, "Comparative Customs and the Patriarchal Age," 119, 122, 138.

21. For an ancient Near East parallel, see "The Middle Assyrian Laws," § 55, in *ANET*, 185. The Assyrian law differs from the Mosaic legislation in that it allows the victim's father another option: "The father of the virgin shall take the wife of the virgin's ravisher and give her to be ravished." Mosaic law did not encourage such revenge but only restitution. On the rational for such legislation, see Finkelstein, who argues that a violated virgin would be considered "damaged goods," making it difficult for the father to arrange a future marriage and obtain a fair dowry. "Sex Offenses in Sumerian Laws," 355–72.

22. That this was the intention behind the brothers' proposal is suggested by the fact that they employ the language of God's command to Abraham in Genesis 17:10: compare "Every male among you shall be circumcised [הִמּוֹל לָכֶם כָּל־זָכָר]" with the brothers' demand "that every male of you be circumcised [לְהִמֹּל לָכֶם כָּל־זָכָר]" (34:15b).

degree) salvage Dinah's honor but would also maintain Israel's unique identity.[23] Jacob agrees with the apparent wisdom of his sons.[24]

Finally, the charge that Jacob's final response betrays cowardice, egocentrism, and a lack of moral concern is groundless. Jacob's protest against Simeon and Levi assumes that a morally reprehensible act has been committed.[25] So it is unfair to assert that Jacob is solely concerned about *the consequences* of his sons' deeds and not *the morality* of their deeds.[26] Nor can Jacob be charged with "egocentrism" since his concern

23. Of course, that such a union would preserve Israel's unique identity is only a *prima facie* conclusion. Patriarchal and Mosaic legislation allowed foreigners to assimilate into Israel through circumcision (Gen 17:12, 27; Exod 12:48–49). This allowance, however, assumed that the alien desired to worship Israel's God and submit to Israel's laws. It is unlikely that the Shechemites possessed such theological and ethical motivations. On this basis and in light of later Mosaic legislation forbidding assimilation with the Canaanite population but calling for its complete annihilation (e.g., Deut 7:1–5), many commentators argue that the brothers' proposal should have appeared inappropriate to Jacob and that the patriarch should have quickly rejected it out of hand. But the laws calling for Canaanite genocide were unique to a later period of Israel's history and did not apply during the patriarchal period since the patriarchs were allowed to make treaties with the peoples of Canaan (Gen 14:13, 24; 20:22–32; 26:26–31). That Jacob should have discerned that a confederacy with the Shechemites even under the condition of circumcision was unwise is probably true. But he faced a difficult dilemma. The prospect of arranging a future respectable marriage for Dinah was not only undermined by her defilement but also by the fact that Jacob's ties with his kinsmen in Haran had been effectively severed (Gen 31:5–54). In this case, he deferred to ancient Near Eastern custom and the seemingly "religious-ethical" proposal of Dinah's own brothers.

24. Ironically, a Jewish Targum translates the Hebrew phrase, בְּמִרְמַה, "in deceit," which characterizes the brothers' proposal (34:13) with the Aramaic phrase, בחוכמא, "in wisdom," presumably to justify Simeon and Levi's response and retaliation against the Shechemites. *Onkelos*, 202–3 n. 4. But all things considered, the brothers' response did appear reasonable and fair on the surface. As Fewell and Gunn note, "Their apparent willingness to reach a settlement . . . is presumably as acceptable to [Jacob] as it is to Shechem. Certainly, we are given no indication of his remonstrating with the sons after the visitors' departure. On this reading, then, Jacob's silence derives from caution rather than apathy." "Tipping the Balance," 198.

25. The terminology "to bring trouble upon" denotes the idea of bringing *moral reproach* on a person(s) that will lead to reprisal or negative consequences (Josh 6:18; 7:25; 1 Sam 14:29; 1 Kgs 18:17–18; 1 Chr 2:7; Prov 11:17, 29; 15:6, 27). Wenham suggests that the term would be better translated "bring ruin," and he notes that the term "always seems to involve personal or national disaster." *Genesis 16–50*, 316. The word for "stink" [באשׁ] elsewhere describes the stench of rotting fish (Exod 7:18, 21), moldy manna (Exod 16:20), and, metaphorically, *offensive behavior* that provokes retaliation (Exod 5:21; 1 Sam 13:4; 27:12; 2 Sam 10:6; 16:21). Both of these terms, while highlighting dangerous consequences, also assume that a *morally reprehensible act* has just occurred!

26. Aalders agrees: "Some have charged that Jacob displayed a characteristic weakness in the way he rebuked his sons. . . . Even so, Jacob cannot be rightfully charged with

includes the welfare of his entire family[27] and possibly the future of the divine promise, which has been placed in jeopardy.[28] What is more, the charge that Jacob has morphed into a weak, passive leader is contradicted when he orders the entire family to rid themselves of their foreign gods (some of which may have been pillaged from Shechem),[29] to purify themselves, and to follow him promptly to Bethel (35:1–3). The fact that the entire family obeys Jacob's command shows that some respect for his authority remains, even among his sons. Apparently, Jacob is still wearing the pants in the family![30]

This attempt to provide some vindication of Jacob's character and actions throughout this narrative should not be interpreted as an attempt to make him the hero of the story.[31] On the contrary, Mathews is

---

complicity in or sanction of the crimes of his sons. He charged his sons with having made him, and his family, 'a stench to the Canaanites and Perizzites.' He thereby declared that he considered their action to be worthy of the strongest condemnation and disdain." *Genesis,* 2:159. See also Leupold, *Exposition of Genesis*, 910–11.

27. "My numbers are few, and if they gather and attack me, I shall be destroyed, both I and my household" (34:30b). Some interpreters make much out of the first person personal pronouns, alleging an obsession with self-preservation. See Arnold, *Encountering the Book of Genesis*, 136; Thomas, *Genesis,* 324. But they overlook the fact that Jacob views himself as representative of the entire covenant family: "I shall be destroyed, both I *and my household*." Amusingly, the same writers find no egocentricity in the response of Dinah's brothers when they reply to Shechem's offer: "*We* cannot do this thing . . . for that would be a disgrace *to us*" (34:14).

28. See Luther's comments in *Lectures on Genesis*, 6:218–19.

29. Currid points out that the reference to Jacob's sons plundering "all that was in the houses" (34:29) may actually refer to a Shechemite temple, since the Hebrew actually employs the *singular*, וְאֵת כָּל־אֲשֶׁר בַּבָּיִת, "and all that was in the House." While it is possible that the singular here may be intended as a collective noun, it is also possible that the Canaanite temple, which later became known as "the house of Baal-berith" (Judg 9:4), was in view. *Study Commentary on Genesis*, 2:157.

30. Fewell and Gunn challenge the allegation that Jacob's initial silence and tardy berating betrays a passive and selfish cowardice. They note, "Jacob's initial silence is wisdom in the face of a potentially explosive situation for his family as a whole. . . . His anger is understandable. His sons have usurped his authority, deceived him in the process, and acted without responsibility. They leave him to face the consequences, him and the rest of the family—the women and children. Jacob is still pater-familias and still has to deal with the threat to the family's very existence—a threat that the brothers' actions have exacerbated beyond measure." "Tipping the Balance," 208.

31. It is unclear why Jacob stopped in Shechem. But in light of his earlier vow to return to Bethel, Jacob's decision to settle near Shechem (temporarily?) was probably unwise and may evidence a degree of spiritual decline. However, Jacob's desperate prayer for deliverance (32:9–12), his encounter with God at Penuel (32:22–32), his

correct when he asserts, "There are no heroes in this episode."[32] But there are villains. Shechem is guilty of sexual abuse (34:2) and the Shechemites of opportunistic greed (34:20–24).[33] Yet the real villains of this story are the sons of Jacob, particularly, Simeon and Levi. Dinah's brothers were right to feel grieved and angry at the news of their sister's rape (34:7).[34] But there are several indications in the immediate and larger context that condemn their reaction.

Simeon and Levi: The Serpent's Offspring

The terminology used to characterize Simeon and Levi's response to Shechem and Hamor (בְּמִרְמָה, 34:13) is the same earlier used to describe Jacob and Laban's deceitful intrigues (Gen 27:35; 29:25).[35] Since Moses

---

humility before Esau (33:3, 5–11), and his altar-building near Shechem (33:20) all give evidence of a personal relationship with God. These considerations should mitigate our judgment of his character and behavior in Genesis 34.

32. Mathews is also correct when he observes, "That no person comes across as purely good or wholly wicked is because the author treats the characters as they really were. They are not one-dimensional figures, cardboard images, but flesh-and-blood persons whose moral conduct fluctuates." *Genesis 11:27—50:26*, 578–79. Wenham appears to agree when he writes, "No one in this tale escapes the narrator's implied censure" and later observes, "Within a firm moral framework sure of what constitutes right and wrong, the narrative hints at the multidimensional aspects of conduct, at the mixed motives that make it impossible either to condemn any of the actors absolutely or to exonerate them entirely." *Genesis 16–50*, 317. But Wenham inconsistently concludes his exposition by declaring Simeon and Levi "the heroes of this story." *Genesis 16–50*, 319.

33. See chapter 3 of this study.

34. They "were indignant [וַיִּתְעַצְּבוּ] and very angry [וַיִּחַר לָהֶם מְאֹד]." The Hebrew verb עצב refers to emotional pain and is used of God's reaction to human evil prior to the Flood (Gen 6:6), as well as the emotional distress one may feel towards his own sin (Gen 45:5). The terminology used for their anger may describe either justified or unjustified anger. But Moses leaves no doubt about the appropriateness of their anger by adding his own justification: "[Shechem] had done an outrageous thing in Israel by lying with Jacob's daughter, for such a thing must not be done" (34:7b). The Hebrew term translated "an outrageous thing" (נְבָלָה) often refers to a sexual immorality (Deut 22:21; Judg 19:23–24; 20:6, 10; 2 Sam 13:12; Isa 9:16; Jer 29:23). When used together with the clause "for such a thing must not be done [וְכֵן לֹא יֵעָשֶׂה]," it underscores the gravity of the sin (2 Sam 13:12).

35. The LXX renders the Hebrew here as μετὰ δόλου, "with guile," as in 27:35. The verb used to describe Laban's action in 29:25 is παραλογίζομαι, which means "to cheat out of a thing, to defraud of." *LSGL*, 1316–17. As noted above, Targum Onkelos emends the text here to read "with wisdom" (בחוכמא) and, not surprisingly, gives the same rendering of Jacob's method of obtaining the blessing from Isaac. See *Onkelos*, 164–65; 202–3. But the Targum refrains from whitewashing Laban's action and employs the verb

has consistently censured the oft-repeated deceptive conduct among the patriarchal community, it seems likely he intends the reader to censure the brothers' ruse similarly.[36] The brothers patently break faith with the Shechemites, and their conduct contrasts with Joshua and Israel's leaders who would later honor an oath to the Gibeonites, though the latter obtained the promise through deceit (Josh 9:3ff.).[37]

Second, Simeon and Levi's retribution far exceeds the *lex talionis* since they do not merely execute Shechem for rape but kill his father and every male in the city (34:25–26). As Waltke notes, "Their moral indignation turns to Lamech-like revenge."[38] From a purely human viewpoint, their blitzkrieg-like tactics may have been necessary to reach Shechem, retrieve Dinah, and avoid retaliation, as some scholars contend.[39] But as Yahweh's chosen people, Simeon and Levi did not need to depend ultimately on human stratagems. They had the option of calling on Yahweh in their distress.[40] Moreover, the brothers'[41] comprehensive pillage of the

שקר (176–77), which refers to a "breach of promise or contract" (Gen 21:23; Lev 19:11; 1 Sam 15:29; Pss 44:18; 89:34). The rabbinical commentary in *Genesis Rabbah* denies that the brothers were lying since the Holy Spirit vindicates their action by adding the phrase that links their guile to Dinah's defilement (3:152).

36. After analyzing the terminology of deception used to describe Simeon and Levi's ruse, as well as the deceptive bargaining, killing, and hypocrisy that follows, Michael Williams, who has carefully analyzed the theme of deception in the book of Genesis, agrees that the narrator intends the reader to evaluate this deceptive act negatively. *Deception in Genesis*, 23–24.

37. Ironically, both the Shechemites and the Gibeonites were ethnically Hivites (Gen 34:2; Josh 9:7). In the first case, the Israelites trick the Hivites into making a peaceful agreement (34:13–17) but slaughter them in the end (34:25–26). In the second case, the Hivites trick the Israelites into making a peaceful treaty in order to avoid being slaughtered (Josh 9:3–15), and Joshua and the leaders of Israel keep their word (Josh 9:16–27).

38. Waltke, *Genesis*, 460.

39. So argues Sternberg. *Poetics of Biblical Language*, 468. But Sternberg's reasoning to some degree rests on the assumption that Dinah was being held hostage against her will. Ibid., 456. As Fewell and Gunn note, "That is a very tenuous inference." They suggest that Shechem's attempts to console and woo Dinah after the rape were successful and that "she is now in Shechem's house of her own accord." "Tipping the Balance," 200.

40. As Rebekah sought for God's guidance when troubled by the struggle in her womb (25:22) and as Jacob prayed for God's protection when facing the prospect of meeting Esau (32:9–12).

41. Some scholars argue that the reference to "the sons of Jacob" in verse 27, precludes Simeon and Levi, and they suggest the translation, "the other sons Jacob" (e.g.s., NAB, NJB, NRSV, CSB). This translation, which excludes Simeon and Levi, is preferred

city (34:27–29) demonstrates that they were less than principled.[42] If anyone should be accused of greed and selfishness, it would be Jacob's sons.[43]

on the basis that Hebrew "often expresses the sense of the 'other' through mere juxtaposition" (Speiser, *Genesis*, 265), as well as lack of a *waw* consecutive pattern, which would have been expected if the narrator intended to continue his focus on Simeon and Levi as the subjects of the action depicted (Mathews, *Genesis 11:27—50:26*, 608). However, the phrase, "the sons of Jacob," as used elsewhere in this passage includes Simeon and Levi" (34:7, 13). In the one instance it refers exclusively to Simeon and Levi, the author says so—"two of the sons of Jacob, Simeon and Levi" (34:25). Moreover, the absence of the *waw* consecutive may simply indicate that Simeon and Levi are no longer *the exclusive ringleaders*. New perpetrators of evil are introduced—now their brothers join the action, and they all together as "the sons of Jacob" participate in phase two of the operation. Furthermore, Jacob's deathbed curse against their violence appears to implicate them in the spoiling of the city as well as the murdering of its males: "For in their anger they killed men, and in their willfulness *they hamstrung oxen*" (emphasis added) (49:6). So all of Jacob's ten sons appear complicit in the looting of the city. In light of Jacob's later pledge to Joseph in Genesis 48:22, "Moreover, I have given to you rather than to your brothers *one mountain slope* [שְׁכֶם; "a portion of Shechem"?] that I took from the hand of the Amorites with my sword and with my bow," some Jewish rabbis argued that Jacob reluctantly joined his sons in the looting. For example, one rabbinical tradition asserts, "Now our father, Jacob, had not wanted his sons to do this. But once they had done it, he said, 'Now shall I leave my sons to fall into the hand of the nations of the world?' What did he do? He took his sword and bow and stood at the gate of Shechem." Parashah 80:10 in *GR*, 3:155. But the Hebrew term may refer to a mountain slope or ridge, as reflected in many English versions. Hence, Jacob may be alluding to a different event. This may also be inferred from his reference to "the Amorites," which contrasts with the identification of the Shechemites as "Hivites." Yet, it is possible that Amorite may be used in a more generic sense to indicate one who dwells in Canaan (15:16). Perhaps the best solution is that proposed by Lowenthal who interprets Jacob's statement as a sarcastic jab at Simeon and Levi's evil deed for which he as family head was in a sense responsible. *Joseph Narrative in Genesis*, 143. This interpretation agrees with Jacob's later denunciation of their violent ways (49:5–7) that stand in contrast with his more peaceable interactions with the Canaanites (33:17–18).

42. Ross notes, "The sons' instinct for justice was correct, but their methods were ruthless and excessive." *Creation & Blessing*, 575. Fretheim remarks, "The extensive detail (the accusative particle is used nine times!) yields an 'overkill,' a blood feud mentality. Even more, the fact that the brothers kept their 'spoil' for themselves is highly problematic." "Genesis," 579. Walton also disapproves of their excess: "Beyond the slaughter of the entire male population, the brothers take all the women and children as well as all the goods in the city as plunder. Presumably the brothers rationalize their conduct by insisting that such is the mandated bride price for the violation of their sister. Nevertheless, the level of brutality is incomprehensible and far exceeds any justifiable retribution for the crime of the city's prince." *Genesis*, 630.

43. This hardly agrees with Sternberg's contentions that the brothers reject "financial temptation," and that they operate solely from "the higher ground" of "a national-religious framework." *Poetics of Biblical Language*, 457. As Brueggemann correctly observes, "[Their] passionate vengeance is transparently self-serving. What they seized,

Furthermore, the reference to the brothers' taking "all their little ones and their wives" (34:29) leaves the reader wondering what the brothers did with the wives of their victims. Perhaps they married them.[44] But the reader wonders whether the vengeful brothers did not return evil for evil (Rom 12:17; 1 Thess 5:15; 1 Pet 3:9) and follow Shechem's reversed pattern that placed sex before marriage.[45]

Third and most important, the narrator does *not* permit Simeon and Levi the "last word," as some commentators allege. On the contrary, Jacob himself utters the final and authoritative assessment of Simeon and Levi's actions in his deathbed oracle, when he curses their violence as evil (49:5–7).[46] Hence, a holistic reading of this chapter in its larger

they did not destroy as an act of faithfulness (cf. 1 Sam 15:3, 14–19). Rather, they kept it for themselves so that their taking was not an act of righteous indignation, but an act of confiscation for self gain." *Genesis*, 278.

44. Walton, *Genesis*, 630.

45. Some ancient Near Eastern legislation allowed the defrauded father to take the rapist's own wife and expose her to sexual abuse as punishment for her husband's crime. "The Middle Assyrian Laws," in *ANET*, 185. Even if Jacob's sons did not actually rape the Hivite women, the tragic irony is clear, as Duguid points out: "The initial sin of taking one woman was returned in kind but in multiplied form. It is clear that the Israelites were not in any way morally better than the present inhabitants of the Promised Land." *Relentless Grace*, 141.

46. Fretheim agrees that this deathbed oracle must serve as the key to a canonically consistent interpretation of Simeon and Levi's action when he notes, "Perhaps most important, the sharp and unambiguous judgment (indeed, a curse!) by Jacob on the violence of Simeon and Levi must stand as the primary clue about how we should interpret this chapter (49:5–7)." "Genesis," 576–77. Delitzsch also agrees with the pride-of-place Jacob's deathbed oracle holds for authoritatively assessing Simeon and Levi's actions: "Simeon and Levi have the last word, but Jacob speaks the last of all in his testamentary sayings. The most sinful part of it was their degrading the sacred sign of the covenant to so base a means of malice. And yet it was a noble germ which exploded so sinfully." *New Commentary on Genesis*, 2:225. Those commentators who interpret Simeon and Levi's action in a positive light are forced to downplay or discount the importance of Jacob's deathbed curse on Simeon and Levi. For example, Sternberg concedes, "In his so-called blessing, Jacob will reduce the vengeance taken by Simeon and Levi on the Hivites to an outbreak of blind fury. . . . But," counters Sternberg, "as often in repetition, the narrator tells a different story. As early as this point, he summons his omniscient authority to undermine the reliability of Jacob's late version. His inside view unfolds a more complex, and far more sympathetic, picture of the motives actuating the future revengers." *Poetics of Biblical Language*, 453. This approach ignores the fact that the earlier patriarchal "blessings" and/or "curses" (Gen 9:24–27; 27:26–29, 30–40; 28:3–4) do in fact represent the narrator's viewpoint. Consequently, it is even more disconcerting when an evangelical scholar such as Currid agrees with Sternberg's depreciation of Jacob's deathbed curse upon Simeon and Levi. Currid writes, "The biblical writer is not

canonical context yields a central plot quite distinct from that suggested by such summary descriptions as "The Rape (or Violation, Humbling, Ravishing) of Dinah." George Coats captures the main thrust of the narrative's storyline when he labels it as the "Rape of Shechem."[47] Once again, Moses portrays the patriarchal community in a less favorable light than their sinful pagan neighbors.

In summary, the "Rape of Shechem" narrative advances the spread of sin theme in the Genesis narrative. From Cain's hate-filled murder of Abel (4:8) to Lamech's unwarranted assassination of "a young man" (4:23) to an antediluvian society "filled with violence" (6:11, 13) to Nimrod's imperial tyranny (10:8–12), the primeval narrative was characterized by hated, hostility, and bloodshed (Gen 9:5–6). The transition from primeval history to patriarchal history reveals that matters have not improved. If anything, matters have grown worse. For now, the roles are reversed. Instead of the wicked (Cain) slaying the righteous (Abel), the reader encounters "the righteous" (the sons of Jacob) wantonly murdering "the wicked" (Shechemites).[48] The irony here is the fact that the sons of the promise reveal themselves to be "the seed of the Serpent" (Gen 3:15) since like their "spiritual father" they are portrayed as "liars" and "murderers" (see John 8:44; 1 John 3:10–12). Accordingly, one is inclined to

---

as judgemental as Jacob [!]. He allows the two brothers the final word. . . . Simeon and Levi seem to be much more concerned about the morality of the situation than Jacob, caring more about right and wrong. The author leaves the question hanging, as if he is in agreement with the brothers." *Study Commentary on Genesis*, 2:158.

47. Coats, *Genesis*, 233. Coats writes, "The story unfolds a simple plot focused not on the rape of Dinah by Shechem but on the rape of Shechem [the city] by the brothers of Dinah. . . . The main figures in the story are thus the brothers, principally Simeon and Levi, and the opposition, Shechem with his father Hamor." Ibid., 234. Similarly, Bechtel writes, "Ironically, if there is rape in this story, it is Simeon and Levi who 'rape' the Shechemites. It is their behavior that is violent and hostile, carried out for the purpose of exploitation." "What If Dinah Was Not Raped?" 34. Although Bechtel is correct to censure the action of Simeon and Levi, her analysis is flawed by an attempt to portray Shechem and Dinah's sexual act as mutually consensual, thereby removing any blame that might properly attach to Shechem (27–31). Both the language depicting Shechem's deed (34:2) as well as the narrator's expressed assessment of that deed (34:7), however, preclude such a positive reading. For a more extended rebuttal of Bechtel's position, see Chapter 3 of this study.

48. Although "righteous" in terms of lineage, calling, privilege, and type, Jacob's sons were probably not yet "righteous" in terms of a regenerate nature—at least at this point in the narrative. Here, they—especially Simeon and Levi—show themselves to be the offspring of the Serpent rather than the seed of the woman (1 John 3:10–15).

agree with John Gibson, who concludes, "With its unvarnished picture of raw passion and perfidy, it is one of the darkest tales in the Bible."[49]

REUBEN'S REBELLION

Immediately following the Shechem debacle, Jacob orders his family to leave the scene of the crime and make their way to Bethel, where he may fulfill his earlier vow (35:1–15). From Bethel he travels homeward to Hebron where his aged father, Isaac, is still residing (34:27–29). On the way, Jacob is grieved not only with the deaths of Deborah, his mother's nurse (35:8), and Rachel, his favored wife (35:16–20) but also with the news that his son "Reuben went and lay with Bilhah [Jacob's] concubine" (35:22). Strangely, some scholars find little thematic or theological significance in this brief report regarding Reuben and Bilhah.[50] As the exposition below will demonstrate, however, this report of Reuben's deed calls for serious moral evaluation and, along with the subsequent listing of Jacob's sons, prepares the reader for the main plot of Genesis 37–50.

Most obviously, Reuben's action was a case of incest.[51] The Mosaic law categorically condemns incest (Lev 18:8; 20:11) and prescribes the

49 Gibson, *Genesis,* 2:215. Leupold "cannot venture to offer homiletical suggestions for [the chapter's] treatment" though he concedes that the passage "could be treated to advantage before a men's Bible class." *Exposition of Genesis*, 912.

50. Coats observes, "No plot unfolds here. No conclusion is drawn from the report of Reuben's rebellion. The unit as it stands is simply a report." Or, "more precisely," Coats opines, "The report may be . . . defined as an ANECDOTE." *Genesis,* 242. Fokkelman, whose analysis of "The Cycle about Jacob" is usually careful to find significance in the details, concludes his study with the comment, "The Story of Jacob shows a somewhat fragmented ending. Two short notes have been inserted which we might just take for granted v. 8 and v. 22a." In a footnote, he thinks 22a is inserted merely to prepare the reader for Jacob's curse of Reuben in 49:4. *Narrative Art in Genesis*, 235. Fishbane treats the text as the final verse in the Jacob cycle denouement but provides no commentary on it. *Biblical Text and Texture*, 43–46.

51. Some Jewish rabbis reject this conclusion and posit a different scenario that absolves Reuben of any sexual misdeed: "Whoever maintains that Reuben sinned is merely making an error, for it is said, *Now the sons of Jacob were twelve*, teaching that they were all equal. Then how do I interpret, *and he lay with Bilhah his father's concubine?* This teaches that he transposed his father's couch, and the Writ imputes [blame] to him as though he had lain with her. It was taught, R. Simeon b. Eleazar said: That righteous man was saved from sin and that deed did not come to his hand. . . . He resented his mother's humiliation. Said he, If my mother's sister was a rival to my mother, shall the bondmaid of my mother's sister be a rival to my mother? [Thereupon] he arose and transposed her couch." "Shabbath 55b," in *BabTalmud,* II, 1:256–57. The idea seems to be that Reuben removed (and hid?) Bilhah's bed to prevent Jacob from sleeping with her.

death penalty (Deut 27:20). Up to this point, the patriarchal narratives have exposed the occasional practice of polygamy among the chosen community. More serious cases of immorality such as homosexuality and rape have been limited to pagan society (19:5–9; 34:2), with the exception of the incestuous act of Lot's daughters with their own father (19:30–36). There, Lot was not completely conscious of his evil action. Here both parties appear complicitous since the text gives no indication that Bilhah was raped or sought to resist Reuben's advance. Sadly, Jacob's decision to encamp before Shechem (וַיִּחַן אֶת־פְּנֵי הָעִיר) had degrading moral effects on his family comparable to those resulting from Lot's decision to pitch his tent towards Sodom (וַיֶּאֱהַל עַד־סְדֹם).

But Reuben's action may have been motivated by something more than mere lust. The reader should note that Reuben's incestuous act immediately follows Rachel's death (35:18–20). Since Bilhah was Rachel's handmaid, it is possible that Jacob's favoritism towards Rachel may have passed to Rachel's handmaid—if not *in fact* at least *in the minds* of the Leah's sons, whose mother Jacob had long disfavored and neglected. Consequently, Reuben's sexual act with Bilhah may have been his way of striking back at his father for the years of disfavor Jacob had shown to Leah and her children (see 29:30–35; 33:1–2).[52] Some, noting a parallel story in Homer's Iliad, have even suggested that Leah may have prompted or encouraged Reuben's revenge.[53]

Most interpreters, however, are probably correct to see Reuben's action primarily as a power play. By sleeping with his father's wife, Reuben

52. The rabbis suggested this motivation, as cited above ("Shabbath 55b"), though they denied Reuben used incest as a means to prevent Bilhah's ascendancy. Waltke thinks this may have formed a part of Reuben's motivation and writes, "By defiling Bilhah, he makes certain that with Rachel's death her handmaid cannot supplant Leah as chief wife (cf. 2 Sam 15:16; 16:22; 20:3)." In a footnote, Waltke also reminds the readers of Reuben's earlier concern for his mother's supremacy in gathering the mandrakes (30:14). *Genesis*, 478. See also Nichol, "Genesis xxix. 32 and xxxv. 22a: Reuben's Reversal," 536–39.

53. Gunkel (*Genesis*, 370) notes the parallel, which Skinner (*Genesis*, 427) uses to suggest as a motive for Reuben's shameful deed. The relevant section occurs in Book IX, line 400ff. In that section, Lord Phoinix addresses a speech to Akhilleus in the midst of which he recounts, "I went north/to avoid a feud with Father, Amyntor/Ormenides. His anger against me rose /over a fair-haired slave girl whom he fancied/without respect for his own wife, my mother/Mother embraced my knees and begged that I/make love to this girl, so that afterward/she might be cold to the aging man. I did it/My father guessed the truth at once, and cursed me,/praying the ghostly Furies that no son/of mine should ever rest upon his knees:/a curse fulfilled by the immortals—Lord/Zeus of undergloom and cold Persephone." *Iliad*, 217–18.

attempted to usurp Jacob's role as leader of the clan. Several considerations combine to support this reading. First, later OT narratives include examples of individuals who apparently seek to seize political control from a ruler by sleeping with his concubines. Ishbosheth interprets Abner's affair with Rizpah, the concubine of his deceased father Saul, as an attempt to grab political power over Israel (2 Sam 3:6–8). Later, Absalom follows Ahithophel's counsel and sleeps with David's concubines as public declaration of his intent to lay claim to his father's kingship (2 Sam 16:20–22). And when Adonijah uses Bathsheba to request Solomon's permission to take Abishag, David's former concubine, as wife (1 Kgs 2:13–18), Solomon sees through his veiled request to his true intentions and has him executed for treason (1 Kgs 2:19–25). These examples of power play within Israel's monarchy suggest, as Roland de Vaux observes, "Possession of the harem was a title to the throne."[54]

That this was Reuben's motivation is also suggested by Moses's editorial comment noting that Jacob had twelve sons (35:22b), which is followed by a list of Jacob's sons that identifies Reuben as "Jacob's firstborn [בְּכוֹר יַעֲקֹב]" (35:23). Some modern commentators view the list of Jacob's sons as an intrusion to the narrative and as derived from another source.[55] But there are good reasons for interpreting the list with Reuben's "firstborn" position highlighted as an integral part of the narrative.[56] As Jacob's "firstborn," Reuben stood first in line to receive a

54. *Ancient Israel*, 1:116; Schedi, *History of the OT*, 3:190. Commentators who interpret this as Reuben's primary motivation include Brueggemann, *Genesis*, 284; Currid, *Study Commentary on Genesis*, 2:170–71; Fretheim, "Genesis," 585; Hamilton, *Genesis 18–50*, 387; Mathews, *Genesis 11:27—50:26*, 628; Sarna, *Genesis*, 244–45; Waltke, *Genesis*, 478; Walton, *Genesis*, 636; Wenham, *Genesis 16–50*, 327.

55. Coats, *Genesis*, 243–44; Janzen, *Abraham and All the Families of the Earth*, 144; Speiser, *Genesis*, 274–75; von Rad, *Genesis*, 342; Claus Westermann, *Genesis 12–36*, 556.

56. Steinmetz calls it an "apparent non sequitur" but suggests that its purpose is to highlight Jacob's passivity by including Reuben as "firstborn" in the family list "despite his act of usurpation." *From Father to Son*, 113. But the oft-repeated view that Jacob is completely passive is tenuous in light of his assertive leadership in 35:2–4, as well as the fact that Reuben's plan plainly failed. The subsequent narrative still portrays Jacob as exercising headship over this family (35:27–29; 37:2–4, 12–14; 42:1–2; 43:2, 11–14; 46:28; 48:3–22; 49:1–27, 29–33). Calvin's logic is more persuasive: "Reuben is put the first among them, not for the sake of honour, but that he may be loaded with the greater opprobrium: for the greater the honour which any one receives from the Lord, the more severely is he to be blamed, if he afterwards makes himself the slave of Satan, and deserts his post." *Genesis*, 2:247.

double-portion of the inheritance (Deut 21:15–17) and was the natural candidate for the "blessing." But Jacob's partiality towards Rachel's offspring (33:2) likely created suspicion in Reuben's mind regarding his father's intentions. Jacob's naming Rachel's last son "Benjamin" (literally, "son of my right hand," 35:18b) may have been the proverbial "straw that broke the camel's back." Reuben decided it was time to act decisively and assert himself as the rightful successor to Jacob (35:22a).[57] But his plan evidently failed, as the subsequent narrative demonstrates (35:27–29; 37:2–4, 12–14).[58] Moses's interposition of the list of Jacob's sons, then, provides a transition to the final major narrative in Genesis. Simeon and Levi's act of aggression (34:13–31) and now Reuben's attempted coup d'état (35:22a) have disqualified the first three of Jacob's sons from inheriting the "blessing" (49:3–7).[59] Judah is next in line (35:23). But Judah will have to compete with Rachel's firstborn, Joseph—a major plot in Genesis 37–50.

Jacob's deathbed oracle may also expose Reuben's political motives (Gen 49). Addressing his sons, the ailing Jacob begins with Reuben and utters what is in effect an anti-blessing or curse, similar to the one Isaac pronounced on Esau (27:39–40). After Jacob identifies Reuben as his "firstborn" (49:3a), he twice employs the noun for "preeminence" (יֶתֶר) followed by the cognate verb "to have preeminence" (יתר), which is preceded by the negative particle [אַל־]. The text reads: "preeminent

57. Janzen appears to reason in a similar vein: "Firstborn Reuben now attempts to force the transition to the next generation, by an act that is a clear bid to seize leadership of the family. Coming right after the birth of Benjamin, his act may mean he fears that Jacob intends this youngest son to be his chief heir." *Abraham and All the Families of the Earth*, 143.

58. Perhaps this explains why Reuben later urges his brothers not to kill Joseph but to cast him into a pit (37:21). Although the narrator tells the reader that Reuben's motivation was "that he might rescue him out of their hand to restore him to his father" (37:22), it is likely that a deeper motivation prompted Reuben's seemingly virtuous act. Rather than being motivated by a purely virtuous desire to protect Joseph, he may have been seeking an opportunity to get back in good graces with Jacob. His attempt to grasp at preeminence via incest with his father's concubine had failed. If he is still to obtain the double-inheritance and conferral of lordship among his brothers, he must find a way to repair his fractured relationship with his father, Jacob. By rescuing Joseph from the evil plot of his brothers, Reuben might be able to regain his father's respect and perhaps obtain the family preeminence for which he longed.

59. For a discussion of extrabiblical examples of disinheritance for serious offenses in relation to the biblical accounts, see Selman, "Comparative Customs and the Patriarchal Age," 120, 135–36.

in dignity and preeminent in power. Unstable as water, you shall not have preeminence, because you went up to your father's bed" (49:3b–4a). One might read verse 3 as Jacob's description of what Reuben *should have been* (i.e., the preeminent one) and verse 4 as what Reuben *actually was* (i.e., unstable and immoral) and *would be* (i.e., deprived of preeminence). It is also possible, however, to read the first part of verse 3 as a depiction of what Reuben *was and should have been*, namely, the firstborn who was to represent his father's might and the firstfruits of his strength (כֹּחִ וְרֵאשִׁית אוֹנִי בְּכֹרִי אַתָּה). One may read the second part of verse 3 as Jacob's *satire of Reuben's aspirations*—to be "preeminent in dignity and preeminent in power [יֶתֶר שְׂאֵת וְיֶתֶר עָז]." The first clause of verse 4 shifts from a satirical exposure to *a metaphorical censure*, describing Reuben's moral character as "unstable as water [פַּחַז כַּמַּיִם]." The word פַּחַז may be a noun or verbal substantive. In its verbal form, the term elsewhere depicts a lack of moral restraint, that is, moral laxity or reckless behavior (Judg 9:4; Zeph 3:4; Sir 19:2). The instability of water provides a suitable metaphor for Reuben's lack of moral stability. Consequently, the remainder of verse 4 contains Jacob's curse ("you shall not have preeminence [אַל־תּוֹתַר]"), which is the very object Reuben sought and Jacob's grounds for the curse: "Because you went up to your father's bed; then you defiled it—he went up to my couch!"[60]

In conclusion, Reuben's contempt for his father parallels Ham's contempt for Noah (9:22–27), and he deserves Jacob's curse (49:3–4).[61] Moreover, Reuben's autonomous and inordinate grasping for "the blessing" follows in the line of his primordial parents, who grasped for the blessing in disobedience to and contempt for Yahweh's law and authority. The avalanche of sin that began in primeval history continues to gather speed and increases in severity as it tumbles through the successive generations of patriarchal history.

60. The writer of Chronicles specifically alludes to Jacob's curse as the basis for the double-portion passing from Reuben to Joseph (1 Chr 5:1).

61. This is not to suggest, as some have, that Ham committed a sexual crime against his father. Ham gazed upon "the nakedness of his father and told his two brothers outside," an act of blatant disrespect. Reuben, on the other hand, "uncovered his father's nakedness" by committing incest with his step-mother (see Lev 18:7–8). In both cases, the son disgraces the father, but in Reuben's case the crime is more severe.

CAIN(S) REDIVIVUS

The violent aggression and power play tactics of Jacob's sons come to their full expression in the beginning of Jacob's תֹּלְדוֹת, Genesis 37. The opening verses introduce a tension between Joseph and his brothers that escalates from animosity to jealously to murderous plotting as the narrative progresses.

Nursing Malice

At least three factors contribute to a growing animosity between Joseph and his brothers. First, Joseph brings Jacob *a negative report* (אֶת־דִּבָּתָם רָעָה) concerning his half-brothers, the sons of Bilhah and Zilpah (37:2). At this time, Joseph was seventeen years old and apparently served as a shepherd alongside his brothers. Although the text does not explicitly reveal the brothers' reaction to Joseph's disclosure, the subsequent flow of the narrative suggests that Joseph's negative report contributed to unfriendly relations with his siblings. Because the Hebrew terminology employed to describe Joseph's "bad report" is commonly employed for *a false or negatively biased report* (Num 13:32; 14:36, 37; Ps 31:14; Prov 10:18; 25:10; Jer 20:10; Ezek 36:3), some commentators charge Joseph with slander or accuse him of being a tattletale.[62] But at least three considerations suggest that the reader view Joseph's report in a more positive light. The noun דִּבָּה with the modifier רָעָה may, in this case, refer to *a negative yet accurate report* concerning the "evil" deeds of his brothers.[63] On the other hand, one may interpret the pronominal

62. For example, Gibson remarks, "In view of this so deep-seated Hebrew aversion to the mischievous use of words, it is very unlikely that any of this story's original audiences could have been tempted to justify Joseph's conduct as stemming from a respect for truth, or filial loyalty, or some other admirable sentiment. Nor should we." *Genesis*, 2:226. Garland and Garland also provide a negative reading of Joseph's report concerning his brothers as well as his account of his dreams: "Joseph foolishly flaunted his status as the favorite child, tattled on his older brothers to Dad (Gen 37:2), and bragged about his grandiose dreams in which he would lord it over all of them. He fanned the embers of sibling rivalry into flames of murderous hatred (Gen 37:5–8)." *Flawed Families of the Bible*, 105. See also Aalders, *Genesis*, 2:181; Delitzsch, *New Commentary on Genesis*, 2:255; Hamilton, *Genesis 18–50*, 406; Hartley, *Genesis*, 310; Mathews, *Genesis 11:27—50:26*, 671; Waltke, *Genesis*, 499; Wenham, *Genesis 16–50*, 350. A few commentators refrain from any moral assessment of Joseph's report. See Fretheim, "Genesis," 598; Sarna, *Genesis*, 255; Westermann, *Genesis 37–50*, 36.

63. *HALOT* offers the generic glosses of "report [which could be true or false]," and "rumour [which has a negative connotation]" (208). *BDB* suggests the definition

suffix ם affixed to the noun דִּבָּתָם as a *subjective* rather than an *objective* genitive.[64] In this case, Joseph is reporting the slanderous things *his brothers are saying* rather than acting as the perpetrator of slander himself. The subsequent narratives that portray Joseph as a man of integrity and contrast his moral behavior with that of his brothers would seem to constrain a more positive interpretation of his actions here.[65] Moreover, Joseph's "bad report" concerning the "sons of Bilhah and Zilpah" fills out the overall negative picture of Jacob's sons. Moses has already portrayed Simeon, Levi, and Reuben in a negative light (34:13–31; 35:22a). Here,

---

"a (true) report of evil doing" (179) but can only offer Genesis 37:2 as an example of this meaning. Ross takes the adjective "evil" as describing the brothers' actions and insists that Joseph is simply telling the truth which "shows that Joseph was faithful to his father." From this assessment Ross draws the following lesson: "Those who would be leaders must prove faithful in the smaller responsibilities." *Creation & Blessing*, 598. Sailhamer also views the "evil report" about the brothers as true and suggests that the adjective "foreshadows the brothers' intended evil (rāʿāh; NIV, "harm") spoken of in 50:20." "Genesis," 226.

64. For the subjective genitive of the pronominal suffix, see *GBH* § 146f [2:543]; *IBHS* § 16.4d [303]. Instances of דִּבָּה used with a subjective genitive include Jer 20:10 and Ps 31:14. Peck also notes that the LXX employs ψόγος, which is "elsewhere only used where *dibbah* has a subjective genitive." "Note on Genesis 37:2 and Joseph's Character," 343. Janzen, like Peck, notes the cases where דִּבָּה is used with a subjective genitive and argues, "Our first picture of Joseph, then, is of an individual surrounded like Jeremiah or the innocent psalmist by those who wish him evil. This picture is repeated with deepening gravity for several episodes, before Joseph's saving reversal comes." *Abraham and All the Families of the Earth*, 148.

65. As the present analysis will demonstrate, Joseph is portrayed in the likeness of Abel and his brothers in the likeness of Cain (see below). Furthermore, the narrative later contrasts Judah's lack of sexual restraint (38:15–18) with Joseph's victory over sexual temptation (39:8–12). Moreover, Joseph is portrayed as a man of integrity (39:9) who enjoys God's special presence and favor (39:2, 21) in contrast with the brothers who are deceivers and who suffer God's judgment for their deceit (38:26; 42:22; 50:15). Finally, Joseph refuses to take revenge on the very brothers who vengefully wanted to kill him and sold him into slavery (37:4, 5, 8, 11, 18–20, 26–28) but instead seeks to preserve them alive and do them good (45:5–7; 50:20). Noting the predominantly positive portrayal of Joseph's character throughout chapters 37–50, modern critics are compelled to posit a different source for 37:2b. This supposedly negative depiction of Joseph is attributed to the hand of P (who negatively portrays the tribes of Ephraim and Manasseh in the Prophets) in contrast to the idealistic depiction of Joseph attributed to J and E throughout the rest of the "Joseph Story." See Hilgert, "The Dual Image of Joseph in Hebrew and Early Jewish Literature," 5–7; von Rad, *Genesis*, 350; Westermann, *Genesis 37–50*, 36; idem, *Joseph*, 3–4. Strangely, Westermann does not attribute this verse to P because of its negative portrayal of Joseph but because of the detail of Joseph's age, which he sees as characteristic of P's interests in chronological details.

he exposes the sons of the concubines (37:2). Judah still remains, and Moses will expose his negative character later in the narrative.

Second, the brothers' animosity is aggravated when Jacob treats Joseph with the kind of favoritism he had shown to Joseph's mother[66] and publicizes his partiality by having a *special garment* (כְּתֹנֶת פַּסִּים) tailored for Joseph (37:3).[67] The practical significance of this type of clothing is its unsuitableness for manual labor.[68] Consequently, Jacob's gift to Joseph is not merely an expression of his love but also a kind of promotion from a "blue-collar" shepherd (alongside his brothers) to Jacob's assistant supervisor (over his brothers). This may be the first sign that Jacob intends to pass on the position of family leadership to his favored son.[69] This reading fits well with the subsequent narrative, which

66. Compare the language of 37:3a, וְיִשְׂרָאֵל אָהַב אֶת־יוֹסֵף מִכָּל־בָּנָיו, with that of 29:30, וַיֶּאֱהַב גַּם־אֶת־רָחֵל מִלֵּאָה.

67. Scholars debate the precise nature of the garment. Following the LXX's χιτῶνα ποικίλον and the Vulgate's *tunicam polymitam,* many versions render it as multi-colored tunic (KJV, DRA, ASV, NAS, ESV, CSB). Although the Greek term often refers to variegated colors, its basic meaning simply denotes *that which is varied in appearance or kind* (e.g., Gen 30:37, 39, 40; 31:8, 10, 12; 2 Macc 15:21; 3 Macc 1:21; 2:6; 4 Macc 17:7; 18:21; Matt 4:24; Mark 1:34; Luke 4:40; 2 Tim 3:6). Perhaps because of this or in light of a possible connection between the Hebrew and the Akkadian kitû pishannu, "ornamented garment," some versions render Jacob's gift to Joseph as "an ornamented tunic" (TNK), "a richly ornamented robe" (NIV), or "a decorated tunic" (NJB). However, the Hebrew phrase is used elsewhere to refer to a garment worn by a daughter of an Israelite king (2 Sam 13:18–19). There the LXX translates it as χιτὼν καρπωτός, "a long-sleeved robe," which more closely resembles the Hebrew wording כְּתֹנֶת פַּסִּים, literally, "a tunic of palms of hands/soles of feet." These considerations have led some translators to part from the traditional rendering and opt for "a long tunic" (NAB) or "a long robe with sleeves" (NRSV). A few translations allow for a degree of ambiguity and offer renderings like "a special tunic" (NET) or "a beautiful robe" (NLT).

68. According to von Rad, "It was a luxury which only those who did not have to work could think of having." *Genesis,* 351. See also Gibson, *Genesis,* 2:227; Gunkel, *Genesis,* 390; Hartley, *Genesis,* 310.

69. Waltke notes the royal connotations of the special tunic and argues, "By this regal apparel (see 2 Sam 13:18) Jacob publicly designates Joseph as the ruler over the family." *Genesis,* 500. One exegetical detail that may undermine such a conclusion is the fact that Jacob later rebukes Joseph for relaying a dream portraying himself as the future family ruler (37:10). Jacob's rebuke, then, would seem to indicate that the patriarch has not yet finally determined to whom he will pass the leadership. It is possible, however, to interpret Jacob's rebuke as a public front designed to cloak his enthusiasm regarding the implications of the dream. Jacob has already allowed some of his cards to show by his obvious favoritism and the royal tunic he has had tailored for his son (37:3–4). But by the time Joseph relates this second dream to Jacob, the father has become aware of the brothers' growing resentment towards Joseph and decides that a public "rebuke"

describes Jacob sending Joseph on an assignment to inspect his brothers' doings and report back to his father (37:12–14). Jacob's partiality provokes the brothers to hate Joseph and renders them unable to speak kindly to him (34:4).

Third, the brothers' hostility towards Joseph is increased by two dreams that Joseph freely relates to them. Joseph's first dream depicts his brothers doing obeisance to him (37:5–7). His brothers sarcastically reject the implications of his dreams with a double rhetorical question (37:8).[70] Joseph's second dream portrays the entire family as bowing before him (37:9). This time Jacob rebukes him (וַיִּגְעַר־בּוֹ)[71] and seems to discount the implications of his dream (37:10).[72] In both cases, Joseph's

---

may serve to mitigate their growing animosity towards Joseph and suspicions regarding their father's future intentions for the younger brother. The possibility that Jacob's public rebuke was only a façade is also suggested when Moses informs the reader of Jacob's inward reaction to the dream in the subsequent verse: "And his brothers were jealous of him, *but his father kept the saying in mind*" (37:11), literally, "but his father tended the matter [שָׁמַר אֶת־הַדָּבָר]." One might say that Jacob inwardly *cherished the idea*. Of course, it is also possible that Jacob's gift to Joseph of regal attire conveyed truth about Joseph that exceeded Jacob's initial intent. Only after Joseph's dreams does it begin to "dawn" on Jacob that Joseph may be the son God intends to receive the blessing.

70. The doubling of the question along with the repeated use of the infinitive absolute to strengthen the finite verb serve to intensify the brothers' rejection of the dream's implications.

71. The Hebrew verb גער is sometimes used metaphorically to refer to God controlling or restraining some force of nature (Isa 7:12; Nah 1:4; Ps 106:9). More often, though, it is used in a more literal sense for *one person reproving another person for a perceived wrong*. In Ruth 2:16, Boaz informs his workers that they are to allow Ruth the Moabitess to glean behind them and admonishes them, "Do not rebuke her." God "rebukes" the proud who stray from His commandments (Ps 119:21). In some cases, though, the perception of the one who rebukes is wrong (Jer 29:26–28). Hence, the fact that a rebuke is given does not necessarily imply that an actual wrong has been committed. So in the present case, Jacob may have rebuked Joseph because he perceived either nonsense in Joseph's dream or pride in Joseph's relating of that dream. But Jacob's rebuke does not necessarily mean his perception of Joseph's motives were correct. Perhaps Joseph is betraying a degree of youthful naïveté in that he fails to perceive that by relating such dreams, especially to his brothers, he is only aggravating their hatred of him. But the narrator gives no clear indication that Joseph was guilty of pride. Moreover, as noted above, it is possible that Jacob's public "rebuke" was only a front designed to mitigate the brother's growing suspicions regarding their father's future intentions to make Joseph the family head.

72. Once again, the two rhetorical questions along with the infinitive absolute serve to emphasize Jacob's initial rejection (which he later rethinks, v. 11) of the implications of Joseph's dream.

brothers respond with intensifying hatred and jealousy (37:5, 8, 11), which prepares the reader for the next stage in the narrative.

Plotting Murder

Jacob sends Joseph to check up on his brothers (37:12–14), and Joseph eventually finds them in Dothan (37:15–17). Here the growing tension between him and his brothers will reach its "resolution." When the brothers see Joseph approaching from a distance, they plot murder (37:18). Moses relates some of the details of this murder conspiracy. First, the brothers begin to vent their hatred with the mocking announcement: "Here comes this dreamer" (37:19). Then they appear to reach an initial consensus on a murder plot that includes the disposing of his body and the covering up of the crime. In this way, they hope to frustrate the realization of Joseph's rulership dreams (39:20). But Reuben, who was likely absent during the initial planning,[73] opposes Joseph's bloodshed and desires to "rescue him out of their hand to restore him to his father." So he suggests that they simply throw Joseph into an empty cistern (37:21–22).[74] The brothers yield to the firstborn (37:23–24), at least for the moment. Reuben departs temporarily, probably to contrive a plan of deliverance.[75] Meanwhile, the other brothers sit down to eat a meal, and a trading caravan happens to pass by (37:25). Quickly, Judah hatches an alternative plan to sell Joseph to slave-traders (37:26–27a).

73. That Reuben shared the brothers' animosity towards Joseph is intimated throughout the earlier narrative (37:4, 5, 8, 11). It may be possible that Reuben was present with the other brothers as they saw Joseph approaching and began to vent their disgust and commence their conspiracy. Then, at the first suggestion of murder, Reuben objected. More likely, though, Reuben was not initially present when the conspiracy began. When he returned (as Joseph was still approaching), the brothers apprised him of the plan, and he quickly rejected the proposal of bloodshed.

74. The narrator indicates that Reuben's motive was "that he might rescue [Joseph] from their hand and restore him to his father" (37:22). The fact that Reuben shared the brothers' hatred for Joseph makes it unlikely that his motives for rescuing the lad are pure. Otherwise, why does Reuben remain silent about the brothers' evil deed and go along with the cover up plot (37:31–32, 35)? Most likely, Reuben is looking for an opportunity to regain Jacob's favor for his earlier crime (35:22a). When that opportunity is lost, Reuben's "noble" concern for Joseph's welfare evaporates.

75. That Reuben has departed at this point in the narrative becomes clear later when he returns to find Joseph missing and complains to the other brothers (37:29–30).

Virtual Murder

Judah's plan deserves special consideration for several reasons. Judah is the only brother specifically identified besides Reuben (37:21, 29). So the narrator appears to be drawing a deliberate contrast or comparison between the two. Judah's plan also demonstrates shrewd cunning. The initial consensus among the brothers was to get rid of Joseph permanently (37:18–20). But Reuben's objection to kin-slaying apparently swayed a majority (37:21–24). Judah deftly proposes a *via media*. By refraining from cold-blooded murder, the brothers could satisfy Reuben's scruples.[76] Yet by selling Joseph into slavery, they could still gratify their lust for revenge and rid themselves of Joseph's annoying presence. What is more, they could make a little money in the process! Third, Judah's role in hatching this plan throws him forward in the narrative for the reader's evaluation. Up to this point, all the brothers have been evaluated negatively, except Judah and Joseph.[77] Now Moses exposes Judah's evil heart, and he will reveal more of Judah's ungodly character in chapter 38. When Reuben returns and finds Joseph gone, he expresses grief and complains to his brothers (37:29–30). But Reuben's duplicity and complicity are evident when he goes along with the plan to cover up Joseph's disappearance with a "slain-by-a-wild animal" ruse (37:20, 31–32). Adding deceit to virtual murder, the brothers complete the conspiracy and bring their aged father to mourn inconsolably the "death" of his favored son (37:33–35).[78] Meanwhile, Joseph is sold into Egyptian slavery (37:36).

76. Some suggest that Judah himself may have been swayed by Reuben's argument, perhaps fearing divine retribution for spilled blood (Gen 4:10; Isa 26:21; Ezek 24:7–8; Rev 6:10). See Hamilton, *Genesis 18–50*, 421. Judah's reservations, however, are more likely motivated by "the polls." He wants to get rid of Joseph, but he fears he may not have enough votes from the nine brothers. So he pretends to share Reuben's aversion to murder when in fact he does not. So contends Ackerman when he notes, "The text makes no mention that Judah's interest is to rescue Joseph. Instead Judah piously speaks of not laying a hand on a brother; but the effect of his suggestion is not so different from murder: Joseph will be removed from their midst and reduced to slavery. In many ways biblical law equates selling a person into slavery with murder. Judah wants the same results as his other brothers, but he seeks profit from the deed." "Joseph, Judah, and Jacob," 2:85–113. See also Bryan Smith's analysis of Judah's speech and motivation. "The Presentation of Judah in Genesis 37–50 and Its Implications for the Narrative's Structure and Thematic Unity," 59–63.

77. Benjamin is still a young child at this time.

78. The brothers' ruse has its intended effect, leading Jacob to believe that Joseph is dead. That the brothers persist in covering their crime while their father pines away in grief serves to accentuate their guilt. Hamilton observes, "They attempt to comfort

So a narrative that began with sibling rivalry ends in virtual murder. In a number of ways, this story parallels that of Cain and Abel. In both cases, the unrighteous despises the righteous because God favors the latter (4:4–5; 37:4, 5, 8, 11).[79] As Cain's anger and hatred intensify to the point of plotting murder (4:7),[80] so the hatred of Joseph's brothers mounts (37:4, 5, 8, 11) until it results in an assassination conspiracy (37:18–20).[81] Cain actually murders Abel (4:8); Joseph's brothers stop short of murder and sell him into slavery (37:21–28). Yet their deed amounts to a virtual murder.[82] To the relief of his brothers and the grief

---

their father, all the time restraining their glee at the demise of Joseph, and just after they deceived their father about Joseph's alleged horrible death. Deceivers become (pseudo-) comforters." *Genesis 18–50,* 427. Indeed, there was a sense in which they robbed their own father of many years of life since, by Jacob's own testimony, he responded to the news of Joseph's "death" as a man living with one foot in the grave (37:35).

79. Jacob's preference for Joseph above his other sons may have been initially conditioned by his preference for Joseph's mother and the fact that Joseph, like Benjamin, was born "out of due time," making him special. But Jacob's later preference for Joseph may also have been based on the quality of Joseph's character in contrast to the brothers (37:2b, 12–14). Moreover, the fact that Joseph was the recipient of revelatory dreams made him the apparent favorite of Yahweh, a fact that did not escape the notice of his brothers and provoked not merely anger (37:5, 8) but envy (37:11).

80. That God confronts Cain regarding his anger towards Abel, warns him, "Sin is crouching at the door," and admonishes him to "rule over it," shows that the Lord knew Cain's anger was beginning to give way to dark thoughts and murderous plotting.

81. The narrator highlights the brothers' growing hatred of Joseph by moving from a mere statement of fact, וַיִּשְׂנְאוּ (v. 4), to a double expression of intensification, using the verb וַיּוֹסִפוּ followed by the adverb עוֹד followed by the infinitive construct שְׂנֹא (vv. 5, 8), which in turn leads to jealous rage, וַיְקַנְאוּ־בוֹ אֶחָיו (v. 11). The clause in verse 5b, "they hated him even more [וַיּוֹסִפוּ עוֹד שְׂנֹא אֹתוֹ]," is absent in the LXX. As a result, many scholars view it as a later gloss that crept into the Masoretic text. Becking, however, defends the clause as original by calling attention to the literary technique of "retrospective achrony (*Nachholende Erzählung*)." "In this technique," writes Becking, "the final result of a group of events and/or acts is told first and [then] the way in which this climax was achieved is narrated afterwards." He sees Jonah 4:4–9 as a parallel, where the section begins and ends with God's rhetorical question, "Are you justly angry?" The implication for the narrative of Genesis 37 is that the "primary emphasis in the story is not on the dreams as such; but on the growing alienation between Joseph and his brothers. Their hatred, provoked by the love of Jacob/Israel and the כְּתֹנֶת פַּסִּים gift, is increased by their interpretation of Joseph's first dream and turned, thus, into jealousy after the second dream. Their jealousy forms the basis for their actions, by which they try to prevent Joseph's dreams from coming true (Gen 37:12–36)." "They Hated Him Even More," 40–47.

82. First, the unwarranted theft of a man's freedom and consignment of his life to slavery is treated with the same gravity in the ancient Near East as the unwarranted

of his father, "Joseph is no more" (42:36), at least for the next twenty years.[83] Finally, the brothers take no responsibility for the crime. Worse, they attempt to cover the evil deed with deceit (37:31–33, 35), just as Cain lied about his murderous act and denied accountability (4:9). Once again, it appears that the seed of the Serpent has fatally struck the heel of the woman's offspring.[84]

JUDAH'S SPIRITUAL BLINDNESS

After Joseph is separated from his family and "brought down [הוּרַד]" to Egypt as a slave (37:28, 36; 39:1), Judah "went down [וַיֵּרֶד] from his brothers and turned aside to a certain Adullamite, whose name was Hirah" (38:1).[85] In the subsequent narratives (Gen 38), Moses under-

theft of a man's life—as a capital offense punishable by death (Exod 21:16; Deut 24:7). Compare also stipulation no. 14 in "The Code of Hammurabi," which reads, "If a seignior has stolen the young son of a(nother) seignior, he shall be put to death." *ANET*, 166. Second, one of the most painful elements of death is the prospect of being separated from those whom the person loves, especially family (Gen 21:16; 23:2; 50:1; 2 Sam 12:16–18, 22; Isa 38:11, 17–19). Joseph had to suffer this pain (41:51–52), as did his father (37:34–35; 42:36, 38), at least for a time. Third, for all intents and purposes, the brothers themselves treat Joseph as if he were "no more" (42:13, 32). Fourth, by ending with Joseph's consignment to slavery in Egypt (37:36) and transitioning to the Judah-Tamar narrative (ch. 38), the narrator has left the reader with the gnawing fear that Joseph—the one son who has not yet manifested a negative character (besides Benjamin) and who, therefore, remains the most likely candidate for the blessing—has been eliminated from the picture and is "no more"!

83. Following the narrator's chronology, Joseph was seventeen years old when his brothers sold him into slavery (37:2), thirty years old when the seven years of plenty started (41:46), and thirty-seven years old at the beginning of the famine (41:53–54). The brothers probably came to Egypt for grain not long after the famine began (42:1–7), so at least twenty years have passed since they sold him into slavery.

84. Ronning makes the perceptive connection between Joseph/the brothers, Abel/Cain, and the seed of the woman/the seed of the Serpent. Ronning notes, "Hatred and jealousy are distinctly Cainite reactions to God's favor. Joseph and his ten older brothers thus represent the two seeds of Genesis 3:15 once again at enmity, once again in the same family" (204). Thankfully, though, this later narrative takes a positive turn in the end. Unlike Abel, Joseph "rises from the grave," as it were, and is used of God to preserve the covenant family and to bring his Cain-like brothers to repentance. "So the story of Joseph, in terms of Genesis 3:15," says Ronning, "is a story about how ten brothers cast as the offspring of the Serpent are brought instead to be 'the servants of your father's God' (Gen 50:17), thus sharing in the promises to the righteous seed of Gen 3:15 as spoken to their father Abraham" (206).

85. Judah's plot to eliminate Jacob's favorite backfires. He can remove Joseph physically from the family, but he cannot remove Joseph from Jacob's affections. Prodded by

scores Judah's lack of spiritual perception and contrasts him with Joseph who is portrayed as a man with spiritual insight and moral values (Gen 39–41).[86] In this regard, Judah resembles his uncle Esau, a worldly opportunist who lives for the here-and-now.[87] And as was true of Esau, Judah's spiritual blindness renders him unfit to be the recipient of the blessing.[88]

The Closing of Judah's Eyes

Judah's spiritual blindness is highlighted in several ways throughout the narrative. First, Judah shows no signs of genuine remorse for his crime against his brother and father. Selling a brother into slavery was a capital offense under Mosaic law (Exod 21:16; Deut 24:7). Judah compounds this sin by deceiving his father into thinking Joseph had been killed (37:31–32)[89] and, what is worse, he aggravates the cruel nature of that

---

the realization that his prospects for gaining his father's favor are slim and perhaps also by a sense of nagging guilt for his conspiracy and evil deed against Joseph, Judah decides to remove himself from the covenant family and pursue an independent destiny. See Mathews, *Genesis 11:27—50:26,* 714; Bryan Smith, "The Presentation of Judah in Genesis 37–50 and Its Implications for the Narrative's Structure and Thematic Unity," 81–85.

86. Many commentators have struggled to understand the relationship of the narrative in chapter 38, commonly called, "The Judah and Tamar Story," with the preceding and subsequent narratives (chs. 37, 39–50), commonly called, "The Joseph Story." See von Rad, *Genesis,* 351. Brueggemann, *Genesis,* 307; Hamilton, *Genesis 18–50,* 431. A number of recent literary analyses, however, have demonstrated incontestable connections between chapter 38 and its surrounding context. See Ackerman, "Joseph, Judah, and Jacob," 3–12; Cassuto, "Tamar and Judah Story," 1:30–31; Childs, *Introduction to the OT as Scripture,* 156–57; Golding, "Youngest Son; or, Where Does Genesis 38 Belong?" 27–44; Mathewson, "Exegetical Study of Genesis 38," 373–92; Bryan Smith, "Presentation of Judah in Genesis 37–50 and Its Implications for the Narrative's Structure and Thematic Unity," 55–311.

87. Esau sells his birthright for a bowl of stew (25:29–34; Judah sells his brother (the destined recipient of the birthright) for twenty shekels of silver (37:28). Esau commits exogamy, taking two Canaanite wives (26:34); Judah marries a Canaanite woman (38:2). Esau separates himself from the covenant family to pursue his own destiny and make a name for himself (36:1–43); Judah too separates from the covenant family with the apparent intention of pursuing a destiny unconnected with the Abrahamic promise (38:1ff.). For an extended development of these and other parallels, see Bryan Smith, "The Presentation of Judah in Genesis 37–50 and Its Implications for the Narrative's Structure and Thematic Unity," 71–85.

88. Yet, unlike Esau, Judah repents (38:26), shows the fruit of repentance (44:14–34), and, as a result, shares the blessing with Joseph in the end (Gen 49:8–12; 22–26).

89. That Judah was the mastermind behind the "killed-by-a-wild animal" ruse is suggested by the following. First, Moses presents Judah as an assertive leader and major

deception by attempting to "comfort" his father in the face of Jacob's loss (37:35). In doing so, Judah provides a striking illustration of the proverb, "the mercy of the wicked is cruel" (Prov 12:10). Although a degree of gnawing guilt may have prompted Judah to withdraw from his family, it fails to produce in him genuine remorse and repentance for his sin.[90] The first twenty-five verses of chapter 38 depict Judah marrying, building a family, and carrying out his vocation as if he had committed no crime.

Second, Judah disassociates himself from the covenant family and intermingles with the pagan population (38:1), even marrying a Canaanite woman (38:2). Of course, one must not fault Judah merely for having some associations with the Canaanite population since his forefathers sometimes made appropriate alliances and engaged in lawful commerce with certain of Canaan's inhabitants (Gen 14:13; 21:22–32; 23:3–20; 26:26–31; 33:19). The narrator, however, portrays Judah's association with the Canaanite population as *a reaction against* his relationship to the covenant family: "Judah *left his brothers* [מֵאֵת אֶחָיו][91] and went down *to stay with a man* [וַיֵּט עַד־אִישׁ][92] of Adullam named Hirah" (38:1,

---

spokesman for his brothers (37:26–27; 43:3, 8; 44:14ff.; 46:28; 49:8–10). Second, the "poetic justice" or *lex talionis* principle operative in chapter 38 indicts Judah as the primary guilty party in the sale of Joseph and deception of Jacob. Judah bereaves Jacob of a son, so God bereaves Judah of two sons (38:6, 10). More striking is the parallel between Tamar's message to Judah, "Please identify whose these are, the signet and the cord and the staff [הַכֶּר־נָא לְמִי הַחֹתֶמֶת וְהַפְּתִילִים וְהַמַּטֶּה הָאֵלֶּה]" (38:25b) and the heartless message Joseph's brothers conveyed to Jacob, "Please identify whether it is your son's robe or not [הַכֶּר־נָא הַכְּתֹנֶת בִּנְךָ הִוא אִם־לֹא]" (37:32b), a parallel that implies that Judah was paying the price for his own prior deception. As Alter aptly remarks, "This precise recurrence of the verb in identical forms at the ends of Genesis 37 and 38 respectively is manifestly the result not of some automatic mechanism of interpolating traditional materials but of careful splicing of sources by a brilliant literary artist. The first use of the formula was an act of deception; the second use is for an act of unmasking. Judah with Tamar after Judah with his brothers is an exemplary narrative instance of the deceiver deceived." *Art of Biblical Narrative*, 10.

90. Stigers notes the lack of repentance-producing sorrow when he remarks, "The motivation of Judah in his move to the Shephelah is suggested in the statement 'Judah went down from his brothers,' suggesting a falling out with them relative to their treatment of Joseph, but not to the point of his going to Jacob and revealing the shameful deed." *A Commentary on Genesis*, 278.

91. Here the preposition מִן designates "movement *away from* a specified beginning point" (*IBHS* § 11.2.11b).

92. The Hebrew Qal of נטה can refer to the inclination of one's heart or the direction of one's behavior, whether good or evil (1 Sam 14:7; 2 Sam 19:14; Pss 21:11; 119:112). Elsewhere, it is used to depict the turning aside to engage in a sinful way of behavior

NIV). As the subsequent narrative shows, Hirah failed to provide Judah with a godly influence and more likely encouraged him in the opposite direction.[93] Moreover, Judah's marriage to a Canaanite woman evidences a calloused disregard for the dangers of exogamy, which the earlier bearers of the promise sought to avoid (24:3; 26:35; 27:46—28:2),[94] and suggests that his choice of a bride was guided more by physical attraction than by spiritual virtue (Prov 31:30).[95] In sum, Judah's disassociation with his covenant family and alliance with the Canaanite population betray a lack of spiritual vision. As Waltke remarks,

> Judah enters as a slave trader who has turned his back on Abraham's God-given vision. He is callous toward his father and cynical about the covenant family. The narrator's report that he

---

(1 Sam 8:3) or to the forming of an unhealthy alliance (Exod 23:2; Judg 9:3). This latter usage seems to be in view here.

93. First, the flow of verses 1 and 2 suggests that Hirah may have introduced Judah to the Canaanite woman whom Judah would marry. Second, the account seems to imply that Hirah was with Judah when the latter pursued an illicit relationship with a prostitute (38:12) and rather than dissuading Judah from this immoral act, Hirah is willing to act as an accomplice in covering the crime (38:20–23). Moreover, when Judah demands the death penalty for Tamar on account of her supposed harlotries, Hirah makes no attempt to point out Judah's grave hypocrisy (38:24–25). Judah's friendship with Hirah reminds the reader of Solomon's warning, "Whoever walks with the wise becomes wise, but the companion of fools will suffer harm" (Prov 13:20).

94. Notes Wenham, "Though the narrative does not underline it here, marrying Canaanites was hardly respectable in Israel. Abraham was most insistent that Isaac should not marry a Canaanite (24:3), and Isaac and Rebekah strongly objected to Esau's marriage with Canaanites and forbade Jacob to do so (27:46—28:1). So it may be presumed that Jacob felt similarly about his son's marriage. Yet knowing his father's antipathy, Judah went ahead, showing once again his callous disregard for his father's feelings. Simeon (46:10) also married a Canaanite, and Joseph an Egyptian (41:45), so by marrying a foreigner, Judah anticipates his brothers' actions." *Genesis 16–50*, 365.

95. According to verse 2, "There Judah saw [וַיַּרְא־שָׁם יְהוּדָה] the daughter of a certain Canaanite whose name was Shua. He took her [וַיִּקָּחֶהָ] and went in to her [וַיָּבֹא אֵלֶיהָ]." Elsewhere in Genesis the combination of the verbs ראה and לקח carry negative connotations, implying a pursuit to gratify sensual desire (Gen 3:6; 6:2; 12:15; 34:2). Indeed, Judah's relationship to his unnamed Canaanite wife differs from his sexual liaison with Tamar "the prostitute" only in one particular. Both relationships begin with the verb ראה and end with the phrase "went into her [וַיָּבֹא אֵלֶיהָ]" (38:2, 15, 18). Judah's relationship with Tamar simply excludes the formality of marriage (i.e., לקח). These considerations lead Wenham to suggest, "Judah's marriage may have been based on mere lust. The fact that his wife's name is not mentioned . . . may point in the same direction." *Genesis 16–50*, 366. Kidner notes the parallel with Samson's choice of a Philistine bride who remains unnamed in the narrative (Judg 14:1–4). *Genesis*, 187.

> has entered intimate relationships with Canaanites speaks volumes (cf. 24:3; 27:46—28:8; 34:1).[96]

Third, Judah's spiritual blindness is underscored by his inability to perceive the true cause behind his sons' premature deaths. Although the character development of Er and Onan is minimal, they are both described as either being or doing what is "wicked in the sight of the Lord" (38:7a, 9–10a).[97] And on this account, God "put [them] to death" (38:7b, 10b).[98] Yet Judah suspects that Tamar, whom he first gave to his firstborn Er in marriage (38:6) and then to his second son Onan after Er's death in keeping with the levirate custom (38:8),[99] is the real cause behind his

96. Waltke, *Genesis*, 508.

97. The expression "evil in the sight of the Lord" occurs elsewhere in connection with unbelief, disobedience, idolatry, or wicked behavior in general (Num 22:34; 32:13; Deut 4:25; 1 Sam 15:19; 2 Sam 12:9; Jer 7:30; 32:30; Mal 2:17; see especially Judges, Kings, and Chricles). Er's sin is not identified. Some commentators have deduced from the language describing Onan's death (38:10) that Er must have committed a similar offense, that is, some sexual perversion. For example, H. Freedman interprets גַּם as meaning "for that reason" and deduces a similar sin for Er as that of Onan. "The Book of Genesis," 237. According to parashah 85:4 of *Genesis Rabbah*, Er committed a form of sodomy euphemistically called, "plowing on the roof." *GR*, 3:209. But the language at best emphasizes the magnitude of both sins without necessarily equating them. Apparently, Moses did not view it necessary to the plot to reveal the precise nature of Er's evil.

98. The Hebrew verb מות appears both times in the Hiphil causative and is elsewhere employed for capital punishment either by human or divine agency (Gen 18:25; Exod 4:24; Num 35:19, 21; 2 Sam 14:7; Isa 11:4).

99. The phrase "and perform the duty of a brother-in-law" translates a single Hebrew verb with the copula וְיַבֵּם. The verb also appears in Deuteronomy 25:5 along with the cognate noun יָבָם (vv. 5, 7), which refers to the brother of a widow's deceased husband. The existence and use of this terminology in the OT bears witness to a common custom in the ancient Near East in which the brother of a barren widow's deceased husband was responsible to have sexual intercourse with the barren widow in order to provide his deceased brother with an enduring lineage and his widow with a son who could later provide for his mother economically. According to some extrabiblical ancient Near East legal codes, the father-in-law himself could provide the levirate obligation. See Hittite Code, no. 193 in *ANET*, 196; Middle Assyrian Laws, no. 33, in *ANET*, 182. The Mosaic legislation, however, limited the obligation to the deceased's brother (Deut 25:5–6) and even made provision for the deceased's brother to decline the obligation, though he would have to accept public shaming (Deut 25:7–10; see also Ruth 4:1–12). Some scholars believe the OT levirate laws actually required the brother to take his deceased brother's widow and live with her permanently as a wife. See Davies, "Inheritance Rights and the Hebrew Levirate Marriage: Part 1," 143. Other scholars contend that once the widow conceived, the brother's obligation was fulfilled and marriage was unnecessary. See Coats, "Widow's Rights: A Crux in the Structure of Gen 38," 463.

sons' premature deaths (38:11).[100] By shifting the blame to Tamar, Judah shows that he is blind to the crooked character of his own flesh and blood[101] and reminds the reader of Isaac's blindness to Esau's faults.[102]

Fourth, Judah's lack of spiritual perception is most poignantly displayed in the main plot of the narrative by his refusal to fulfill the levirate obligation he owed to Tamar, which was simultaneously his obligation to fulfill the creation mandate and advance the realization of the Abrahamic promise. As most commentators correctly observe, the events of the first eleven verses set the stage for the real crux of the narrative. The heart of the narrative begins with the death of Judah's wife. After a period of mourning, Judah went with Hirah to supervise his sheepshearers (38:12). Once apprised of Judah's itinerary (38:13), Tamar, who all this time[103] has been waiting at her father's home as a widow until Judah should give her to his third son, Shelah (38:11), takes a risky course of action. She takes off her widow's garments and clothes herself in such a way so as to prevent Judah from recognizing her and to present herself as a prostitute (38:14a). Noteworthy is the location she chooses to position herself (34:14b). Not only does she select a location where Judah must pass on his way to Timnah, but the very name of the place—"at the entrance to Enaim," which may be translated, "at the Opening of Eyes"—suggests one or more intentional wordplays. It may allude proleptically to the lustful gaze Judah will cast toward Tamar when he sees her sitting in this location (38:15). Conversely, it may allude to the

100. Leupold says, "He believed Tamar was a woman who brought bad luck." *Exposition of Genesis*, 981.

101. As Stigers observes, "Some have believed that the superstition of Tobit 3:7 concerning the fateful marriage, was operating here. But here, as there, the cause of death was removal by God. Judah had refused to connect the evil conduct of his sons with their early demise. It would appear that he had become spiritually unperceptive, further evidence of the unsuitability of the land of Canaan for the clan of Israel to develop there into the nation of God's purpose." *Commentary on Genesis*, 279. Leupold also notes Judah's failure: "As we have just been informed, the reasons for the death of the first two sons lay in their own sinfulness. Somehow the father failed to see this and instead became obsessed with a kind of superstitious notion, worthy rather of a heathen Canaanite than of a member of the chosen family." *Exposition of Genesis*, 981.

102. See the discussion in chapter 5 of this study.

103. The exact period is not known, but the opening phrase of verse 13, which literally reads, "Now after many days [וַיִּרְבּוּ הַיָּמִים]," suggests something like "a considerable time" (NAU) or "a long time" (NIV). Furthermore, verse 14 indicates that enough time had elapsed for Shelah to have matured and become eligible for marriage.

manner of Tamar's veiled identity, with only her eyes visible to Judah.[104] Most likely, the wordplay ironically exposes Judah's failure to recognize Tamar's true identity and, therefore, his own guilt.[105] Indeed, Tamar's ruse will prove to be a real "eye-opener" for Judah when his sin and hypocrisy are later exposed (38:25–26).[106] What is more, the phrase may also highlight Tamar's acute knowledge of Judah and his ways. Judah does not know Tamar, but Tamar knows Judah all too well.

Not surprisingly, Tamar has accurately predicted Judah's proclivities and the circumstances that would make him ripe for her ruse.[107] Judah takes the bait and seeks sexual congress with Tamar "for he did not how that she was his daughter-in-law" (38:15–16a). Tamar allows Judah to name the price (38:16b)—he offers a goat (38:17a)—but she reserves the right to name the pledge (38:17b). With cunning foresight, she asks for Judah's "identification seal and its cord and the walking stick you are car-

104. Mathews, *Genesis 11:27—50:26*, 718–19.

105. Ira Robinson has compared the phrase with the somewhat antithetical phrase in Genesis 20:16. There, the phrase "covering of the eyes" signifies, metaphorically, *exoneration from guilt*. Conversely, the phrase "opening of the eyes" may figuratively connote *exposure of guilt*. "bĕpetaḥ ʿênayim in Genesis 38:14," 569; Bos, "Out of the Shadows," 42; Good, "Deception and Women: A Response," 116–17.

106. Garland and Garland attempt to bring out the various possible ironies conveyed by the play on words: "Tamar covers her eyes with a veil to deceive Judah. When he came to the place where Tamar sat, however, he was blinded by his lust and saw what he thought was only a hooker willing to sell her body to him, not his daughter-in-law. His eyes would be opened much later, when it was too late, but his eyes would be opened to his duty in new ways, and he would also view Tamar in an entirely new light." Again they note, "Judah's blindness is not so surprising, however. He had never really seen Tamar as a person with needs and for whom he was responsible. He had made an early attempt to care for her by ordering Onan to lie with her. But evidently he never asked why no pregnancy ensued. He went through the motions, just as Onan had done. . . . It is ironic that only now, when she was wearing a veil, that he finally 'saw' Tamar. As a sexual object—not as a person—she attracted his notice." *Flawed Families of the Bible*, 113.

107. Moses portrays Judah as a man largely governed by his sensual proclivities. Tamar has probably picked up on this. Moreover, she knows that as a widower, Judah will be more susceptible to sexual temptation. Furthermore, as Kidner notes, "Sheep-shearing was a festive time (cf. 1 Sam 25:4, 11, 36), when sexual temptation would be sharpened by the Canaanite cult, which encouraged ritual fornication as fertility magic" (188). Since wine-drinking often accompanied such events (2 Sam 25:18, 16), Judah's empirical senses would be dulled and moral inhibitions relaxed (Gen 19:32–36).

rying" (38:18a, NLT),[108] which he surrenders foolishly[109] and completes the shady transaction, unwittingly and providentially impregnating his own daughter-in-law (38:18b). Quickly following the liaison, Tamar returns to her state of widowhood (38:19). Meanwhile, Judah does not waste any time sending Hirah to deliver payment and retrieve his pledge (38:20).

Ironically, some commentators pause at this point to admire Judah's integrity. Claus Westermann, for example, opines,

> The episode serves further to portray Judah as an honorable man. The narrator does not regard Judah's going to a prostitute as something dishonorable; but it would have been dishonorable had Judah reneged on the payment. Hence it is stated in v. 23b that he had done all to deliver the promised kid.[110]

But such a positive assessment of Judah goes contrary to the grain of the narrative. It is more likely that Judah's speedy payment is motivated by an eagerness to retrieve incriminating evidence (i.e., his identity markers) than by a noble business ethic. This fact becomes more apparent when the reader notes that Judah sends Hirah to fulfill the errand rather than personally delivering the payment. After Hirah makes a thorough but unsuccessful search for the "cult prostitute" (38:21–22), Judah decides,

108. Literally, Tamar says to Judah, "your seal and your cord and your staff which is in your hand [חֹתָמְךָ וּפְתִילֶךָ וּמַטְּךָ אֲשֶׁר בְּיָדֶךָ]." The "seal" (חֹתָם) was a stone or metal cylinder ornament that was engraved with the owner's identification markings and suspended from the owner's neck by a "cord" (פָּתִיל). Speiser suggests the first two nouns be interpreted as a hendiadys and translated, "the seal on the cord." *Genesis,* 298–99. For more information about this form of identification and its uses in the ancient Near East, see Millard, "חתם," *NIDOTTE*, 2:324; Magnes-Gardiner, "Seals, Mesopotamian," in *ABD*, 5:1062–64. For pictures of various cylinder seals, see *ANEP*, 219–23 ns. 672–706. The "staff" (מַטֶּה) was also an identity marker, often bearing the mark of ownership engraved on its head. According to the Greek historian Herodotus, it was customary for Mesopotamian men to carry such a staff with an ornately decorated top. *Herodotus*, 1:195. For examples of such staffs in the ancient Near East, see *ANEP*, 6 n. 14; 134 n. 383; 153 n. 445; 174 n. 513; 179 n. 530; 192 n. 576; 199 n. 609. Hence, as Vawter points out, "What Judah does is surrender his ID card." *On Genesis*, 398).

109. Gunn and Fewell call attention to the stupidity of Judah's surrendering his personal identification markers when they emote, "Left his credit cards with a prostitute? Unbelievable! What a fool!" *Narrative in the Hebrew Bible*, 40. Perhaps Solomon had Judah's folly in mind when he wrote, "Suddenly he went after her like an ox that goes to the slaughter, like a stag prancing into a trapper's snare" (Prov 7:22, NET).

110. Westermann, *Genesis 37–50*, 53–54. See also Gunkel's praise of Judah, *Genesis*, 401.

"Let her keep the things as her own, or we shall be laughed at" (38:23a). In other words, Judah's governing motivation is the drive to avoid embarrassment.[111] And the fear of embarrassment usually presupposes that a shameful act has been committed (Gen 3:7–10). Judah's final words to Hirah, "You see, I sent the young goat, and you did not find her" (38:23b), are not the evidence of a good conscience but the rationalizations of a guilty conscience attempting to place a positive spin on the attempted cover-up.

The Opening of Judah's Eyes

That the narrator intends the reader to see Judah's actions in a negative light becomes even clearer as the story progresses. Within three months, news of Tamar's pregnancy leaks out to Judah, and she is accused of adultery (38:24a).[112] Without pause or a proper hearing,[113] Judah acts as judge and pronounces a death-penalty verdict (38:24b).[114] But just as she

111. Bryan Smith aptly notes, "Judah knows that the longer he attempts to find this harlot, the greater the chances are that others will find out that he not only stooped to sleeping with a harlot but also that he was foolish enough to leave important pieces of identification with her. He is not afraid to engage in shameful pleasure, but he is afraid of being shamed by it. Thus, he values his reputation more than his character." "The Presentation of Judah in Genesis 37–50 and Its Implications for the Narrative's Structure and Thematic Unity," 67.

112. Tamar's accusers are not identified, but they appear to accuse her not only of *an immoral act* but also of *an immoral character*. First, they assert, "Tamar your daughter-in-law has been immoral." The verb translated "immoral [זנה]" is semantically broad enough to include various forms of sexual immorality. Since the accusers are probably unaware of how Tamar became pregnant, the reader should interpret her alleged crime as "adultery." Second, they add, "Moreover, she is pregnant by immorality." Here, the plural noun זְנוּנִים is used, which cannot logically refer to impregnation through multiple acts of immorality but which must refer to a character disposition or habitual behavior (see *IBHS* § 7.4.2c). Hence, Tamar's character is being assassinated.

113. Judah does not summon witnesses or allow the defendant to speak before rendering the verdict, both of which are procedures commended in the OT (Deut 17:6; 19:15; Prov 18:13, 17). Of course, Tamar's pregnancy would have counted as circumstantial evidence. But she at least deserved an opportunity to speak before judgment was rendered. One is reminded of Nicodemus's rhetorical question put to his fellow Pharisees, as they made allegations against Jesus of Nazareth: "Does our law judge a man without first giving him a hearing and learning what he does?" (John 7:51).

114. The OT prescribed stoning for adultery (Deut 22:20–24) and reserved burning for a man who married a mother and daughter simultaneously (Lev 20:14) or a priest's daughter who was guilty of prostitution (Lev 21:9). In light of this, some scholars view Judah's sentence as severe. Sarna thinks that a stoning would have prefaced the burning, as in the case of Achan (Josh 7:25–26). *Genesis*, 270.

is being led to her execution, she sends a message and some incriminating evidence to Judah (38:25). When Judah looks at exhibits A, B, and C (38:26a), he realizes he's been had![115] Judah's eyes are now opened to his sin. Finally, Judah does act with honor and acknowledges his own guilt publicly. His self-condemnation contains the verdict proper as well as the grounds for the verdict (38:26b). Since Judah's self-condemnation is the turning point of the plot,[116] an accurate interpretation of its meaning is vital for understanding the narrative's central message. In the Hebrew, the verdict reads, צָדְקָה מִמֶּנִּי. Grammatically, the *min* may function as *a comparison of exclusion*[117] and be translated, "She was right and I was wrong" (NJB). This interpretation of Judah's statement would find a parallel in Saul's confession to David, when the former declares, "You are in the right rather than I" (NAB). In such a case, the object of the comparative preposition (i.e., Judah/Saul) is not righteous; whereas the referent (i.e., Tamar/David) is righteous. Such a reading, however, would require the reader either to excuse Tamar's deception and incestuous act with her father-in-law or to limit the semantic range of "righteous" to mere conformity to a social convention (i.e., the levirate custom) rather than conformity to God's moral law.[118] The first option is ruled out by Judah's own sense of shame for immorality committed (38:20–23) and by Judah's condemnation of Tamar (38:24b), which was technically justified, though hypocritical.[119] The second option overlooks that fact that

115. The sight of his identity markers together with Tamar's message, "Please identify whose these are," immediately reminded Judah of the message he had sent to his father with Joseph's identity marker (i.e., the special tunic covered with blood) in order to cover up Judah's evil deed. God has exposed his own wickedness!

116. According to Brueggemann, "That concession on [Judah's] part constitutes the main turn in the narrative." *Genesis,* 309. Mathewson agrees that the "verdict from Judah in verse 26 is the normative (authoritative) viewpoint of the story." "An Exegetical Study of Genesis 38," 380.

117. *IBHS* §14.4e.

118. The term "righteous" refers to conformity to a standard, and though its use overwhelmingly has an ethical standard in view, it may sometimes simply refer to social conventions or man-made standards, as possibly in Ecclesiastes 7:16.

119. Judah not only attempts to execute Tamar for the same *kind* of crime he has just committed but also, ironically, for the very *same crime*. Nevertheless, Tamar was pledged to Shelah (38:11), and her ruse, therefore, was both deceitful and adulterous. Hence, Judah cannot be unqualifiedly justifying her moral actions. One should also note that Judah's refusal to have any further sexual relations with Tamar following his confession bears witness to his recognition that such a relationship between a father-in-law and daughter-in-law was inappropriate (Lev 18:15). Those interpreters who attempt to

she herself technically violated the social agreement. The agreement was for her to wait until Judah gave her Shelah (38:11). True, Judah never intended to fulfill his pledge (38:14b). Nevertheless, that was the agreement, which Tamar in fact violated by her deceitful ruse.[120] It seems preferable, therefore, to interpret the מִן preposition as *a positive comparison* wherein the subject (i.e., Tamar) possesses a quality (i.e., innocence) to *a greater degree than* the referent (i.e., Judah).[121] More precisely, the comparison serves to underscore *the greater guilt* of one above another. This usage of the מִן of comparison with the root צדק occurs in four other texts where neither the preposition's object nor its referent is completely innocent. When Yahweh declares, "Faithless Israel has shown herself more righteous than treacherous Judah [צִדְּקָה נַפְשָׁהּ מְשֻׁבָה יִשְׂרָאֵל מִבֹּגֵדָה יְהוּדָה]" (Jer 3:11), the real point is *relative guilt*. Similarly, when Habakkuk wonders why Yahweh "remain[s] silent when the wicked [i.e., the Babylonians] swallows up the man more righteous [i.e., the Jews] than he [תַּחֲרִישׁ בְּבַלַּע רָשָׁע צַדִּיק מִמֶּנּוּ]?" he is not exonerating the nation of Judah

---

justify Tamar's deceitful sexual liaison on the basis that "the ends justify the means" are misguided. Fretheim provides an example of such reasoning when he suggests, "It may be necessary to go beyond the law in order to fulfill the law, which should enable life and well-being to a community (see Deut 6:4; Jesus' sabbath-breaking, Mark 2:27). Here the OT narrative gives especially high value to the future of the community, in view of which individual acts, which might be normally condemned, are viewed positively. Relationships are more important than rules; faithfulness may mean going beyond the law. We cannot help wondering whether this story has informed Jesus' saying that 'the prostitutes are going into the kingdom of God ahead of you' (Matt 21:31 NRSV) as well as his open response to the woman who was a 'sinner' (Luke 7:36–50)." "Genesis," 607. Ironically, in an article entitled "Survival Must Not be Gained through Sin," Wildavsky argues in a similar vein, viewing the preservation of the purity of Abraham's family line as "the moral law" that Judah almost violated (but did not thanks to Tamar) and that Joseph actually violated by marrying an Egyptian! (43). But the reasoning of Fretheim and Wildavsky is precarious. Tamar was certainly right to expect Judah to support her until Shelah was old enough for marriage and to expect Judah to give his blessing to the marriage so that offspring could be raised up. In this sense, she was more righteous than Judah and even evidenced a greater concern for the promise than the patriarch himself. For this we may commend her. But like many of the members of the patriarchal community, she employs deceptive and sinful means to achieve a righteous end. For this, she must not be excused.

120. Most English versions reflect this meaning (KJV, ASV, RSV, NAS, NIV, NLT, NRSV, ESV, CSB). The fact Tamar's deceitful ruse follows in a line of deceitful schemes that are perpetrated within the patriarchal community and that are almost always explicitly or implicitly condemned by the narrator suggests a negative evaluation for Tamar's deed.

121. GKC § 133a; *GBH* § 133e; 141g; *IBHS* § 11.2.11e; 14.4d.

from its deserved punishment. The comparison serves to highlight the relatively greater guilt of one party over the other (see also 1 Kgs 2:32; Ezek 16:52). So Judah is not exonerating Tamar. Judah's indignation against a perceived act of sexual immorality on the part of Tamar was not without some justification. Judah, however, acknowledges and accepts that he bears the greater blame.

As the grounds for Judah's self-condemnation, he asserts, "on account of the fact that [כִּי־עַל־כֵּן] I did not give her to Shelah my son" (38:26b; author's translation). The reference is obviously to Judah's failure to keep his levirate obligation to Tamar (38:11a). Judah admits that his breach of good faith served as the occasion that led Tamar to the desperate measures she took in order to ensure the propagation of a seed and the preservation of Judah's line.[122] Neither Tamar nor Judah may be commended for their deception or immoral sexual affair.[123] Tamar's guilt is mitigated, however, by the fact that she showed more concern than Judah for the maintenance of the family line—an essential element of the Abrahamic promise. This interpretation is supported by the fact that Tamar's words, "Please identify whose these are [הַכֶּר־נָא לְמִי הָאֵלֶּה]," would have immediately reminded Judah of his sinful cover up of the heartless sale of Joseph into slavery—itself a grievous disregard for the maintenance of the family line and an act of contempt for the divine promise. Moreover, the birth of Judah's two sons through Tamar, with

122. This is how Bush interprets the passage: "*She hath been more righteous than I.* That is, less culpable. The conduct of neither had much to commend it, on the score of *righteousness*, nor does he perhaps intend to say that she had *in this matter* committed a less sin than himself, but that *his wrong-doing in another instance had been the occasion of hers, at this time*" (emphasis his). *Notes on Genesis*, 244.

123. Hence, the reader must reject the attempt of some early church fathers to minimize or absolve Tamar and Judah's guilt on the basis that their sexual liaison fulfilled the divine plan. Chrysostom advances this view when he warns, "Let no one who hears this condemn Tamar. As I said before, she was carrying out the divine plan, and hence neither did she incur any blame, nor did Judah lay himself open to any charge." *Homilies on Genesis*, 62.5, *ACCS*, 2:244. Ephrem of Syria suggests that Judah's attraction to Tamar and solicitation were contrary to his true nature but were a response to God's prompting which came about in answer to Tamar's prayer: "While Tamar was making supplication to God for these things, behold, Judah came out and saw her. The prayer of Tamar inclined him [Judah], contrary to his usual habit, [to go] to a harlot. When she saw him, she was veiled, for she was afraid. After the word of the sign for which she had asked had been spoken, she knew that God was pleased with what she was doing. Afterward she revealed her face without fear and even demanded remuneration from the lord of the treasure." *Commentary on Genesis* 34.4, *ACCS* 2:44.

which the story concludes, demonstrates for the reader that the continuity of Abraham's promised offspring was at stake.[124] Consequently, Tamar's deceitful ruse exposes Judah's spiritual blindness to his responsibility to advance rather than to oppose the historical fulfillment of the Abrahamic covenant. Accordingly, one may, in a qualified sense, refer to Tamar as the heroine of the story.[125] But in reality, the true hero is God himself, who once again has overruled human sin to accomplish the divine purpose.

In summary, the fourth generation of the patriarchal community has not escaped the contamination of Adam's first transgression. What is more, there appears to be an intensification of sin as the reader moves from one generation to the next. On the one hand, the reader notes a progression in God's fulfillment of his redemptive promise, given first to Adam and Eve (Gen 3:15), passed down through Noah (Gen 6:18; 9:1–17), and handed to Abraham and his offspring (Gen 12:1–3; 15:5–21; 17:1–21; 22:16–18; 26:2–5, 24; 27:27–29; 28:3–4, 13–15; 32:12, 29; 35:9–12; 37:5–9; 48:14; 49:8–12, 22–26). On the other hand, he observes a general moral decline in each successive generation of Abraham's offspring. Mathewson accurately captures the flow of both primeval as well as patriarchal history when he writes,

> Each תּוֹלֵדוֹת explains what became of a line, all the while narrowing down and following the line, through which God would bring blessing. In addition, each תּוֹלֵדוֹת shows a marked deterioration. Up to Genesis 12, the deterioration ends in judgment by God. After chapter 12, there is a continual deterioration among those striving for the blessing.[126]

So God's grace does abound in chapters 12–50 of Genesis. But the glorious beauty of God's grace is displayed against the dark backdrop of human sin abounding.

124. The parallels with the birth of Esau and Jacob are notable (Gen 25:22–26).

125. Such is the assessment of Waltke who writes, "Although the narrator describes little of Tamar's character development, she is the heroine of this scene. She rejects her Canaanite father's house and remains loyal to Judah. Presumably she could have married a Canaanite man or have become a cult prostitute in a Canaanite temple, but like Ruth, who will chose her flawed Israelite family over her Moabite roots, Tamar remains true to her Israelite family in spite of its glaring failures and becomes absorbed into it." *Genesis*, 508.

126. Mathewson, "Exegetical Study on Genesis 38," 389.

8

The Spread of the Curse in the Patriarchal Narratives

ACCORDING TO THE LAW of causality, "for every effect there is a cause." If this axiom holds true in the narrative of primeval and patriarchal history, then the reader may deduce the motif of sin's spread from the varied manifestations of sin's effects. This final chapter will complement the previous chapters by noting the varied expressions of Yahweh's implemented *curse-sanction* against human sin as revealed in the patriarchal narrative. The reader will recall that when God is subject of the Hebrew verb ארר ("curse"), it expresses a divine verdict of covenant-breach as well as divine intention to mete out punishment proportionate to the crime, which is usually specified in the curse-sanction. An analysis of Yahweh's curse-verdict in the Fall narrative as well as an examination of his curse-enactment throughout the primeval and patriarchal narratives reveals two basic categories of punishment: *general* and *discriminate.*

GENERAL PUNISHMENT IN THE PATRIARCHAL NARRATIVE

Many echoes of Yahweh's primordial curse on Adam and Eve in the Fall narrative reverberate throughout the patriarchal narrative.

The Woes of Motherhood

Yahweh declares that the woman will experience great pain in connection with her role as mother (3:16a). The primeval narrative does not appear to highlight instances of this facet of the curse. The patriarchal narrative, however, provides several examples. Most notably, the narrator commences the patriarchal narrative by introducing an immediate tension into the redemptive historical plot. Before Yahweh announces the Abrahamic promise, which includes numerous progeny who will ultimately become a nation (12:2), Moses notes, "Now Sarai was barren; she had no child" (11:30). Since fertility is consistently portrayed as a facet of divine blessing (1:22, 28; 8:17; 9:1, 7), then infertility may be interpreted as a facet of divine curse.[1] So promise and curse collide.[2] And this tension is not immediately resolved. Sarah remains barren beyond the years of menopause (17:17; 18:11–12), so that the eventual birth of the promised offspring requires a divine miracle (18:13–14; 21:1–2; Rom 4:17–21; Heb 11:11). What is more, Sarah is not the only matriarch to suffer barrenness. Both Rebekah and also Rachel must endure this curse for a time (25:21a; 29:31b; 30:1–2).[3] In addition to barrenness, Rachel will suffer painful complications during the birth of her second child (35:16–17), resulting in her premature death (35:18–19). So Moses makes it abundantly clear that even the recipients of promise are not exempt from God's primordial curse on the woman's maternal calling.

An Inharmonious Union

Not only does the curse affect the woman's maternal role, but it also spoils the harmony of her marital union (3:16b). Several examples of marital disharmony appear in the patriarchal narrative. Both Abraham and Isaac abuse their headship when they order their wives to pose as their sisters, thereby exposing them to danger (12:11–13; 20:2, 13; 26:6–7).[4] Later,

1. Later Mosaic revelation confirms this interpretation (Lev 26:9; Deut 28:4, 18).

2. Brueggemann calls attention to the strategic placement of this notice: "Sarah is barren! This innocent little verse is too carefully placed and too cryptic to be regarded simply as a historical observation. It is, in fact, a quite intentional theological notice. The blessing, mandate, and promise was to 'Be fruitful and multiply' (Gen. 1:28; 9:1). And now barrenness! The incongruity between what is intended and what happens is overwhelming. The tale could be nuanced differently if ended in [10:32]. But the narrative refuses to end with the nations. It insists on ending with Israel. Its object has been Israel. But quite clearly Israel is a major disappointment in terms of the purposes of creation." *Genesis*, 95–96. Brueggemann then draws a connection between the formless and empty void over which God pronounced the creative blessing (1:2ff.) and the barren womb over which he will declare the redemptive blessing (11:30ff.). In Brueggeman's words, "The first call of God has created a context in which a second call now needs to be issued. The first call was spoken over the *void*. When it is given, the second word will be spoken over a creation gone *barren*." *Genesis*, 97.

3. Rebekah is barren for approximately nineteen years (25:20–21, 26b) and Rachel for approximately thirteen years (29:28, 31; 30:1–2, 22–26).

4. Lot's demeaning abuse of his paternal authority over his daughters (Gen 19:8) also evidences the general climate of the demeaning of women characteristic of the ancient Near East.

Isaac appears insensitive to Rebekah's perspective of Esau and Jacob when he secretly arranges to bless the former (27:1–4). Jacob's special affection for Rachel was not wrong per se, and a polygamous marriage will always introduce a degree of irresolvable tension into husband-wife relationships (especially one that involves sisters!). Nevertheless, the narrative indicates that Jacob not only loved Rachel more than Leah but that he acted unlovingly towards Leah (29:30–35; 30:15–16).[5] Conversely, the reader finds the matriarchs sometimes imitating Eve's role as temptress and leading their husbands astray (16:2; 30:3–4; 9). Isaac's insensitivity towards Rebekah's viewpoint regarding their sons was inappropriate. But his sin does not justify her insubordinate act of deception (27:5–13). So the curse of marital strife plagued even the patriarchal home.

The Cursed Earth

As God shaped the woman's penalty according to her role (mother/wife), so he shaped man's penalty according to his God-given task. Yahweh cursed the ground that Adam was to cultivate (3:17–18). It must be admitted that a superficial reading of the patriarchal narratives gives the impression that God's elect are not affected by this aspect of the curse. Abram is described as materially prosperous (12:2; 24:35). "Isaac," the reader is told, "sowed in that land and reaped in the same year a hundredfold. The Lord blessed him, and the man became rich, and gained more and more until he became very wealthy" (26:12–13). Jacob also prospered materially (31:9–12; 32:10, 13–21; 33:8–11). But a more careful inspection of the patriarchal narrative leads the reader to discover that the patriarchs did not entirely escape this aspect of the curse. For instance, each generation of the patriarchal community had to contend with a major famine (12:10; 26:1; 41:54–57; 43:1; 47:4, 13, 20). Each of these famines was "severe" (כָּבֵד),[6] and the third lasted seven years (41:27, 30–31, 36, 54), affecting the entire inhabited earth (41:57)[7] and placing

5. See the discussion in chapter 6.

6. The adjective literally means "heavy" and is used once to describe the famine in Abraham's day (12:10) and seven times (twice with the adverb מְאֹד, "very") to describe the famine in the days of Jacob and his sons (41:31, 56, 57; 43:1; 47:4, 13, 20).

7. According to Moses, "all the earth came to Egypt to Joseph to buy grain, because the famine was severe over all the earth" (41:57). The phrase כָּל־הָאָרֶץ need not imply a global famine but probably refers to the entire Fertile Crescent region, which included Egypt and Mesopotamia.

the well-being of the covenant community in jeopardy (42:1–2; 45:7). Moreover, the patriarchs' enjoyment of Yahweh's blessing did not exempt them from toil. Laban, Jacob's "benefactor," treated his nephew like a virtual slave,[8] exposing him to the extremities of heat and cold and robbing him of many a night's sleep (31:40). In light of these observations, it seems best to view God's blessing on the patriarchs as provisional and in no way exempting them from the effects of God's general punishment of humanity (3:17–19a).

To Dust You Shall Return

Yahweh capped off his curse on mankind with haunting words, "To dust you shall return" (3:19b). The primeval narrative had a lot to say about death. But the patriarchal narrative also contributes to this motif. All the major patriarchs, Abraham, Isaac, Jacob, and Joseph, breathed their last breath and died (25:8; 35:29; 49:33; 50:26). An entire chapter is devoted to Sarah's death and burial (chap. 23).[9] Rebekah's death is not mentioned explicitly. But Moses seems to imply her death when he notes the death of her personal nurse, Deborah (35:8).[10] Rachel's premature death is recorded (35:18–20), and Leah's death is later implied by the reference to her interment (49:31). Even the deaths of secondary characters such as Ishmael (25:17) and Esau's descendants (36:33–39) are noted. One of the most important contributions of the patriarchal narrative to this theme is death's ever-increasing encroachment on human longevity. Before the Flood men almost attain the millennial mark.[11] After the Flood, however, human longevity begins to decline. This decline is first highlighted in the Shem genealogy (11:10–26), which the reader may view simultaneously as the conclusion of primeval and the beginning of patriarchal history.[12] The decline continues till one reaches the end of the patriarchal

8. Jacob's labor for Laban is repeatedly described with the verb עָבַד (29:15, 18, 20, 25, 27, 30; 30:26, 29; 31:6, 41), which probably reminded Moses's original readers of their servitude in Egypt. Jacob strengthens this connection when he speaks of his "service" as *his affliction and laborious toil* (אֶת־עָנְיִי וְאֶת־יְגִיעַ, 31:42).

9. Jacob's death and burial also receive a fairly lengthy treatment (49:33—50:14).

10. After Rebekah's death and on learning that Jacob was on his way, Deborah apparently went to meet Jacob to give him the news. Ironically, she dies sometime shortly afterwards.

11. Methuselah is longest-lived at 969 years according to the Genesis 5 genealogy.

12. As Clines remarks, "In the final form of Genesis, there is at no point a break between primeaval and patriarchal history. What follows immediately upon the Babel

narrative, which ends with Joseph's death (50:22–26). The table below illustrates this decline:

Table 4: Decreasing Longevity from the Flood to Joseph's Death

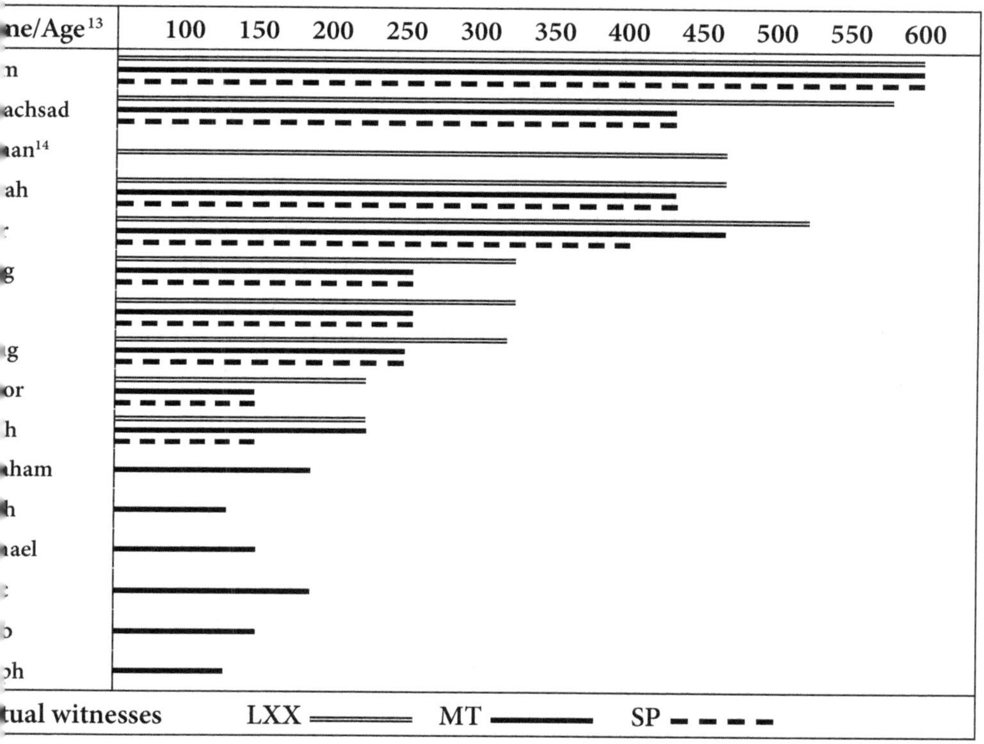

ne/Age[13]	100	150	200	250	300	350	400	450	500	550	600
n											
achsad											
an[14]											
ah											
g											
g											
or											
h											
ham											
h											
ael											
h											
tual witnesses	LXX ═══			MT ───			SP - - - -				

story (11:1–9) is the genealogical table leading from Seth to Terah (11:10–26). . . . Its function is equally to trace the ancestry of Abram—so it is attached to what follows—*and* to follow the line of descent from Shem—so it is attached to what precedes." *The Theme of the Pentateuch*, 84–85.

13. The precise ages are as follows: Shem (LXX-600; MT-600; SP-600), Arpachsad (LXX-565; MT-438; SP-438), Cainan (LXX-460), Shelah (LXX-460; MT-433; SP-433), Eber (LXX-504; MT-464; SP-404), Peleg (LXX-339; MT-239; SP-239), Reu (LXX-339; MT-239; SP-239), Serug (LXX-330; MT-230; SP-230), Nahor (LXX-208; MT-149; SP-148), Terah (LXX-205; MT-205; SP-145), Abraham (MT-175), Sarah (MT-127), Ishmael (MT-137), Isaac (MT-180), Jacob (MT-147), and Joseph (MT-110).

14. The name "Cainan" appears in the LXX and in Luke's genealogy (Luke 3:36). For a thorough discussion of the textual witnesses in relationship to the genealogy of Genesis 11, see Shaw, "The Genealogies of Genesis 5 and 11 and Their Significance for Chronology," 62–75.

Many scholars fail to detect any connection between the decreasing life-spans and the motif of sin and death. Some commentators note the decline but draw no theological conclusion.[15] Modern scholars often suggest that the transition from extraordinary lifespans to those closer to the reader's present experience signals a shift from "primeval history" to real history, from a more mythical and legendary account of the past to an account that more closely approximates actual history.[16] However, the תּוֹלְדֹת literary structure of the Genesis narrative resists any attempt to treat the primeval narratives as any less historical than the patriarchal narratives. Moreover, the interpreter who is committed to the inspiration of all Scripture must affirm the historicity of the primeval account along with the chronicler, Luke, Jesus and the apostles. Other interpreters note that the Shem genealogy differs from the Adam-Seth genealogy in that it omits a reference to the person's total age as well as the death formula, "and he died." Two conclusions are commonly drawn from these omissions. First, the author wanted to quicken the narrative's pace to accelerate the transition from primeval to patriarchal history.[17] This observation is valid. The second conclusion, however, is problematic: namely, that the narrator is attempting to direct the reader's mind away from the motif of death. In the words of Ross, "Genesis 5:1—6:8 stressed that death prevailed in the race; but *Genesis 11:10–26 stresses a movement away from death toward the promise, and it stresses life and expansion, even though longevity was declining*" (emphasis his).[18]

15. Jeske, for example, remarks, "The first detail to catch our eye is the shortened life spans of the patriarchs who lived after the flood. . . . We don't know the reasons for the sharp drop in the span of human life. It is enough for us to know that God knows." *Genesis*, 112.

16. According to Gowan, "The ages given gradually diminish to approach life spans known to us, as a way of saying that the primeval materials are now giving way to historical existence as we know it." *From Eden to Babel*, 121. See also Westermann, *Genesis 1–11*, 565–66.

17. Observes Stigers, "There is need to take up the subject of Abram so as to exhibit the basic truths in the redemptive scheme of God as soon as possible." *A Commentary on Genesis*, 132. "The main purpose of the Genesis 11 genealogy," writes Youngblood, "seems to be to provide the briefest possible transition between Shem and Abram." *The Book of Genesis*, 132. Similarly, Mathews remarks, "Chapter 11's omissions make for a swifter sequence of names, which propels the reader quickly down the line to 'Abram.'" *Genesis 1—11:26*, 489.

18 Ross, *Creation & Blessing*, 252. Likewise, Stigers opines, "In the case of Adam's history, the specific mention of death is made of each person to emphasize that sin was terminating the life. . . . But now in this new genealogy we are to remember that God

There are significant problems with such a reading. First, if Moses wants to emphasize "a movement away from death" and stress "life and expansion," why does he bother to include numerical data that patently conveys the idea of a waning of human life? Why not simply exclude that information? In reality, an objective assessment of the numerical data of the Shem genealogy together with that provided in the patriarchal death-notices leads the reader to discern an accelerated movement not *away from* but *towards* death.[19] In the second place, this overly optimistic and life-oriented reading of the Shem genealogy and rest of the patriarchal narrative conflicts with Paul's reading of this stage of redemptive history. In developing his theology of sin and death, the apostle does not confine himself either to the Fall narrative or to primeval history. Instead, he is careful to point out that "death reigned from Adam to Moses" (Rom 4:14a).[20] This leads to the third objection to the approach that sees a shift from death to life at this juncture in the narrative: such a reading introduces an unwarranted bifurcation between the message of the primeval narrative and that of the patriarchal narrative. There is only

henceforth bears with the sin of men, and it is not agreeable to his thought to announce the death of any person." *Commentary on Genesis*, 132. So too Mathews concludes, "The startling omission of the death notice, however, does more than push the narrative ahead. It also is consistent with the optimism that the new era of Abraham brought. The absence of 'death' is the author's reflection on God's patience toward sinful man." *Genesis 1—11:26*, 490. This reading of the Genesis 11 genealogy is surprising especially considering that Mathews earlier interpreted the divine judgment portended in 6:3 (i.e., man's days shall be 120 years) as a decrease in man's longevity and as partially fulfilled in this genealogy. To be consistent with his interpretation of 6:3, Mathews would have to conclude that God's patience from antediluvian days to postdiluvian days has shortened. That does not sound terribly optimistic!

19. One is compelled to agree with Ward when he remarks, "We are given the impression of time running out, of a deterioration which ought to make us look more expectantly for the promised Deliverer." *Foundations in Genesis*, 203. Concerning the omission of the death-notices, Ward offers a reasonable suggestion when he observes, "The refrain 'and he died' and the total length of life do not appear, since there is no Enoch whose passing from this world without death needs to be highlighted. Death in the second genealogy was the universal experience and it was unnecessary to note it." *Ibid.*, 203.

20. Interestingly, commentators who interpret the Genesis 11 genealogy optimistically concede that Paul viewed it otherwise. Mathews, for instance, admits, "Despite this exception to death in chap. 11, the apostle Paul assumed death had its way from 'Adam to Moses' (Rom 5:14), an allusion to Genesis 5 and 11. The Genesis author's optimism was founded on the arrival of Abraham, but for Paul the reign of death's terror was finally undone by the arrival of the last Adam, Jesus Christ." *Genesis 1—11:26*, 490. Stigers also adds a parenthetic concession to Paul's viewpoint. *Commentary on Genesis*, 132.

one point in Genesis where a clear disjunction exists between blessing and the curse, between life and death—namely, the point at which sin enters the world (Gen 3:6). From that point onward, the general out-working of Yahweh's curse, including death, constitutes a vital element of the *entire* Genesis narrative. Consistent with this conclusion is the often-overlooked fact that the final verse of Genesis closes with Joseph's death and burial (50:26). Thus, in the so-called narrative of "promise," death has the last word!

DISCRIMINATE PUNISHMENT IN THE PATRIARCHAL NARRATIVE

Not only did Yahweh's primordial curse set in motion *general punishments* that affect all mankind indiscriminately. His curse-sanction also established the principle of divine retribution that results in *discriminate punishments* for individuals or collective societies who are guilty of specific crimes. Three discernable kinds of retribution find prominence in patriarchal history. The first resembles the Flood judgment and may be viewed as a typical eschatological intrusion of the Final Judgment. The second is like the first but on a much smaller scale. It involves supernatural retaliatory interventions against individuals or groups that threaten God's promise community. The third kind of retribution, often missed, may be termed "poetic justice," or more appropriately "providential payback," and is often the chastening rod God uses on his people.

Sodom and Gomorrah: A Harbinger of Judgment Day

Chapter 3 not only surveyed various allusions to the spread of sin among pagan society in the patriarchal narrative, but it made special note of the notorious example of Sodom and Gomorrah. The narrator's repeated and poignant ways of underlining the extreme perversity and anti-God hubris of the Sodomites were documented.[21] The Sodomites were guilty of an inordinate love for material prosperity (13:10–12; 19:16, 18–20, 26; see also Ezek 16:49) and an inordinate lust for sexual pleasure (19:4–9; see also 2 Pet 2:7; Jude 7). Their sin is *so grave* (כָּבְדָה מְאֹד) that even the intercession of Yahweh's righteous servant cannot stay the divine

21. Moses distinguished the Sodomites from ordinary sinners with the addition of the adverb מְאֹד, the use of a hendiadys, and the characterization of their sin as "in God's face" so to speak: "Now the men of Sodom were exceedingly wicked sinners before Yahweh [וְאַנְשֵׁי סְדֹם רָעִים וְחַטָּאִים לַיהוָה מְאֹד]" (13:13; author's translation).

gauntlet of judgment (18:20–33). Since the Sodomites *abuse the gift of fertility* both materially and sexually, Yahweh will give them their due recompense. In succinct yet sweeping language, the act of judgment is described. As Yahweh *caused to rain* (מַמְטִיר) a deluge of watery judgment on the world that then was (7:4, 11), so now he *causes to rain* (הִמְטִיר) a deluge of fiery sulfur on the cities of the plain (19:24–25). The vengeance originates "from Yahweh out of heaven" (מֵאֵת יְהוָה מִן־הַשָּׁמָיִם), and it obliterates not only the cities and their inhabitants but, ironically, "what grew on the ground" (וְצֶמַח הָאֲדָמָה).[22] What once was as fertile as Eden (13:10) has now become a wasteland of salt (19:26)! Not only does the reader hear echoes of Eden's curse, but he also sees a preview of Final Judgment (Luke 17:26–30; 2 Pet 2:4–9). Like the watery judgment of primeval history, the fiery judgment of patriarchal history proves nothing less than a supernatural[23] intrusion of eschatological judgment into the sphere of pre-consummate history.[24]

22. Note the progression: in Eden, Yahweh-Elohim *causes to spring out of the ground* (וַיַּצְמַח ... מִן־הָאֲדָמָה) every tree pleasant to the sight and good for food (2:9). After man's fall into sin, Yahweh warns Adam that *the cursed ground* (אֲרוּרָה הָאֲדָמָה) *will bring forth* (תַּצְמִיחַ) thorns and thistles (3:17–18). Now, at the Sodom and Gomorrah site nothing at all *springs from the ground* (וְצֶמַח הָאֲדָמָה).

23. Some commentators attempt to look for some natural cause to explain the ruin of Sodom and Gomorrah. For example, Harland conjectures, "A great earthquake, perhaps accompanied by lightning, brought utter ruin and a terrible conflagration to Sodom and the other communities in the vicinity. The destructive fire may have been caused by the ignition of gases and of seepages of asphalt emanating from the region, through lightning or the scattering of fires from hearths." "Sodom and Gomorrah," 58. For similar "natural" explanations, see Skinner, *Genesis*, 309–10; Sarna, *Genesis*, 138; Vawter, *On Genesis*, 239–40. Waltke also suggests the combination of an earthquake and lightning as a possible scientific explanation, adding the caution, "It is theologically mischievous to dismiss either the scientific causes of historical events because of theological explanation or vise versa." *Genesis*, 279. Yet, the phrase מֵאֵת יְהוָה מִן־הַשָּׁמָיִם emphasizes an supernatural divine intervention that these "naturalistic" explanations often downplay or minimize. As Mathews remarks, "This heaven's rain cannot be explained solely as a natural phenomenon, such as an earthquake; it was exceptional, never again repeated, providing the parade illustration of the fiery eschatological judgment against the wicked (e.g., 2 Pet 2:6–9). The twin calamities of Noah and Lot illustrate Jesus' teaching on the suddenness of the coming of the Son of Man (Luke 17:26–30)." *Genesis 11:27—50:26*, 241. See also Hamilton, *Genesis: 18–50*, 47.

24. For the concept of intrusions of eschatological judgment into redemptive history, see Kline, *Kingdom Prologue*, 212–20; idem, *Structure of Biblical Authority*, 154–67.

Divine Retaliations: Whoever Curses You I Will Curse

In the Abrahamic promise, God avows *to curse* (ארר) anyone who *treats with contempt* (קלל) his chosen agent of blessing (12:3). The patriarchal narrative supplies us with at least four striking examples of a divine retributory response to individuals who threatened the promise. The first two examples involve pagan kings who threaten the promise unwittingly, and the second two examples involve patriarchal sons who despise the promise high-handedly. In the first incident, Pharaoh of Egypt takes Sarah, Abraham's wife, into his harem because of her reputed beauty (12:15). Although Pharaoh did not realize he had taken another man's wife (12:11–13), his ignorance does not spare him from judgment. Yahweh smites Pharaoh and his house with severe plagues (12:17). The vocabulary used to describe the punishment suggests some kind of serious sickness or disease,[25] but the narrator does not identify the precise form of punishment. The second incident, however, is quite parallel and may imply the same kind of punishment in Pharaoh's case. More than twenty years later Abimelech in Gerar does the same thing, once again, unwittingly (20:1–2). This time the narrator provides more detail. God communicates to Abimelech in a dream, threatening the monarch and his household with death if he does not promptly return the patriarch's wife (20:3–7). The pagan ruler wastes no time and quickly restores Sarah to Abraham (20:8–16). In return, Abraham prays for Abimelech, and God heals Abimelech, his wives, and his concubines "so that they bore children. For the Lord had closed all the wombs of the house of Abimelech because of Sarah, Abraham's wife" (20:17–18). Some commentators have conjectured some disorder like a genital discharge or venereal disease that prevented sexual intercourse and threatened the prospect of a royal offspring.[26] God's death-threat was probably a potential judgment in addition to the infertility already inflicted on the royal household. Thus, Moses provides the reader with a second example of divine intervention and judgment in a situation where the promise was in jeopardy.

25. "And Yahweh afflicted [וַיְנַגַּע יְהוָה]" is followed by the amplified cognate noun "great plagues [נְגָעִים גְּדֹלִים]." The vocabulary is used elsewhere for sickness and disease, which at times may be lethal (Exod 11:1; 1 Kgs 8:37; 2 Kgs 15:5; 2 Chr 6:28; 26:20; Pss 39:10 [Heb 11]; 91:10). The use of the adjective גְּדֹלִים indicates something severe.

26. Keil and Delitzsch, *Pentateuch*, 1:241–42; Skinner, *Genesis*, 320; Walton, *Genesis*, 495.

The next two cases of divine retaliation involve two brothers, namely, the first two sons of Judah. Judah selects Tamar to be the wife of his firstborn, Er (38:6). But because the man was wicked in Yahweh's sight, Yahweh killed him (38:7). Moses chooses not to disclose the precise nature of Er's sin but moves quickly to the levirate marriage of Tamar to Er's brother Onan (38:8). Like Er, Onan commits evil in God's sight, and God slays him (38:10). In this case, Moses describes the sin. Onan refuses to impregnate Tamar by deceitfully and repeatedly engaging in coitus interruptus (38:9). Because of the similar vocabulary used to describe the brothers' crime as well as Yahweh's penalty,[27] some infer that Er must have committed some kind of sexual act similar to his brother Onan.[28] Whatever the precise nature of Er's wickedness, he likely shared in common with his brother a high-handed contempt for the Abrahamic promise. The Lord's severer retaliation in the case of Er and Onan in contrast with the non-lethal punishment of Pharaoh and Abimelech is probably due to the fact that the pagan kings sinned ignorantly whereas Abraham's great-grandsons sinned knowingly against greater light and privilege.

Providential Payback: What Goes Around Comes Around

Some interpreters underscore what they perceive to be a lack of censure of the patriarchs' immoral behavior in the patriarchal narrative. In other words, while God judges the sins of men in primeval history and the sins of pagans in patriarchal history, he appears to let the patriarchs themselves "off the hook." Speaking primarily of the patriarchal narrative, Childs remarks, "It is astonishing to see the extent to which the ethical difficulties of the Genesis story are completely disregarded."[29] After noting that the patriarchs engaged in "highly questionable behavior," Hamilton makes the observation that "God never clearly rebukes any

27. Their character/act is described with the same root idea (רעע/רַע). In both cases their sin is described as בְּעֵינֵי יְהוָה. And God inflicts death (מות) on both.

28. As noted previously, Freedman interprets גַּם in the clause "and he put him to death *also* [גַּם]" (38:10) as meaning "for that reason" and deduces a similar sin for Er as that of Onan (237). According to Parashah 85:4 of *Genesis Rabbah*, as previously cited, Er committed a form of sodomy (euphemistically called, "plowing on the roof"). *GR*, 3:209).

29. Childs, *OT Theology in a Canonical Context*, 215.

of the patriarchs." Advancing this observation a step further, Hamilton opines,

> The patriarchs escape prosecution. In fact, after the Tower of Babel story in Gen 11, one does not encounter any story before Exod 32 in which the followers of God experience the voice of judgment. (except for Er and Onan, the sons of Judah, Gen 38)[30]

Although comments like these contain an element of truth and are motivated by a laudable effort to underscore God's relentless faithfulness to his promise, they can blind the reader to real yet subtle forms of divine retribution suffered by the patriarchal community. Indeed, one of the most common forms of retribution in the patriarchal narratives is that of "poetic justice."[31] However, since retribution in the biblical narrative is not merely the product of literary artistry but the outworking of providential justice, then "providential payback" is a preferable epithet.[32] A careful reading of the patriarchal stories reveals the age-old axiom: what a person sows he eventually reaps (Job 4:8; Hos 8:7; 10:12; Gal 6:7–8).

The reader will recall, for example, Abraham's cowardly ruse in Egypt, where he virtually pawns his wife Sarah to the Egyptian Pharaoh in return for personal safety as well as material gain (12:10–16). Yahweh punishes Pharaoh, but he appears to let Abraham escape scot-free. Indeed, Abraham leaves Egypt with all the livestock and human servants he had acquired as dowry from Pharaoh (12:16, 13:1–2). But the patriarch will live to regret his detour to Egypt. For no more than ten years following the Egypt debacle, Abraham's own wife pawns her husband off to an Egyptian (16:1–4a)![33] In fact, it is highly probable that

30. Hamilton, *Genesis 1–17*, 43–45.

31. One definition of "poetic justice" is "the rewarding of virtue and the punishment of vice, often in an especially appropriate or ironic manner." *The American Heritage Dictionary of the English Language*, 4th edition (Random House, 2006), s.v. Another dictionary describes it as "an ideal distribution of rewards and punishments such as is common in some poetry and fiction." *Random House Unabridged Dictionary* (Random House, 2006), s.v. Both of these definitions are available from http://dictionary.reference.com/browse/poetic%20justice; Internet; accessed 29 December 2007.

32. Indeed, the poignancy of poetic justice depends on the assumption that events in life are not merely the products of random chance. There seem to be some "moral laws" in the universe that bear some resemblance to "physical laws." Regrettably, many opt for a kind of impersonal, mechanistic "fate" or "karma" in place of the personal, living God who is Creator, Lord, Judge, and Redeemer.

33. It is not without purpose that Moses twice identifies Hagar as an Egyptian (16:1, 3).

Hagar the maidservant was part of Abraham's "spoil" obtained from Pharaoh (12:16). Not only does the Hagar-as-surrogate-mother scheme end in family strife (16:4b–6) and fail to produce the son of promise (17:18–21), but it also serves as God's chastening rod for the patriarch's early sin of unbelief, deceit, and cowardice. Conversely, God will also make Sarah regret her impatient attempt to make the promise happen and obtain her coveted offspring. Years later the son of Sarah's ingenious scheme, Ishmael, will show signs of contempt towards the son of Sarah's own womb, thus threatening the very promise Sarah had sought to secure. And one must not forget the sin of Lot. Will he love possessions more than God (13:10–12)? Then God will take away his possessions (14:12). Will Lot give away his own daughters to be raped (19:8)? Then God will make Lot a victim of rape and Lot's daughters the perpetrators (19:31–36).

The second generation of patriarchs does not escape such providential paybacks. Isaac's blind eye to his favorite son's huge faults and his obstinate determination to give Esau the blessing in stealth will be met with a punishment corresponding to the crime. Isaac's wife will assert her own stubborn will and successfully counter his scheme with a conspiracy of her own. Exploiting Isaac's physical blindness, she persuades Jacob to disguise himself as Esau and steal the blessing. Isaac's terror-stricken shock at the discovery of his being hoodwinked and his subsequent acquiescence to the outcome as an overruling providence (27:33, 35, 37) seem to indicate that he had come to the realization that God himself had exposed his sin. But Rebekah would also suffer for her trickery. Jacob's robbery of Esau's blessing provokes the latter to plot murder (27:44). When Rebekah discovers Esau's intent, she must persuade Isaac to send Jacob away in order to protect him from Esau and secure for him a wife (27:45–46). But what she assumes will be a relatively brief parting with her favorite son (27:44) turns out to be a full twenty-year absence. Sadly, Rebekah dies before she is able to see her beloved Jacob again.[34]

Then there are Esau and Jacob, the third generation. Esau does not care for the promise with its distant prospect of a city whose architect

34. Dods reflects on the consequences of Rebekah's deceitful scheme and remarks, "The fate of all such attempts to manage God's matters by keeping things dark, and misrepresenting fact, is written for all those who care to understand in the results of this scheme of Rebekah's and Jacob's. They gained nothing and they lost a great deal by their wicked interference. . . . The mother lost her son; Jacob had to flee for his life, and, for all we know, Rebekah never saw him more." *Book of Genesis*, 274.

and builder is God (Heb 11:8–10). He prefers immediate gratification (25:29–34). So God grants Esau's wish and gives him an earthly inheritance—but nothing more (Gen 36:1–43; Heb 12:16–17)! Jacob does care about the promise. But he will use his own wits to fleece Esau of the birthright (בְּכֹרָה) (26:29–34) and pull the wool over his father's eyes to secure the blessing (בְּרָכָה) (27:18–29). Accordingly, God gives the shyster a bitter taste of his own medicine. First, God uses Uncle Laban as a whip to chasten Jacob. Laban promises to give his daughter Rachel to Jacob as wife in exchange for seven years of labor (29:15–20). But on the wedding night, when Jacob's senses are dulled by wine and darkness, Laban deceives (רמה) his nephew by substituting Leah, the firstborn (הַבְּכִירָה), for Rachel, the second-born (29:21–30). Hence, the stone Jacob rolled onto Esau to obtain the בְּכֹרָה comes rolling back on him (Prov 26:27b),[35] and the deceit (מִרְמָה) he employed on his father (27:35) returns to stun Jacob "like a boomerang."[36] Later, God will give Jacob a second dose of his own medicine when Jacob's own sons use a garment and a goat to deceive their own father (37:31–33), just as Jacob had earlier used to deceive Isaac (27:14–16, 19–27).[37]

35. Friedman notes the poetic justice when he observes, as previously quoted, that "the man who took away the firstborn privilege of his brother has now suffered because of the firstborn privilege of his beloved's [i.e., Rachel's] sister." "Deception for Deception," 134.

36. The phrase is borrowed from Fokkelmann, who wryly comments on the word Isaac uses to describe Jacob's deceit (i.e., מִרְמָה), "That word will return like a boomerang in the Story of Jacob!" *Narrative Art in Genesis*, 119. Fishbane has also caught the irony: "Genesis 29–31 thus counterpoint the surrounding tale of Esau. Indeed, on reading Genesis 29 (E), one has the distinct sense of déja à vu. . . . The counterpoint with Genesis 27 is obvious: there Jacob was the younger (tzaᶜir/qaton) who misappropriated the birthright (bekhorah) of his elder brother (ra / gadol) by deception (stem: *rimmah*, 27:35). With [Jacob's] indignant protest to Laban, Jacob unwittingly condemns himself." *Biblical Text and Texture*, 55.

37. As Friedman observes, "Jacob once deceived *his* father with his *brother's clothing* and the meat and hide of a *goat*. Now his sons deceive with their *brother's clothing* and the blood of a *goat*. . . . Worse still, the word that is used for 'goat' in the Joseph story is ṣēᶜîr; śeᶜir is the name of the place where Esau settles (Genesis 33:16). We are thus subtly reminded of the connection between the two stories." "Deception for Deception," 135. The reader should also recall that Jacob suffered disgrace and potential annihilation when Simeon and Levi treat the men of Shechem, as Jacob had treated Isaac, *deceitfully* (בְּמִרְמָה) (Gen 34:13ff.). Duguid perceptively remarks, "They had learned well at their father's knee. The children inherit the sins of the parents, often in greater measure. . . . We sow the wind; our children reap the whirlwind." *Relentless Grace*, 138–39.

The Lord also repays Jacob's sons for the evil they committed against him and against their brother Joseph. Judah, the mastermind not only of the sale of Joseph into slavery (37:26–27) but probably also of the robe-dipped-in-blood cover-up (37:19–20, 31–33), is found out when his daughter-in-law exposes his own sin using the same language he had earlier used to deceive Jacob (38:25).[38] Indeed, Tamar deceives Judah into fathering the very offspring (38:13–19, 27–30) that he himself had deceitfully withheld from her by refusing his levirate obligation (38:11).[39] Moreover, Joseph's brothers are made to pay in two ways for their abuse of him. First, the hand of Providence forces them to make a trip to Egypt, (42:1–5) where Joseph, the once-slave-now-vizier, cunningly[40] pricks their conscience and makes them painfully recall their former misdeed.[41] Second, God leads the sons of Israel to Egypt to protect them from the corrupting influences of Canaan (chaps. 34, 38) and preserve them from starvation (45:5–7; 50:20), but he also has an account to settle. Did they sell their brother into Egyptian slavery? What goes around (eventually)

38. Under Judah's leadership, the brothers send Joseph's bloodstained robe to Jacob with the message, "Please identify [הַכֶּר־נָא] whether it is you son's robe or not" (37:32b). Similarly, Tamar sends Judah's identity-markers to him with the message, "Please identify [הַכֶּר־נָא] whose these are, the signet and the cord and the staff" (38:25b).

39. Comments Friedman, "The deceiver has been deceived. . . . And the retribution fits the original deception. He denies her a man; she makes him her man." "Deception for Deception," 139.

40. After analyzing and comparing the various cases of deception in Genesis, Michael Williams concludes that Joseph's deception towards his brothers (42:7–28; 44:1–34) was not a case of sinful deception because "the perpetrator deceives one who has previously wronged him in order to restore his own condition to what it would have been had it not been disrupted, while, at the same time, not harming the victim. This license to act deceptively in order to restore the previous status quo appears to intersect with the biblical concept of *shalom*. . . . In Genesis, deception is justified when it is used by one previously wronged against the one who has done the wrong in order to restore *shalom*." *Deception in Genesis*, 13–29, 56.

41. After Joseph treats them as spies and forces them to return with Benjamin in order to free the now captive Simeon (42:7–20), "they said to one another, 'In truth we are guilty concerning our brother [i.e., Joseph], in that we saw the distress of his soul, when he begged us and we did not listen. That is why this distress has come upon us.' And Reuben answered them 'Did not I tell you not to sin against the boy? But you did not listen. So now there comes a reckoning for his blood'" (42:21–22). As earlier cited, Buis notes, "Not only Special Revelation but also the conscience of man is deeply imbued with the conviction that a man will be punished according to his deeds." "Retribution," *ZPEB*, 5:84.

comes around. Not surprisingly, the Genesis-sequel (Exodus) opens with the "sons of Israel" suffering Egyptian bondage (Exod 1:1–14).

CONCLUSION

The careful reader encounters various manifestations of God's curse on human sin in the patriarchal narrative. Indeed, the patriarchal narrative is replete not only with examples of the general effects of the curse but also with specific instances of divine retribution on pagans and patriarchs alike. Of course, God's punishment of the patriarchal community is usually subtler and has a remedial purpose in view. Nevertheless, the prevalence of sin's consequences in the patriarchal narrative only strengthens the thesis of this study. Namely, the spread of sin is a major theme in both the primeval and patriarchal narratives of Genesis.

Conclusion

THE OBJECTIVE OF THIS study is to provide a comprehensive and detailed exegetical and theological analysis of the spread of human sin and the divine curse in the book of Genesis with a special emphasis on the patriarchal narrative. Below is a review of the study, a synthesis of the findings, and a reflection on its implications for the original audience as well as today's reader.

REVIEW OF ANALYSIS

First, the need for an analysis of the spread of sin and the curse in the book of Genesis, particularly the patriarchal narratives, was established. Second, an examination of the Fall narrative laid the theological foundation and provided the historical backdrop for the spread of sin theme. Third, a detailed analysis of the spread of sin and the curse in the primeval narratives and the patriarchal narratives was conducted.

Sin and the Curse in the Fall Narrative

Adam and Eve's fall was first situated in its creational and covenantal context to make the reader aware of the pristine conditions of man's existence and the covenantal nature of his obligations as vassal-image to Yahweh-Elohim. This awareness enables the reader to appreciate the gravity and nature of man's primordial sin. The Fall narrative was then explored in several stages. First, the agent of temptation (the Serpent) was identified as ultimately Satan, an angelic being who became the archenemy of God's kingdom. Second, the temptation was identified as both a solicitation to evil (from the perspective of Satan's intention) and also as a test of mankind's fealty (from the perspective of Yahweh's intention). Satan tempted the humans by attacking the integrity of Yahweh's word and the goodness of his character. Satan invited humanity to pursue wisdom and eschatological fullness (i.e., life in the fullest sense) autonomously rather than in dependence on Yahweh's revealed will and in devotion to Yahweh's supreme glory. Third, Adam and Eve's primordial sin consisted in a transgression of the divine command and a breach of the creation covenant, and it was motivated by pride. Fourth, Yahweh responded to this act of mutiny with a judicial inquest, verdict, and punishment. Having carefully investigated the crime, Yahweh issued a guilty verdict, consisting of a direct curse on the Serpent and an indirect curse on the human couple. Yahweh's curse on humanity, however, contained an element of grace. The woman would still bear children and the man would till the ground, albeit in pain and with frustration. More importantly, the prediction of the Serpent's eventual defeat through the agency of the woman's offspring foreshadows a realignment of man's loyalty towards his Creator-Suzerain and restoration of God's original intentions for humanity. This expression of grace in the midst of the curse prompted a response of faith in Adam. Yahweh reciprocated with a token of forgiveness and expression of goodwill. Finally, Yahweh banished Adam and Eve from the royal Garden, signaling the commencement of the curse-sanction and officially marking the beginning of redemptive history.

Sin and the Curse in the Primeval Narrative

The proliferation of human sin and the manifestation of the divine curse appear as major themes in the primeval narrative. Adam and Eve's progeny inherited existence in a sin-cursed world outside the paradisiacal Garden. Moreover, their firstborn son, Cain, soon manifested an inward disaffection towards God. These two facts suggest that Adam's altered status as covenant-breaker and his moral condition as estranged sinner are conveyed to his progeny. Cain's enmity toward God devolved into envy, hatred, and murder directed toward his brother. Worse, Cain showed no signs of repentance, even after God mitigated Cain's punishment. The pattern of temptation, fall, inquest, curse-sanction, and banishment, which had characterized the Fall narrative is repeated in the Cain-Abel story, but now in darker hue, indicating an intensification of human sin.

Cain's subsequent history confirms his impenitence. He refused to trust Yahweh's safe-conduct edict and rebelled against his divinely decreed punishment. He settled down in the land of Nod and built a city for protection as well as to secure an enduring dynasty and lasting name. Cain's unbelief, ungodliness, and recalcitrance came to maturity in his offspring. Though Cain's descendants were notable for their cultural advances, they excelled most in evil. This fact is highlighted in Cain's seventh descendant, Lamech, who was the first bigamist and a boastful perpetrator of violence.

The next stage in the primeval narrative features Adam's history through the line of Seth. In spite of a renewed hope in God's promise connected with the birth of Seth and a revival of Yahwehism connected with the birth of Seth's son (Enosh), the spread of sin and the curse continued. Far from an interruption of or respite from sin's doleful encroachment on human life, the Adam-Seth genealogy reminds the reader that God meant business when he issued his death threat in the Garden.

Some of the same motifs in the earlier Cain narratives reappear in the next stage of the primeval narrative—only now in aggravated form. Lamech's bigamy developed into harem-building. His tyrannous violence grew into titan proportions as primeval suzerains assumed the epithet "sons of God" and sired mighty warriors who filled the earth with violence and corruption. Yahweh assessed the human condition as profoundly wicked, grieved in his heart, and decided to take action with judgment. Sin's invasive and enveloping spread throughout the human race provoked a catastrophic flood that destroyed all life on earth except Noah, his family, and representatives from the animal kingdom.

Antediluvian history gives way to postdiluvian history and the "new beginning" Yahweh graciously granted humanity through Noah and his family. Regrettably, God's reinstatement of the original creation-mandate objectives was followed by the reemergence of human sin. Noah, a kind of "second Adam," fell into sin, as did the first Adam. Moreover, as Adam's sin occasioned greater sin in his son Cain, Noah's sin became the occasion for the manifestation of greater sin in his offspring. Acting in the capacity of Yahweh's prophet, Noah invoked a divine curse on Canaan and his descendants. Thus, the primeval narrative resumes the theme of the spread of sin and the curse.

The Tower of Babel story and the account of Nimrod included in the Table of Nations constitute the final stage of primeval history. Human sin spread and grew into mammoth proportions that rivaled the antediluvian hubris. Moses depicts a good portion if not all of Noah's descendants in language that parallels the earlier Cain narratives. Like Cain, collective humanity is portrayed as sojourning in an easterly direction, signaling a movement away from God. They also decided to build a city and secure a lasting name. But their defiant enterprise exceeded Cain's in one important respect. The Babelites attempted to build the "Gate of God," an artificial mountain that mimicked the primordial Holy Mountain of Eden. This human enterprise signals a sinful effort to reenter the sphere from which mankind had been banished and serves as a paramount example of human rebellion on an international scale. Yahweh, however, frustrated the project by disrupting human communication. Nevertheless, Nimrod, whom the text portrays as a warrior-king and empire-builder, refused to submit to Yahweh's judgment and continued to perpetuate the Babel-tradition. In summary, the repeated outbreaks of sin as well as the references to human death and divine judgment lead to the irresistible conclusion that the spread of human sin and the divine curse serve as major themes in the primeval narrative.

Sin and the Curse in the Patriarchal Narrative

Since the patriarchal history emerges out of the context of the Babel enterprise, it is not surprising to find many allusions in the patriarchal narratives to the prevalence of sin in pagan cultures. Harem-building and political tyranny, both notable in the primeval history, reoccur in the patriarchal history. Yahweh's reference to the collective sins of Canaan's inhabitants increasing in magnitude to the point at which divine forbearance reaches its limit resembles his earlier warning concerning the Deluge-provoking sin of antediluvian history. Sodom's wickedness is comparable to the pre- and postdiluvian evil in the primeval history. Indeed, the primeval pattern of sin, discovery, speech, mitigation, and judgment surfaces again in the Sodom and Gomorrah account.

The patriarchal narratives do not merely provide allusions or instances of sin among pagans. They also highlight the spread of sin in the successive generations of the patriarchal community. Abraham's initial response to Yahweh's call is not as commendable as many have assumed. When he did finally arrive in Canaan, God tested his faith with a famine. Abraham disobeyed by relocating to Egypt. There, he forced Sarah to pose as his sister, placing her in danger in order to protect his own life. His ruse not only employed deception (a Serpent-like tactic) but also jeopardized "the offspring of the woman." Sadly, Abraham repeated this ruse over twenty years later. Sarah also fell into sin when she tried to obtain the promised offspring through a surrogate mother. In this case, she played the role of a "second Eve," tempting her husband to take what

God had forbidden. Later, when God assured Abraham and Sarah that they would conceive and bear the child of promise, they each laughed with a degree of incredulity that exposed their weak faith. Hence, these paragons of faith had repeated moments of weakness, though their faith triumphed in the end. If the narrator portrays Abraham and Sarah as less than plaster saints, he depicts Lot as barely a saint. In parallel to Eve's lustful glance at the forbidden fruit, Lot cast his eyes in the direction of the Jordan valley, which the narrator remarkably compares to "the garden of Yahweh." Lot's decision to move east of the Promised Land paralleled the eastward movement of Cain and the Babelites. Lot continued to decline morally until he became hardly distinguishable from his degenerate neighbors. Only Abraham's prayers and divine grace spared Lot from Sodom's terrible fate. Similarities and contrasts between Noah and Lot serve to advance the theme of sin's spread in the patriarchal narratives.

The sins of the parents were sometimes repeated in their children. Abraham and Sarah laughed with incredulity at the prospect of the promised offspring when they were advanced in age. Their son Ishmael also laughed at the son of promise. But Ishmael's laughter betrayed mocking unbelief and a rejection of Isaac's role in the divine plan, and it resembled Cain's contempt for Abel's favor with God. Isaac's early life looked promising. But before long, he utilized the same wife-sister ruse his father had earlier employed. Isaac's (and Abraham's) lack of godly fear and inordinate fear of man served as poor examples before a pagan world. Later, Isaac stealthily attempted to confer the blessing on an unworthy firstborn son, and Rebekah deceitfully schemed to overrule her husband's error in favor of the second-born. In this incident, Isaac's weakness for savory food led to his fall much like Adam and Eve's attraction to the forbidden fruit led to their fall. Moreover, Rebekah adopted a Serpent-like tactic to advance the promise. So neither the first nor second generations of the patriarchal family escaped the gravity of sin.

Esau and Jacob are the major characters in the third generation of the patriarchal family. Esau provides a tragic example of religious defection. Moses's depiction of him as a hunter provides a textual link with Nimrod. Like Nimrod, Esau turned out to be a worldly opportunist with no concern for Yahweh's kingdom. His polygamy repeated the marital distortions of the primeval Lamech and the "sons of God," and his angry plot to murder Jacob echoed Cain's enmity toward the divinely favored

Abel. Though Jacob manifested an early interest in the promise, his motives and tactics for advancing the promise could not be commended. First, he snatched at the birthright with Serpent-like cunning. Then he became willingly complicit in his mother's conspiracy and snatched at the blessing with Serpent-like deception. Such tactics earned him the epithet "Heel-Grabber," which reminds the reader of the Serpent's modus operandi in attacking the woman's offspring. By exploiting Esau, Jacob placed his own life at risk and was forced to move eastward in exile, which in turn placed the promise at risk. In exile Jacob entered into a bigamous relationship with two sisters through the trickery of their father. The marital tension was then aggravated when the two rival sisters enticed Jacob into marrying their maidservants in order to obtain more offspring. The result was greater tensions within the family fueled by undue favoritism on Jacob's part. This intra-familial strife set the stage for the fourth generation.

The sons of Israel constitute the fourth generation. Simeon and Levi treacherously deceived and slaughtered the Shechemites. The violence of primeval history is not just repeated; in this case the roles were reversed. Instead of the wicked (Cain) slaying the righteous (Abel), "the righteous" (Jacob's sons) wantonly murdered "the wicked" (the Shechemites). In this act, Simeon and Levi revealed their true identity as "the seed" of the Serpent, who was a liar and murderer from the beginning. Following the tragedy at Shechem, Reuben committed an incestuous act with his father's concubine. Reuben's act was not merely a case of unbridled lust and immorality. As a preemptive assertion of his birthright, he attempted to usurp his father's role as leader of the clan. Reuben's contempt for his father paralleled Ham's contempt for Noah, as Jacob's consequent curse on Reuben echoed Noah's curse on Ham's descendants. The next stage of the narrative draws attention to the mounting animosity of Jacob's sons toward their younger brother Joseph, whom Jacob (and God) favors. Once again, there is a Cain-like murder plot. But instead of killing Joseph, the brothers, at Judah's prompting, sold him into Egyptian slavery (a kind of virtual murder) and concealed their crime from Jacob with the same kind of cunning trickery Jacob had used to deceive his father, Isaac. Judah separated from the covenant family and associated with the Canaanites when he realized that Jacob would not be consoled over Joseph's "death." Judah's calloused conscience was matched only by his spiritual blindness, which prevented him from perceiving the cause of his sons' premature deaths. He deceived Tamar, his daughter-in-law, into believing he would give her his third-born to fulfill his levirate obligation. But Tamar turned the tables on her father-in-law. She stealthily posed as a prostitute and lured Judah into a sexual liaison in order to obtain the offspring she desired. When Judah learned of her illegitimate pregnancy, he harshly and hypocritically condemned her to death. But Judah's eyes were finally opened when she exposed him as the true culprit. His confession served not only as an admission of sin but also as an indication that his Canaanite daughter-in-law had shown more concern to perpetuate the offspring of promise than a flesh-and-blood descendant of Abraham. A downward trajectory of piety from the first to the forth generation of the patriarchal community is patent.

The patriarchal narrative not only provides many expressions of sin among the patriarchal family but also highlights the effects of sin. The barren matriarchal womb (Sarah, Rebekah, Rachel) as well as Rachel's premature death in childbearing reflected Yahweh's curse on the woman in her role as mother. The portended spousal strife in Yahweh's original curse also features prominently in the patriarchal narrative. Abraham and Isaac forced their wives to pose as sisters and exposed them to danger. Isaac was insensitive toward Rebekah, and Jacob neglected Leah. Conversely, the matriarchs played Eve's role of temptress in leading their husbands to make wrong decisions. The three major famines that occurred during the lives of all four generations of patriarchs echoed Yahweh's curse on the ground. The death notices in patriarchal history indicate that the vigor and longevity of human life is waning and its pace toward death quickening. In addition to the general effects of Yahweh's curse, there are examples of discriminate punishments in the patriarchal narrative. The cataclysmic destruction of Sodom and Gomorrah is to patriarchal history what the Flood is to primeval history. God temporally punished pagan kings who threatened the promise unwittingly, and he lethally punished Judah's two sons who threatened the promise highhandedly. Finally, certain sins that the patriarchs or matriarchs commit against others are in turn committed against them. Thus, poetic justice is served and what goes around (eventually) comes around. The prevalence of sin's consequences in the patriarchal narrative supports the overall thesis that the spread of sin and the curse is a major theme in the entire Genesis narrative.

SYNTHESIS OF FINDINGS

The theme of human sin and the divine curse not only serve as the main themes of the Fall narrative, but they also continue to function as major themes in both the primeval and patriarchal narratives that follow.[1] More particularly, human sin appears to increase at both individual and societal levels. Moreover, just as the primordial sin threatened to derail the advance of God's kingdom and fulfillment of the creation mandate, so the spread of human sin in postlapsarian history threatens to thwart God's redemptive plan, which consists in the restoration of his original creational intentions for divine and human eschatological fullness. This proves true even in the patriarchal narratives where the sins of God's chosen often threaten the very promise intended for their ultimate good. The patriarchal narrative leaves the reader with the impression that not merely humanity but even God's people left to themselves would eventually come to ruin. Only intrusions of divine grace (common and special) or judgment (punitive or remedial) can stem sin's rising tide. Yet, primeval and patriarchal history bear witness to a kind of cyclical pattern. The proliferation of human sin is followed by instances of mitigating grace and retributive judgment. Then human sin begins to increase once more, and the divine promise is under threat yet again. The patriarchal narrative concludes on a mixed note. On the one hand, God's grace and remedial judgment overrule the patriarchal family's evil with good and preserve the promise intact (Gen 50:20). On the other hand, this act of overruling grace and remedial judgment is (like prior instances) only provisional. For in the end, Joseph (Yahweh's agent for blessing and the savior of the promise) ends up dead in a coffin and the sons of Israel stranded in Egypt, far from the Land of Promise. So the patriarchal narrative, like the primeval narrative, leaves the problem of sin and the curse ultimately unsolved.[2]

Sin threatens God's plans ?

1. Garrett advances the thesis that "alienation" is *the* theme of Genesis (235–37), a proposal that supports the prominence of sin and curse in Genesis since the theme of alienation embraces both. Nevertheless, the conclusions of this study do not necessarily prove that sin and curse are *the* main themes of Genesis, only that they function as major themes.

2. Mann calls attention to both the "completeness" and "incompleteness" of the Genesis narrative when he writes, "The stories of the family of Abraham *are* stories in the sense that they move from tension to resolution. In this sense, they are complete in themselves, and the Book of Genesis comes to a satisfying conclusion. Yet it is obvious that the book does not stand on its own but looks beyond its own content to *un*resolved issues" (emphasis his). "All the Families of the Earth," 350.

IMPLICATIONS OF THE STUDY

The results of this study lead to practical implications regarding Genesis's thematic structure, the patriarchal narrative's message for God's people, and the maintenance of a biblical view of sanctification.

The Thematic Structure of Genesis

William Dumbrell represents the majority opinion when he writes, "Genesis 11:1–9 culminates the spread-of-sin narratives, which began in Genesis 3."[3] This study has definitely called that view into question. The tendency among scholars to bifurcate primeval and patriarchal history on the supposition that the spread of sin theme is replaced by such themes as election, promise, redemption and blessing reflects a superficial reading of the Genesis narrative and leads to faulty conclusions. For example, after citing approvingly Gerhard von Rad's distinction between pre-sacred history (Gen 1–11) and sacred history (Gen 12–50), Henri Blocher asserts, "With Abram . . . begins the decisive implementation of the plan of God."[4] But God's redemptive plan began the moment he uttered his first curse in Eden (Gen 3:14–15). According to Victor Hamilton, the Genesis narrative transitions "from generation (chs. 1–2), to degeneration (chs. 3–11), to regeneration (chs. 12–50)."[5] But regeneration occurs in primeval history (Gen 3:20; 4:25–26; 5:22–24; 6:8–9), and there are abundant examples of degeneration (individually and corporately) in patriarchal history. LaSor, Hubbard, and Bush find the themes of the "Problem of Sin" and "God's Judgment on Human Sin" in the primeval prologue (Gen 1–11). But in their estimation these themes disappear when the narrative transitions to patriarchal history and are replaced by "Election and the Promises of God," "Faith and Righteousness," and "Covenant."[6] Such a portrayal of the two major storylines in Genesis is

3. Dumbrell, *Search for Order*, 32.

4. Blocher, *In the Beginning*, 211. Likewise, Atkinson sees primeval history as establishing the pattern that "sin leads to punishment" and avers, "Through Abraham the covenant story of sacred history begins." *Message of Genesis 1–11*, 184–85. According to Gibson, God does not "set the Gospel story in motion" until "the call of Abraham." *Genesis*, 2:213.

5. Hamilton, *Genesis 1–17*, 11. Of course, Hamilton would deny neither instances of regeneration in primeval history nor examples of degeneracy in patriarchal history. But for that reason, his representation of the thematic shifts in the Genesis narrative is unwarranted.

6. LaSor, Hubbard, and Bush, *OT Survey*, 80–85, 111–16.

overly simplistic. Election, promise, faith, righteousness, and covenant appear at strategic places in the primeval narrative. Conversely, the problem of human sin and the manifestation of divine judgment are found throughout the patriarchal narratives.

One may borrow a statement from the apostle Paul (which comes very close to epitomizing the Genesis message) to illustrate the common mistake most interpreters make in their characterization of Genesis's thematic structure. Bringing his Adam-Christ comparison in Romans 5 to a close, Paul asserts, "Where sin abounded, grace did much more abound" (5:20b, KJV). Judging from the thematic disjunction most commentators see in the Genesis narrative, it would seem reasonable to conclude that their application of this Pauline statement to Genesis would take the following form: "Where sin abounded [primeval history, Gen 1–11], grace did much more abound [patriarchal history, Gen 12–50]." This study, however, has demonstrated that both halves of Paul's statement apply to the entire Genesis narrative. A few interpreters are coming to this realization. Terence Fretheim, for instance, perceptively remarks,

> It is striking the extent to which the more emphatic themes of chaps. 12–50 are grounded in chaps. 1–11, wherein God promises and blesses, elects and saves. . . . God's work of blessing in the world does not begin with Abraham; it is integral to chaps. 1–11 (see 9:1, 26) and so God's blessing work through Abraham must involve intensification and pervasiveness, not a new reality. . . . Issues of creation and redemption are integrated throughout Genesis.[7]

Nevertheless, Fretheim's observation provides only a partial solution. He rightly suggests that the interpreter look for the roots of promise, blessing, election, and salvation in the soil of primeval history. But the

7. Fretheim, "Genesis," 328–29. Mann argues in a similar vein when he observes that the Abrahamic "promise of blessing 'to all the families of the earth' in 12:3 appears as a *reiteration* of 1:28." "All the Families of the Earth," 345. Most recently, McKeown has questioned a thematic dichotomy between the primeval and patriarchal narratives. He notes, "While this is a convenient way of dividing the material, it can mislead the reader by giving the impression that the first 11 chapters are merely introductory and unrelated to chapters 12–50. But this would be a gross underestimation of the value and function of these early chapters, *since they establish principles and themes that provide a foundation and, indeed, an interpretative key for the events of chapters 12–50*" (emphasis added). *Genesis*, 2. Unfortunately, McKeown lists "descendents," "blessing," and "land" as major themes in Genesis but, aside from a discussion of the Fall, fails to list human sin as a major theme of the narrative.

reader should equally note that the seeds of human sin planted in Eden's garden grow into vines that spread beyond the parameters of the primeval narrative and bear much evil fruit in the patriarchal narratives. Adapting Fretheim's own language, *it is striking the extent to which the more emphatic themes of chs. 1–11 are further developed in chs. 12–50, wherein human society in general and the patriarchal community in particular continue to sin and experience God's curse.*[8] Thus, Paul's statement comes very close to epitomizing *the entire* message of Genesis. Yet Paul's statement assumes that the ultimate solution to the human problem has arrived. It assumes that grace has triumphed over sin in a definitive way. The Genesis narrative, however, does not bring the reader to that point. While grace produces definitive changes in certain individuals, it triumphs over human sin at the redemptive historical level *only provisionally*. Sin abounds in the entire Genesis narrative, and so does grace.[9] The "much more" redemptive historical triumph of grace, however, will have to await the crucifixion and resurrection of Jesus Christ. As the writer of Hebrews expresses it, "These were all commended for their faith, yet none of them received what had been promised. God had planned something better for us so that only together with us would they be made perfect" (Heb 11:39–40).

The Patriarchal Narrative's Message for Israel (and the Church)

Moses had an original audience in view when he wrote Genesis. Israel had just been redeemed from Egypt and was about to take possession of Canaan. It is likely Moses intended the Genesis narratives to do

8. Fishbane comes close to this observation when remarking about the tension between birth, blessing, and land, on the one hand, and barrenness and exile, on the other hand, in the Jacob cycle in particular and the patriarchal narrative in general. Observes Fishbane, "It is, finally, most striking that these tensions in the patriarchal cycles . . . constitute the inner structure of the Eden narrative (Genesis 3). Eden was a sacred spatial center in which all manner of blessing and life abounded. The primary life values of fertile womb and fertile earth, of life and blessing, were lost through the action of Adam and Eve; earth and womb were cursed, and mankind was exiled from sacred space." *Biblical Text and Texture*, 62.

9. Lim's assessment of the primeval narrative applies to the entire book of Genesis: "Whenever there is a spread of sin on the human part, there is a corresponding parallel spread of grace on God's part. . . . No matter how drastic human sin becomes, even to the point of destroying what God has made good and bringing the world to the brink of uncreation, God's grace always comes to the rescue." *Grace in the Midst of Judgment*, 192.

more than provide Israel with a historical record of humanity's origins and Israel's ancestral roots. Moses had a theological message for Israel. Unfortunately, a review of Israel's history, as recorded in both the Old and New Testaments, reveals that many Israelites made the same mistake many modern interpreters have made. They concluded that the story of sin ended where Israel's history began. For some of these ancient Israelites, the result was more tragic. They assumed, wrongly, that the patriarchal narratives were mainly about good people (in contrast with bad people who predominated primeval history) and that God's promises to these pious patriarchs were grounded on their personal merit. From this reading, it was only a small step to the conclusion that Yahweh had ransomed Israel from Egypt and was about to gift them the Promised Land on the basis of their intrinsic worth. Moses detected this self-righteous mindset among some of his contemporaries and warned them with words that allude to the patriarchal narrative:

> Do not say in your heart, after the Lord your God has thrust them out before you, "It is because of my righteousness that the Lord has brought me in to possess this land," whereas it is because of the wickedness of these nations that the Lord is driving them out before you. Not because of your righteousness or the uprightness of your heart are you going in to possess their land, but because of the wickedness of these nations the Lord your God is driving them out from before you, and that he may confirm the word that the Lord swore to your fathers, to Abraham, to Isaac, and to Jacob. (Deut 9:4–5)

With these strong words, Moses eliminates any fantasy his contemporaries may have entertained regarding their supposed superiority to their pagan neighbors! "Ah!" says one of Moses's fellow Israelites. "I agree that we have not established a good track record with Yahweh in our wilderness wanderings. But as your concluding words indicate, we will enjoy Yahweh's blessing because of the fathers, that is, on account of their merit!" Moses replies, "My dear kinsman, you have greatly misunderstood the meaning of my words. It is not on account of the fathers' merits that you will inherit the land. Rather, the land will become yours on account of God's gracious promise to the ill-deserving among whom the fathers are included!" Then Moses encourages his Israelite neighbor to reread Genesis—*especially the patriarchal narratives*. There he will not find plaster saints and huge reservoirs of human merit. On the contrary, he will find that his patriarchs and matriarchs sometimes behaved worse than the pagans around them. There he will learn that salvation is by grace alone and not by works.

Moses did not write Genesis for his generation only. He also wrote it for future generations. Fourteen centuries later a Jew named Saul of Tarsus would come to see that Genesis was not written to set off the Jews as the sole heirs of salvation, nor was it written to ground their hope in the piety of their ancestors (or their own for that matter). Once converted, this Saul-turned-Paul would argue that sin's sway over Israel functioned as a portrait of sin's sway over every man thereby condemning the entire human race (Rom 3:9–19).[10] Paul would even use Abraham as an example of one over whom sin had sway, placing him on the same level as the penitent yet forgiven King David—a sinner who rejoiced in the God who "justifies the ungodly" (Rom 4:3–8).[11]

Abraham was ungodly? But did not God "count him righteous" (Gen 15:6)? "Yes," says Paul. "But God reckoned him so *on account of faith in the promise* (Rom 4:3–5). In fact, Paul would go on to argue that one of the primary functions of the law (of which the patriarchal narrative was an essential part!) was to increase the magnitude of Adam's original trespass by means of displaying its spread among Adam's prog-

10. Specifically, Paul concludes that "the law speaks to *those who are under the law* [i.e., Jews], so that every mouth may be stopped, and *the whole world* [i.e., Jews and Gentiles] may be held accountable to God" (3:19, emphasis added). Murray insists that the phrase τοῖς ἐν τῷ νόμῳ includes all people in light of the following universal descriptions πᾶν στόμα and πᾶς ὁ κόσμος, as well as the teaching of Rom 2:14–15. *Epistle to the Romans*, 1:106–7. The phrase ἐν νόμῳ, however, is also used more restrictively to refer to the Jews (2:12). Consequently, Paul seems to be arguing that the law's condemnation of the Jews (which is found throughout the OT canon) serves as an indictment on the entire human race. See Moo, *Epistle to the Romans*, 204–6.

11. Paul's characterization of Abraham as "ungodly" (ἀσεβῆ) cannot be limited to Abraham's pre-conversion state. Paul bases his portrayal of Abraham as an ungodly man justified on Genesis 15:6, a text characterizing the patriarch some time after his initial conversion (compare Gen 12:1–6 with Acts 7:2–4; Heb 11:8). Although Abraham was justified once and for all a number of years before his act of faith described in Genesis 15:6, that simple faith remained paradigmatic of the patriarch's first act of saving faith. Moreover, the blessing attributed to Abraham in 15:6, namely, being credited as righteous, continues to contemplate his state as "ungodly," that is, as a sinner in need of saving grace. Similarly, Paul's citation of David's words in Psalm 32 applies to post-conversion experience (Ps 32:1–2; Rom 4:7–8). Thus, it seems likely that Paul's characterization of Abraham as "ungodly" is not based merely on the patriarch's pre-Canaan life (Josh 24:2; Neh 9:7) but embraces the totality of the patriarch's life as depicted in the patriarchal narrative.

eny among whom death reigned (5:14a, 20–21)[12] and thus underscore man's desperate need for saving grace.

In summary, reading the patriarchal narrative in a way that does not turn a blind eye to the many and sometimes large faults of the fathers will serve as a powerful antidote to a works-based religion. This point has relevance not merely for the Jewish contemporaries of Moses or Paul. It needs to be proclaimed in the church in every generation—especially today when contemporary Protestant scholars are conflating faith and obedience as the instruments of justification.[13] A reading of the

12. Romans 5:20 is key: "Now the law came in to increase the trespass, but where sin increased, grace abounded all the more." Interestingly, the Greek word translated "trespass" is singular and includes the article: τὸ παράπτωμα. In every other case it is used in this passage, it refers specifically to Adam's one act of disobedience (5:15 [twice], 16, 17, 18; see also verses 14 [τῆς παραβάσεως], 16 [ἑνὸς ἁμαρτήσαντος], 18 [τῆς παρακοῆς τοῦ ἑνὸς ἀνθρώπου]. Hence, Lenski translates the verse, "Now the law came in besides so that *the fall* increased" (emphasis added). *Interpretation of St. Paul's Epistle to the Romans*, 383–84. This raises the question of how the law, which was given millennia after Adam's sin could cause his one sin to increase. Sensing the difficulty, some commentators interpret the singular τὸ παράπτωμα as a collective noun, referring to the sins of men in general or Israelites in particular. See Hodge, *Epistle to the Romans*, 177. In this context, however, Adam's transgression is chiefly in view, and whatever sins follow Adam actually point back to his own transgression. Accordingly, Leon Morris suggests that "the word may be chosen as a way of bringing out the continuity between his sin and that of his descendants." *Epistle to the Romans*, 241. See also Haldane, *An Exposition of Romans*, 227. Hence, Paul's allusion to the reign of death between the time of Adam and Moses as indicative of sin's presence in the world (5:13–14) and his continuance of the sin-death-reign connection in the next verse (5:21) would seem to suggest that one of the law's purposes is to "increase" Adam-like transgressions. The book of Genesis, as part of the Torah, certainly functions as a magnifying glass that demonstrates the spread of "the trespass" and "the reign of death." Thus, even though men may not have reckoned their sinful behavior as transgression against the will of God prior to the law, the law, particularly Genesis, demonstrates that such sinful behavior is linked to Adam's transgression and is therefore a violation of God's will and worthy of his wrath.

13. Some modern scholars argue that the faith that justifies must be understood in its active sense, namely, obedient faith or faithfulness. Hence, they understand Paul and James to be referring to the same genus of justification in their appeal to Abraham's faith in Genesis 15:6 (see Rom 4:3–5; Jas 2:21–24). For example, Fuller argues that it was *the combination* of Abraham's initial act of faith whereby he left Ur together with his ongoing perseverance in faith that served as the condition for his justification. *The Unity of the Bible*, 310. Not surprisingly, Fuller goes on to fault Luther and Calvin for interpreting Paul and James to be referring to two different kinds of justification. Ibid., 311. Garlington avers, "In keeping with the Hebrew term ᵓemunah, the Greek noun translated 'faith,' pistis, is two-sided: faith and faithfulness. Given this set of data, righteousness does consist of *pistis* in the expansive sense of ᵓemunah, that is, covenant conformity." "Imputation or Union with Christ?" 52. Wright appears to be moving in the

patriarchal narrative that overemphasizes patriarchal piety and minimizes the many patriarchal and matriarchal failings will soon lose sight of God's corresponding grace.

Simul Iustus et Peccator

When describing the believer who is simultaneously a righteous man and a sinner, Martin Luther coined the phraseology, *simil iustus et peccator.*[14] Luther applied this description not only to the believer's legal status before God (i.e., justification)[15] but also to his moral condition as a result of the "already-not yet" tension of sanctification. Hence, commenting on the believer's inward struggle with remaining sin depicted by Paul in Romans 7, Luther remarks, "Therefore I am at the same time a sinner and a righteous man, for I do evil and I hate the evil which I do."[16] Luther's

---

same direction when he remarks, "Faith and obedience are not antithetical. They belong exactly together. Indeed, the word 'faith' itself could properly be translated as 'faithfulness,' which makes the point just as well." Wright quickly assures the reader that his definition of faith does not compromise the doctrine of justification by faith alone by adding, "Faith, even in this active sense, is never and in no way a qualification, provided from the human side, either for getting into God's family or for staying there once in. It is the God-given badge of membership, neither more nor less." *What Saint Paul Really Said,* 160. Wright does not appear to understand the Protestant doctrine of *sola fide.* The Reformers never denied that true faith eventuates in good works. What they taught was that the one and the same faith responds differently to divine promise than it does to divine law. Faith responding to promise is *passive* or *receptive.* Faith responding to law is *active* or *obedient.* Faith in its passive or receptive role is alone the instrument of justification. Faith in its active or obedient role may be viewed as the instrument of sanctification, as well as the evidence of one's justification. For an analysis of Luther and Calvin's conception of justifying faith, see Waldron, *Faith, Obedience, and Justification*, 13–71. Paul was focusing on faith in its receptive role. James was focusing on faith in its active role. For this reason, they were each using the term "justification" differently. Buchanan calls attention to this distinction in his classic work on the subject: "While 'Justification' is a forensic or judicial term, it is used in Scripture to denote, sometimes the acceptance of a sinner as righteous in the sight of God [e.g., Paul's usage]—sometimes the manifestation or proof of his acceptance, by which it is attested and made sure [e.g., James's usage]: and this variety in the application of it is the ground of an important theological distinction—the distinction between actual [Paul's focus] and declarative [James' focus] Justification." *Doctrine of Justification*, 233. For a helpful exegetical analysis of the respective ways in which Paul and James use Genesis 15:6, see Beale and Carson, eds., *Commentary on the New Testament Use of the OT*, 622–24, 1003– 5.

14. Or something similar, like *simul iustus, simul peccator.*

15. *Lectures on Romans: Glosses and Scholia*, 260; *Lectures on Galatians 1545:1–4*, 232; *Lectures on Galatians 1519:1–6*, 231.

16. *Lectures on Romans*, 25:63. Later in his *Scholia*, Luther uses different words to express the same idea: "In the same way man is at the same time both flesh and spirit"

portrayal of the believer underscores the same reality highlighted in the patriarchal narrative: namely, true saints are still sinners.

Unfortunately, the tendency to ignore or minimize the spread of sin theme in the patriarchal narratives deprives the reader of this important doctrine. The patriarchs and matriarchs were men and women of genuine faith and piety. Abraham's displayed unqualified devotion to Yahweh in his willingness to sacrifice Isaac, the very son of promise (Gen 22:1–19).[17] Jacob was unrelenting in his determination to obtain Yahweh's blessing (Gen 32:22–32). Joseph believed that God had used his brother's evil intentions for the ultimate good of the promise (Gen 50:20) and that God would one day restore the sons of Israel to the Land of Promise (50:24–25). No doubt, Moses intended his readers to be inspired by the positive examples of faith and obedience portrayed in the patriarchal narratives. Accordingly, the writer of Hebrews calls attention to these exemplars in his famous "Hall of Faith" (Heb 11:1–40). But he was familiar with the patriarchal narrative and the fact that sin sometimes prevailed even among the patriarchal community. Thus, when he follows up the "Hall of Faith" with an application to his Christian audience, he exhorts believers not only to persevere in faith, as did these OT saints, but also to "lay aside every encumbrance and the sin which so easily entangles [them]" (Heb 12:1, NAU). The implication is that these paragons of faith whom he has set forth as "so great a cloud of witnesses" also had to strive against remaining sins that sometimes encumbered and entangled their steps in the path of devotion to God.

The spread of sin and the curse in the patriarchal narratives support this biblical and experiential tension that characterizes the life of every true believer. Moses's realistic depiction of the life of faith in the patriarchal narrative provides the church with a biblically balanced view of sanctification[18] as well as an exemplar for preaching character studies

(25:339). For further discussion of Luther's application of this description to the believer's sanctification, see Althaus, *Theology of Martin Luther*, 242–45.

17. Ryken sees chapter 22 as the climax of the plot in which the conflict between faith and expediency are resolved. *Words of Delight*, 69.

18. In reacting to errors such as easy-believism or the carnal Christian theory, which in their extreme forms advocate the idea that one may receive a new legal status before God (i.e., forgiveness and imputed righteousness) without experiencing a moral change (i.e., regeneration and sanctification), one must beware the opposite extreme that leaves no room (or very little) for the reality of remaining sin in the heart of true believers, as well as the fact that a truly pious believer may have periods of backsliding and even

or writing Christian biography.[19] Finally, by "telling it like it is," Moses does not undermine but actually reinforces the doctrine of inspiration.[20]

stumble into serious sin. Like the patriarchs and matriarchs, other biblical characters of significant spiritual stature who experienced a "fall" include Moses (Num 20:11–12), David (2 Sam 11), and Peter (Luke 22:54–62). Of course, the reality of remaining sin and the failures of godly saints must not be abused in the other direction (see Rom 6:1ff.). Nevertheless, the patriarchal narratives, like the rest of Scripture, remind us of the need for balance in our self-expectations as well as our expectations of others.

19. Bryan Smith's remarks concerning the portrayal of Judah in Genesis 38 apply to the entire patriarchal narrative: "The Jews' concern to ameliorate the reputation of one of their most illustrious progenitors is understandable. However, the fact that Moses refused to do so when writing the history of the Israelites should teach all interpreters that they too should avoid hagiography and that there is more to be gained by viewing the characters as they are presented in Scripture and not as one may wish they were presented." "Presentation of Judah in Genesis 37–50 and Its Implications for the Narrative's Structure and Thematic Unity," 91 n. 39.

20. What Pink says regarding the historiography of the OT writers especially applies to Moses's presentation of the nation's founding fathers: "In the repeated mention which we have in the OT of Israel's sins, we discover, in light as clear as day, the absolute honesty and candor of those who recorded Israel's history. No attempt whatever is made to conceal their folly, their unbelief, and their wickedness; instead, the corrupt condition of their hearts is made fully manifest, and this, by writers who belonged to, and were born of the same nation. In the whole realm of literature there is no parallel. The record of Israel's history is absolutely unique. The careful reader would at first conclude that Israel as a nation was more depraved than any other, yet further reflection will show that the inference is a false one and that the real fact is that the history of Israel has been more faithfully transmitted than that of any other nation. We mean the history of Israel as it is recorded in the Holy Scriptures, for in striking contrast thereto and in exemplification of all that we have written above, it is noteworthy that Josephus passes over in silence whatever appeared unfavorable to his nation!!" *Divine Inspiration of the Bible*, 32. Leupold states it succinctly, "Israel's past was not glorified at the expense of truth." *Exposition of Genesis*, 977.

Appendix

Instances of Sin and the Curse in the Genesis Corpus

The following tables divide the Genesis narratives into separate literary units and endeavors to note the varied instances of sin or curse occurring in each.

Instances of Sin and the Curse in the Primeval History

Unit	*Title*	*Expressions of Sin*	*Effects of Sin (Curse)*
1:1–2:3	*Creation*	None	None
2:4–2:25	*Man in Eden*	None (though first mention of "evil" in connection with Tree of Knowledge)	None (though God warns man of death as punishment for disobedience)
3:1–3:24	*The Fall*	Deception; distrust; disobedience; treason; blame-shifting	Guilt; alienation; divine curse-pain, toil, death; banishment and forfeiture of access to Tree of Life
4:1–4:16	*Cain & Abel*	Heartless worship; anger, envy, hatred; murder; impenitence	Death of innocent; banishment; alienation from God and family
4:17–4:24	*Cain's Line*	Rebellion; bigamy; murder; arrogance	Death of innocent
4:25–4:26	*Seth's Birth*	Reference to Cain's murder	Reference to Abel's death
5:1–5:32	*Adam-Seth Line*	None	Divine image mediated through fractured image; death (9x); pain

Unit	*Title*	*Expressions of Sin*	*Effects of Sin (Curse)*
6:1–6:8	*Escalation of Sin*	Lust and polygamy (or ungodly marriage alliances); totally depraved heart; widespread evil	Oppression/suffering probably implied in ref. to tyrannous Nephilim and Gibborim; portended withdrawal of Spirit
6:9–7:5	*Flood Portended*	Widespread corruption and violence	Universal flood-judgment announced
7:6–8:19	*Flood Judgment*	Implied impenitence of mankind	Universal flood-judgment executed; universal death
8:20–9:17	*Noachian Covenant*	Man's sinful nature remains; capital punishment portends future violence	None (though death-threat for murders parallels curse-threat in Garden [2:17])
9:18–9:29	*Noah's Curse*	Drunkenness; contempt and mockery	Curse invoked; slavery portended; Noah's death
10:1–10:32	*Table of Nations*	Human pride and tyranny (Nimrod)	Dispersion and different languages possibly an allusion to Babel-judgment
11:1–11:9	*Tower of Babel*	Collective human pride and rebellion	Divinely imposed communication impediment
11:10–11:26	*Shem's Line*	None	Decreased longevity and death (implied)
11:27–12:9	*Abram's Call*	Weak faith; false start	Haran's premature death; Sarai's barrenness; Terah's death
12:10–12:20	*Abram in Egypt*	Weak faith; disobedience; fear of man; deception; polygamy	Famine; threat to divine promise; divinely inflicted plagues
13:1–13:18	*Abram & Lot Split*	Interfamilial strife; greed; weak faith; wickedness in Sodom	Lot and family separated from agent and sphere of blessing

Unit	*Title*	*Expressions of Sin*	*Effects of Sin (Curse)*
14:1–14:24	*Abram Rescues Lot*	Tyranny (Mesopotamian rulers); rebellion (Jordan valley vassals)	War; despoilment; death
15:1–15:21	*God's Oath to Abram*	Weak faith; allusion to the increasing sin of Amorites	Barrenness; portended slavery of Hebrews; portended judgment on Egyptians and Canaanites
16:1–16:16	*Sarai, Abram & Hagar*	Weak faith; bigamy; contempt; envy; interfamilial strife; violence	Marital disharmony; child born who will threaten promise
17:1–17:27	*Circumcision-Covenant*	Incredulous laughter (weak faith)	Barrenness; pain of circumcision
18:1–18:15	*Visit of Angels*	Incredulous laughter (weak faith)	Barrenness; debilitating effects of age; divine rebuke
18:16–18:33	*Abraham's Intercession*	Sodom's "sin is very grave"—very few righteous	Portended divine judgment
19:1–19:38	*Lot Rescued & Raped*	Inhospitality; attempted homosexual rape; violence; greed; weak faith; daughters "rape" Lot (incest)	Catastrophic judgment on cities; loss of possessions and family; cursed offspring
20:1–20:20	*Abraham in Gerar*	Weak faith; fear of man; deception; polygamy	Promise threatened; death-threat; infertility
21:1–21:21	*Isaac vs. Ishmael*	Contemptuous unbelief (Ishmael); weak faith (Abraham)	Interfamilial strife; Ishmael's life in danger
21:22–21:34	*Treaty with Abimelech*	Theft (Gerarites)	Climate of mistrust between Abraham and Gerarites
22:1–22:19	*The Binding of Isaac*	None	Sacrifice of offspring assumes context of a cursed world

Unit	*Title*	*Expressions of Sin*	*Effects of Sin (Curse)*
22:20–22:24	*Nahor's Twelve Sons*	Bigamy (Nahor)	None
23:1–23:20	*Sarah's Death & Burial*	Extortion (Ephron the Hittite)	Death and grief
24:1–24:67	*A Bride for Isaac*	Greed (Laban)	Difficulty of finding good wife; Isaac's lingering grief
25:1–25:11	*Abraham's Death*	Polygamy; weak faith (Abraham)	Death and grief
25:12–25:18	*Ishmael's Genealogy*	Possible allusion to Ishmael's hostile posture towards kinsmen	Death
25:19–25:28	*Esau & Jacob's Birth*	Fraternal strife portended; favoritism and familial strife	Barrenness
25:29–25:34	*Esau Sells Birthright*	Unbelief and contempt for religious privilege (Esau); manipulation (Jacob)	Loss of religious privileges
26:1–26:16	*Isaac in Gerar*	Weak faith; fear of man; deception	Promise threatened
26:17–26:33	*Treaty with Abimelech*	Envy; strife	Climate of mistrust between Isaac and Gerarites
26:34–27:40	*Jacob Gets the Blessing*	Bigamy and exogamy (Esau); spiritual blindness (Isaac); deception (Isaac, Rebekah, Jacob)	Parental grief; marital disharmony; climate of mistrust; loss of blessing (Esau)
27:41–28:9	*Jacob Sent to Laban*	Hatred and potential fratricide; (partial) deception; polygamy (Esau)	Mother "bereft" of favored son; Jacob exiled from Promised Land
28:10–28:22	*Jacob's Bethel-Dream*	Perhaps an opportunist motive behind Jacob's vow?	Jacob's forced exile

Unit	*Title*	*Expressions of Sin*	*Effects of Sin (Curse)*
29:1–29:30	*Jacob Marries Sisters*	Greed and deception (Laban); Bigamy (Jacob); undue favoritism	Familial strife
29:31–30:34	*Leah & Rachel Strive*	Undue favoritism; weak faith; polygamy (concubines)	Marital disharmony; barrenness; familial strife
30:25–30:43	*God Blesses Jacob*	Greed and deception (Laban); weak faith (Jacob)	Familial strife
31:1–31:55	*Jacob Flees from Laban*	Deception; theft (Rachel); allusion to idolatry (idols)	Familial strife
32:1–32:21	*Jacob Prepares for Esau*	Perhaps weak faith (Jacob)?	Promise threatened
32:22–32:32	*Jacob Wrestles Angel*	None	Anticipated fraternal strife
33:1–33:19	*Jacob Meets Esau*	Undue favoritism (Jacob); lack of concern for promise (Esau)	Fear and distress
33:18–34:31	*Shechem Ravaged*	Lust and rape; excessive anger; deception; greed; murder	Destruction and death
35:1–35:29	*To Bethel & Hebron*	Allusion to idolatry (idols); incest and attempted usurpation (Reuben); interfamilial strife	Great pain and death in childbearing (Rachel); more death (Deborah, Isaac); loss of birthright (Reuben)
36:1–37:1	*Esau's Genealogy*	Polygamy; worldly-mindedness	Esau's temporal blessing contrasts with Jacob's future blessing
37:2–37:11	*Joseph's Dreams*	Unwise parental favoritism (?); Sibling rivalry, hatred, jealousy	Familial strife

Unit	*Title*	*Expressions of Sin*	*Effects of Sin (Curse)*
37:12–37:36	*Joseph Sold as Slave*	Unwise parental favoritism (?); sibling rivalry; hatred; murder-plot; man-stealing; allusion to forced servitude; deceit	Emotional grief; familial strife
38:1–38:30	*Judah & Tamar*	Contempt for religious privilege; exogamy; spiritual blindness; great evil (Judah's sons); deceit (Judah and Tamar); lust and immorality; attempted cover-up; hypocrisy	Premature death (Judah's sons); familial strife
39:1–39:23	*Joseph & Potiphar's Wife*	Man-stealing; seduction; deception; injustice	Suffering injustice (Joseph)
40:1–40:32	*Joseph in Prison*	Continued injustice; un-neighborly neglect (cup-bearer)	Suffering injustice (Joseph); death of baker
41:1–41:57	*Joseph Rises to Power*	None	Famine portended
42:1–42:38	*Brothers Go to Egypt*	Blame-shifting and rash vow (Reuben); Weak faith (Jacob)	Famine; guilty conscience; distress; detention (Simeon)
43:1–43:34	*Brothers Return to Egypt*	None	Famine; guilty conscience
44:1–44:34	*Judah's Speech*	None	Guilty conscience; allusion to bereavement (Jacob's)
45:1–45:15	*Brothers Reconciled*	None	Famine
45:16–45:28	*Joseph Sends for Jacob*	None	Famine; chosen family must leave Promised Land; allusion to Jacob's approaching death

Unit	*Title*	*Expressions of Sin*	*Effects of Sin (Curse)*
46:1–46:30	*Jacob & Joseph Reunited*	None	Famine (assumed); allusion to Jacob's approaching death
46:31–47:12	*Jacob Blesses Pharaoh*	Allusion to ethnic prejudice	Famine (assumed)
47:13–47:27	*Joseph, Egypt's Vizier*	None	Famine (very severe)
47:28–47:31	*Jacob's Burial Wishes*	None	Death (anticipated)
48:1–48:22	*Joseph's Double-Portion*	None	Jacob's blindness and decline of health
49:1–49:28	*Jacob's Deathbed Oracle*	Allusions to past sins and ongoing character defects (Jacob's sons)	Forfeiture of blessing (Reuben, Simeon, Levi)
49:29–50:21	*Jacob's Death & Burial*	None	Death; grief of bereavement; fear of retaliation (Joseph's brothers)
50:21–50:26	*Joseph's Death*	None	Death

Note: Narrative units in bold print indicate the beginning of a *toledot* section.

Bibliography

Aalders, G. Charles. *Genesis*. 2 vols. Translated by William Heynen. *BSC*. Grand Rapids: Zondervan, 1981.

Ackerman, Joseph. "Joseph, Judah, and Jacob." In vol. 2 of *Literary Interpretations of Biblical Narratives*. 2 vols. Edited by Kenneth R. R. Gros Louis. Nashville: Abingdon Press, 1974–1982.

Albright, William Foxwell, and David Noel Freedman, editors. *Genesis*, vol. 1 of *AB*. New York: Doubleday, 1964.

Alexander, P. S. "The Targumim and Early Exegesis of the 'Sons of God' in Genesis 6," *JSS* 23 (1972) 60–71.

Alexander, T. D. *Abraham in the Negev: A Source-Critical Investigation of Genesis 20:1—22:19*. Carlisle, PA: Paternoster, 1997.

———. *From Paradise to the Promised Land: An Introduction to the Pentateuch*. 2nd ed. Grand Rapids: Baker Academic, 2002.

———. "Further Observations on the Term 'Seed' in Genesis." *TB* 48 (1997) 363–67.

———. "Genealogies, Seed and the Compositional Unity of Genesis." *TB* 44 (1993) 255–70.

———, and Brian S. Rosner, editors. *New Dictionary of Biblical Theology*. Downers Grove, IL: InterVarsity Press, 2000.

———. "The Old Testament View of Life After Death." *Themelios* 11 (1986) 41–46.

———. "Royal Expectations in Genesis to Kings: Their Importance for Biblical Theology." *TB* 49 (1998) 191–212.

Allen, Leslie C. *Ezekiel 20–48*. *WBC*. Edited by David A. Hubbard. Nashville: Nelson, 1990.

Allen, Ronald B. *The Majesty of Man: The Dignity of Being Human*. 2nd ed. Grand Rapids: Kregel, 2000.

Allis, Oswald T. "The Birth-Oracle to Rebekah (Genesis 25:23)." *EQ* 11 (1939) 97–117.

———. *The Five Books of Moses*. Phillipsburg, NJ: Presbyterian and Reformed, 1949.

———. *God Spake By Moses: An Exposition of the Pentateuch*. Phillipsburg, NJ: Presbyterian and Reformed, 1951.

Alter, Robert. *The Art of Biblical Narrative*. New York: Basic, 1981.

———. *The Art of Biblical Poetry*. Basic, 1985.

———. *Genesis: A Translation and Commentary*. New York: Norton, 1996.

Althaus, Paul. *The Theology of Martin Luther*. Translated by Robert C. Schultz. Philadelphia: Fortress, 1966.

Ambrose. *On Noah* 4.8. In *ACCS*, 1:126.

Anderson, Gary A. *The Genesis of Perfection: Adam and Eve in Jewish and Christian Imagination*. Louisville: Westminster John Knox, 2001.

Anderson, W. "The Curse of Work in Qoheleth: An Expose of Genesis 3:17–19 in Ecclesiastes," *EQ* 70 (1998) 99–113.

Ansell, Nicholas John. "The Call of Wisdom/The Voice of the Serpent: A Canonical Approach to the Tree of Knowledge." *Christian Scholar's Review* 31 (2001) 31–57.

Archer, Gleason, Jr. *A Survey of Old Testament Introduction*. 3rd ed. Chicago: Moody Press, 1994.

Arnold, Bill T. *Encountering the Book of Genesis. EBS*. Edited by Walter A. Elwell and Eugene H. Merrill. Grand Rapids: Baker, 1998.

Atkinson, David. *The Message of Genesis 1–11: The Dawn of Creation*. In *BST*. Edited by J. Alec Motyer and John Stott. Downers Grove, IL: InterVarsity, 1990.

Augustine. *The City of God*. Translated by Marcus Dods. Books XII–XVI. New York: Random, 1950.

———. "Reply to Faustus the Manichean." Book XII, 33–40. Translated by R. Stothert. Vol. 4 of *NPNF*. Edited by Philip Schaff. Grand Rapids: Eerdmans, 1956.

Austel, Herman J. *TWOT*, 2:944–45.

Bahnsen, Greg L. *Homosexuality: A Biblical View*. Grand Rapids: Baker, 1978.

Bailey, Lloyd R., Sr. *Biblical Perspectives on Death*. Overtures to Biblical Theology. Edited by Walter Brueggemann and John R. Donahue. Philadelphia: Fortress, 1979.

Baldwin, Joyce. *The Message of Genesis 12–50. BST(OT)*. Edited by J. Alec Motyer and John Stott. Downers Grove, IL: InterVarsity, 1986.

Baloian, Bruce. "שׂטם (śṭm)." In *NIDOTTE*, 3:1230–31.

Barr, James. *The Garden of Eden and the Hope of Immortality*. Minneapolis: Fortress, 1992.

Barton, John. "Natural Law and Poetic Justice in the Old Testament. *JTS* 30 (1979) 1–14.

Bassett, F. W. "Noah's Nakedness and the Curse of Canaan: A Case of Incest?" *VT* 21 (1971) 232–37.

Batchelor, Edward, Jr., ed. *Homosexuality and Ethics*. New York: Pilgrim, 1980.

Beale, G. K. *The Temple and the Church's Mission: A Biblical Theology of the Dwelling Place of God. NSBT*. Edited by D. A. Carson. Downers Grove, IL: InterVarsity, 2004.

Beale, G. K., and D. A. Carson, editors. *Commentary on the New Testament Use of the Old Testament*. Grand Rapids: Baker Academic, 2007.

Bechtel, Lyn M. "What If Dinah Is Not Raped? (Genesis 34)." *JSOT* 62 (1994) 19–36.

Becking, Bob. "They Hated Him Even More: Literary Technique in Genesis 37:1–11." *BN* 60 (1991) 40–47.

Berg, Werner. "Der Sündenfall Abrahams und Saras nach Gen 16:1–6." *BN* 19 (1982) 7–14.

———. "Nochmals: ein Sündenfall Abrahams—der erste—in Gen 12:10–20." *BN* 21 (1983) 7–15.

Berkhof, Louis. *Systematic Theology*. Grand Rapids: Eerdmans, 1941.

Berkhouwer, G. C. *Man: The Image of God*. Translated by Dirk W. Jellema. Studies in Dogmatics. Grand Rapids: Eerdmans, 1962.

———. *Sin*. Translated by Philip C. Holtrop. Studies in Dogmatics. Grand Rapids: Eerdmans, 1971.

Biddle, Mark E. *Missing the Mark: Sin and Its Consequences in Biblical Theology*. Nashville: Abingdon, 2005.

Blenkinsopp, Joseph. *Ezekiel. Interpretation*. Edited by James Luther Mays. Louisville: Knox, 1990.

———. *The Pentateuch: An Introduction to the First Five Books of the Bible*. New York: Doubleday, 1992.

Blocher, Henri. *In the Beginning: The Opening Chapters of Genesis*. Translated by David G. Preston. Downers Grove, IL: InterVarsity, 1984.

———. *Original Sin: Illuminating the Riddle*. New Studies in Biblical Theology. Edited by D. A. Carson. Downers Grove, IL: InterVarsity, 1997.

Block, Daniel I. "Table of Nations." *ISBE*rev, 4:707–13.

Boice, James Montgomery. *Genesis: An Expositional Commentary*. 3 vols. 1985. Reprint, Grand Rapids: Baker, 2006.

Bonhoeffer, Dietrich. *Creation and Fall: A Theological Interpretation of Genesis 1–3*. New York: MacMillan, 1959.

Borowski, Oded. "Agriculture." *ABD*. Edited by Noel David Freedman, 1:96. New York: Doubleday, 1992.

Bos, J. W. H. "Out of the Shadows: Genesis 38; Judges 4:17–22; Ruth 3." In *Reasoning with the Foxes: Female Wit in a World of Male Power*. Edited by J. C. Exum and J. W. H. Bos, 37–67. Atlanta: Scholars, 1988.

Boswell, John. *Christianity, Social Tolerance, and Homosexuality*. Chicago: University of Chicago Press, 1980.

Bramer, Stephen J. *Genesis*. Vol. 1 of *HOTC*. Edited by Max Anders. Nashville: Broadman & Holman Publishers, 2002.

Bratcher, Margaret Dee. "The Pattern of Sin and Judgment in Genesis 1–11." PhD diss., Southern Baptist Theological Seminary, 1984.

Bray, Gerald. "The Significance of God's Image in Man." *TB* 42 (1991) 195–225.

Brichto, Herbert Chanan. *The Problem of "Curse" in the Hebrew Bible*. JBL Monograph Series XIII. Philadelphia: Society of Biblical Literature, 1963.

Briggs Charles. *Messianic Prophecy: The Prediction of the Fulfillment of Redemption Through the Messiah*.New York: Scribner's, 1886.

Briscoe, D. Stuart. *Genesis*. *The Communicator's Commentary*. Edited by Lloyd J. Olgivie. Waco, TX: Word, 1987.

Brown, John. *Hebrews*. 1862. Reprint, Edinburgh: The Banner of Truth Trust, 1983.

Brown, Walter E. "Noah: Sot or Saint? Genesis 9:20–27." *The Way of Wisdom: Essays in Honor of Bruce K. Waltke*. Edited by J. I. Packer and Sven K. Soderlund. Grand Rapids: Zondervan, 2000.

Bruce, F. F. *The Epistle to the Hebrews*. *NICNT*. Edited by F. F. Bruce. Grand Rapids: Eerdmans, 1988.

———. *The Epistle of Paul to the Romans*. *TNTC*. Edited by R. V. G. Tasker. Grand Rapids: Eerdmans, 1963.

Bruckner, James K. *Implied Law in the Abraham Narrative: A Literary and Theological Analysis*. JSOT Supplement Series 335. Edited by David J. A. Clines and Philip R. Davies. London: Sheffield Academic, 2001.

Brueggemann, Walter. "From Dust to Kingship." *ZAW* 84 (1972) 1–18.

———. *Genesis, Interpretation: A Biblical Commentary for Teaching and Preaching*. Edited by James Luther Mays. Atlanta: Knox, 1982.

Buchanan, George. *The Doctrine of Justification: An Outline of Its History in the Church and of Its Exposition from Scripture*. 1867. Reprint, Edinburgh: The Banner of Truth Trust, 1991.

———. *To the Hebrews*.In *AB*. Edited by William Foxwell Albright and David Noel Freedman. Garden City, NY: Doubleday, 1976.

Buis Harry. "Retribution," in *ZPEB*, 5:84.

Bush, George. *Notes on Genesis*. 2 vols. 1860. Reprint, Minneapolis: James Family Christian, 1979.

Buswell, Oliver J. *A Systematic Theology of the Christian Religion*. Grand Rapids: Zondervan, 1962.

Calvin, John. *Commentaries on the First Book of Moses Called Genesis*. 2 vols. Translated by John King. 1845. Reprint, Grand Rapids: Baker, 2003.

———. *The Institutes of the Christian Religion*. Translated by Ford Lewis Battles. Edited by John T. McNeill. Philadelphia: Westminster, 1960.

Candlish, Robert S. *Studies in Genesis*. 1868. Reprint, Grand Rapids: Kregel Publications, 1979.

Carey, George. *I Believe in Man*. Grand Rapids: Eerdmans, 1977.

Carson, Donald A. *The Difficult Doctrine of the Love of God*. Wheaton: Crossway, 2000.

———. *Exegetical Fallacies*. Grand Rapids: Baker, 1984.

———. *How Long, O Lord? Reflections on Suffering and Evil*. 2nd ed. Grand Rapids: Baker, 2006.

Caspi, Mishael Maswari. "The Story of the Rape of Dinah: The Narrator and the Reader." *HS* 26 (1985) 25–45.

Cassuto, Umberto. *A Commentary on the Book of Genesis I: From Adam to Noah (Genesis 1—6:8)*. Translated by Israel Abrahams. Jerusalem: Magnes, 1961.

———. *A Commentary on the Book of Genesis II: From Noah to Abraham (Genesis 6:9—11:32)*. Translated by Israel Abrahams. Jerusalem: Magnes, 1964.

———. "The Episode of the Sons of God and the Daughters of Man (Genesis 6:1–4)"; "The Story of Tamar and Judah." In vol. 1 of *Biblical and Oriental Studies*. Translated by Israel Abrahams. Jerusalem: Magnes, 1973–1975.

———. "The Tamar and Judah Story." In *Biblical and Oriental Studies*. Translated by Israel Abrahams. Jerusalem: Magnes, 1973–1975.

Chafer, Lewis Sperry. *Satan*. Chicago: Moody, 1942.

Childs, Brevard. *Biblical Theology of the Old and New Testaments: Theological Reflections on the Christian Bible*. Minneapolis: Fortress, 1992.

———. *Introduction to the Old Testament as Scripture*. Philadelphia: Fortress, 1979.

———. *Old Testament Theology in a Canonical Context*. Philadelphia: Fortress, 1989.

Chysostom. "Homilies on Genesis 53:3," *ACCS*, 2:169.

Clark, William Malcolm. "The Flood and the Structure of the Pre-patriarchal History," *ZAW* 83 (1971) 184–211.

———. "A Legal Background to the Yahwist's Use of 'Good and Evil' in Genesis 2–3." *JBL* 88 (1969) 266–78.

Clemens, David M. "The Law of Sin and Death: Ecclesiastes and Genesis 1–3." *Themelios* 19 (1994) 5–8.

Clement of Alexandria. *Christ the Educator*, 3.2.14. In *ACCS*, 1:124.

Clines, David J. A. "The Image of God in Man." *TB* 19 (1968) 53–103.

———. "The Significance of the 'Sons of God' Episode (Genesis 6:1–4) in the Context of the 'Primeval History' (Genesis 1–11)." *JSOT* 13 (1979) 33–46.

———. "Theme in Genesis 1–11." *CBQ* 38 (1976) 483–507.

———. *The Theme of the Pentateuch*. 2nd ed. *JSOT Supplement Series* 10. Editors David J. A. Clines and Philip R. Davies. Sheffield, UK: Sheffield Academic, 1997.

Coats, George W. *Genesis with an Introduction to Narrative Literature*, vol. 1 of *The Forms of the Old Testament Literature*. Edited by Rolf Knierim and Gene M. Tucker. Grand Rapids: Eerdmans, 1983.

———. "God of Death: Power and Obedience in the Primeval History." *Int* 29 (1975) 227–39.

———. "Widow's Rights: A Crux in the Structure of Gen. 38." *CBQ* 34 (1972) 463.

Collins, C. John. *Genesis 1–4: A Linguistic, Literary, and Theological Commentary.* Phillipsburg, NJ: Presbyterian and Reformed, 2006.

Collins, Jack. "A Syntactical Note (Genesis 3:15): Is the Woman's Seed Singular or Plural?" *TB* 48 (1997) 139–48.

Craigie, Peter C. *The Book of Deuteronomy.* In *NICOT*. Edited by R. K. Harrison. Grand Rapids: Eerdmans, 1976.

Cranfield, C. E. B. *Romans 1–8, ICC.* Edited by G. I. Davies and G. N. Stanton. 1975. Reprint, London: T. & T. Clark, 2006.

Culver, Robert D. "The Traditional View," *Women in Ministry*, ed. Bonnidell Clouse and Robert G. Clouse. Downers Grove, IL: InterVarsity, 1989.

Currid, John D. *A Study Commentary on Genesis.* 2 vols. Webster, NY: Evangelical, 2003.

Curtis, Byron G. "Hosea 6:7 and Covenant Breaking Like/At Adam." In *The Law Is Not of Faith: Essays on Works and Grace in the Mosaic Covenant.* Edited by Bryan D. Estelle, J. V. Fesko, and David VanDrunen. Phillipsburg: Presbyterian and Reformed, 2009.

Dahood, Michel. "Abraham's Reply in Genesis 20:11." *Biblica* 61 (1980) 90–91.

———. "Hebrew-Ugaritic Lexicography iv." *Biblica* 47 (1966) 414.

———. "Northwest Semitic Notes on Genesis." *Biblica* 55 (1974) 78.

Dandamavev, Muhammed A. "Slavery (ANE)," "Slavery (OT)." In *ABD.* Edited by Noel David Freedman, 6:58–65. New York: Doubleday, 1992.

Daube, D., and R. Yaron, "Jacob's Reception by Laban." *JSS* 1 (1956) 60–62.

Davies, E. W. "Inheritance Rights and the Hebrew Levirate Marriage: Part 1." *VT* 31 (1981) 143.

Davis, John J. *From Paradise to Prison: Studies in Genesis.* Grand Rapids: Baker, 1975.

de Boer P. A. H. *Nederlands theologisch tijdshrift* 31 (1942) 197–212.

Delitzsch, Franz. *A New Commentary on Genesis.* 2 vols. Translated by Sophia Taylor. New York: Scribner & Welford, 1889.

Dempster, Stephen G. *Dominion and Dynasty: A Theology of the Hebrew Bible. NSBT.* Edited by D. A. Carson. Downers Grove: InterVarsity, 2003.

De Vaux, Roland. *Ancient Israel: Its Life and Institutions.* New York: McGraw Hill, 1961.

Dever, Mark. *The Message of the Old Testament: Promises Made.* Wheaton: Crossway, 2006.

DeWitt, Dale S. "The Historical Background of Genesis 11:1–9: Babel or Ur?" *JETS* 22 (1979) 15–26.

Dillard, Raymond B., and Tremper Longman III. *An Introduction to the Old Testament.* 2nd ed. Grand Rapids: Zondervan, 2006.

Dillman, A. *Genesis: Critically and Exegetically Expounded.* 2 vols. Translated by William B. Stevenson. Edinburgh: T. & T. Clark, 1897.

Dods, Marcus. *The Book of Genesis* in *The Expositor's Bible*. Edited by W. R. Nicoll. New York: Armstrong, 1901.

Dorsey, David A. *The Literary Structure of the Old Testament: A Commentary on Genesis—Malachi.* Grand Rapids: Baker, 1999.

Doyle, Brian. "The Sin of Sodom: yāḏaᶜ, yāḏaᶜ, yāḏaᶜ? A Reading of the Mamre-Sodom Narrative of Genesis 18–19." *Theology & Sexuality* 9 (1998) 84–100.

Dresner, Samuel. "Rachel and Leah: Sibling Tragedy or the Triumph of Piety and Compassion?" In *Abraham & Family: New Insights into the Patriarchal Narratives*. Edited by Hershel Shanks. Washington, D.C.: Biblical Archaeological Society, 2000.

Driver, S. R. *The Book of Genesis. Westminster Commentaries*. Edited by Walter Lock. London: Methuen, 1904.

Duguid, Iain M. *Ezekiel. Living in the Gap Between Promise and Reality: The Gospel According to Abraham. The Gospel According to the Old Testament*. Edited by Tremper Longman III and Alan Groves. Phillipsburg, NJ: Presbyterian and Reformed, 1999.

———. *Living in the Grip of Relentless Grace: The Gospel in the Lives of Isaac and Jacob. The Gospel According to the Old Testament*. Edited by Tremper Longman III and Alan Groves. Phillipsburg, NJ: Presbyterian and Reformed, 2002.

———. *The NIV Application Commentary*. Edited by Terry Muck. Grand Rapids: Zondervan, 1999.

Dumbrell, William. *Covenant and Creation: A Theology of the Old Testament Covenants*. Carlisle, UK: Paternoster, 1984.

———. "Life and Death in God's Creative Purposes (Genesis 1–3)." *The Ethics of Life and Death*. Edited by B. G. Webb. Homebush West, Australia: Lancer, 1990.

———. *Search for Order: Biblical Eschatology in Focus*. Grand Rapids: Baker, 1994.

Dunn, James. *Romans 1–8*, vol. 38 of *WBC*. Edited by Bruce M. Metzger and David A. Hubbard. Nashville: Nelson, 1988.

Dyrness, William. "Stewardship of the Earth in the Old Testament." In *Tending the Garden: Essays on the Gospel and the Earth*. Edited by Wesley Granberg-Michaelson. Grand Rapids: Eerdmans, 1987.

Edersheim, Alfred. *The Life and Times of Jesus the Messiah*. 1886. Reprint, Grand Rapids: Eerdmans, 1987.

Eichrodt, Walther. *Theology of the Old Testament*. 2 vols. Translated by J. A. Baker. Philadelphia: Westminster, 1961.

Ellingworth, Paul. *The Epistle to the Hebrews: A Commentary on the Greek Text*. In *NIGNTC*. Edited by I. Howard Marshall and W. Ward Gasque. Grand Rapids: Eerdmans, 1993.

Elliott, E. "Esau." *Expository Times* 29 (1917–1918) 44–45.

Elliott, Matthew A. *Faithful Feelings: Rethinking Emotion in the New Testament*. Grand Rapids: Kregel, 2006.

Ellul, Jacques. *The Meaning of the City*. Translated by Dennis Pardee. Grand Rapids: Eerdmans, 1970.

Emanueli, M. "The Sons of God Took Wives Whomever They Chose." *Bet Mikra* 20 (1974) 150–52.

Engnell, Ivan. *Studies in Divine Kingship in the Ancient Near East*. Oxford, UK: Basil Blackwell, 1967.

Ephrem the Syrian. *Commentary on Genesis*, 6.3.1. In *ACCS*, 1:124.

Epstein, Isidore , ed. *The Babylonian Talmud*. London: Soncino, 1935–1948.

Eslinger, L. "A Contextual Identification of the bene haʾelohim and benoth haʾadam," *JSOT* 13 (1979) 65–73.

Evans, Carl D. "The Patriarch Jacob: An 'Innocent Man.'" In *Abraham & Family: New Insights into the Patriarchal Narratives*. Edited by Hershel Shanks. Washington, D.C.: Biblical Archaeological Society, 2000.

Eveson, Philip. *The Book of Origins: Genesis Simply Explained*. Welwyn Commentary Series. Webster, NY: Evangelical, 2003.

Feinberg, Charles Lee. "Image of God." *BibSac* 129 (1972) 235–46.

———. *The Prophecy of Ezekiel: The Glory of the Lord.* Chicago: Moody, 1969.

Fewell, Danna Nolan, and David M. Gunn. "Tipping the Balance: Sternberg's Reader and the Rape of Dinah." *JBL* 110 (1991) 193–211.

Finkelstein, J. J. "Sex Offenses in Sumerian Laws." *JAOS* (1986) 355–72.

———. "The Antediluvian Kings: A University of California Tablet." *Journal of Cuneiform Studies* 17 (1963) 39–51.

Firmage, Edwin. "Genesis 1 and the Priestly Agenda." *JSOT* 82 (1992) 97–114.

Fishbane, Michael. *Biblical Text and Texture: A Literary Reading of Selected Texts.* Oxford, UK: Oneworld, 1998.

Foh, Susan T. "What Is the Woman's Desire," WTJ 37 (1975) 376–83.

Fokkelmann, Jan P. *Narrative Art in Genesis: Specimens of Stylistic and Structural Analysis.* 2nd ed. The Biblical Seminar. Edited by David E. Orton. 1991. Reprint, Eugene, OR: Wipf & Stock, 2004.

Frame, John M. *Apologetics to the Glory of God: An Introduction.* Phillipsburg, NJ: Presbyterian & Reformed, 1994.

———. *The Doctrine of God.* Phillipsburg, NJ: Presbyterian & Reformed, 2002.

Frankfort, Henri. *Kingship and the Gods: A Study of Ancient Near Eastern Religion as the Integration of Society and Nature.* Chicago: University of Chicago Press, 1948.

Freedman, H. "The Book of Genesis." In *The Soncino Chumash: The Five Books of Moses with Hapthtaroth.* Edited by A. Cohen. London: Soncino, 1947.

Fretheim, Terence E. "Genesis." In vol. 1 of *NIB*. Edited by Leander E. Keck. Nashville: Abingdon, 1994.

———. *Creation, Fall, and Flood: Studies in Genesis 1–11.* Minneapolis: Augsburg, 1969.

———. "Is Genesis 3 a Fall Story?" *Word & World* 14 (1994) 144–53.

———. *The Suffering of God: An Old Testament Perspective.* Overtures to Biblical Theology. Edited by Walter Brueggemann, John R. Donahue, Sharyn Dowd, and Christopher R. Seitz. Philadelphia: Fortress, 1984.

Frick, Frank S. *The City in Ancient Israel.* Society of Biblical Literature Dissertation Series 36. Edited by Howard C. Kee and Douglas A. Knight. Missoula, MT: Scholars, 1977.

Friedman, Richard Elliott. "Deception for Deception: Who Breaks the Cycle?" In *Abraham & Family: New Insights into the Patriarchal Narratives.* Edited by Hershel Shanks. Washington, D.C.: Biblical Archaeological Society, 2000.

Frymer-Kensky, T. "Patriarchal Family Relationship and Near Eastern Law." *BA* 44 (1981) 209–14.

Fuller, Daniel P. *The Unity of the Bible: Unfolding God's Plan for Humanity.* Grand Rapids: Zondervan, 1992.

Gage, Warren Austin. *The Gospel of Genesis: Studies in Protology and Eschatology.* 1984. Reprint, Eugene, OR: Wipf & Stock, 2001.

Gangel, Kenneth O., and Stephen J. Bramer. *Genesis.* Vol. 1 in *The Holman Old Testament Commentary.* Edited by Max Anders. Nashville: Holman, 2002.

Garland, David E. and Diana R. Garland. *Flawed Families of the Bible: How God's Grace Works Through Imperfect Relationships.* Grand Rapids: Brazos, 2007.

Garlington, Don. "Imputation or Union with Christ? A Response to John Piper." *Reformation & Revival* 2:4 (2003) 49–52.

Garrett, Duane. *Rethinking Genesis: The Sources and Authorship of the First Book of the Pentateuch.* 1991; reprint, Ross-shire, UK: Christian Focus, 2000.

Geisler, Norman L. *A Popular Survey of the Old Testament.* Grand Rapids: Baker, 2004.

Gestrich, Christof. *The Return of Splendor in the World: The Christian Doctrine of Sin and Forgiveness.* Translated by Daniel W. Bloesch. Grand Rapids: Eerdmans, 1997.

Getz, Gene A. *Abraham: Holding Fast to the Will of God.* Nashville: Broadman & Holman, 1996.

———. *Jacob: Following God Without Looking Back.* Nashville: Broadman & Holman, 1996.

———. *Joseph: Overcoming Obstacles Through Faithfulness.* Nashville: Broadman & Holman, 1996.

Gibson, John C. L. *Genesis*, 2 vols. *DSBS (OT)*. Edited by John C. L. Gibson. Philadelphia: Westminster, 1982.

Godet, Frederick. *Commentary on St. Paul's Epistle to the Romans.* Translated by A. Cusin, edited by Talbot W. Chambers. New York: Funk & Wagnalls, 1889.

Goertzen, John. "The Bible and Pterosaurs: Archaeological and Linguistic Studies of Jurassic Animals that Lived Recently." An article presented at the 1998 Midwestern Evangelical Theological Society Conference held at Grand Rapids Baptist Seminary, Grand Rapids, September 30, 1998; available at www.rae.org/pteroets.html; accessed 19 January 2008.

Golding, Judah. "The Youngest Son; or, Where Does Genesis 38 Belong?" *JBL* 96 (1977) 27–44.

Gonzales, Robert R., Jr. "The Covenantal Context of the Fall: Did God Make a Primeval Covenant with Adam?" *RBTR* 4:2 (2007) 5–32.

Good, E. M. "Deception and Women: A Response." *Semeia* 42 (1988) 116–17.

Goodfriend, E. A. "Adultery."In *ABD.* Edited by Noel David Freedman, 1:82–86. New York: Doubleday, 1992.

Gordis, Robert. "Homosexuality and the Homosexual." In *Homosexuality and Ethics.* Edited by E. Batchelor, Jr. New York: Pilgrim, 1980.

Gordon, Cyrus H. "Biblical Customs and the Nuzu Tablets." *BA* 3 (1940) 3.

———. "Hagar: A Throw-Away Character Among the Matriarchs?" In *Society of Biblical Literature Abstracts and Seminar Papers*, 271–77. Atlanta: Scholars, 1985.

———. "'In' of Predication or Equivalence." *JBL* 100 (1981) 612–13.

Gowan, Donald E. *From Eden to Babel: A Commentary on the Book of Genesis 1–11. ITC.* Edited by Fredrick Carlson Holmgren and George A. F. Knight. Grand Rapids: Eerdmans, 1988.

———. *When Man Becomes God: Humanism and Hybris in the Old Testament.* Pittsburgh Theological Monograph Series. Eugene, OR: Pickwick, 1975.

Green, William Henry. "Primeval Chronology." In *Classical Evangelical Essays in Old Testament Interpretation.* Edited by Walter C. Kaiser, Jr. Grand Rapids: Baker, 1972.

Greidanus, Sidney. *Preaching Christ from Genesis: Foundations for Expository Sermons.* Grand Rapids: Eerdmans, 2007.

Griffith, Howard. "Eschatology Begins with Creation." *WTJ* 49 (1987) 387–96.

Grisanti, Michael A. "בזה (bzh)." *NIDOTTE*, 628–30.

Grundtke, Christopher. "A Tempest in a Teapot? Genesis 3:8 Again." *VT* 51 (2001) 548–51.

Gunkel, Hermann. *Genesis.* Translated by Mark E. Biddle. Macon, GA: Mercer University, 1997.

Gunn, David M., and Danna Nolan Fewell. *Narrative in the Hebrew Bible*. Oxford Bible Series. Edited by P. R. Ackroyd and G. N. Stanton. New York: Oxford University Press, 1993.

Haldane, Robert. *An Exposition of Romans*. 1839. Reprint, MacDill AFB, Florida: MacDonald, 1958.

Hall, Kevin. "The Theology of Genesis 1–11." *Southwestern Journal of Theology* 44 (2001) 56–75.

Ham, Ken. *The Great Dinosaur Mystery Explained!* Green Forest, AR: Master, 1999.

Hamilton, Victor P. *The Book of Genesis: Chapters 1–17*. *NICOT*. Edited by R. K. Harrison and Robert L. Hubbard Jr. Grand Rapids: Eerdmans, 1990.

———. *The Book of Genesis: Chapters 18–50*. *NICOT*. Edited by R. K. Harrison and Robert L. Hubbard Jr. Grand Rapids: Eerdmans, 1995.

———. *Handbook on the Pentateuch*. Grand Rapids: Baker, 1982.

Hanson, Richard S. *The Serpent Was Wiser: A New Look at Genesis 1–11*. Minneapolis: Augsburg, 1972.

Harland, J. Penrose. "Sodom and Gomorrah." In *The Biblical Archaeologist Reader*. Edited by G. Ernest Wright and David N. Freedman, 41–75. New York: Doubleday, 1961.

Harris, J. Gordon. *Biblical Perspectives on Aging: God and the Elderly*. Overtures to Biblical Theology. Edited by Walter Brueggemann and John R. Donahue. Philadelphia: Fortress, 1987.

Harris, John L. "An Exposition of Genesis 2:4—11:32." *Southwestern Journal of Theology* 44 (2001) 39–55.

Harris, R. Laird. "Leviticus." In vol. 2 of *EBC*. Edited by Frank E. Gaebelein. Grand Rapids: Zondervan, 1990.

Harrison, R. K. *Introduction to the Old Testament: Including a Comprehensive Review of Old Testament Studies and a Special Supplement on the Apocrypha*. 1969; reprint, Peabody, MA: Hendrickson, 2004.

Hartley, John E. *Genesis*. *NIBC* (Old Testament Series). Edited by Robert L. Hubbard Jr. and Robert K. Johnston. Grand Rapids: Peabody, MA: Hendrickson, 2000.

Helminiak, Daniel A. *What the Bible Really Says About Homosexuality*. San Francisco: Alamo Square, 1994.

Helyer, Larry R. "Abraham's Eight Crises." In *Abraham & Family: New Insights Into the Patriarchal Narratives*. Edited by Hershel Shanks. Washington, D.C.: Biblical Archaelology Society, 2000.

———. "The Separation of Abram and Lot: Its Significance in the Patriarchal Narratives." *JSOT* 26 (1983) 77–88.

———. *Yesterday, Today, and Forever: The Continuing Relevance of the Old Testament*. 2nd ed. Salem, WI: Sheffield, 2004.

Hendricksen, William. *Exposition of Paul's Epistle to the Romans: Chapters 1–8, New Testament Commentary*. Grand Rapids: Baker, 1980.

Henry, Matthew. "Genesis to Deuteronomy." Vol. 1 of *Mathew Henry's Commentary on the Whole Bible*. 1706; reprint ed., Old Tappan, NJ: Revell, n.d.

Hess, Richard S. "The Roles of the Woman and the Man in Genesis 3." *Themelios* (1993) 15–19.

Hesselgrave, David J. "Polygamy."In *Baker's Dictionary of Christian Ethics*. Edited by Carl F. H. Henry. Grand Rapids: Baker, 1973.

Higgins, Jean M. "The Myth of Eve: The Temptress." *JAAR* 44 (1976) 639–47.

Hilgert, Earle. "The Dual Image of Joseph in Hebrew and Early Jewish Literature." *Biblical Research* 30 (1985) 5–21.

Hill, Andrew E., and John H. Walton. *A Survey of the Old Testament*. 2nd ed. Grand Rapids: Zondervan, 2000.

Hodge, Charles. *Epistle to the Romans*. Edinburgh: The Banner of Truth Trust, 1835, reprint ed. 1972.

Hoekema, Anthony A. *Created in God's Image*. Grand Rapids: Eerdmans, 1986.

Hoeksema, Homer C. *Unfolding Covenant History*. Volumes 1–3. Edited by Mark H. Hoeksema. Grandville, MI: Reformed Free, 2001–2003.

Hoffmeier, J. K. "The Wives' Tales of Genesis 12:20 and 26 and the Covenants at Beer-Sheba," *TB* 43 (1992) 81–99.

Holloway, Jeph. "'From the Beginning': The Moral Vision of Genesis 1–11." *Southwest Journal of Theology* 44 (2001) 76–92.

Homer. *The Iliad*. Translated by Robert Fitzgerald. Garden City, NY: International Collectors Library, 1974.

Horton, Michael. *God of Promise: Introducing Covenant Theology*. Grand Rapids: Baker, 2006.

House, Paul R. *Old Testament Theology*. Downers Grove: InterVarsity, 1998.

Houston, J. M. "City." *ZPEB*. 1:873–80.

Hughes, Philip Edgcumbe. *A Commentary on the Epistle to the Hebrews*. Grand Rapids: Eerdmans, 1977.

Hughes, Philip Edgcumbe. *The True Image: The Origin and Destiny of Man in Christ*. Grand Rapids: Eerdmans, 1989.

Hughes, R. Kent. *Genesis: Beginning and Blessing*. Preaching the Word. Wheaton: Crossway, 2004.

Jacob, Benno. *The First Book of the Bible: Genesis*. Edited and translated by Ernest I. Jacob and Walter Jacob. New York: KTAV, 1974.

Jacobs, Mignon R. "The Conceptual Dynamics of Good and Evil in the Joseph Story: An Exegetical and Hermeneutical Inquiry." *JSOT* 27 (2003) 309–38.

Janzen, J. Gerald. *Abraham and All the Families of the Earth: A Commentary on the Book of Genesis 12–50*. In *ITC*. Edited by Fredrick Carlson Holmgren and George A. F. Knight. Grand Rapids: Eerdmans, 1993.

Jeske, John C. *Genesis. People's Bible Commentary*. St. Louis: Concordia, 1992.

Johnson, Aubrey R. *Sacral Kingship in Ancient Israel*. Cardiff: University of Wales Press, 1967.

Joines, Karen Randolph. *Serpent Symbolism in the Old Testament: A Linguistic, Archaeological, and Literary Study*. Haddonfield, NJ: Haddonfield, 1974.

Jones, Peter. *Spirit Wars: Pagan Revival in Christian America*. Mukilteo, WA: WinePress, 1997.

Jordan, James B. "Merit Verses Maturity: What Did Jesus Do for Us?" In *The Federal Vision*. Edited by Steve Wilkins and Duane Garner. Monroe, LA: Athanasius, 2004.

———. *Primeval Saints: Studies in the Patriarchs of Genesis*. Moscow, ID: Canon, 2001.

———. *Through New Eyes: Developing a Biblical View of the World*. 1988; reprint, Eugene, OR: Wipf & Stock, 1999.

Josephus. *Antiquities of the Jews*, 1.3.1. *The Complete Works of Josephus*. Translated by William Whiston. Grand Rapids: Kregel, 1981.

Joüon, Paul. *A Grammar of Biblical Hebrew*. Translated and revised by T. Muraoka. Rome: Editrice Pontificio Istituto Biblico, 1992.

Kaiser, Walter C., Jr. *Toward Old Testament Ethics*. Grand Rapids: Eerdmans, 1983.

———. *Toward an Old Testament Theology*. Grand Rapids: Zondervan, 1978.

Karlberg, Mark W. "Justification in Redemptive History." *WTJ* 43 (1981) 213–46.

Keil, C. F. *Ezekiel & Daniel*. Translated by James Martin. Vol. 9 of *Commentary on the Old Testament*. Reprint. Grand Rapids: Eerdmans, 1986.

———. *Jeremiah & Lamentations*. Translated by James Kennedy. Vol. 8 of *Commentary on the Old Testament*. Grand Rapids: Eerdmans, 1988.

———, and F. Delitzsch. *Joshua, Judges, Ruth, 1 & 2 Samuel*. Translated by James Martin. Vol. 2 of *Commentary on the Old Testament*. Grand Rapids: Eerdmans, 1986.

———, and F. Delitzsch. *The Pentateuch*. Translated by James Martin. Vol. 1 of *Commentary on the Old Testament*. 1866. Reprint, Grand Rapids: Eerdmans, 1986.

Kessler, Martin. "Genesis 34—An Interpretation." *Reformed Review* 19 (1965–66) 3–8.

Kidner, Derek. *Genesis: An Introduction and Commentary*. *TOTC*. Edited by D. J. Wiseman. Downers Grove, IL: InterVarsity, 1967.

Kirsh, Jonathan. "What Did Sarah See?" In *Abraham and Family: New Insights into the Patriarchal Narratives*. Edited by Hershel Shanks. Washington, D.C.: Biblical Archaeological Society, 2000.

Kitchen, Kenneth A. *On the Reliability of the Old Testament*. Grand Rapids: Eerdmans, 2003.

Kline, Meredith G. "Abram's Amen." *WTJ* 31 (1968) 1–11.

———. "Divine Kingship and Genesis 6:1–4." *WTJ 24* (1965) 187–204.

———. *God, Heaven, and Har Magedon: A Covenantal Tale of Telos and Cosmos*. Eugene, OR: Wipf & Stock, 2006.

———. "Gospel Until the Law: Rom 5:13–14 and the Old Covenant." *JETS* 34 (1991) 433–46.

———. *Images of the Spirit*. 1980. Reprint, Eugene, OR: Wipf & Stock, 1999.

———. *Kingdom Prologue: Genesis Foundations for a Covenantal Worldview*. Eugene, OR: Wipf & Stock, 2006.

———. "The Oracular Origin of the State." *Biblical and Near Eastern Studies: Essays in Honor of William Sanford LaSor*. Edited by Gary A. Tuttle. Grand Rapids: Eerdmans, 1978.

———. *The Structure of Biblical Authority*. 2nd ed. Grand Rapids: Eerdmans, 1975.

Knierim, Rolf P. "On the Contours of Old Testament and Biblical Hamartiology." In *The Task of Old Testament Theology: Substance, Method, and Cases*. Grand Rapids: Eerdmans, 1995.

Kraeling, Emil G. "The Significance and Origins of Genesis 6:1–4." *JNES* 6:4 (1947) 197.

Laidlaw, John. *The Bible Doctrine of Man*. Edinburgh: T. & T. Clark, 1879.

Lambdin, Thomas O. *Introduction to Biblical Hebrew*. New York: Scribner's, 1971.

Lane, William L. *Hebrews 9–13*. In *WBC*. Edited by David A. Hubbard. Dallas: Word, 1991.

Lange, John Peter. *Genesis or the First Book of Moses*. 5th ed. Translated by Tayler Lewis and A. Gosman. Vol. 1 of *Lange's Commentary*. Edited by Philip Schaff. New York: Scribner, Armstrong, 1873.

LaSor, William Sanford. *Great Personalities of the Old Testament: Their Lives and Times*. Westwood, NJ: Revell, 1959.

———, David Allen Hubbard, and Frederic William Bush. *Old Testament Survey: The Message, Form, and Background of the Old Testament*. Grand Rapids: Eerdmans, 1982.

Laurin, Robert B. "The Tower of Babel Revisited." *Biblical and Near Eastern Studies: Essays in Honor of William Sanford LaSor*. Edited by Gary A. Tuttle. Grand Rapids: Eerdmans, 1978.

Lenski, Richard. *Interpretation of St. Paul's Epistle to the Romans*. Colombus: Wartburg, 1945.

Leupold, H. C. *Exposition of Genesis*. 2 vols. 1942. Reprint, Grand Rapids: Baker, 1987.

Lichtheim, Miriam. *Ancient Egyptian Literature*, 2:203–11. Berkeley: University of California Press, 1973–80.

Liddell, Henry George, and Robert Scott, editors. *A Greek-English Lexicon*. Oxford: Claredon, 1968.

Lim, Johnson T. K. *Grace in the Midst of Judgment: Grappling with Genesis 1–11*. Behiefte zur Zeitschrift für die alttestamentliche Wissenschaft. Edited by Otto Kaiser. Berlin: Walter de Gruyter, 2002.

———. "The Sin Theology of the Cain and Abel Story: An Analysis of Narrative Themes Within the Context of Genesis 1–11." PhD diss., Marquette University, 1988.

Long, V. Phillips. "Historiography of the Old Testament," in *The Face of Old Testament Studies: A Survey of Contemporary Approaches*. Edited by David W. Baker and Bill T. Arnold. Grand Rapids: Baker, 1999.

———. *The Art of Biblical History*, vol. 4 of *Foundations of Contemporary Interpretation: Six Volumes in One*. Edited by Moisés Silva. Grand Rapids: Zondervan, 1996.

Longman, Tremper, III. *How to Read Genesis*. Downers Grove, IL: InterVarsity, 2005.

Louth, Andrew, ed. *Genesis 1–11*. Vol. 1 of *ACCS*. Edited by Thomas C. Oden. Downers Grove, IL: InterVarsity, 2001.

Lowenthal, Eric I. *The Joseph Narrative in Genesis*. New York: KTAV, 1973.

Luther, Martin. *Lectures on Galatians 1519:1–6*. Translated by Richard Jungkuntz. Vol. 27 of *Luther's Works*. Edited by Jaroslav Pelikan. St. Louis: Concordia, 1964.

———. *Lectures on Galatians 1545: 1–4*. Translated by Jaroslav Pelikan. Vol. 26 of *Luther's Works*. Edited by Jaroslav Pelikan. St. Louis: Concordia, 1963.

———. *Lectures on Genesis*. Vols. 1–8 in *LW*. Edited by Jaroslav Pelikan. Translated by George V. Schick. St. Louis: Concordia, 1958–1966.

———. *Lectures on Romans: Glosses and Scholia*.Vol. 25 of *Luther's Works*. Edited by Hilton C. Oswald. St. Louis: Concordia, 1972.

Maclaren, Alexander. *Genesis*. Vol. 1 of *Expositions of Holy Scripture*. New York: Hodder & Stoughton, n.d.

Magnes-Gardiner, B. S. "Seals, Mesopotamian." In *ABD*. Edited by Noel David Freedman, 5:1062–64. New York: Doubleday, 1992.

Mann, Thomas M. "All the Families of the Earth: The Theological Unity of Genesis." *Intrepretation* 45 (1991) 341–53.

Mathews, Kenneth A. *Genesis 1—11:26*. Vol. 1a of *NAC*. Edited by E. Ray Clendenen. Nashville: Broadman & Holman, 1996.

———. *Genesis 11:27—50:26*. Vol. 1b of *NAC*. Edited by E. Ray Clendenen. Nashville: Broadman & Holman, 2005.

———. "Genesis." In *New Dictionary of Biblical Theology*. Edited by T. Desmond Alexander and Brian S. Rosner. Downers Grove, IL: InterVarsity, 2000.

Mathewson, Stephen D. "An Exegetical Study of Genesis 38." *BibSac* 146 (1989) 373–92.

Mazar, Amthai. "The Fortifications of Cities in the Ancient Near East" *CANE*. 3:1523–37.

McComiskey, Thomas Edward. *The Covenants of Promise: A Theology of the Old Testament Covenants*. Grand Rapids: Baker, 1985.

———. *Hosea*. In vol. 1 of *The Minor Prophets: An Exegetical and Expositional Commentary*. Edited by Thomas McComiskey. Grand Rapids: Baker, 1992.

McConville, J. G. *Deuteronomy*. Vol. 5 of *AOTC*. Edited by David W. Baker and Gordon J. Wenham. Downers Grove, IL: InterVarsity, 2002.

McKeown, James. *Genesis*. *THOTC*. Edited by J. Gordon McConville and Craig Bartholomew. Grand Rapids: Eerdmans, 2008.

Menninger, Karl. *Whatever Became of Sin?* New York: Hawthorn, 1973.

Merrill, Eugene H. *Deuteronomy*. Vol. 4 of *NAC*. Edited by E. Ray Clendenen. Nashville: Broadman & Holman, 1994.

———. *Everlasting Dominion: A Theology of the Old Testament*. Nashville: Broadman & Holman, 2006.

Metzger, Bruce M. *Introduction to the Aprocrypha*. New York: Oxford University, 1957.

Middleton, J. Richard. *The Liberating Image: The Imago Dei in Genesis 1*. Grand Rapids: Brazos, 2005.

———. "A New Babylonian 'Genesis Story.'" *TB* 18 (1967) 12.

Miller, J. Maxwell. "In the 'Image' and 'Likeness' of God." *JBL* 91 (1972) 289–304.

Minear, Paul Sevier. *Christians and the New Creation: Genesis Motifs in the New Testament*. Louisville: Westminster Knox, 1994.

Moffatt, James. *Epistle to the Hebrews*. In *ICC*. Edited by Theodore H. Robinson. New York: Scribner's, 1924.

Moo, Douglas. *The Epistle to the Romans*, *NICNT*. Edited by Gordon D. Fee. Grand Rapids: Eerdmans, 1996.

Moran, W. L. "The Scandal of the 'Great Sin' at Ugarit." *JNES 18* (1956) 280–81.

Morris, Henry M. *The Genesis Record: A Scientific and Devotional Commentary on the Book of Beginnings*. Grand Rapids: Baker, 1976.

Morris, Henry, III. *After Eden: Understanding Creation, the Curse, and the Cross*. Green Forest, AZ: Master, 2003.

Morris, Leon. *The Epistle to the Romans*, *PNTC*. Edited by D. A. Carson. Grand Rapids: Eerdmans, 1988.

Morris, Leon L. "Justification By Faith: The Old Testament and Rabbinic Anticipation." *EQ* 24 (1952) 24–36.

———. *The Wages of Sin: An Examination of the New Testament Teaching on Death*. London: Tyndale, 1954.

Motyer, Alec. *The Story of the Old Testament: Men with a Message*. Revised by John Stott. Grand Rapids: Baker, 2001.

Munday, John C., Jr. "Creature Mortality: From Creation or Fall?" *JETS* 35 (1992) 51–68.

Murray, John. *Collected Writings of John Murray*, ed. Iain Murray (Edinburgh: The Banner of Truth Trust, 1976.

———. *The Epistle to the Romans*, *NICNT*. Edited by F. F. Bruce. Grand Rapids: Eerdmans, 1959, 1965.

———. "The Fall of Man." In vol. 2 of *Collected Writings of John Murray*. Edited by Iain Murray. Edinburgh: The Banner of Truth Trust, 1977.

———. *The Imputation of Adam's Sin*. Nutley, NJ: Presbyterian and Reformed, 1957.

———. *Principles of Conduct: Aspects of Biblical Ethics*. Grand Rapids: Eerdmans, 1957.

Neusner, Jacob, ed. and trans. *Genesis Rabbah: The Judaic Commentary to the Book of Genesis.* 3 vols. Atlanta: Scholars, 1985.

Newman, R. C. "The Ancient Exegesis of Genesis 6:2, 4," *GTJ* 5 (1984) 13–36.

Nichol, G. C. "Genesis 29:32 and 35:22a: Reuben's Reversal." *JTS* 31 (1980) 536–39.

Nichols, Gregory G. "The Emotivity of God," *RBTR* 1:2 (2004) 95–143.

Niditch, Susan. "Genesis." In *The Woman's Bible Commentary.* Edited by Carol A. Newsom and Sharon H. Ringe. Louisville: Westminster Knox, 1992.

Niehaus, Jeffrey J. *God at Sinai: Covenant & Theophany in the Bible and Ancient Near East. Studies in Old Testament Biblical Theology.* Edited by Willem VanGemeren. Carlisle, UK: Paternoster, 1995.

Oehler, Gustav Friedrich. *Theology of the Old Testament.* 4th ed. Translated by George E. Day. London: Funk & Wagnalls, 1888.

Ortlund, Raymond C. Jr. "Male-Female Equality and Male Headship." In *Recovering Biblical Manhood & Womanhood: A Response to Evangelical Feminism.* Edited by John Piper and Wayne Grudem. Wheaton: Crossway, 1991.

Oswalt, John. *The Book of Isaiah: Chapters 1–39. NICOT.* Edited by Robert L. Hubbard Jr. Grand Rapids: Eerdmans, 1986.

Owen, John. *Epistle to the Hebrews.* Edited by W. H. Goold. London: Johnstone & Hunter, 1855. Reprint, Grand Rapids: Baker, 1980.

Parker, Joseph. *Genesis.* The People's Bible. Reprint, Chicago: Moody, 1951.

Parrot, Andre. *The Tower of Babel.* London: SCM, 1955.

Payne, J. Barton. *The Theology of the Older Testament.* Grand Rapids: Zondervan, 1962.

Peck, John. "Note on Genesis 37:2 and Joseph's Character." *The Expository Times* 82 (1971) 342–43.

Peters, Ted. *Sin: Radical Evil in Soul and Society.* Grand Rapids: Eerdmans, 1994.

Pink, Arthur W. *The Divine Inspiration of the Bible.* Swengel, PA: Bible Truth Depot, 1917.

Piper, John. "A Response to Don Garlington on Imputation." *Reformation & Revival* 2:4 (2003) 121–29.

Plantinga, Cornelius, Jr. *Not the Way It's Supposed to Be: A Breviary of Sin.* Grand Rapids: Eerdmans, 1995.

Porúbčan, Štefan. *Sin in the Old Testament: A Soteriological Study.* Rome: Herder, 1963.

Powell, Tim. "תעע (tᶜᶜ)." In *NIDOTTE,* 4:320–21.

Pratt, Richard L. "Pictures, Windows, and Mirrors in Old Testament Exegesis." *WTJ* 45 (1983) 156–67.

Rabinowitz, J. J. "The 'Great Sin' in Ancient Egyptian Marriages Contracts." *JNES* 18 (1956) 73.

Ramm, Bernard. *Offense to Reason: A Theology of Sin.* San Francisco: Harper & Row, 1985.

Reimann, Paul A. "Am I My Brother's Keeper?" *Int* 24 (1970) 482–91.

Rendtorff, Rolf. "Genesis 821 und die Urgeschichte des Jahwisten." *Kerygma und Dogma* 7 (1961) 69–78.

Reymond, Robert L. "An Investigation of the Covenants of the Old Testament and Their Significance in the Theocratic Program of God." PhD diss., Bob Jones University, 1962.

———. *A New Systematic Theology of the Christian Faith.* Nashville: Nelson, 1998.

Rice, G. "The Curse That Never Was," *JRT* 29 (1972) 11–13.

Ricoeur, Paul. *The Symbolism of Evil*. Translated by Emerson Buchanan. New York: Harper & Row, 1967.

Roberts, Linleigh J. *Let Us Make Man*. Edinburgh: The Banner of Truth Trust, 1988.

Robertson, O. Palmer. *The Christ of the Covenants*. Phillipsburg, NJ: Presbyterian and Reformed, 1980.

———. "Genesis 15:6: New Covenant Expositions of an Old Covenant Text." *WTJ* 42 (1980) 259–90.

———. *The Genesis of Sex: Sexual Relationships in the First Book of the Bible*. Phillipsburg, NJ: Presbyterian and Reformed, 2002.

Robinson, H. Wheeler. *The Christian Doctrine of Man*. Edinburgh: T. & T. Clark, 1911.

Robinson, Ira. "bĕpetaḥ ʿênayim in Genesis 38:14." *JBL* 96 (1977) 569.

Robinson, Robert B. "Literary Functions of the Genealogies of Genesis." *CBQ* 48 (1986) 595–608.

Roehrs, Walter R. "Covenant and Justification in the Old Testament." *Concordia Theological Monthly* 35 (1964) 583–602.

Ronning, John L. "The Curse on the Serpent (Genesis 3:15) in Biblical Theology and Hermeneutics." PhD diss., Westminster Theological Seminary, 1997.

Roop, Eugene F. *Genesis*. *BCBC (OT)*. Edited by Elmer A. Martens. Scottdale, PA: Herald, 1987.

Ross, Allen P. *Creation & Blessing: A Guide to the Study and Exposition of Genesis*. Grand Rapids: Baker, 1998.

———. *Holiness to the Lord: A Guide to the Exposition of the Book of Leviticus*. Grand Rapids: Baker, 2002.

———. "The Table of Nations in Genesis 10—Its Structure." *BibSac* 137 (1980) 340–53.

———. "The Table of Nations in Genesis 10—Its Content," *BibSac* 138 (1981) 22–34.

Rupprecht, A. "Slave, Slavery." *ZPEB*, 5:453–60.

Ryken, Leland. *Words of Delight: A Literary Introduction to the Bible*. Grand Rapids: Baker Academic, 1992.

Ryken, Leland, and Tremper Longman III. *A Complete Literary Guide to the Bible*. Grand Rapids: Zondervan, 1993.

Sailhamer, John. "Creation, Genesis 1–11, and the Canon." *Bulletin for Biblical Research* 10 (2000) 89–106.

———. "Genesis." In *A Complete Literary Guide to the Bible*. Edited by Leland Ryken and Tremper Longman III, 108–20. Grand Rapids: Zondervan, 1993.

———. "Genesis." In vol. 2 of *EBC*. Edited by Frank E. Gaebelein. Grand Rapids: Zondervan, 1990.

———. *The Pentateuch as Narrative: A Biblical-Theological Commentary*. Grand Rapids: Zondervan, 1992.

Sarna, Nahum M. *Genesis*. *The JPS Torah Commentary*. Edited by Nahum M. Sarna. Philadelphia: Jewish Publication Society, 1989.

Schaeffer, Francis A. "Genesis in Space and Time." In vol. 2 of *The Complete Works of Francis Schaeffer: A Christian Worldview*. 2nd ed. Westchester, IL: Crossway, 1982.

Schaff, Philip, and David S. Schaff , eds. Vol. 3 of *The Creeds of Christendom*. 2nd ed. 1931. Reprint, Grand Rapids: Baker, 1990.

Schedi, Claus. *History of the Old Testament*. Staten Island, NY: Alba, 1972.

Schreiner, Thomas R. *Romans, Baker Exegetical Commentary on the New Testament*. Edited Moisés Silva. Grand Rapids: Baker Academic, 1998.

Schimmel, S. "Joseph and His Brothers: A Paradigm for Repentance." *Judaism* 37 (1988) 60–65.

Selman, M. J. "Comparative Customs and the Patriarchal Age." In *Essays on the Patriarchal Narratives*. Edited by A. R. Millard and D. J. Wiseman. Winona Lake, IN: Eisenbrauns, 1983.

Shank, Harold. "The Sin Theology of the Cain and Abel Story: An Analysis of Narrative Themes Within the Context of Genesis 1–11." PhD diss., Marquette University, 1988.

Shapira, A. "Be Silent: An Immoral Behavior?" *Beit Mikra* 39 (1994) 232–44.

Shaw, Benjamin. "The Genealogies of Genesis 5 and 11 and Their Significance for Chronology." PhD diss., Bob Jones University, 2004.

Sheridan, Mark, ed. *Genesis 12–50*. Vol. 2 of *ACCS*. Edited by Thomas C. Oden. Downers Grove, IL: InterVarsity, 2002.

Sherlock, Charles. *The Doctrine of Humanity*. Contours of Christian Theology. Edited by Gerald Bray. Downers Grove, IL: InterVarsity, 1996.

Sherwood, S. K. *"Had Not God Been On My Side": An Examination of the Narrative Technique of the Story of Jacob and Laban, Genesis 29:1—32:2*. Frankfurt: Lang, 1990.

Shuster, Marguerite. *The Fall and Sin: What We Have Become as Sinners*. Grand Rapids: Eerdmans, 2004.

Silberman, Lou H. "Death in the Hebrew Bible and Apocalyptic Literature." *Perspectives on Death*. Edited by Liston O. Mills. Nashville: Abingdon, 1969.

Simeon, Charles. "Genesis through Leviticus." Vol. 1 of *Expository Outlines on the Whole Bible*. 1847. Reprint, Grand Rapids: Zondervan, 1956.

Skinner, John. *A Critical and Exegetical Commentary on Genesis*. *ICC*. Edited by Samuel Rolles Driver, Alfred Plummer, and Charles Augustus Briggs. Edinburgh: T. & T. Clark, 1910.

Smalley, Gary, and John Trent. *The Blessing*. Nashville: Thomas Nelson Publishers, 1986.

Smith, Bryan. "The Presentation of Judah in Genesis 37–50 and Its Implications for the Narrative's Structural and Thematic Unity." PhD diss., Bob Jones University, 2002.

Smith, C. Ryder. *The Bible Doctrine of Sin and of the Ways of God with Sinners*. London: Epworth, 1953.

Smith, David L. *With Willful Intent: A Theology of Sin*. Wheaton: Victor, 1994.

Smith, Gary V. "Structure and Purpose in Genesis 1–11." *JETS* 20 (1977) 307–18.

Speiser, Ephraim A. *Genesis*. 3rd ed. Vol. 1 of *AB*. Edited by William Foxwell Albright and David Noel Freedman. Garden City, NY: Doubleday, 1964.

———. "New Kirkuk Documents Relating to Family Laws." In *AASOR* 10 (1930) 31–32.

———. "The Wife-Sister Motif in the Patriarchal Narratives." In *Biblical and Other Studies*. Cambridge: Harvard University, 1963.

Spurgeon, C. H. "The Sin of Unbelief." *New Park Street Pulpit*, January 14, 1855. Cited from The C. H. Spurgeon Collection, Ages Digital Library, 1998.

Stambaugh, John E. "Cities." *ABD*. Edited by Noel David Freedman, 1:1031–48. New York: Doubleday, 1992.

Starikov, Vyacheslav V. "The Mercy of Vanity: An Examination of the Canonical Purpose of Ecclesiastes." PhD diss., Bob Jones University, 2004, 124–30.

Steinmetz, Devora. *From Father to Son: Kinship, Conflict, and Continuity in Genesis*. *LCBI*. Edited by Danna Noel Fewell and David M. Gunn. Louisville: Knox, 1991.

Stek, John H. "What Says the Scripture?" In *Portraits of Creation: Biblical and Scientific Perspectives on the World's Formation*. Edited by Howard J. VanTill. Grand Rapids: Eerdmans, 1990.

Sternberg, Meir. *The Poetics of Biblical Narrative: Ideological Literature and the Drama of Reading*. Bloomington, IN: Indiana University, 1987.

Stigers, Harold G. *A Commentary on Genesis*. Grand Rapids: Zondervan, 1976.

Stone, Elizabeth C. "The Development of Cities in Ancient Mesopotamia." *CANE*. 1:235–48.

Stordalen, Terje. *Echoes of Eden: Genesis 2–3 and Symbolism of the Eden Garden in Biblical Hebrew Literature. Contributions to Biblical Exegesis and Theology* 25. Edited by Tj. Baarda, A. van der Kooij, A. S. van der Woude, and K. De Troyer. Leiden, Netherlands: Peeters, 2000.

Surburg, Raymond F. "Justification as a Doctrine of the Old Testament: A Comparative Study in Confessional and Biblical Theology." *Concordia Theological Monthly* 46 (1982) 129–46.

Tanner, J. Paul. "The Message of the Song of Songs." *BibSac* 154:614 (April 1997) 143–62.

Taylor, John B. *Ezekiel: An Introduction and Commentary. TOTC*. Edited by D. J. Wiseman. Downers Grove, IL: InterVarsity, 1969.

Terreros, Marco T. "Death Before the Sin of Adam: A Fundamental Concept in Theistic Evolution and Its Implications for Evangelical Theology." PhD diss., Andrews University, 1994.

Theophilus. *Theophilus to Autolycus*. Translated by Marcus Dod. Vol. 2 of *The Ante-Nicene Fathers*. Edited by Alexander Roberts and James Donaldson. Grand Rapids: Eerdmans, 1956.

Thomas, W. H. Griffith. *Genesis: A Devotional Commentary*. Grand Rapids: Eerdmans, 1946.

Tomasino, A. "History Repeats Itself: the 'Fall' and Noah's Drunkenness," *VT* 42 (1992) 128–30.

Toon, Peter T. "Polygamy."In *Encyclopedia of Biblical and Christian Ethics*. Edited by R. K. Harrison. Nashville: Nelson, 1987.

Toppin, Ian N. *Biblical Patriarchs and Their Legacy of Family Dysfunctions*. New York: iUniverse, 2006.

Towner, W. Sibley. "Interpretations and Reinterpretations of the Fall." *Modern Scholarship: Its Impact on Theology and Proclamation*. Edited by Francis A. Eigo. Villanova, PA: Villanova University Press, 1984.

Travis, Stephen H. "The Problem of Judgment." *Themelios* 11 (1986) 52–57.

Trible, Phyllis. *God and the Rhetoric of Sexuality. OBT*. Edited by Walter Brueggemann and John R. Donahue. Philadelphia: Fortress, 1978.

Tsumura, David. "A Note on הרון (Gen 3:16)," *Biblica* 75 (1994) 398–400.

Tucker, Gordon. "Jacob's Terrible Burden: In the Shadow of the Text." In *Abraham and Family: New Insights into the Patriarchal Narratives*. Edited by Hershel Shanks. Washington, D.C.: Biblical Archaeological Society, 2000.

Unger, Merrill. *Biblical Demonology: A Study of the Spiritual Forces Behind the Present World Unrest*. Wheaton: Van Kampen, 1952.

Van Der Zee, William B. *Ape or Adam? Our Roots According to the Book of Genesis*. Translated by Gerard M. Verschuuren. North Andover, MA: Genesis, 1995.

Van Seters, John. *Abraham in History and Tradition*. New Haven: Yale University Press, 1975.

———. "The Creation of Man and the Creation of the King." *ZAW* 101 (1989) 333–42.

Van Til, Cornelius. *Common Grace and the Gospel*. Philadelphia: Presbyterian and Reformed, 1972.

VanGemeren, Willem A. *The Progress of Redemption: The Story of Salvation from Creation to the New Jerusalem*. 1988. Reprint, Grand Rapids: Baker, 2000.

———. "The Sons of God in Genesis 6:1–4 (An Example of Evangelical Demythologization?)." *WTJ* (1981) 320–48.

van Wolde, Ellen. "The Story of Cain and Abel: A Narrative Study." *JSOT* 52 (1991) 25–41.

Vawter, Bruce. *On Genesis: A New Reading*. New York: Doubleday, 1977.

Visotsky, Burton L. *The Genesis of Ethics: How the Tormented Family of Genesis Leads Us to Moral Development*. New York: Three Rivers, 1996.

von Rad, Gerhard. *Genesis: A Commentary*. 2nd ed. Translated by John H. Marks. *The Old Testament Library*. Philadelphia: Westminster, 1972.

———. *Old Testament Theology*. 2 vols. Translated by D. M. G. Stalker. 1962–65. Reprint, Peabody: Prince, 2005.

Vos, Geerhardus. *Biblical Theology: Old and New Testaments*. 1948. Reprint, Grand Rapids: Eerdmans, 1988.

———. *The Eschatology of the Old Testament*. Edited by James T. Dennison Jr. Phillipsburg: Presbyterian and Reformed, 2001.

Vriezen, Theodorus C. *An Outline of Old Testament Theology*. Translated by S. Neuijen, 2nd ed. Oxford: Blackwell, 1960.

Waldron, Samuel E. *Faith, Obedience, and Justification: Current Evangelical Departures from Sola Fide*. Palmdale, CA: Reformed Baptist Academic Press, 2006.

———. "The Suffering of God: An Old Testament Perspective, Terence E. Fretheim," *RBTR* IV:1 (Jan 2007) 128–37.

Wallace, Daniel. *Greek Grammar Beyond the Basics: An Exegetical Syntax of the New Testament*. Grand Rapids: Zondervan, 1996.

Walsh, Jerome T. "Genesis 2:4b-3:24: A Synchronic Approach." *JBL* 96 (1977) 161–77.

Waltke, Bruce K. "בָּזָה (bāzā^{h}) *to despise, disdain, hold in contempt.*" *TWOT*, 1:98–99.

———. "Cain and His Offering." *WTJ* 48 (1986) 363–72.

———. *Genesis: A Commentary*. Grand Rapids: Zondervan, 2001.

———. *An Old Testament Theology: An Exegetical, Canonical, and Thematic Approach*. Grand Rapids: Zondervan, 2007.

Walton, John H. "Are the 'Sons of God' in Genesis 6 Angels? No." In *The Genesis Debate*. Edited by Ronald Youngblood. Nashville: Nelson, 1986.

Walton, John H. *Covenant: God's Purpose, God's Plan*. Grand Rapids: Zondervan, 1994.

———. *Genesis. The NIV Application Commentary*. Edited by Terry Muck. Grand Rapids: Zondervan, 2001.

Ward, Rowland S. *Foundations in Genesis: Genesis 1–11 Today*. Wantirna, Australia: New Melbourne, 1998.

Ware, Bruce. *God & Adam: Reformed Theology and the Creation Covenant*. Wantirna, Australia: New Melbourne, 2003.

———. *God's Greater Glory: The Exalted God fo Scripture and the Christian Faith*. Crossway, 2004.

Warfield, B. B. "Antiquity and Unity of the Human Race." In *Biblical and Theological Studies*. Edited by Samuel Craig. Philadelphia: Presbyterian & Reformed, 1968.

———. "Hosea vi.7: Adam or Man?" In *Selected Shorter Writings of Benjamin B. Warfield*. Edited by John E. Meeter. Nutley, NJ: Presbyterian & Reformed, 1970.

Watson, Francis. "Strategies of Recovery and Resistance: Hermeneutical Reflections on Genesis 1–3 and its Pauline Reception," *Journal for the Study of the New Testament* 45 (1992) 103.

Weeks, Noel. *Gateway to the Old Testament*. Edinburgh: The Banner of Truth Trust, 1995.

Wenham, Gordon J. "Original Sin in Genesis 1–11." *Churchman* 104 (1990) 309–28.

———. *Genesis 1–15*. Vol. 1 of *WBC*. Edited by David A. Hubbard and Glenn W. Barker. Nashville: Nelson, 1987.

———. *Genesis 16–50*. Vol. 2 of *WBC*. Edited by David A. Hubbard and Glenn W. Barker. Nashville: Nelson, 1994.

Werner, Berg. "Der Sündenfall Abrahams und Saras nach Gen 16,1–6." *BN* 19 (1982) 7–14.

———. "Nochmals: Ein Sündenfall Abrahams—der erste—in Gen 12,10–20." *BN* 21 (1983) 7–15.

Westcott, B. F. *The Epistle to the Hebrews*. Reprint, Grand Rapids: Eerdmans, 1952.

Westermann, Claus. "Arten der Erzählung in der Genesis." In *Forschung am Alten Testament: Gesammelte Studien*. Munich: Chr. Kaiser, 1964.

———. *Genesis 1–11: A Continental Commentary*. Translated by John J. Scullion. Minneapolis: Fortress, 1994.

———. *Genesis 12–36: A Continental Commentary*. Translated by John J. Scullion. Minneapolis: Fortress, 1995.

———. *Genesis 37–50: A Continental Commentary*. Translated by John J. Scullion. Minneapolis: Fortress, 2002.

———. *Joseph: Eleven Bible Studies on Genesis*. Translated by Omar Kaste. Minneapolis: Fortress, 1996.

———. *The Promises to the Fathers: Studies on the Patriarchal Narratives*. Translated by David E. Green. Philadelphia: Fortress, 1976.

White, H. C. "Reuben and Judah: Duplicates or Complements?" In *Understanding the Word: Essays in Honor of Bernhard W. Anderson*. Edited by J. T. Butler, E. W. Conrad, and B. C. Ollenburger. *JSOTSup* 37. Sheffield, UK: JSOT, 1985.

Whyte, Alexander. *Bible Characters From the Old and New Testaments*. 1896. Reprint, Grand Rapids: Kregel, 1990.

Wickham, L. R. "The Sons of God and the Daughters of Men: Genesis 6:2 in Early Christian Exegesis." In *Language and Meaning, OTS* 19. Edited by James Barr, 135–47. Leiden, The Netherlands: Brill, 1974.

Wildasvsky, Aaron. "Survival Must Not Be Gained Through Sin: The Moral of the Joseph Stories Prefigured Through Judah and Tamar." *JSOT* 62 (1994) 37–48.

Williams, Michael D. *Far as the Curse Is Found: The Covenant Story of Redemption*. Phillipsburg, NJ: Presbyterian and Reformed, 2005.

Williams, Michael James. *Deception in Genesis: An Investigation into the Morality of a Unique Biblical Phenomenon*. New York: Peter Lang, 2001.

Williams, Peter. *From Eden to Egypt: Exploring the Genesis Themes*. Epsom, UK: Day One, 2001.

Williams, Ronald J. *Hebrew Syntax: An Outline*, 2nd ed. Toronto: The University of Toronto Press, 1976.

Williamson, Paul R. *Sealed with an Oath: Covenant in God's Unfolding Purpose. NSBT*. Edited by D. A. Carson. Downers Grove, IL: InterVarsity, 2007.

Wilson, J. M., and R. K. Harrison. "Birthright." In *ISBE*, 1:515.

Wilson, Marvin R. *Our Father Abraham: Jewish Roots of the Christian Faith*. Grand Rapids: Eerdmans, 1989.

Wilson, Robert R. *Genealogy and History in the Biblical World*. Yale Near Eastern Researches 7. Edited by William W. Hallo. New Haven: Yale University Press, 1977.

Wisdom, Thurman. *A Royal Destiny: The Reign of Man in God's Kingdom*. Greenville, SC: Bob Jones University Press, 2006.

Wiseman, D. J., editor. *Peoples of Old Testament Times*.Oxford: Clarendon, 1973.

Wolters, Albert M. *Creation Regained: Biblical Basics for a Reformational Worldview*. 2nd ed. Grand Rapids: Eerdmans, 2005.

Woudstra, M. H. "The *Toledot* of the Book of Genesis and Their Redemptive-Historical Significance." *CTJ* (1970) 184–89.

Wright, Thomas. *What Saint Paul Really Said: Was Saul of Tarsus the Real Founder of Christianity?* Grand Rapids: Eerdmans, 1997.

Young, Edward J. *The Book of Isaiah*. Grand Rapids: Eerdmans, 1969.

———. *In the Beginning: Genesis 1–3 and the Authority of Scripture*. Edinburgh: The Banner of Truth Trust, 1976.

———. *An Introduction to the Old Testament*. 2nd ed. Grand Rapids: Eerdmans, 1964.

Youngblood, Ronald F. *The Book of Genesis: An Introductory Commentary*. 2nd ed. Grand Rapids: Baker, 1991.

———. "A New Look at Three Old Testament Roots for 'Sin.'" *Biblical and Near Eastern Studies: Essays in Honor of William Sanford LaSor*. Edited by Gary A. Tuttle. Grand Rapids: Eerdmans, 1978.

Zimmerli, Walther. *A Commentary on the Book of the Prophet Ezekiel*. In *Hermeneia*. Translated by James D. Martin. Edited by Paul D. Hanson. Philadelphia: Fortress, 1983.

Zuck, Roy B., ed. *A Biblical Theology of the Old Testament*. Chicago: Moody, 1991.

CPSIA information can be obtained
at www.ICGtesting.com
Printed in the USA
LVHW021220030921
696794LV00013B/1339

9 781606 087473